The Foundations of Modern Terrorism

Why is it that terrorism has become such a central factor in our lives, despite all the efforts to eradicate it? Ranging from early modern Europe to the contemporary Middle East, Martin A. Miller reveals the foundations of modern terrorism. He argues that the French Revolution was a watershed moment, as it was then that ordinary citizens first claimed the right to govern. The traditional notion of state legitimacy was forever altered, and terrorism became part of a violent contest over control of state power between officials in government and insurgents in society. In the nineteenth and twentieth centuries terrorism evolved into a way of seeing the world and a way of life for both insurgents and state security forces, with the two sides drawn ever closer in their behaviour and tactics. This is a groundbreaking history of terrorism which, for the first time, integrates the violence of governments and insurgencies.

Martin A. Miller is Professor in the Department of History and the Department of Slavic and Eurasian Studies at Duke University. A specialist in Russian revolutionary movements, his earlier books include *Freud and the Bolsheviks* (1998) and *The Russian Revolution* (2001).

The Foundations of Modern Terrorism

State, Society and the Dynamics of Political Violence

Martin A. Miller
Duke University

CAMBRIDGE
UNIVERSITY PRESS

CAMBRIDGE
UNIVERSITY PRESS

University Printing House, Cambridge CB2 8BS, United Kingdom

Cambridge University Press is part of the University of Cambridge.

It furthers the University's mission by disseminating knowledge in the pursuit of education, learning and research at the highest international levels of excellence.

www.cambridge.org
Information on this title: www.cambridge.org/9781107621084

First published 2013
Reprinted 2015

Printed in the United States of America by Sheridan Books, Inc.

A catalogue record for this publication is available from the British Library

Library of Congress Cataloguing in Publication data

Miller, Martin A. (Martin Alan), 1938– author.
    The foundations of modern terrorism: state, society and the dynamics of political violence / Martin A. Miller, Duke University.
    pages cm
ISBN 978-1-107-02530-1 (Hardback) – ISBN 978-1-107-62108-4 (Paperback)
    1. Terrorism.   I. Title.
    HV6431.M57345 2012
    363.325–dc23

                                                                    2012021046

ISBN 978-1-107-02530-1 Hardback
ISBN 978-1-107-62108-4 Paperback

In memory of Lily and Alfred Feiler

It is just that what is just must be followed. It is necessary that what is strongest must be followed. Justice without force is impotent. Force without justice is tyrannical...

So one must combine justice and force, and in so doing, making that which is just, strong, and what is strong, just. Justice is subject to dispute. Force is very recognizable and indisputable. Thus one cannot give force to justice because force contradicts justice, having said that it [justice] was unjust and that it was itself [force] just. And thus being unable to make that which is just, stronger, one has made what is strong, more just.

BLAISE PASCAL *(1623–1662), OPUSCULES ET PENSEES, edited by Leon Brunschvicg (Paris: Hachette, 1897), no. 298, p. 470.*

CONTENTS

Acknowledgments   x

1   Writing the history of terrorism   1

2   The origins of political violence in the pre-modern era   10

3   Trajectories of terrorism in the transition to modernity   32

4   Nineteenth-century Russian revolutionary and tsarist terrorisms   58

5   European nation state terrorism and its antagonists, at home and abroad, 1848–1914   98

6   Terrorism in a democracy: the United States   137

7   Communist and fascist authoritarian terror   163

8   Global ideological terror during the Cold War   197

9   Toward the present: terrorism in theory and practice   240

Bibliography   259
Index   285

ACKNOWLEDGMENTS

One of the great pleasures of completing a book is the opportunity it provides to express gratitude to the people who were so helpful in the process. My journey into the world of political violence as a research project began a couple of books ago thanks to an invitation from Martha Crenshaw and Philip Pomper to present a paper on Western European conceptions of terrorism in historical perspective at an international conference held at Wesleyan University. Ann Larabee and Arthur Versluis provided the chance to sharpen my thinking on the subject by including me at the Conference on Radical History at Michigan State University. Thanks to David Rapoport for his invitations to present papers at two of the conferences he organized on the history of terrorism in New Orleans and Arlington, Virginia. I also wish to thank Charles Strozier for inviting me to discuss my research at a stimulating workshop on terrorism at John Jay College for Criminal Justice. For a challenging seminar at Harvard University's Kennedy School on the problems of writing the history of terrorism, I am grateful to Alex Keyssar. Thanks also to the kind invitation arranged by Dominic Sachsenmaier, I gave lectures on several chapters of this book at the Free University in Berlin and also at the Transnational Studies Seminar at Leipzig University, where Matthias Middell served as a gracious host. Responses from colleagues and graduate students at all of these venues were extremely helpful as well in raising important questions about my arguments and evidence.

Most of the materials upon which I have relied have been published, but I would not have been able to find a good number of them without expert help from the research librarians at Perkins and Lilly Libraries at Duke University. In particular, Ernest Zitzer and Carson Holloway were indispensable in locating these items. I have also leaned on the knowledge of colleagues here at Duke for sources in fields far from my own specializations. Jocelyn Olcott and John French were especially helpful in suggesting Latin American materials. Luca Pec shared his expertise on postwar Italy with me during my semester at Venice International University. Discussions with my colleagues and our invited guests in the Triangle Intellectual History seminar, which meets monthly at the National Humanities Center, have been very useful in the difficult task of thinking things out. I have also been fortunate to have had an array of talented students in my courses at Duke while I was researching and writing this book; their interventions in class and their research papers have proven to be continual sources of stimulation.

Some of my mentors who became friends as well as lifelong colleagues are, sadly, no longer with us. Leopold Haimson, Michel Confino and Reggie Zelnik provided models of scholarship that included theoretical and empirical dimensions as well as comparative and transnational historical analysis that have influenced my work over the decades in many ways.

My editor at Cambridge, Michael Watson, deserves special thanks for his role in bringing this book to fruition. From the outset, he was encouraging, in supporting me to refine my interpretation of terrorism in historical perspective. In addition, he read the entire book more closely than I had any right to expect, and provided many incisive comments. Flaws and problems undoubtedly remain in this book, but it certainly is a better product as a result of his attention to detail. The readers for Cambridge, though anonymous and unknown to me, took the thesis of my work seriously and provided significant constructive criticism.

Lastly and most importantly, I wish to add a few words about the huge debt of gratitude I owe to my family. My very grown-up children, Joshua L. Miller and Zinaida A. Miller, have moved into professional lives of their own that, luckily for me, were located close enough to my interests that they could provide suggestions and criticism from their own fields of knowledge as well as support because of the sensitive, exceptional people they are. Further good fortune was added when they chose partners, Ruby Tapia and Robert Blecher respectively, who have also made important contributions that have helped me to better understand the problems involved in conceptualizing the dynamics of terrorism. No one, however, has meant more to the realization of this project than my life-long partner and closest colleague, Ylana N. Miller. Without her initial encouragement, I would not have even pursued the argument that defines this book. She has read, with great critical acumen, various drafts from start to finish, improving many aspects of the original manuscript. I could not have been more fortunate in having such a perceptive in-the-house editor.

Though it should go without saying, I must nonetheless make clear that no one is responsible for any aspect of the material contained in these pages except the author.

1 WRITING THE HISTORY OF TERRORISM

This book is an effort to understand the phenomenon of terrorism in a historical perspective. Because of the global breadth this necessarily entails, there is no dominating geographic center to my inquiry. By following the primary chronological pathways, we begin in the Biblical Near East and extend to Europe, the US, Latin America and Africa. The narrative and analysis of the historical evolution of terrorism as approached here will seek to clarify the conditions which have given rise to terrorism, the goals sought by those relying on its violent tactics, and the dynamics that evolved over time, leading to its becoming a permanent force in the politics of the modern world.

Terrorism is one of a number of genres of political violence, which also include war, genocide and ethnic cleansing among its main categories. All of these forms make use of violence for political reasons, but terrorism is distinguished from the others in several ways. First, it involves repeated acts of violence that create an atmosphere of fear, insecurity and mistrust in civilian society; second, it involves a dynamic interaction between groups or individuals in both government and society who choose it as a means of accomplishing specific political objectives; and third, terrorism is a response to the contestation over what constitutes legitimate authority within a territorial nation state in periods of political vulnerability.

We have become accustomed to conceptualizing "terrorism" as an illegitimate effort by subnational, clandestine factions to sabotage existing governing systems and do great harm to innocent civilians in the process. In addition, the word "terror" is conventionally understood as a signifier for extremely violent regimes, such as the state terror of the Soviet Union under Stalin, Hitler's Third Reich, Pol Pot's Khmer Rouge regime in Cambodia, Idi Amin's Uganda, and Mao's Cultural Revolution in China, to mention some of the more notorious. Indeed, much of the vast literature on the subject has reflected these divisions for many decades, and the distinction has only been enhanced by the global response to the attacks in the US on September 11, 2001.

The interpretation presented here is a departure from this separation of struggles over power. Rather than emphasizing one perspective over the other, I will be integrating the violence of governments and insurgencies into a single narrative format as a way of understanding terrorism in its broadest historical representation. To demonstrate this approach, I have selected a number of historical moments from a variety of countries, while proceeding chronologically across the last two centuries. I have chosen them because I believe they best reveal and reflect the characteristics and variations that illuminate the essence of terrorist realities in historical perspective. In each example, the antagonistic interplay between state officials and insurgent leaders proves to be the decisive factor in understanding why violence is so vital to the realization of their intentions. They are deeply linked with one another, and neither can easily move to non-violent alternatives, once committed to the path defined by the conditions of terror.

The dominant problematic that gives rise to the resort to terrorist violence is the ongoing contestation found in the conflicts over the legitimacy of state power. The watershed moment in which terrorism entered the politics of modern Europe was during the French Revolution, when ordinary citizens claimed the right to govern. The traditional notion of state legitimacy was forever altered as a result of this upheaval. Among the many consequences resulting from the establishment of a democratic republic in the wake of the overthrown monarchy was the opening of the doorway to a multitude of potential forms of governance. No single form had the hegemonic authority that divine right monarchies once possessed, thereby creating the opportunity for a wide spectrum of proposals to justify the format and functions of the successor. Further, at least in principle, any individual or group in this competitive atmosphere could make a claim to realize a future social order governed by rulers and leaders truly responsive to the needs and desires of the citizens under their authority.

This combination of new political space in an elected legisla-
ture with unprecedented levels of popular participation in state functioning led to the need to redefine the tactics and strategy of
governance. Activism took precedence over passive complicity. Theories that were formerly the preserve of educated, if not learned, men,
now were open to transformation into policies to be implemented by
newly empowered citizens. In the midst of these heightened expectations and tumultuous experiences, the tactics of violence proved to be
an attractive alternative as the means to achieve certain political ends
and positions of power in the evolving contestation over post-monarchical, political legitimacy. Would *Ancien Régime* loyalists accept their
status in a republic without the privileges of their estate? Was the
church to have a place in this new secular constellation of power?
Was there a compromise possible in which the authority of the sovereign could be limited, rather than absolute? In the absence of clear
answers, political violence with secular justification would assume a
huge role in seeking resolution to these questions.

Terrorism, from the French Revolutionary era onward, was
positioned as an evolving complex of forces in civilian zones of violent
combat over control of state power between officials in government
and insurgents in society. There is no uniform model that explains
either the nature of the varying contexts in which the violence becomes
pronounced, or predicts the many sites in which terrorism can occur.
There are periods of terror that break out because of specific antagonisms in contestations over power that the parties have decided cannot
be resolved by peaceful negotiated means. There are no terrorist states,
but there are *states of terror* in which regimes utilize policies of political
violence to end perceived threats to their authority. Similarly, there are
no permanent insurgent terrorist organizations, but rather such organizations are mobilized in certain historical situations with the intention
of violently contesting a government's authority. The interpretive
framework in this book departs from the tendency to focus on one side
or the other, but rather seeks to demonstrate that both of these agents
are necessary in order for terrorism to function over a period of time.
To do otherwise obscures the fact that both are, however incommensur-
ately, in some way responsible.

Securing consent, cooperation and, ultimately, the active participation of a constituency is crucial for the endurance of terrorism as
a dynamic, either in the hands of governments or insurgencies, though

it does not guarantee success. Promises are made: force from below will end the abusive government's reign; force from above against the state's (and, according to the logic, society's) enemies will end the fearful violence that they conduct. The disputes lying at the center of terrorist situations are frequently focused on the right to use violence and control over access to advanced weaponry to accomplish their particular goals. States have traditionally reserved this as an exclusive right in order to enforce their legitimacy in power when it is questioned. Insurgencies have sought this right for themselves precisely because they no longer accept that legitimacy and exclusivity. The resulting violent combat between the two in the competitive civilian space of the social order is the driving component in the dynamic of terrorism.

Perhaps because those in power are inherently suspicious of claims challenging the legitimacy of their authority, and because those who are without political power covet it so desperately, all the parties involved in the violence are vulnerable to exaggerating their roles in creating what they imagine will be a more ameliorative political future order in which relentless conflicts and unanswered demands will at last be resolved. These heartfelt aspirations are dominated by powerful expectations that are expressed in a milieu of heightened vulnerability and anxiety precisely because of the palpable political instability created when daily life is so affected by these divisive issues. At such moments, political goals often come to be understood as unrealizable without terror. Entire groups are then conceptualized as threatening, whether in government or in the underground, and are targeted for repression or elimination. Governments declare states of emergency and alter laws to accomplish their ends, while insurgents invent new moral codes to transcend the existing legal system and, in the process, transform themselves into permanent outlaws in order to realize their grandiose plans. Both sides nonetheless feel the need to reach out to convince the larger society to accept their perspectives on the crisis at hand and the necessity of resolution by violence. In this process, both sides often create victims in sectors of the civilian population, which, at different times and sites, is either intentional or unintentional. From the state's point of view, those who are targeted are meant to be harmed in order to defuse their role as a threat to existing authority. For the insurgents, the objects of attack are chosen because of the positions they occupy in the state system of perceived repression and injustice. The other casualties are what strategists coldly refer to as collateral damage.

The centrality of the terror rests in those assumptions. For the state, its officials come to believe that they must have extensive control to exorcise the demons that lurk secretively within the gates of the civil order, while the insurgents are convinced they can foment widespread discontent against the brutalizing state to fatally wound it. Both must create this structure of belief in which terror is conceptualized as the solution to the resolution of its discontents. Both tend to invest enormous, even excessive power, in imagining the capacities of violence of which their enemies are capable. Leaders emerge, whether elected or selected, endowed with qualities approaching charismatic significance by their opponents as well as their followers and supporters; this then entitles or grants them the authority to command and justify the tactics of violence to be used against one another.

There are, of course, many forms of violence, both political and otherwise, that have not been included here. Violence that is fundamentally non-political, such as the domestic abuse of spouses and children, horrible and criminal as this is, does not really qualify as terrorism as conceptualized in this study. Mass violence that is political, such as civil and transnational wars, ethnic cleansing and cases of genocide, are not examined in detail only because they are violent by nature and often occur within the framework of organized or declared warfare between governments. Moreover, these episodes of violence are frequently the consequence of ongoing violent events, rather than being part of the foundational structure of terrorism. We can learn much about the forms of brutality from these instances of extreme violence, but much less about the essence of terrorism.

Terrorism is also a way of seeing the world, of understanding (or, in many cases, misunderstanding) the dominant political paradigm of the particular historical moment. It involves public commitments based on specific perspectives rooted in deeply felt responses to, and interpretations of, social and political problems. The salient motivations range from perceptions of survival and conquest, to imaginaries of eschatological dimensions that are experienced as desperately needed and attainable only through violence. Terrorism as a phenomenon and dynamic also includes acceptance of the hermetically enclosed, secretive universe that defines the quotidian of both the state's clandestine security agencies and the equally furtive radical insurgency centers and operations at such times. In a sense, both sides come to accept the need to live with an alternative morality from which, once committed, exiting back into public space becomes virtually impossible.

Terrorism is also a way of life. Living so intensely in such a guarded, secretive world produces the tendency to imitate each other's behavior and tactics, a phenomenon I refer to in this study as "mirroring." There are many examples referenced in the pages that follow, but in general, this term refers to the close and, at times, intimate connection that security counter-terrorism has with its antagonists. Among the characteristics of this experience one finds the employment of surveillance techniques, the presence of spies and agents pretending loyalties to one side while reporting to the other, and provoking acts while undercover that permit the opposing forces to act with repressive violence during the periods of terror. In other cases, such as the culture of lynching in the American South, and the spasmodic anti-Semitic pogroms in tsarist Russia, a shared set of beliefs and justifications mirrored and unified ordinary citizens with forces of authority in terrorizing the targeted population.

Moreover, the attitudes toward declared enemies fostered during terrorist periods frequently remain fixed. Whether the danger was communism in power or communism threatening power, categories of defining exactly who was dangerous, and assessing how valid the evidence was, proved very expansive and elastic. Similarly, in cases of aroused racial, religious or ethnic fears, citizens can be convinced of the danger posed by the threatening "other," and thus have been relatively easy to mobilize and recruit to become participants in the violent path to find solace and solutions. At such vulnerable moments, notions of state (il)legitimacy and feelings of individual (in)security mesh together and can become virtually indistinguishable.

Further, terrorism involves adopting an idiom, a language and a collective identity. Codes become expressions of words that cannot, for security reasons, be communicated directly. Concepts of danger posed by threatening forces become dominant patterns of understanding and processing information. Becoming so exclusively involved in the adrenalin-heightened clandestine activities of terrorism, whether for government security agencies or underground insurgencies, provides a sense of belonging to a larger community with a grand purpose, devoted to rectifying what are perceived to be unacceptable and menacing conditions in quotidian existence. In this way, nuances and avenues for compromise are lost, the extraordinary becomes the ordinary, and what should be understood as abnormal is transformed into the normative.

Despite the appalling tragedy of lost and mangled lives, terrorism has rarely succeeded in achieving its goals. Regimes of terror have always, in the end, proved transient, though the damage they have wrought while in power has certainly been significant. Hitler did not manage to annihilate every Jew, Stalin never created his classless utopia no matter how many enemies of the state he did away with, Pinochet could not "disappear" every suspected participant in the opposition, and neither Catholics nor Protestants in Northern Ireland found a way to completely disentangle themselves from one another's living space.

Similarly, insurgencies of terror have been responsible for enormous damage to life and property, but have usually fallen short of their intentions. Russian populists and European anarchists killed many rulers and their subordinates in their rampages against governments in the decades before the First World War, but could not achieve through assassinations their desired political goals. Rulers and systems of government, they learned, were endlessly replaceable. So too, the Ku Klux Klan never succeeded in its quest to literally strangle the efforts by former slaves to become fully empowered and equal citizens as promised to all citizens by the 15th amendment of the US constitution.

That said, there clearly have been historical moments when terrorism was nonetheless an important ingredient in the achievement of intended political goals. Outlaw parties advocating violence did come to power in Russia in 1917, Italy in 1921, and Germany in 1933. Violence was instrumental in the eventual victory over the French colonial regime by the FLN in Algeria in 1962.

This is not to say that forms of terrorism must be the sole alternative in seeking the amelioration of the social order. With regard to states, the South African apartheid regime fell without mass, insurrectionary violence. The Soviet Union came to an end through peaceful negotiations. Chile's military terrorism under President Augusto Pinochet collapsed through a non-violent referendum. On the insurgent side, the Red Brigades in Italy and the Weather Underground in the US, both of which espoused violence, came to an end in the 1970s without government-legislated states of emergency that would have included an excessive reliance on police terror over protracted periods of time.

Terrorist periods are dominated by proclamations, denunciations and demands from insurgents, by decrees and legislation from parliaments and executive offices, and by a multitude of voices from the expansive media ranging from state controlled sources to those run by the illegal underground and their exiled comrades in the global diasporas. All will have positions to propound with regard to the problems of the day. The agents of violence in power and in the groups seeking it will state repeatedly that they are acting in the name of the people, and that they know how to solve the problems gnawing at the bodies and souls of their constituencies. More often than not, however, these problems of injustice, abuse, poverty and the desire for political liberty, which have existed from time immemorial, are neither the causes of the violence nor is the violence a solution to correct them. Blinded by grandiose intentions, terrorists frequently use these issues for their own purposes of enforcement, repression or revolution as well as to gain the support of the people to strengthen their own agenda.

The chapters that follow begin with a prelude that discusses the pre-modern religious origins of political violence in Europe, and continues in greater depth with an examination of the French Revolutionary era when the representative, constitutional nation state was established. Further chapters trace the history of terrorism in the Restoration years in Europe, and the political violence in nineteenth-century Russia in which revolutionaries and state security forces engaged in brutal combat that had far-reaching international influences. I also consider the role of terrorism in the US, particularly with regard to the violent expulsion of Native Americans from their tribal lands in flagrant violation of negotiated treaties, and the astonishing success of the Ku Klux Klan and its offshoots in their long campaign of victimizing African Americans over issues of political empowerment. Further chapters consider the conflict between governments and anarchists before the First World War, the violence imposed by Europeans on Africans in the late nineteenth and early twentieth centuries, the authoritarian state terror in Germany during the Third Reich and in the Soviet Union under Stalin's rule, the "dirty wars" in Latin America, and the clashes of political cultures during the 1960s and 1970s, "from Berkeley to Berlin." The narrative closes with the end of the Cold War in 1991.

This book is not designed to provide a comprehensive history of terrorism in the Western world. There are many other instances of terrorism that deserve to be included. My approach and selection of events, however, are intended to illustrate the historical conditions for the emergence of the terrorist dynamic, and its evolving development over the last two centuries by focusing on specific crisis situations. Much of this material is not necessarily new, and all of it deserves far greater attention than given here, but if I have advanced the conversation about terrorism at all, it is because of the manner in which I have placed the forces of state and insurgent violence in historical and synchronic dialogue with each other. One of the reasons for this is that nations have buried, repressed or sanitized much of their violent pasts. It is my view that until every country can open its national closet and honestly confront the skeletons of its own history, which may reveal some of the most atrocious excesses committed by individuals or groups in the name of either patriotism or revolution, we shall continue to live with the ingredients of terrorism. These ingredients can, unfortunately, be stoked from quietly burning embers to violent conflagrations once the appropriate conditions emerge. If there is a message in this historical narrative, it is that we should not have to repeat it.

2 THE ORIGINS OF POLITICAL VIOLENCE IN THE PRE-MODERN ERA

In the minds of many, all things political begin either with God or Aristotle. In the case of political violence, both originators are relevant. The complex dynamic between the forces of authority on the one hand, and the society over which it presides on the other, has been at work since time immemorial. Violence has always been a necessary part of the contestation over the legitimacy of that authority, and aspirations to power have perpetually suffered from the temptation to seek consequences beyond the realistic possibilities at hand. Rulers, whether religious or secular, who seek to enforce authority and insurgents who contest that power have been drawn to violence across the centuries.

This chapter examines a huge swath of chronological time, from Biblical and classical Greco-Roman cultures through the medieval and early modern eras of European history. Although my survey through these periods is of necessity far too brief, the intention is to present the emergence of some of the characteristics of terrorism that would much later coalesce into a functioning and integral part of the contentious relationship between the governments of the modern nation state and their challenging antagonists. The violence of these earlier centuries was presented in both religious and secular frameworks; indeed, often the two were merged so as to be almost indistinguishable. These frameworks include two formats. One focuses on the intellectual products written by the prominent and influential theorists of violence, who felt it necessary to justify their critique, whether of a threatening minority in society or an abusive ruler in government. The other is concerned with the acts of political violence that took place. These events on occasion developed from episodic moments of brutality to periods of widespread fear and repression, which more closely resemble aspects of the core ingredients of modern terrorism that developed later.

The Old Testament is filled with tales of battles over political power as clans and tribes fought over the quest to establish an enduring form of governance under divine ordinance. In the absence of corroborating archeological or textual evidence, we may never know to what extent we are dealing with belief and faith, as opposed to factual events. However, by comparison with Greco-Roman standards, "Jehovah's children produced no definitions of legitimacy, leadership or representation likely to sustain enduring institutions of state. They did not, for example, produce any coherent notion of how authority might be transferred in the face of conflicting personal interests."[1]

Indeed, the Bible is more than accepting of the necessity of violence in the resolution of political disputations over legitimate rule, whether it is the king committing atrocities against his declared enemies, or individuals killing those in power. Interestingly, women have played an important part in this narrative. In one example, from the Book of Judges, Jael, wife of Heber, tricked the fleeing and defeated Canaanite general Sisera into accepting her hospitality, after which she battered his skull with a hammer when he fell asleep. In another more visually celebrated case, Judith murdered Holofernes, presumed to be an Assyrian ruler, beheading him at night in the privacy of her bedroom. There are numerous paintings across the centuries depicting Judith as a political heroine as she holds the unruly severed, bloodied head of her adversary and lover. In the version by Bernardo Cavallino (1616–56), she has taken care to bandage his head to contain the flow of blood, while in others the rivulets drip onto the floor with abandon. Regardless of the intentions of the various artists, the indelibly imprinted image is one of justified assassination.

The annals of ancient Judaic culture also have preserved the extraordinary episode of what has been considered one of the earliest instances of insurgent terrorism. During the reign of King Herod (37–4 BCE), with the occupation of the eastern province of the Roman Empire, Palestine, under full control, political divisions broke out

[1] Ford, *Political Murder*, 23.

among factions within the Jewish community. Though it is difficult to know percentages, the majority seemed to support the position of the Sadducees, who were willing to cooperate fully with the occupying authorities in Jerusalem and who were also willing to assimilate Rome's more worldly pagan culture into their own. The Pharisees were compromisers as well, but insisted on practicing their own religion in Jewish temples and in their homes. Another group, the Essenes, who would later become identified with the preservation of the Dead Sea Scrolls, seemingly were on the fringes of these political and religious controversies in their devotion to ancient ascetic rituals. Finally, there were the Zealots, who were actively oppositional.

The Romans referred to the Zealots as Sicarii, or men of the daggers, their weapon of choice. The political goal of the Jewish Zealots was to reclaim their homeland and free it from the occupation. To accomplish this, they engaged in a daring campaign of violent assassinations of not only Roman soldiers and politicians, but Jewish Sadducees, whom they saw as collaborators with the enemy occupiers. During the years 66–70, according to Flavius Josephus, the main source on the aptly named Jewish Wars, the Zealots managed to destroy an entire brigade of Roman soldiers, at which point the imperial forces were ordered to wage a merciless campaign to eliminate the Zealots entirely. They ultimately succeeded in this in a dramatic climax atop the mountain plateau of Masada near Jerusalem. Trapped there after their retreat, the entire remains of the Zealot community, including wives and children, committed mass suicide rather than surrender to the Roman legions that had found their way up the steep slopes.[2] Thus ended one of history's emblematic violent confrontations between what in more modern terminology might be called a resistance movement, or a liberation front, and the state that repressed its demand for liberty.

The development of both the theory and the practice of political violence intensified during the classical Greek and Roman periods, which established the foundation for much of what was later defined as terrorism. The problem of defining the form of misrule designated as tyranny was present from our earliest surviving historical records. For Herodotus, the tyrant's most identifiable characteristics were unbridled and defiant acts of arrogance. He attempted a psychological analysis of

---

[2] Josephus, *The Jewish Wars*. Of the many commentators who have written on this topic, see Rapoport, "Fear and Trembling" 658–78.

sorts by claiming that such men were driven by excessive pride, jealousy and envy, which led them to lawless, reckless, brutal behavior toward their subjects, including the execution and raping of citizens of all social classes.

Herodotus made two other important contributions to the understanding of political violence. First, he noted that tyrants were compelled to commit such outrageous actions because of the impossibility of ever stabilizing their rule in perpetuity. They were in a state of constant anxiety over the competitiveness of rivals, real or imagined, since their own accession to power was illegitimate. Thus, his second point was that it was the method of gaining power, rather than the abuse of that power once obtained, that made tyrants so dangerous.[3] The usurper, rather than the abuser, was the essence of Herodotus' notion of tyranny in government.

Two later historians of classical Greece, Thucydides and Xenophon, took the emerging discourse on the nature of despotic rule a step farther. It was not enough merely to define what tyranny was; the more difficult question was what to do about it. Xenophon uses Simonides as his spokesman when he states that while there should be a revulsion against overthrowing a constitutional government, "with tyrants, the very reverse is the case. For states, instead of avenging their deaths, bestow great honor on him who kills a tyrant; and instead of excluding tyrannicides from their temples, as they exclude the murderers of private citizens, they even place in their temples the statues of those who have been guilty of tyrannicide."[4]

Aristotle's deliberations on the nature of despotic authority and societal responses are, unsurprisingly, far more comprehensive than those of any previous writer for whom we have extant records. He also brought the concept of the state into sharper focus than his predecessors. His political analysis rests on a taxonomy of categories of legitimate and illegitimate forms of state authority. There were three forms of polities that he considered genuine – monarchy, aristocracy and democracy. If misruled, each one would degenerate into its illegitimate form, which he called, respectively, tyranny, oligarchy and "extreme democracy," or ochlocracy (authority of the crowd, or mob).

---

[3] For this discussion, see Strassler, *The Landmark Herodotus*, 835–7.
[4] Quoted in Ford, *Political Murder*, 42. See also Strauss, *Xenophon's Socrates*. Thucydides' classic is his *The Peloponnesian War*, books V and VI.

As always, starting with the foundation of his inquiry, Aristotle asks "what is a state?" His answer is that it is a composite of the relationship between a ruler and those over whom he rules. There are many kinds of rulers and a variety of people in society, the qualified sector of which is entitled to be called the citizenry. Although there are the three forms of constitution, states do not correspond neatly to one or another. Some states undergo transformations from one into another, and some are composed of mixtures of two or more of those forms.

Regarding the problem of misrule, Aristotle discusses the characteristics of tyrants and what can be done to limit or overthrow their authority. Tyrants generally came to power by force, and ruled more in their own interests than in the interests of the common good, which is the purpose of the virtuous state. Tyrannies are also distinguished by the tendency to abolish the participation of the citizenry in governance, which can also occur in monarchies as well as aristocracies and democracies. Monarchs, so long as they rule over a citizenry according to law and in the interests of the common good, may avoid tyranny, while democratic assemblies can succumb to violence common to abusive rulers in any kind of state in what Aristotle termed "elective tyranny."[5]

With his knowledge of the 157 city state constitutions in the Greek political system, and armed with Plato's prior interrogations into the nature of the state, Aristotle was able to describe the problem of state violence from above and insurgent violence from below using a vast array of evidence that was both factual and theoretical. He recognized that while rulers employ brutal tactics to maintain their power when uncertain about their survival, citizens attack their sovereign when they have been provoked and abused. Fear of excessive power is another motive, he writes, which has led to conspiracies against the state in both monarchies and democracies. Those who commit these daring acts to avenge abuse or dishonor sometimes believe they will achieve fame and respect for their deed of violence against the contemptible tyrant. They also know that they must be prepared to lose their own lives in the process, either through success or failure.

Aristotle also devotes a section of his *Politics* to exactly how the tyrannical ruler must behave, which reads like a manual for

[5] This discussion is taken from Aristotle's *Politics*, Book 3, 578–617.

authoritarian rulers of any century. To preserve his unjust authority, he should "lop off those who are too high, put to death men of spirit, allow no common meals, clubs or education, or the like, be on his guard against anything likely to inspire either courage or confidence among his subjects, prohibit literary assemblies or other meetings for discussion, and take every means to prevent his people from knowing one another, for acquaintance begets mutual confidence."[6] Further, the tyrant should employ spies and eavesdroppers for "the fear of informants prevents people from speaking their minds, and when they do, they are easily found out." The tyrant must learn the art of sowing quarrels among the citizens, turning friends and family members against one another. Tyrants also are fond of making wars in order to keep their subjects distracted, fearful of external threats, and thereby circumvent the efforts to overthrow them. Aristotle even mentions the necessity for the tyrant to enlist wives and slaves to inform against their husbands and masters, since they are entirely vulnerable to the entreaties of the higher power.

At the same time, Aristotle also looked at the psychological dimension of state tyrants. Because they enjoy being flattered and having obsequious servants to carry out their orders, they will choose men of lesser talent for these important government positions. One of the chief traits of tyrants is the tendency to "dislike everyone who has dignity or independence." Such men are threats to the overwhelming desire for personal glory that drives the perpetually insecure despot, and humiliating them can therefore be the abusive ruler's most effective weapon.

At the same time, Aristotle cleverly shows how the tyrant can appear to be the opposite of what he actually is. Among his concerns must be the improvement of the territory under his control, which will make it appear that he is the guardian of the state and acting for the common good. He should maintain a façade of respect for religion and the gods that will evoke signs of respect from the people. He should make promotions as though his citizens "had a free government." Punishments should be distributed to lesser officials and courts of law under his control. Tyrants should "abstain from all outrage, in particular from personal violence and wanton conduct toward the young." Concluding, Aristotle mentions that most tyrants cannot in fact follow

---

[6] Aristotle, *On Man in the Universe*, 371.

this code of morality. For this reason, he believed that "tyrannies generally have been of quite short duration."[7]

Not all of Aristotle's comments are original, and many can be traced to Plato, who devoted a section of *The Republic* to the inter-related problems of rulers and their citizens in despotic states which lead one side or the other to resort to tactics of political violence. Socrates lectures at some length on the need for the tyrant to make use of informers while posing as a champion of the people whom he allegedly is protecting against internal and external enemies. He must nevertheless be careful to avoid being deceived by his own informers. The tyrant's brutalities will, however, breed those "who conspire to assassinate him" if he cannot "be condemned to death by a public accusation" for his misdeeds. Socrates also cites the need for the despotic ruler to conduct constant warfare in order to deflect resistance to his authority and to have a supply of citizens who can be blamed for the government's brutal actions against its enemies. Socrates in add-ition characterizes the tyrant as a wolf who must hunt his prey, and as "the most miserable of all men" because he can never cease his restless and relentless pursuit of security amidst overwhelming conditions of fear. His authority will be constantly challenged because of the unjust manner in which he either gained power or utilized it.[8]

The savage struggle over state power that brought about the collapse of the period of the Roman Republic and the early decades of the subsequent Roman Empire brought forth truly graphic descriptions of the causes and casualties of political violence that went beyond even the imaginations of the Greeks. Wars, civilian atrocities and unbridled violence from below and above brought numerous governments to their end, culminating in the assassinations of Tiberius Gracchus (133 BCE) and Julius Caesar (44 BCE). Marcus Tullius Cicero, who experienced the fall of the Republic, wrote passionately of the threat posed by despotic regimes and provided one of the earliest unqualified justifications for tyrannicide in the long discourse on political violence. He paid dearly for his critique of Mark Antony, whose supporters caught Cicero as he was fleeing a certain death sentence and executed

---

[7] There was one exception that he noted, claiming that Orthagoras and his sons at Sicyon in the Peloponnesus ruled tyrannically for 100 years. For this general discussion on the tyrant's methods of rule, see ibid., 372–7, which is the latter part of Book 5 of Aristotle's *Politics*.

[8] Plato, *The Republic*, 455–66. The sections relied on here are from the end of Book 8 and the start of Book 9.

him on the spot on December 7, 43 BCE, after which his head and hands were delivered to Antony as conclusive proof of his demise. Before that event, Cicero managed to produce the following declaration:

> *For we have not fellowship with tyrants, but rather are separated from them by the widest gulf; nor is it contrary to nature to despoil, if we can, him whom it is honorable to kill. And this whole pestiferous and impious race ought to be exterminated from the community of men. For even as a limb is amputated when the lifeblood ceases to circulate in it and it becomes injurious to other parts of the body, so that fierce and savage beast in human form ought to be severed from the body of mankind.[9]*

Perhaps no description of political violence at the state level in the ancient world matches that of Gaius Cornelius Tacitus (c. 56–117). Though he comprehensively covered the reigns of some of the most prominent emperors of Rome, including Augustus and Nero, he reserved a special term for the chapter on the era of Emperor Tiberius (42 BCE–37 AD), which he called "The Reign of Terror." In a particularly revealing passage, he wrote of the emperor:

> *It was indeed a horrible feature of the period that leading senators become informers even on trivial matters, some openly, many secretly. Friends and relatives were as suspected as strangers, old stories as damaging as new. In the main square, at a dinner party, a remark on any subject might mean prosecution. Everyone competed for priority in marking down the victim. Sometimes this was self-defense, but mostly it was a sort of contagion, like an epidemic.[10]*

Charges of treason were assigned with abandon by Tiberius and his closest advisors. Plots against the state and the Emperor's life abounded. Denunciations were frequently followed by suicide, to avoid the public spectacle of a humiliating trial in which one's entire family could be ostracized or exiled. Women were accused of

---

[9] Quoted in Jászi and Lewis, *Against the Tyrant*, 10.
[10] Tacitus, *The Annals of Imperial Rome*, 198.

lamenting their dishonored sons' executions, and even some of the Emperor's closest friends were sentenced to death. Tiberius reproved senators whom he felt "were not using their authority to restrain popular demonstrations," and similarly rebuked judicial officials for the occasional leniency shown to certain defendants. The killings by state command reached such proportions that Tacitus frequently resorted to terms like "frenzied with bloodshed" and "massacres" in his descriptions. On occasion, Tiberius, not satisfied with the death of the accused, would attack him and his relatives for years afterward, continually claiming to have uncovered conspiracies within the victim's family against the government, motivated by the lust for revenge. "Transformed and deranged by absolute power," Tiberius' reign of state terror, a period characterized by Tacitus in his conclusion as one of "unrestrained crime and infamy,"[11] came to an end only with his death.

In the aftermath of the demise of the Roman Empire, Europe underwent a huge transformation largely dictated by an emergent Catholic theology and a feudal economic system. Centers of authority gradually coalesced around powerful lords controlling large tracts of land made agriculturally productive by the labor of privately owned serfs. Over the course of several centuries, in spite of a great deal of regional autonomy, these centers were gradually subordinated to control by the papacy in Rome and a network of royal families across the continent who claimed their right to rule on the basis of divine and familial inheritance. With very few local exceptions, what the Greek and Roman theorists understood as the state evolved into national monarchies with kings on their thrones located on palatial sites in capital cities in control of vast stretches of territory and subjects. The expectations of these rulers and those who challenged them were grandiose and, at times, unrealistic.

There was much appeal to law – natural, royal and constitutional – in this period, but the associated problems of violence by and against rulers, as well as their justifications, seemed impervious to these established regulations and codes. Writers who wielded great influence wrestled – indeed, at times, agonized – over these issues, including the Dominican priest and philosopher Thomas Aquinas

---

[11] For the evidence in this discussion, see Tacitus, *The Annals*, ch. 8, "The Reign of Terror," 193–221.

(1225–74), the Franciscan theologian William of Occam (1288–1348) and the early English legal expert Henry de Bracton (1210–68).

However, the clearest argument that essentially reignited the discourse on tyrannicide was John of Salisbury's treatise, *Policraticus*. John (1120–80) received a superior theological education, largely in France, prior to becoming Bishop of Chartres and secretary to Thomas à Becket, the Archbishop of Canterbury during the reign of Henry II, whose politics they both criticized. Far from being a rebel against the principle of monarchy, John held it in the highest esteem. Indeed, his distinction between a legitimate prince and an illegitimate tyrant rested on a single and simple principle – the former obeys the law in his treatment of his subjects, while the latter brings "not justice but oppression and bases his rule not on law but on force." While the prince has the likeness of divinity, the tyrant represented "the likeness of the devil."[12]

This principle led John to two conclusions. First, with regard to those who commit offensive or harmful acts against the legitimate ruler, John spares no punishment, including torture and execution, in accord with the law. Precisely because the prince possesses the earthly likeness of divinity upon earth, an attempt on him is an assault against God. The examples of crimes that he mentions are soliciting rebellion against the prince, forsaking him with disrespect or disloyalty in any way, or deserting him or his causes in the course of battle. For these criminal actions, the penalty is for him to be "put to the sword" and for his sons to be left without title to any property.

On the other hand, because tyrants are "raised to power by sin ..., it is just for public tyrants to be killed and the people thus set free for the service of God." He found ample evidence in the Bible to support this interpretation. He did, however, have conditions. One was that the use of poison was forbidden, since it was "adapted by infidels" and was contrary to church teachings. Another was that "tyrants ought to be removed from our midst, but it should be done without loss of religion and honor." Lastly, no one should undertake this portentous task if he is "bound by oath or the obligation of fealty" to the tyrant.[13]

---

[12] Quoted in Jászi and Lewis, *Against the Tyrant*, 24.
[13] For this discussion, see *The Statesman's Book of John of Salisbury*, 369–70. Dickinson's lengthy introduction is informative. The most useful complete edition currently available is John of Salisbury, *Policraticus*.

Everyday reality has a way of altering expected outcomes in spite of the most thoughtful and careful planning. Theories justifying tyrannicide under certain conditions continued to evolve through the medieval and early modern eras of European history, as did far more prominent theories of authority in which standards of loyalty and punishments were drawn up to stabilize the authority of the national monarchs by maintaining increasingly severe control over their subjects. Although, as will shortly be made evident, it proved impossible to contain both regimes and insurgents within the prescribed frameworks each had designed, the theories from above and below filtered their way into the discourses and deeds of the ensuing centuries of political violence.

Another contributor to the growing literature on the subject of tyrannicide was Jean Petit (d. 1411). His theory, which incidentally makes explicit reference to the direct influence of John of Salisbury, was brought into the public domain as a result of one of the more obvious interactive moments where the theory and reality of political violence blend simultaneously. The context for Petit's entrance into this fray was the assassination of the Duke of Orleans, brother of the French king, Charles VI, which was ordered by his rival the Duke of Burgundy in 1407. Jean Petit, a Dominican theologian who also had studied law, in an address to the royal council that he called his "Justification," defended his patron, John of Burgundy, who clearly was responsible for the murder. Petit cited the most prominent authorities of the past, including his interpretation of both Aristotle's and Thomas Aquinas' views on removing tyrants from power in his treatise defending the Duke. The phrase in his speech that has often been cited is the passage in which he states that "it is lawful for any subject, without any order or command, according to moral, divine, and natural law, to kill or cause to be killed a traitor and disloyal tyrant." The point was that, given the Duke of Orleans' brutal behavior, were he to succeed to the throne of his brother, he would become a tyrant to the entire country and all its subjects.[14]

---

[14] For the basic details, see Jászi and Lewis, *Against the Tyrant*, 28–9, and Ford, *Political Murder*, 132–3. Most of what we know of Petit still is taken mainly from Coville, *Jean Petit*, which remains the definitive biography. Petit's speech was later critiqued at some length by the Chancellor of the University of Paris, Jean Gerson, who argued for trials and due process over assassination in resolving such disputes about the nature of tyranny.

In terms of actual violence, however, the terror of the Spanish Inquisition has no rivals among the rulers of royal authority discussed in the tyrannicide discourse. As far back as the thirteenth century, the Catholic Church began to enforce its monopoly on the theory and practice of Christendom with tactics of terrorism in the territories under Rome's clerical jurisdiction. The Cathars were the first group to be targeted as heretics by the church for repression, which reached its bloody climax during the Albigensian Crusade, when thousands were tortured and burned to death. The Inquisition was officially established by the Pope in 1478. At that time, its victims were mainly Muslim and Jewish *conversos* who, despite their formal acceptance of Catholicism, were viewed by the church as unbelievers practicing their heresies in secret. The Protestant Reformation and the rise of new scientific experimentation provided the Inquisition with whole new sectors of the population to repress as the authority of the papacy confronted extraordinary challenges to its doctrinal authority. The threat was perceived as serious enough that a separate branch of the Inquisition was created in Rome in 1542. In the words of one bishop, the struggle against satanic evil was so overwhelming that "the use of every means is sanctified, even cunning, treachery, violence, simony, prison, death."[15]

The long period between the outbreak of the Reformation in the early sixteenth century and the Treaty of Westphalia ending the Thirty Years War in 1648 was crucial in understanding the increasing reliance on political violence by both rulers and insurgents in Europe. In particular, notions of political legitimacy underwent a radical change that saw not only the breakdown of Catholicism's virtual monopoly over Western Christendom, but also the empowerment of secular rulers across the continent who sought to justify monarchical nation states as possessing uncontested sovereignty over the territories and subjects under their authority, inviolably distinct from jurisdiction emanating from the papacy as well as from one another.

The violence of the Reformation and the Wars of Religion that followed has been described in many accounts. Horrific as many of these events were, they were episodic, spontaneous and generally not politically motivated. When Martin Luther challenged the authority of the papacy in matters of the definition, practice and symbols of

[15] Quoted in Kirsch, *The Grand Inquisitor's Manual*, 13.

Christian faith, he touched on an undercurrent of antagonism felt in various ways by sectors of society across the continent. Insurgencies emerged quickly. Territorial princes within the loose boundaries of the Holy Roman Empire took advantage of the unstable situation by making military advances to either consolidate or expand their holdings, often "secularizing" church property in the process. Zealots arose, claiming their own versions of authentic Christian belief. One of the more bizarre religious rebellions of the period was the Anabaptist commune set up in the city of Munster in 1534 under the rigid control of a former tailor from Holland, John of Leyden. His reforms and the following he attracted so threatened the established church authorities that, in this one instance, Catholics and the nascent Lutheran movement combined forces to lay siege to Munster, burning much of it to the ground and executing John after forcing him to endure bouts of torture.

The other form of protest from below concerned the economically driven rebellions that punctuated the sixteenth century. Perhaps the single largest affair was the massive Peasant War (1524–6), which involved tens of thousands of mainly southeastern German peasants seeking the abolition of conditions of serfdom that deprived them of owning land and having access to agricultural resources necessary for their well-being and, indeed, survival in many instances. The loss of life remains incalculable, due to inadequate records, but there is little doubt that it was extraordinarily high. Luther, in a rare instance of consensual agreement on his part with his Catholic opponents, wrote very critically against the peasant disorders.[16] In addition, riots that often turned violent were experienced in many areas of France throughout the sixteenth century as urban workers protested about laboring conditions, merchants in town councils sought expanded rights, artisans fought for guild representation, and combinations of grain failures and price rises stirred rebellions in the countryside. Again, these were punctuating moments rather than expanded political competitions, largely leaderless and mostly unorganized.[17]

Debates remain among scholars over the degree to which these protests were direct consequences of the Reformation battles between Catholics and Lutherans, as opposed to trajectories of longstanding

[16] Luther, *Against the Thieving, Murderous Hordes of Peasants*.
[17] See Collins, *From Tribes to Nation*, 217–27.

conflicts more deeply rooted in the transformation of Europe from the last vestiges of a feudal economy into a more comprehensive capitalist system. There is, however, little doubt about the fact that the continent's governance and the justifications of legitimacy underwent a dramatic alteration in the post-Reformation era. The complexity of the situation can be seen from the solidifying alliances and antagonisms. Domestically, church and rulers united to preserve the status of powerful secular nation states, justified by divine providence, with a single national religion dominant in most cases. Across national borders royal houses battled against the religious authorities of competing states, to the point where no Catholic could ever reign in Prussia or Holland, while no Protestant could ever come to power in France, Spain or Austria. Religious diversity was repressed. Efforts to the contrary ended in regicide, as was the case with Henry III (d. 1589) and Henry IV (d. 1610) of France, both of whom were murdered by religious antagonists. There is also little controversy over the main consequence of the Thirty Years War, which finally brought the religious wars to an end by instituting the primacy of royal absolutism across the European continent in domestic and international relations.

As events were to show, however, the resolutions established at the postwar Westphalia Conference in 1648 did little to stem the development of continuing conflicts, directly involving political violence, between the competing forces of state and society. Some examples from France during this era illuminate these problems quite graphically. With the Reformation still in full force across the continent, one of the most important Protestant treatises on the subject of despotic rule was published in 1579. Though the author felt obliged to publish it anonymously, it is assumed by most scholars to have been written by the Huguenot scholar Philippe Duplessis-Mornay, under the classical Roman pseudonym of Junius Brutus.[18] Titled *Vindiciae contra Tyrannos* ("Justification Against Tyrants"), it was clearly a response to the massacre of French Protestants on St Bartholomew's Day in 1572, ordered by the Catholic king.

[18] The other candidate for authorship of the *Vindiciae* is the Protestant diplomat Hubert Languet (1518–81), who served a number of Lutheran princes in Germany in the interests of reconciling rancor with Catholics.

The reverberations of the Reformation's challenge to the supremacy of Catholicism came to a climax during the sixteenth century, beginning with Francis I's chilling declaration in 1535 to banish all heresy from his kingdom. This was to be accomplished, he proclaimed, "in such manner that if one of the arms of my body was infected with this [Huguenot] corruption, I would cut it off, and if my children were tainted with it, I would myself offer them in sacrifice."[19]

In 1563, rival terrorist groups assassinated Catholic and Huguenot leaders, with each side conspiring to plan for revenge attacks. In the summer of 1572, Gaspard, the Count of Coligny and widely regarded as the country's most revered Protestant, was murdered. The assassins were hired by a clique responsible for carrying out the orders of the son of the Catholic duke who had been killed in the 1563 affair, and which had the permission of the de facto ruler of France, Catherine de' Medici, mother of the young and inexperienced Charles IX. Many of the country's most prominent Huguenots had assembled in Paris for the St Bartholomew's Day festivities to celebrate the interfaith marriage of Henri of Navarre and Marguerite of Valois, sister of the king. Clearly under the impression that the court was favorable to their participation, the Protestants were obviously taken by surprise and shocked at the reaction. News of the death of Coligny provoked the simmering tensions into palpable hostilities. The Huguenot nobles and their entourages were directed to the huge courtyard of the Louvre, where they were summarily massacred. Detachments of soldiers were sent out to destroy all Huguenots, and were joined by mobs of ordinary Catholic residents of the city in a slaughter that cost the lives of anywhere from 2,000 to 5,000 people in the capital, and even greater numbers also in provincial centers where encouragement was widespread to imitate the carnage in Paris.[20]

The *Vindiciae* is a detailed inquiry into one of the crucial problems of the legitimacy of political authority: what means could

---

[19] Diefendorf, *Beneath the Cross*, 47, and Kaplan, *Divided by Faith*, 1.

[20] Much has been written about this event, but one of the most comprehensive studies remains Kingdon, *Myths about the St Bartholemew's Day Massacre*, esp. 28–50. For a convenient summary of the larger diplomatic and religious contexts, see Ford, *Political Murder*, 158–60. The estimates of victims vary widely with the accounts. Anthony Marx, e.g., writes: "Within several days, between two and four thousand were slaughtered in Paris; within weeks, at least another 4,000 or as many as 10,000 outside the capital, including many more than those listed by the authorities, lost their lives." See his *Faith in Nation*, 90.

be used, and by what justification, to oppose a ruler who seeks to destroy the state, or who violates divine law by devastating the church? The answer provided involved a new formulation of the traditional concept of the prince ruling with divine investiture. The *Vindiciae* argues for the doctrine of a tripartite contract involving God, the ruler and his earthly subjects. The sovereign's legitimacy was regarded as based on both the carrying out of God's commands and on a range of secular obligations to the people under his authority. This was, in a real sense, a social contractual theory *avant la lettre*, presaging not only the Lockian and Rousseauian notions, but Hobbes' as well, where the contractual relationship was bipartite in the absence of a divine partner. It was also, therefore, the construction of the legitimacy of the modern secular state, which was, somewhat ironically, being empowered by these religious justifications.

On the matter of resistance and opposition to the sovereign, the *Vindiciae* makes two points clear. First, any ruler who assumes power illegitimately is considered a usurper, in the Aristotelian model, and may be slain by a subject of the realm in the name of God.[21] As for the more elusively defined problem of the legitimate ruler who through misrule becomes identified as a tyrant, the *Vindiciae* painstakingly describes the many acts that characterize this form of despotism, which include instances of subverting the state, offending God, breaking sacred and civil obligations and having committed extraordinary crimes against his people. In such cases, it is the duty of "officers of the kingdom, either all or some good number of them, to suppress a tyrant." Indeed, if they choose to refuse this task under such circumstances, they themselves become classifiable as tyrants, by virtue of their complicity.[22] To be sure, the examples in the document remain cast in Biblical modes ("It is then lawful for Israel to resist the king who would overthrow the law of God and abolish his Church"), but its conceptualization is pathbreaking in its attention to having a responsible elite (officials such as officers, magistrates, tribunal authorities, etc.) acting in the name of the people. They are assigned

---

[21] Laski, *A Defense of Liberty against Tyrants*, 121. Laski's edition was essentially a republication of the 1689 English translation of the *Vindiciae*. See his thoughtful introduction, 1–60. For a discussion of other Protestant contemporary theorists seeking both to define and confine violent tyranny, including François Hotman and Theodore Beza, see Kingdon, *Myths about the St Bartholemew's Day Massacres*, 172–82.

[22] Laski, *A Defense of Liberty*, 137.

the moral duty of resisting the tyrant's rule because they "represent the whole body of the people."[23]

At the same time, individuals far closer to the centers of political authority than those writing about how to resist the crown's despotism were working out notions of even more powerful forms of state sovereignty. The reverberations from both the St Bartholomew's Day massacre and the Protestant resolve as presented in the *Vindiciae* sent shock waves into the heart of the monarchy's officialdom. The distinguished political theorist Jean Bodin (1530–96), a French diplomat in the service of the king's brother, fashioned a theory of sovereignty in his influential work, *Six Books of the Commonwealth* (1576), which was designed to ward off the disorder and chaos of the continuing combat between Catholics and Protestants seeking increasing influence over secular political authority that reached a bloody climax in the 1572 mass killings.

For Bodin, the primary concern was to justify a powerful sovereign in a way which would preserve the state and defend it and society against the clashes of factionalism, whether religious or secular in nature. His response was to demonstrate with comprehensive evidence from past legal traditions as well as scriptural sources that the state was to be recognized as the supreme and indeed exclusive source of legitimate political authority and public order. Although legal rulers had long been invested with divine legitimacy, their power had been variously challenged, weakened, neutralized and, at certain historical moments, overthrown with apparent justification. To avoid the simple but legally indefensible principle of might makes right, and to make the ruler able to do more than merely follow traditional laws and codes of conduct, Bodin invented the principle of legislative sovereignty. This capacity for law-making powers would henceforth be the exclusive responsibility of the absolutist king, justified by divine doctrine and natural law.

Regarding resistance to the sovereign, Bodin believed that since the powers of the king in the state were modeled on God's in the universe, any attack on him or his authority was tantamount to an assault on the Lord. In direct opposition to the tyrannicide theorists, Bodin argued that there was no justification for violence against the sovereign. If he was a legitimate ruler, meaning he had come to power

---

[23] Quoted from the original document in Laqueur, *Voices of Terror*, 30.

according to law, the presumption was that he transcended all affairs of ordinary men. Short of defiling the church, or some unthinkable outrage against God, the ruler could do no wrong to justify using violence against him. Indeed, if conflicts continued to exist in the civil order in matters of church or state, it was the fault of inferior human intervention. To consider taking up arms against the sovereign meant only that "the magistrates themselves are the authors of this failure." The king was the resolver of disputes, not the cause of them.[24]

Neither Bodin nor the author of the *Vindiciae*, despite their competing narratives, could alter or redirect the flow of violence that continued to undermine the social fabric of European society and threaten the national monarchies. The pattern that would dominate the modern era was already cast at this point. Although the violence was justified on predominantly religious grounds, ultimately Protestant and Catholic secular authorities controlled much of it. To put it another way, religious identity was become increasingly contingent upon secular political power. Without the protection of the sovereign prince, quotidian existence was bound to be full of anxiety and uncertainty, making the search for the higher authority to protect oneself and family a necessity. At the same time, the regimes and their hardened oppositions continued to fashion grandiose theories to respond to these insecurities, even though they were often provoking the very forces they sought to reduce in the process.

Some examples should make this tendency clearer, all of which followed in the wake of the traumatic events of the St Bartholomew's Day's mass violence that brought new anxieties to rulers and provided the impetus to push the Reformation's rebellion against Rome further to challenge the traditional modes of power. The more ordinary events that triggered clashes between Catholics and Protestants included public gatherings for funerals, holiday celebrations and religious processions passing through mixed neighborhoods, where the strict codes of respectful behavior could be challenged. Another category of such clashes was the schism over the abolition of the Julian calendar and the adoption of a new calendar by Pope Gregory in 1582. Gregory had already offended Protestants by celebrating the St Bartholomew's Day killings with an official holiday, in addition to issuing a medal commemorating the Catholic triumph in 1572 and

---

[24] On Bodin, see the recent book by Engster, *Divine Sovereignty*, esp. 47–80.

publicizing an additional room devoted to the event in the Sistine Chapel. Revolts broke out in German and Swiss cities with large Protestant populations when demands were made to show public obedience, for example, during Catholic processions honoring the town square on this holiday. To repeat, these protests, which at times turned quite violent, were frequently resolved by secular authorities. City officials and wealthy burghers were called upon to restore order, which they usually managed to do.

The Gunpowder Plot in London in 1605 was another revealing example of the fusion of religious and secular forces in conflict. While it is true that the St Bartholomew's Day massacre was probably the single most violent event apart from battles in war during the early modern era, the Gunpowder Plot could have been as deadly or worse, had it succeeded. Robert Catesby and Henry Garnet, two passionate Catholic supporters, planned the tactics of the conspiracy. At the last moment, a demolition team led by Guy Fawkes was discovered as they prepared to explode a large amount of gunpowder which could have brought down Westminster Palace, the houses of Parliament and untold numbers of MPs in and around the buildings, including King James and members of the royal family. Although often considered part of the religious warfare of the age, it was the secular officialdom and military who were responsible for preventing the carnage that had been planned mainly by a group of conspirators who, though sympathetic to the Catholic hierarchy, were not clerics themselves.[25] The important factor, nevertheless, remains the larger context. Queen Elizabeth had overseen the torture and execution of Catholic priests and their sympathizers for years.[26] The real significance of this affair is the fact that it represents one of the earliest forms of attempted insurgent terrorism. It also invites speculation about possible alterations in the course of England's political history that might have occurred, had the conspiracy succeeded.

[25] For a comprehensive study, see Hogge, *God's Secret Agents*, esp. 328–78. Fawkes was executed along with seven other participants. Evidence suggests that Elizabeth herself was the target of insurgent terror attacks from discontented Catholics, including the Ridolfi Plot, the Babington Plot and the Throckmorton Plot, among others. See also Kyle, "Early Modern Terrorism," 42–55.

[26] Some of these instances were particularly cruel, such as Margaret Clitherow's barbaric execution in 1586 and that of Robert Southwell in 1595, not to mention the numerous missionaries "martyred" on the rack. See Hogge, *God's Secret Agents*, 142–4, 184–90, 209–11.

In the French rural town of Agen in 1618, town magistrates intervened to halt what would have been a mob execution of a Calvinist who refused to remove his hat as a measure of fealty when a Catholic funeral procession passed in front of him. In 1718, during the Corpus Christi ritual in Augsburg, Catholics used the occasion to smash their way into Lutheran homes, torching as many as they could, before military guardsmen, ordered by the royal administration, stopped the violence by firing on the Catholic mobs. Finally, in Warsaw in 1724, the national tribunal of the crown convicted 16 Lutheran citizens and the burgomaster of the town of Thorn to be executed after being proclaimed guilty of sedition. The burgomaster, with the support of his officials, had arrested a Catholic who had refused to kneel as ordered by Jesuits leading a Eucharistic procession through the region, for which they received the ultimate punishment by the Crown's judiciary.[27] With few exceptions, in each instance the secular forces of political authority prevailed in the conflict of Christianities.

Both Protestants and Catholics were driven by powerful fantasies of purification through violence. Moreover, throughout the seventeenth century, during the height of mass assaults by each side on the other, the ubiquitous role of secular authorities in mobilizing, leading and utilizing the unleashed passions of the *menu peuple* to achieve these grandiose goals of containing or removing the religious enemy is clearly visible.[28] This fusion congealed to the point where it becomes increasingly difficult to make a clear distinction between what is purely religious and ecclesiastical on the one hand, and distinctly political and secular on the other. Even when trying to tease out the current of religious riots in the sixteenth century as a phenomenon separate from actions traceable directly to agents of political and clerical authority, the interaction of the two is almost always the dominant theme, whether we speak about grain riots or assaults on churches. If the religious motive of the crowds seems to have been rescuing the faith from competing heresies, the secular officialdom was deeply involved

[27] For a recent discussion of many of these instances, see Kaplan, *Divided by Faith*, 78–92. Kaplan is more concerned with tracing toleration to the pre-Enlightenment, than with the theme of state resolution of violent religious conflicts in this period. Many more earlier examples can be found in Davis, "The Rites of Violence," 152–87.

[28] For a convenient listing of 35 of the more prominent assassinations of both church and state officials from 1535 to 1649, see Ford, *Political Murder*, 147–50.

because of its own interests in regime consolidation. Often, political officers, along with lawyers and merchants, assisted favored clerics actively by participating in the violence themselves, judges in the royal courts could be counted on to render approving verdicts, and court edicts both encouraged certain acts of violence they favored, while punishing others they feared.[29]

As we move closer to the watershed of the French Revolution, the mechanisms of state control become ever more dominant in generating the support previously organized around religious affiliation. The royal houses in power found new ways to mobilize the religious passions of the past, recruiting allies in the solidification of nationalism as the primary social identity for subjects of the realm, defining which groups to include and which to exclude. The state's role was organized around a clever balance between engendering conflicts and reconciling them. The tension was a delicate one in which rewards and punishments were issued simultaneously. As the process of the institutional convergence of church and state took place, the consequence was the overall secularization of religious loyalties and identities on the eve of the eighteenth century Enlightenment. State rulers learned to attack heretics as a tactic to "enflame religious passion and redirect it" for their own ends.[30] Opponents of the crown learned the same lesson. The casualties were huge as the violence was directed toward new goals. The operating motive was for rulers to resolve the questions surrounding the legitimacies of their authority, gained, as we have seen, through this complex process of frequently fostering religious conflicts while presenting the attractions of secular protection against them. This fusion of the religious and the secular currents of the period was also visible in the violent events of the English Civil War, which included the spectacular trial and execution of King Charles I in 1649, following his conviction on charges of high treason by a special High Court of Justice. Charles was convinced his authority was justified by divine ordination; Parliament thought otherwise.[31] The ensuing decade of violence brought forth a spectrum of both religious and political radicalism.

---

[29] See Davis, "Rites of Violence," 165, 167, 169, 184.
[30] Marx, *Faith in Nation: Exclusionary Origins of Nationalism*, 193.
[31] See the interesting discussion of regicide legitimacy with regard to Charles' trial and execution in Burgiss, "The English Regicides and the Legitimation of Political Violence," 56–76.

The larger framework at work in this period prior to the French Revolution was one of advancing state centralization over previously powerful authorities in the provinces. With regard to violence, the state's role was "imposing some degree of security in the face of civilian armaments." Monarchs in power, from London and Paris to Berlin and Vienna, gradually gained control over weapons and agents of violence. Security forces, judicial courts and police constabularies replaced local magistrates and armed retinues of landowners and rulers of regional principalities. As one scholar of this period has put it, "The growth of state power, evident in police forces, arms control, and the expanding power of the state judiciaries, increasingly contained the [forms of] early modern popular protest."[32] As the religious motifs of the era became increasingly blended into political struggles, the accompanying violence was concomitantly secularized.

[32] Ruff, *Violence in Early Modern Europe*, 45, 253.

3 TRAJECTORIES OF TERRORISM IN THE TRANSITION TO MODERNITY

The eighteenth century witnessed further refinements in the discourse on political violence which both accompanied the transformative events of the French Revolution and its aftermath as well as, at the same time, providing conceptual tools to understand these paradigm shifts. Between the conclusion of the Thirty Years War in 1648 and the death of Louis XIV in 1715, national monarchies had largely succeeded in taming the passions of the religious conflicts between Catholics and Protestants, and had created vast networks of loyal functionaries who gradually broke down many of the deeply rooted feudal practices in the provinces on behalf of the centralizing governments. In addition, perhaps most significantly, the monarchs essentially demilitarized the territory under royal authority by abolishing the private militias formerly responsible to powerful regional lords. If Max Weber is correct in defining the stability of the modern state as requiring superiority in the use of legitimate force, it is in this period that such a reality took concrete shape. In a parallel trend at work at the same time, the notion of absolutist monarchical government, as conceptualized by Jean Bodin and ultimately realized by Cardinal Richelieu in France, sought to conclusively end the regional and religious competitiveness of the past over the control of political authority by creating a sense of consensual acceptance (if not agreement) on sovereign rule by a central and supreme legitimate power, or what Charles Taylor has called the "social imaginary" of the nation.[1]

---

[1] Taylor, *Modern Social Imaginaries*. Charles Tilly has taken this theme a bit farther by comparing the national monarchy in France to a protection racket legalizing

As the legal and moral parameters of the state expanded, the government bureaucracy gradually gained supremacy over a growing system of surveillance and regulation that replaced the vanishing provincial forms of authority. Imperial ordinances, regulatory acts and codes of punishment were either legislated or decreed across the continent, from St Petersburg, where Peter the Great founded his new Russian capital, to the centers of Hapsburg and Bourbon authority, which both mobilized and controlled the subjects of their realms.[2] Kings and emperors were to monopolize supreme positions of authority within clearly delimited territories, while projecting a pervasive presence throughout the territory, all intended to fashion a unified social order, free of the feudal disparities in landholding practices, trade, currency, taxes, and military power.

One of the most important contributors to this growing force of centralized royal power was Jean-Baptiste Colbert, who, until his death in 1683, could justly be called Louis XIV's *ministre extraordinaire*. Although mainly celebrated for his sponsorship of the French mercantilist economic system, and his unparalleled private library, Colbert also was responsible for establishing a structure of state control over policing and intelligence that made his sovereign the most powerful king in Europe. In 1666, Colbert established a special office, the Police Council, reporting directly to him and armed with the task of sending agents across the country to printing houses and booksellers to ensure they were adhering to the regime's strict censorship code. These controls over the production and distribution of knowledge, and the emphasis upon secrecy to protect the image of the state, with severe penalties for disobedience, led to a kind of "terrorism of the word." The significance of these developments was to be quite far-reaching. As a recent historian has put it, "[Colbert's] secret sphere of state power would rear its head again during the police states of the Terror and Napoleon, and nestle itself into the administrative frameworks of the nineteenth and twentieth centuries."[3]

Despite these currents of change, resistance to the process of state formation remained and, in some cases, assumed the guise of

organized crime. See Tilly, "War Making and State Making as Organized Crime," 169–91.
[2] See, among many works on this topic, Engster, *Divine Sovereignty* and Raeff, *The Well Ordered Police State*.
[3] Soll, *The Information Master*, 165.

violent rhetoric. Emmerich de Vattel, a legal theorist influenced by Hugo Grotius and Christian Wolff and who also conducted diplomacy for the Kingdom of Saxony during the 1740s, wrote a clear reminder of the dangers of despotic rule:

> The sovereign who has recourse to such execrable means (as assassination and poisoning) should be regarded as the enemy of the human race; and the common safety of mankind calls on all nations to unite against him and join their forces to punish him.[4]

The most influential critiques of the new absolutism emerged from the Enlightenment thinkers primarily during the second half of the eighteenth century. Despite the rigidities of royal censorship restrictions, they managed to pen and publish a veritable avalanche of theories concerning social contracts and utopian proposals, from Rousseau's concept of the General Will, to Condorcet's project on the historical development of the human spirit. Rich with possibilities for future social orders in the absence of tyrants in power, few were concerned directly with issues of political violence. The one exception was Montesquieu who, even earlier, showed that he was well aware of the possibilities for outbreaks of "wild terror" from below during periods of political upheaval, as well as the spread of fear in society fostered by regimes of despotism. Indeed, he even understood the insurrectionary danger of "the avengers establishing a tyranny under the pretext of avenging the republic."[5]

Once the revolution erupted in 1789, the theories were surpassed by the reality of widespread violence, provoking outbursts of alarm from a variety of observers, including examples as varied as parliamentarian Edmund Burke in London, and Catherine the Great, Empress of Russia, in St Petersburg. The narrative of the revolution has been explored in what is now a truly vast literature. Our purpose here

---

[4] From Vattel's Law of Nations, originally published in 1758, as quoted in Edelstein, "War and Terror: The Law of Nations from Grotius to the French Revolution," 243. See also the discussion of early modern theories of political violence in Thorup, An Intellectual History of Terror, 80–6.

[5] Quoted in Mayer, The Furies: Violence and Terror in the French and Russian Revolutions, 100–1. See also the discussion in Robbin, Fear: The History of a Political Idea, 51–72. Thorup states that it is "Montesquieu more than anyone who lays the groundwork for the subsequent politicization of the concept" of terror. See An Intellectual History of Terror, 85.

is, more modestly, to examine the currents of political violence within the larger framework of the revolution. From the moment of the seizure of the Bastille in Paris on July 14, 1789 by an aroused citizenry, the moorings of quotidian life were undermined by unplanned and, in many cases, unprecedented acts.

The very boundaries of state legitimacy were called into question as the monarchy ceased to maintain its authority and competing factions vied to fill the vacuum of power. The governing elements of what was quickly being termed the *Ancien Régime* – the palace and its exalted inhabitants, the clergy and its virtual monopolization of religious authority, and the loyal bureaucratic agents who enforced the functioning mechanisms of the monarchical state system – were cast out of the emerging political wilderness into either prison or exile. New institutions rapidly were invented to replace those now discredited, including a new representative legislative assembly. Amidst the feverish atmosphere, with new frameworks of political legitimacy being invented almost daily, opponents real and imagined were accused and condemned by a freshly empowered network of judicial tribunals, who found execution to be the most effective means of protecting the revolutionary regime against its enemies.

Interestingly, among the many zones of violence that preoccupied France in these years, the wars of religion disappeared quickly. There was a short-lived traditional outbreak of hostilities between Catholics and the minority Protestants in Nîmes in the spring of 1790, but it dissipated within months once the National Assembly promulgated the Civil Constitution of the Clergy in July. This measure effectively nationalized the entire ecclesiastical institution of the church by abolishing papal control over appointments to high office in the French clerical hierarchy, mandating in their place civil elections for those offices.

As the Jacobin party gained supremacy over the Girondins in the Assembly, the question of what to do with the king became the symbolic central issue of the revolution. While the king lived essentially as a prisoner under house arrest from the first year of the revolution, the Jacobin leadership led by Marat, St-Just and Robespierre succeeded in having the Bourbon monarchy officially abolished. Following this, they brought charges of treason against Louis XVI in an impassioned trial, where he was found guilty and sentenced to death for his crimes against the people of France. In an astonishing legal act of tyrannicide, the revolutionary government ordered him to be executed in a public ceremony in January, 1793. His wife, Marie-Antoinette, was also taken to the scaffold, seven months later.

Within the next year, the Jacobin-controlled Committee of Public Safety essentially assumed authority over the divided National Convention (which had succeeded the National Assembly) and inaugurated a self-proclaimed Reign of Terror. The centerpiece of this regime violence was the newly invented beheading machine, named after its leading advocate, the physician and medical reformer Joseph-Ignace Guillotin (d. 1814). First tested in the spring of 1792, the Convention leaders decided to have it mass-produced and distributed around the country. This decapitation device was believed to be more effective than hanging (no dangling and writhing bodies due to rope breaks or noose slippage), more economical than using expensive munitions to shoot the condemned, and more humane than the suffering and pain caused by medieval racks that pulled limbs apart, and jailors' whips that tore apart flesh. One part of the ritual did not change, however: the severed head was frequently displayed, as had been the case following royal executions in previous centuries, to the cheering throng watching in prepared wooden stands and from windows in nearby buildings. Though the estimates vary, it is generally assumed that some 18,000 people were executed on the guillotine during the year of Jacobin Terror, with staggering numbers of additional victims resulting from the summary justice of the revolutionary tribunals and the wars of the Vendée around the country.[6]

The atmosphere in the capital and beyond was truly feverish and chaotic. Every week brought yet another crisis, some growing out of unconfirmed rumors while others were based on quite realistic fears. They varied from dangers of economic underproduction and distribution of essentials like grain, to the sounds of approaching armies from alarmed regimes at France's borders, who felt immediately threatened by the republic's rebellion against the traditional legitimacy of monarchical rule.

---

[6] The most accepted data come from Greer, *The Incidence of the Terror during the French Revolution*. A more recent analysis claims there were at least 20,000 victims beyond the "official figure" of 18,000. In addition, there may have been as many as 200,000 to 300,000 casualties, counting the Vendée civil war, out of a total population of around 28 million. See Chaliand and Blin, *The History of Terrorism from Antiquity to Al Qaeda*, 102. One of the ironies of the new method of execution by guillotine is that Dr Guillotin himself was opposed to the death penalty, and hoped that the new mechanical form of execution would lead to the growth of an opposition to all forms of capital punishment in France.

One of the more imaginative of the numerous rumors circulating in Paris and throughout the country was one claiming Robespierre's collusion with the royal family. The centerpiece of this plot purported his intention to marry the daughter of the executed king (now referred to by his common name, Louis Capet) with the intention of having himself crowned king of France. The rumor had the impact, in the words of the historian who has studied the affair, of "verbal violence." As fantastic as it was to believe, the milieu of fear that dominated the new regime and its citizens contributed to its plausibility. The reality behind the outrageous rumor in this case turned out to be quite diabolical. The creators of the fictitious plot were none other than members of Robespierre's own Committee on Public Safety. Their intent was to fabricate a plot against the republic that could be blamed on the exiled royalists, which would then turn into a groundswell of support for the state's need to enact further emergency legislation to protect the revolution against its violent enemies. And this it proceeded to do, with roundups and executions to "liquidate" the factions of Dantonists and Hébertists, who were presented as mortal threats to the foundations of natural law upon which the republic was being structured.[7]

The language of Robespierre's speeches was dominated by this sense of persistent fear. The anxiety pervading the overall political situation is palpable in his public addresses and proclamations, as though with each word he could somehow compress the evident chaos of this uncharted journey into a world designed to combine the promise of equality and liberty with the tactics of democratic authoritarianism. He seems never to have understood the contradictions of this political fantasy.

For Robespierre, terror was conceptualized as either a weapon of oppression when utilized by despots of monarchical rule, or as a means of liberation when dispensed in the name of the people. "Terror," he wrote, for the maintenance of the republic against its enemies, "is merely justice, prompt, severe and inflexible. It is therefore an emanation of virtue and results from the application of democracy to the most pressing needs of the country."[8] On another occasion, in a speech to the governing Convention, he stated that "the terrifyingly

---

[7] This affair of "the King" is analyzed in Baczko, *Ending the Terror*, 1–32. The "factions" referred to anyone suspected of association with the politics of Georges Jacques Danton or Jacques-René Hébert.

[8] Quoted in Scurr, *Fatal Purity*, 304.

swift sword of the law should hang over the heads of all conspirators, striking terror in the hearts of their accomplices and of all enemies of the *patrie*."[9] His enthusiastic comrade, St-Just, formulated policy recommendations to the Convention that were even more draconian: "You have no longer any reason for restraint against enemies of the new order," he told the delegates in the winter of 1793–4 as the Terror was reaching its zenith. "You must punish not only traitors but the apathetic as well; you must punish whoever is passive in the Republic ... We must rule by iron those who cannot be ruled by justice."[10]

At the same time, St-Just was implementing increasingly severe police laws, permitting the authorities to make sweeping arrests on the basis of little more than suspicion and rumor. Newspapers that dared to criticize the regime's policies were shut down and their editors arrested, including public figures like Camille Desmoulins. Similarly, previously untouchable popular political leaders with large followings, such as the charismatic Danton, and entire political parties, like the Hébertists, were rounded up, convicted and hauled off to mount the staircase to face the gleaming blade of the guillotine. Virtue could not triumph without physically vanquishing "the enemies of the homeland," as Robespierre frequently put it.[11] The very choice of words used by Robespierre clearly reveals the psychological state of siege that dominated his thinking and emotions.

One of the most alarming pieces of legislation that clearly intensified the atmosphere of fear was the "Law of Suspects," a decree authored by the Committee on Public Safety and accepted by the National Convention on September 17, 1793. Among its provisions were measures clearly designed to enhance the authority of the newly created Committees of Surveillance and their cooperation with the revolutionary tribunals already in place in Paris and elsewhere throughout the country. The law identified gross categories of political enemies of the republic, which included members of families of the first two estates, namely the clergy and the nobility, as well as those of émigrés

---

[9] Quoted in Mayer, *The Furies*, 196.

[10] See Gough, *The Terror in the French Revolution*, 43, and Wahnich, *La liberté ou la mort*, 24, where the theme of vengeance against the *Ancien Régime* as a motivating factor in the violence of the Republic is discussed.

[11] See the selections in Robespierre, *Virtue and Terror*, especially "On the Principles of Revolutionary Government," 98–107. On St-Just's measures, see Gueniffey, *La politique de la terreur*, 286. On the Hébertistes, see Slavin, *The Hebertistes to the Guillotine*.

who had fled to England or Austria. The Committees of Surveillance were empowered with the ability to issue warrants for the arrest and imprisonment of such suspects. They also had the legal right to seize all private papers of those taken into custody. The suspects were then to be turned over to the authority of the relevant tribunal, where they could be sentenced with or without trial, even if there was insufficient evidence for accusing the suspect of the charge of "not consistently manifesting their attachment to the revolution."[12]

The dynamic of conflict between elements in the government and in society had reached a point at which the violence had become both state policy and state obsession. The fear and insecurity felt by the leaders of the Committee of Public Safety was a consequence of the absence of a consensus of regime legitimation, and the challenges presented by what Robespierre and his associates were convinced was an authentic insurgency of multiple opposition factions. These were realities, to be sure. Danton, Desmoulins and many others had concrete disagreements with the government's program of terror. However, Robespierre and St Just could not tolerate these challenges, and understood them solely as threats to their authority. Political differences in this atmosphere of foreign invasion and domestic chaos were not a sign of healthy debate on the country's future, but an image of threatening subversion that had to be crushed quickly.

The tide eventually turned against Robespierre as the fears of enemies in his midst and of losing control of power that haunted him ultimately served to undermine his own justifications of violent authority. When opinion turned against him by midsummer of 1794, he raged against fanatics opposing him who, he claimed, were loyal only to themselves or to conspiring monarchists still active in France. The Convention was persuaded that the policies of regime terror were no longer justifiable, and ordered his arrest. Robespierre fled to a room in the Hotel de Ville with a few loyalists, still issuing manifestoes when the military broke in and captured him. He was brought to the beheading machine he had made so popular and suffered his own justice when the blade came down on his neck on July 28 (10 Thermidor, according to the revolutionary calendar).[13]

---

[12] The law can be found in Anderson, *The Constitution and Other Select Documents of the History of France, 1789–1907*, 186–7, and in Mason and Rizzo, *The French Revolution: A Document Collection*, 231–2.
[13] Andress, *The Terror*, 344.

Whether this signified "an assassinated revolution"[14] or one that had decayed under the violent weight of attempting to realize its own utopian fantasy, Thermidor brought an end to "The Terror" of the Committee of Public Safety. It did not, however, abolish the uses of political violence that had characterized it. Just as the Revolution had subsumed earlier religious forms of violence, so too did the Reign of Terror install policies that were adapted by the Directory, which succeeded the discredited Convention in Paris. Indeed, according to one historian who has studied this period, state violence became "a strategic instrument and an object of management" of existing social relations in the late 1790s.[15] Far from ending the violence, France under the Directory displayed a continuation of the authoritarianism of the Terror years. Still acting within the framework of a democratic republic, its legislation included enhanced forms of state repression, an expansion of the judicial trials to punish groups led by returning monarchist and aristocratic exiles, as well as members of a variety of factions dissatisfied with the political orientation of the Directory, and also a declaration of a national state of siege, which even Robespierre had not enacted.

The dynamic of interrelated terror at this time is perhaps best exemplified by the activities and grandiose political strategy of François-Noël (Gracchus) Babeuf, the pioneering political activist who influenced militants in France over the next century like Filippo Buonarroti and leaders of the 1871 Paris Commune. Babeuf was involved with political affairs of the revolution since its inception in 1789 and was most prominent for his association with the radical Cordelier Club and as the editor of the populist newspaper, *Le Tribun du Peuple*. He was jailed several times by the security forces of the Directory after the Thermidor events, for his association with Jacobinism. In 1795, he founded the Society of Equals, which proclaimed a dedication to a socialist future in which distinctions between rich and poor would be abolished and which also was to be led by an insurrectionary committee that would chart the way to the final revolution.

The group managed to unsettle the government, with its distribution of pamphlets and graphic broadsides. It was, however, the Society of Equals' manifesto that was most threatening, written by

[14] The phrase comes from Baczko, *Ending the Terror*, 260.
[15] Brown, *Ending the French Revolution*, 50.

the poet and political theorist, Sylvain Maréchal, a comrade of Babeuf's. The revolution had addressed the problem of political rights, Maréchal argued, but had neglected the larger crisis of an economic system that plundered and exploited the peasant masses. With enthusiastic incantations, the document insisted that the existing system was "full of desperation and unhappiness" because of the corruption of the economic elites dominating France. "Evil is at its height; it cannot become worse, and the only remedy is total subversion! Let all return to chaos, and from chaos let a world arise new and regenerated."[16]

This focus on the economic consequences left unaddressed by the leaders of the republic was the main contribution to the emerging radical discourse made by the writings of Babeuf and Maréchal. The latter survived until 1803 by publishing under a *nom de plume*, but Babeuf was discovered in hiding with the help of a double agent working for the police who betrayed him. Babeuf was arrested on May 10, 1796. His trial, in which he was prosecuted by the Directory for being involved with the 1793 Jacobin constitution that ushered in the Reign of Terror, lasted three months and resulted in a sentence of death. Babeuf was executed on May 27, 1797 as part of the continuing effort to cleanse France of associations with the regime of the Committee of Public Safety, which, somewhat paradoxically, tended to prolong the violence.

England also reacted strongly to the threat posed by the political convulsions in France. Suspicion of sympathies with the republican cause echoed strongly in Parliament, where a series of repressive laws were passed to contain activities of British Jacobins, as they were termed. William Pitt, the prime minister, saw the events in France as existential threats to England, particularly once the monarchies surrounding France agreed to take joint military action to halt the progress of the revolution. Pitt proposed suspending the right of habeas corpus in England to contain the danger on the home front, which provoked an acerbic debate in the House of Commons. Among the other acts Pitt sponsored, one of the more significant was the 1795 Seditious Meetings Act, which forbade meetings of more than 50 people without notifying

---

[16] Quoted in Orsini, *Anatomy of the Red Brigades*, 185–6. Maréchal's "Manifesto of Equals" was originally published in 1796. Influenced by Rousseau and Diderot, he has been seen as a precursor of the French utopian socialist movement that emerged during the Restoration era.

the government, aimed mainly at the London Corresponding Society whose members were supportive of the cause of republican liberty in France. Several prominent trials of individuals who refused to renounce their revolutionary views took place in England and Scotland in an effort to criminalize political activities and publications that were considered seditious. There were also acts of violence throughout the 1790s in London and elsewhere during the period. Political fears were aroused and citizens felt justified in taking matters into their own hands by denouncing political meetings that appeared to be republican-oriented and calling for the arrest of anyone suspected of French revolutionary ideas or activities. There were no guillotines, but enough intimidation, discrimination and repression to have the period referred to as Pitt's "reign of terror."[17]

Napoleon Bonaparte sought to bring order to the chaotically insecure political situation, once he engineered the replacing of the Directory with the Consulate as the new governing body in Paris. As the powerful First Consul, he contributed significantly to the formation of the emerging national security state by directing a pronounced wave of repressive terror, particularly after an attempt was made on his life in 1801. Hundreds of suspected and convicted royalists were deported, while the less fortunate were imprisoned and guillotined.[18] Following his successful *coup d'état* in November, 1799, he ended the Republic, proclaimed France an imperial state, had himself crowned Emperor, and over the course of the next 16 years sought to "liberate" the continent of Europe from monarchical authority by military conquest.

Instead of creating a universal empire, Napoleon's occupation of Europe after his initial victories produced nationalistic reactions across the continent. German cities and towns held patriotic festivals, Protestant churches sponsored services of religious piety that revived the earlier antagonisms directed against the papacy and Catholicism, and student organizations formed along nationalistic lines, in some cases openly critical of the Bonapartist regime.

A more extreme reaction appeared in southern Italy in 1809, in the form of secret societies dedicated to overthrowing the despotic French authorities. Calling themselves Carbonari, they were an outgrowth of the Enlightenment Masonic lodges, some of which had

---

[17] Davis, "The British Jacobins and the Unofficial Terror of Loyalism in the 1790s," 92–113.
[18] Brown, *Ending the French Revolution*, 316–17.

operated clandestinely in order to be able to read and discuss books forbidden by royal censorship. The name they chose translates as "charcoal burners," which seems to have been a symbolic reference for their activities. They met in underground settings, often in secluded forests where charcoal artisans had collected tree bark and stored their products in furnaces. According to one of the few extant memoirs by former members, they also used the identification with this respected trade to avoid suspicion from the authorities.[19]

One of the clearest signs that the Carbonari were moving toward alternative conceptualizations of political legitimacy was the manner in which they inaugurated new recruits. Neophytes were put through an elaborate ceremony that deliberately mocked traditional Catholic ritual, in which they performed the Passion of Christ in a political, antidespotic manner the church would have certainly considered blasphemous. The initiates wore crowns of thorns, figuratively walked the road to Calvary and held symbols of Catholicism that were to be used violently against the French occupiers. In the words of a participant, the Cross serves

> to crucify the tyrant who persecutes us ... the Crown of
> Thorns should serve to pierce his head. The thread denotes
> the cord that leads him to the gibbet ... The leaves are nails
> to pierce his hands and feet. The pick-axe will penetrate his
> breast and shed the impure blood that flows in his veins. The
> axe will also separate his head from his body ... The pole
> will serve to put the skull of the tyrant upon the furnace
> which will burn his body ... The fountain will purify us
> from the vile blood we have shed ...[20]

While this language is more reminiscent of *Ancien Régime* era tryannicide treatises, the Carbonari also made clear their political intentions. Membership estimates, which may well be exaggerated, claimed over 24,000 Italian and French activists at the height of their influence. Buonarroti, an ardent follower of Babeuf, was an active member of one of the Carbonari groups. The Napoleonic administration saw the

---

[19] Bertoldi, *Memoirs of the Secret Societies of the South of Italy*, 4–5.
[20] Ibid., 32–3. Also see Rath, "The Carbonari, Their Origins, Initiation Rites and Aims," 353 ff.

mission of the most radical societies in the Italian south as "the subversion and destruction of all governments." Meanwhile, the Carbonari themselves made it clear that they would utilize their resources of "invincible courage" to combat "the government of the military occupation." They even used the word "terror" to describe the methods to be employed, favoring the dagger and poison in the combat against Bonaparte and his Italian ally, the Pope. The ultimate goal of Carbonari activism was the "prospect of establishing an independent republic" after "the yoke of the present government is destroyed."[21]

In 1814, the Carbonari were active in seeking to overthrow the monarchy and establish a constitutional regime in the Kingdom of Naples, by force if necessary. After the collapse of the Bonaparte occupation, the ranks of the Carbonari swelled further, developing military detachments involved in sporadic guerrilla warfare in Lombardy and Piedmont against the French and Austrian authorities still in control of the Italian peninsula. The societies of the Carbonari dissipated in the late 1820s, with many former members continuing the struggle for republicanism and Italian unification in the Young Italy groups under the inspiration of Giuseppe Mazzini. With their systematic campaign of political violence, the Carbonari network left the legacy of being one of the earliest examples in the modern period of a terrorist insurgent movement.

In many respects, Mazzini was the hunted insurgent terrorist of his generation. After finishing law school, he joined one of the surviving Carbonari groups in 1829 but was arrested within a year. Following his release, he fled to Marseilles where he organized the first Young Italy society dedicated to the creation of a united Italian republic. He plunged into the underworld of conspiracies, establishing his radical reputation as the editor of the periodical he created, *Young Italy*. Throughout the 1830s, he led failed urban insurrections in northern Italy, the result of which led to a huge manhunt by the police across much of Restoration Europe. He lived most of his later life as an exile in London, where he issued a stream of pamphlets calling for

---

[21] Bertoldi, *Memoirs of the Secret Societies of the South of Italy*, 54, 90, 154, 177–83. In his mentioning of the Pope, the author refers to the Concordat signed by Napoleon and the Vatican in 1801. The volume also contains an appendix which includes an 1814 document from Rome declaring a ban on the Carbonari (206–12) and a letter to Pope Pius VII in response arguing for a secular democracy over the continuation of a religious monarchy (213–20).

armed revolution. He had his moment in the sun during the 1848 convulsions when the Rome Republic was briefly set up, but was in a Sicilian jail when his dream of a unified Italian national state finally was realized in 1871.[22]

The consequences of the destabilization of monarchical legitimacy in Western Europe, brought into sharp focus by the emergence of French republicanism, the Terror and the Napoleonic imperial aftermath, surfaced also in tsarist Russia at this time. Since the reign of Peter the Great, the country had been pushed, encouraged and at times driven toward the West, but the real integration of the eastern and western branches of Europe occurred as a consequence of Russia's participation in the continent-wide military campaign that finally brought down the French Empire in 1815.

Catherine the Great, even more than her admired predecessor, mobilized the landowning gentry and much of the state bureaucracy to invest in learning to speak French and to become familiar with selected writings of the Enlightenment thinkers, some of whom even came to St Petersburg, like Diderot, at her invitation in 1773. Her Charters to the ruling elites, while designed to consolidate her own power, were full of selectively edited quotations and interpretations, from Montesquieu and the English legal philosopher William Blackstone. The contradictions in her politics between encouraging modest forms of criticism while maintaining autocratic authority over all discourses soon became clear once the revolution broke out in France in 1789. Catherine saw her life's work in ruins, fearing the spread of "the French disease" to Russia. She arrested Alexander Radishchev, a customs official who published a travelogue in 1790 based on the genre developed by Voltaire and Montesquieu. In his book, Radishchev quoted versions of discussions he had with peasants and traders on a journey he took from St Petersburg to Moscow, which included critical comments about the difficulties of life under monarchs and landowning elites. The timing was crucial for Catherine, who saw this book as a mortal threat to her authority and worried that she too could face the dangers that were confronting Louis XVI in Paris if she did not act decisively. All copies of Radishchev's book were seized from bookstores, and the plates on

---

[22] See Isabella, "Mazzini's Internationalism in Context: From the Cosmopolitan Patriotism of the Italian Carbonari to Mazzini's Europe of the Nations," 37–58.

which the publisher had printed it were melted down. Radishchev himself was sent into Siberian exile.[23]

Nevertheless, her "Enlightenment project" for Russia was still visible less than a generation later. When Napoleon attacked Russia in 1812, many Russian officers were fighting an army whose language in some cases they knew better than their own, having been tutored in French since childhood. After pursuing the French forces across Europe, the Russian military was assigned to join in the siege of Paris, together with troops from England, Austria, and Prussia, to ensure the peace. While the statesmen gathered in Vienna to hammer out a new world order, Russian officers, utterly fluent in French and familiar with the country's culture, attended salons and cafes, and found the literature of the revolutionary era in the bookstalls of Paris. Returning home a year later, a small group of these officers with friends who shared their interests formed the Union of Salvation, which changed its name in 1818 to the Union of Welfare, whose members read and discussed the controversial books they had brought back from France, all of which were under official ban.

In 1820, the group split into what they called the Northern Society, based in St Petersburg, and a smaller Southern Society, located in Tulchin, a military garrison in the south. The division occurred at first because of the transfer to Tulchin of one of the most active members, Pavel Pestel, but political differences soon reinforced the separation. Increasingly, both groups entertained ideas of political change; both wanted Russia to move from autocracy to a constitutional state, but the Southern Society, under the more radical leadership of Pestel, advocated a direct transition to a republic. He also was attracted to Robespierrean notions of revolution and overthrow of the tsarist administration. Pestel's economic program included a plan for the emancipation of Russia's huge population of serfs, a subject that could not be even mentioned in print. Of greater significance, he also formulated a conspiracy plan that went farther than any known insurrectionary group, including the Carbonari. In his "Green Book," Pestel outlined the creation of what he termed a *"garde perdue,"* whose responsibility was to assassinate the entire Romanov family.

[23] There are numerous accounts of Catherine's responses to the French Revolution, which also include letters expressing her fears to confidants such as the brothers Jakob and Wilhelm Grimm in Switzerland. See de Madariaga, *Russia in the Age of Catherine the Great* and her *Politics and Culture in Eighteenth Century Russia.*

As the two groups were in the midst of discussions questioning the legitimacy of the tsarist regime, and seeking to formulate their alternatives, Emperor Alexander I suddenly and unexpectedly died. The line of descent was unclear, since he had no sons to succeed him. Moreover, Russia had never put into place a binding law of succession. When Nicholas, Alexander's youngest brother, claimed the throne, a bloody confrontation at the Senate Square in the capital took place on the night of December 14, 1825 between the rebels of the Northern Society and troops loyal to Nicholas. The Northern Society was prepared to support the other claimant to the vacant throne, Nicholas' older brother Constantine, whom they felt would be more interested in accepting a transitional constitutional monarchy in Russia, as a first step toward realizing a democratic republic in the future. Pestel and the Southern Society members never had the opportunity to join forces with the Northern Society, as they were too far away. By morning, the result was a decisive victory for Nicholas' palace guards. The leadership and core membership of both groups were arrested and imprisoned, being given the combined name of "Decembrists" by the police, by which term they have been known ever since. Five of the leaders of both organizations, including Pestel, were executed, and over a hundred rank and file members were sentenced to life terms of "administrative exile," and sent off to detention camps in Siberia, inaugurating the foundations of the infamous Gulag Archipelago.[24]

To ensure that no future rebellions against the regime would be permitted to emerge, whether from officers in the court's elite military units such as the Decembrist leaders, or from below in any form, Nicholas accepted the recommendations of one of his ministers, Count Benckendorff, that he form a national secret police force with extraordinary powers of surveillance and arrest. It was named the Third Section because it was embedded in that division of his Majesty's Chancellery. For the next five decades, the agents of the Third Section hounded intellectuals, publicists, students among others, gathering dossiers of intelligence on them, harassing them and finally, when so ordered by their superiors, making sweeping arrests. Even the most prominent poet in the country, Alexander Pushkin, was unable to escape their repression.

---

[24] This event has received much attention from historians of Russia. The most comprehensive account remains Nechkina, *Dvizhenie Dekabristov.*

By these acts, Russia adopted the ethos and the institutions of the rest of Restoration Europe, where governments were instituting policies of fear, terror and repression. Following the decisions taken at the Congress of Vienna in 1815 to restore the royal houses to their legitimate positions of authority across the continent, citizens of the recreated monarchies in France, Prussia, Austria and elsewhere in Western Europe were subjected to the severe rules established four years later in a document known as the Carlsbad Decrees. The clauses in this joint statement by the leading Restoration monarchies included provisions for the expansion of censorship to deal with an increasingly literate population, the arrest of professors and students considered dangerous to the rulers, and continent-wide curfews that were to be put in place.

The restrictions on universities were particularly rigid. Academic autonomy was reduced by the presence of "special representatives of the ruler of each state" who "shall have their place of residence where the university is located." Their task was to "strictly enforce the existing laws and disciplinary regulations" and to ensure that anyone "presenting harmful ideas hostile to public order or subverting existing governmental instructions" would be removed from their positions on the faculty or in the student body. Once removed, the instructor "becomes ineligible for a position in any other public institution of learning in another state." Finally, laws already in place "directed against secret and unauthorized societies in the universities shall be strictly enforced."[25]

The prime mover behind this reign of fear was Prince Klemens von Metternich, who as the Hapsburg Emperor's state chancellor in Vienna, was the most powerful statesman in Europe at the time. He had dominated the meetings at the negotiations following Bonaparte's defeat and presided at the Diet where the signing of the Carlsbad Decrees took place. His contempt for any serious opposition from below and his willingness to impose what he considered "the legitimate forces of order" to safeguard the stability of the restored administrations is evident from his memoirs as well as his policies. In particular, his 1820 "Profession of Political Faith" describes the "sources of evil" at work led by the arrogant idealists driven by the idea of "universal perfection" and "the absurd idea of the emancipation of the people," concepts

[25] Excerpted from the document in Snyder, *Documents of German History*, 158–9.

Metternich found "contrary to the essence of man and incompatible with the needs of human society."[26] The conservative theorist Joseph de Maistre put it even more bluntly: "All greatness, all power, all order depend upon the executioner. He is the tie that binds society together. Take away this incomprehensible force and at that very moment order is suspended by chaos, thrones fall and states disappear."[27]

To be sure, the Carbonari inaugurated the structure of insurgent terrorism that would be expanded by Louis-Auguste Blanqui and his many secret organizations in Paris in subsequent decades; the rebellions from below from 1830 to 1848, which brought the Restoration to a violent end are also a crucial part of the narrative. And, more significantly, during the 1820s, rebellions advocating constitutionalism, republicanism and, above all, nationalism, broke out in Spain, southern Italy, Portugal and Greece, where, in the latter case, independence from Ottoman control succeeded in an especially violent episode.

However, the larger context of state repression and terror needs to be considered as an integral component of the dynamic at work in the development of modern terrorism. Indeed, de Maistre was not exaggerating when he referred to royal authority's willingness to use force as the necessary factor in guaranteeing the stability of monarchical legitimacy.[28] Aside from the rigid restrictions on granting permission for public gatherings, what could be published, who could vote, what limits of authority the elected bodies would be permitted, among others, the role played by the state's exercise of violent repression, conducted without pause throughout the decades of the Restoration, deserves to be more clearly integrated into the analysis of the history of terrorism in this period. Of the many examples that could be cited to show the path of the growing tide of violence before the 1848 revolutions, among the most brutal were those that formed part of the 1830–1 rebellion in France.

Although there had been confrontations between insurgent groups and the regime throughout this era, this was the most threatening to the government since the fall of Napoleon. The result of the clashes and political party activism was the dissolution of the

---

[26] von Metternich, *Mémoires laissés par le Prince de Metternich*, vol. III, 431.
[27] Quoted in Artz, *Reaction and Revolution, 1814–1832*, 73.
[28] Garrard, "Isaiah Berlin's Joseph de Maistre," 117–31. See also Armenteros, *The French Idea of History*.

Bourbon monarchy that had ruled France for centuries. In its place, a constitutional monarchy was formed, with Louis-Philippe of the House of Orleans as the successor king cooperating closely with the national parliament. Uprisings in Lyons in 1831, mainly among the silk weavers who labored there in large numbers, ended with more than 600 casualties. In Paris that year a funeral for a Napoleonic military hero, General Lamarque, was broken up by the authorities in clashes that left at least 150 people dead.[29]

Many more incidents occurred with lesser numbers of victims. There were no transnational organizational links to these events, although in most of the cases, the clashes were the result of economically desperate workers and artisans, whose protests were seen by the regimes as politically threatening. German authorities assaulted a crowd of laborers in Aachen in August 1830 in which seven unarmed people were killed. During a strike in Lyons in November of 1831, eight workers were shot dead. An attack on workers by Prussian troops in June 1844 in Silesia, to quell what the government considered a labor riot when demands were made for the improvement of conditions, led to 35 people being killed by gunfire.

The tension between elements in society seeking change, on the one hand, and government policies determined to resist these efforts, on the other, was furthered by the network of state surveillance that had become a crucial part of every Restoration state's budgetary calculations since the Carlsbad Decrees were signed. According to one historian who has studied this problem in detail, the repression and legal restrictions imposed by the royal authorities "were so severe in most European countries that opposition groups were forced into conspiratorial activities."[30] The period is often referred to as "the White Terror" – royal rather than revolutionary violence.

The Austrian and Russian police appear to have been masters of these policies. The Hapsburg regime in Vienna had a wide variety of informants on their payroll. These included servants employed on wealthy estates, writers who were willing to inform in return for permission (if not direct sponsorship) to publish, brothel managers and their sex workers, and the ever-watchful doormen and coachmen anxious to enhance their meager salaries by providing notes to the

[29] Harsin, *Barricades: The War of the Streets in Revolutionary Paris, 1830–1848*, 39–144.
[30] Goldstein, *Political Repression in Nineteenth Century Europe*, 69.

police on the activities of the targeted individuals they served. In addition, members of the police acted in dual roles, as they reported on the groups that they infiltrated, but often were also ordered to foment provocative anti-government actions. Once top-secret dossiers, quite thick in many cases, reside in the national archives as revealing windows into these Restoration period surveillance systems.[31]

Similar evidence exists for the work of the notorious Third Section based in St Petersburg.[32] The police aggressively enforced the state's restrictions on academic freedom at universities, as well as comprehensive censorship regulations and the bans on public gatherings. In addition, police officials began to take advantage of the international exchange of intelligence, advocated by Metternich at the Congress of Vienna, by conducting their own surveillance and ordering arrests in cities abroad where oppositional Russians had fled into exile. While the political exile community included well-known figures from Western and Central Europe such as Lajos Kossuth (Hungary), Adam Mickiewicz (Poland), Heinrich Heine (Prussia), Giuseppe Mazzini (Italy) and the Germans Karl Marx and Friedrich Engels, the contingent from Russia was in the process of becoming the largest of all. Already, before 1848, Alexander Herzen and Michael Bakunin had found cafes and neighborhoods in Geneva and Paris populated with their compatriots, where they could speak Russian freely and begin the act of literary sabotage by publishing anti-tsarist journals and newspapers in Russian abroad, with arrangements to smuggle them back to Russia for distribution.[33] Distributed they were. We now

---

[31] For general histories of the police in Europe, see Emsley, *Gendarmes and the State in Nineteenth Century Europe*, Emsley and Weinberger, *Policing Western Europe*, and Torpey, *The Invention of the Passport*. Robert Peel is conventionally credited with being "the father of modern day policing" as a result of his plan for the metropolitan police force in London in 1829, but he was concerned primarily with the prevention of civil crime. To limit thievery and other crimes, he proposed neighborhood police gaining the trust of civilians.

[32] In addition to the standard accounts of the tsarist police by Sidney Monas and R. Squires as well as the definitive Russian language study by Gernet, *Istoriia tsarskoi tiurmy*, see the more recent account by Ruud and Stepanov, *Fontanka 16: The Tsar's Secret Police*, which had the benefit of post-Soviet archival access.

[33] On these activities and individuals, see above all, Herzen's magnificent memoir, *My Past and Thoughts*, as well as Miller, *The Russian Revolutionary Emigres, 1825–1870*. 10,000 Poles are estimated to have fled to the West after the failed uprising in 1830–1 against the Prussian, Austrian and Russian occupiers of the country. The three powers had eliminated Poland from the map of Europe by dividing it up in the late eighteenth century. It would not reappear as a sovereign nation until the conclusion of the First World War.

know that among the numerous subscribers to Herzen's radical paper *Kolokol* ("The Bell") were none other than Emperor Nicholas I and the chief of the Third Section. In the pages of *Kolokol* (and its predecessor, *The Polar Star*), readers found open discussions about previously forbidden and censored topics. These included the political ideas and fate of the Decembrists, the numerous peasant uprisings (and their violent repression) which the mainstream press were unable to report, and documents spirited out of state files by discontented officials with evidence of court corruption at the highest levels.

With the expansion of public education and rising literacy rates, more citizens began to correspond with each other. While this development, largely sponsored by the state administrations through their ministries of education, brought postal systems into high levels of usage, it also provided the police with additional sites to conduct surveillance and collect intelligence on individuals and groups whose loyalties to their governments were questionable. Most post offices in the main European cities allowed space for a spying operation, and employed a permanent staff of agents specially trained in handwriting analysis and in reading codes.

The opposition was far from innocent of using its own violent methods. After a massive arrest of over 1,000 people in Paris in 1834 when the police believed they had prevented an assault on the monarchy of Louis-Philippe, republican groups managed to assemble a huge gun barrel with 25 chambers of ammunition and attempted to kill the king. They failed to achieve their objective, but killed at least 14 innocent people in the process. There were seven other known attempts on Louis-Philippe's life by groups who considered him one more in the long list of royal tyrants abusing their authority.[34] One particularly striking episode unraveled on July 28, 1835, when Giuseppe Fieschi, a Corsican nationalist radical who detested the monarchy's restoration in France, attempted to assassinate the king. Together with a small group of accomplices, he managed to assemble a heavy gun which was capable of firing all of its 20 barrels simultaneously. On that July day, Fieschi released the chambers of his "infernal machine" from a building above the street where the royal procession

---

[34] Rappoport, *1848: Year of Revolution*, 26 and Harsin, *Barricades*, 101–3.

was passing. Eighteen people were killed instantly, but Louis-Philippe escaped unharmed. Fieschi himself was severely burned by the backfire of the large gun, but was nursed back to health in order to stand trial, where he was condemned to death and executed on February 19, 1836.[35]

Louis-Auguste Blanqui, leader of the insurrectionary Society of Seasons, fomented revolutions and seizures of power throughout this period, including a particularly violent confrontation with the regime in the spring of 1839. He was arrested many times, only to reemerge, after serving time or being pardoned, with yet another new conspiratorial group, achieving near legendary status within the insurrectionary underground. Not a systematic writer, he nevertheless produced numerous essays and pamphlets, including during the 1848 upheaval, presenting the case for the violent seizure of power by a select group of conspirators which had a wide influence among insurrectionists, especially in France.[36]

1848 was a crucial moment in the evolution of these trends. Once the angry crowds overwhelmed the forces responsible for the defense of royal authority in Paris, regime after regime collapsed across the continent in an unprecedented series of multiple revolutions. The upheavals caused the largest number of deaths from acts of political violence in half a century.[37] The roots of these rebellions are complex. No one anticipated or planned for this year of multiple revolts that would topple thrones and have republics declared so rapidly across the continent. Marx and Engels famously produced their pamphlet, "The Communist Manifesto," about industrial class struggle on the eve of the revolt in Paris in February, but even they were surprised by the extent of the violence and the overthrow of the monarchies.

Yet, the forces that made 1848 happen were already in progress. A radical intelligentsia had developed, with inspiring theoreticians and activists speaking and writing knowledgeable treatises as well as more journalistic articles advocating the abolition of poverty, and the rights of citizens against the despotisms of the Restoration

---

[35] Harsin, *Barricades*, 147–67.
[36] See especially Dommanget, *Auguste Blanqui et la révolution de 1848*.
[37] Goldstein, *Political Repression*, 65, has collected the following data: 40 killed in Paris on February 23, 1848; 30 shot or stabbed to death in Stockholm in anti-government rioting on March 18; in April in Rouen, France, 59 were killed in election riots; in a particularly bloody week in June in Paris, 3,000 people were summarily executed after a workers' rebellion was finally put down; 30 artisans and factory workers were killed in the labor uprising in Vienna on August 23.

regimes. Some, like Pierre-Joseph Proudhon, Louis Blanc and Guiseppe Mazzini, even found themselves in political office during the brief reign of the republican governments established that year. Liberal nationalists also played a key role in mobilizing public opinion in favor of constitutional republics to replace the monarchies. Above all, discontented urban workers, organized in nascent labor organizations, took to the streets to demand better factory conditions. Equally significant were the rebellions in the countryside where peasants, who wished to hold on to their traditional forests, fields and properties now threatened by the industrialization trends in the cities, attacked landowners, local banks and provincial officials. Under the weight of this violence, Restoration administrations vanished not only in Paris, but also in Vienna, Berlin, Munich and Budapest. In Dresden and Prague, the anarchist Michael Bakunin attracted followers who found meaning in his appeals for rebellion against the established authorities and who were willing to confront the police on the streets in large numbers.[38]

Nevertheless, the unequal nature of the conflicting sides cannot be ignored, nor the huge imbalance in the number of victims, in which victims of the state exponentially exceeded victims of the insurgents. This was especially true once the smoke cleared in the spring of 1849, revealing that the revived armies of the monarchies had crushed every republic, from Paris to Budapest, with many thousands of casualties. France, where it all started, ended the revolution in 1851 under the aegis of another Napoleon, who after seizing power in a *coup d'état*, revived the imperial political structure left in ruins back in 1815.

Amidst the carnage of the 1848 revolution, a document was published that broke new ground in justifying insurgent terrorism. The essay, written by a radicalized former German civil servant, Karl Heinzen and titled simply "Murder," appeared in March of 1849 in an obscure periodical called *Die Evolution*, as the royalist armies of the Hapsburgs and Hohenzollerns were approaching to wipe out the last of the liberal and radical opposition strongholds.

Heinzen's argument proceeded along the lines of a syllogism that had the power to trap its readers into accepting some

---

[38] For a good brief account of the 1848 revolts, see Bayly, *The Birth of the Modern World, 1780–1914*, 155–60. A minor but interesting episode in the Dresden affair in 1848 was the fact that Bakunin, following his subsequent arrest by the authorities after they regained control of the town, shared his cell with another young radical, the future nationalist and composer Richard Wagner.

uncomfortable conclusions. His first premise was that annihilating the life of another human being was "a crime against humanity" and a morally unacceptable act. The second premise followed from Heinzen's review of Western history since ancient times, in which he found governments and their leaders responsible for the destruction of their subjects and citizens in an unbroken succession of violence.

The conclusion to these premises, supported with a large number of examples, was that since the state had committed atrocities against society, members of society had no choice but to adopt similar methods if they were truly to achieve their liberty. Either no one kills, or murder "should be permitted equally to all." In another passage, he wrote: "Even if we have to blow up half a continent or spill a sea of blood in order to finish off the barbarian party, we should have no scruples about doing it. The man who would not joyfully give up his own life for the satisfaction of putting a million barbarians into their coffins carries no republican heart within his breast." Governments proclaim their desire and responsibility for realizing and protecting the liberty of society but in fact have acted to repress it, with virtual unlimited brutality, of which declared warfare is only the most visible form. "Murder," Heinzen resolves, "is the principal agent of historical progress."[39]

Heinzen was prescient in recognizing the importance of technology as a means for "freedom fighters" to overcome the enormous advantages in numbers of troops and advanced weaponry that are always available to the state. To redress this imbalance, he saw no difficulty in making use of new chemical discoveries to construct concealed bomb devices, exploding Congreve missiles and introducing food poisoning as tactics to triumph over the monarchist rulers and their subordinates. He was convinced that he was justifying what was essentially an ongoing civil war for the defense of the rights and liberties of citizens. His conclusion was that the assassins in governments "have left us no other choice than to devote ourselves to the study of murder and refine the art of killing to the highest possible degree."[40]

Heinzen's language in this essay is an unexpected advance without precedent in the radical literature of his time. He personally knew

---

[39] Heinzen, "Murder," 53, 59. Walter Laqueur published an expanded version of these texts as *Voices of Terror* (New York: Reed Press, 2004). A full translation of Heinzen's essay has been published in English for the first time. See Bessner and Stauch, "Karl Heinzen and the Intellectual Origins of Modern Terror," 143–76.

[40] Heinzen, "Murder," 64.

Marx, Engels, Arnold Ruge and other contemporary critics of monarchical rule in Prussia, and indeed they criticized one another with verbal vitriol. He also emerged, as the others did, from the hothouse of Hegelian and Feuerbachian philosophical debates of the 1830s, but no radical before him had justified acts of terrorism against the state with such venom and with such comprehensiveness. As one scholar has put it, "Heinzen does not simply want an unjust king to be killed and replaced. He wishes to see an entire system, and with it all those human beings who represent or are involved in that system, completely wiped out."[41]

Was Heinzen the last of the classical tyrannicide theorists, or the first exponent of modern terrorism?[42] In a sense, he does bring one trend to an end and inaugurates the next. Writing the text within the context of the 1848–9 revolutions that toppled Metternich and his entire state system, Heinzen, while deeply conscious of his predecessors who struggled to justify the killing of a tyrant, had moved this discourse onto new ground. Removing a tyrant, he realized, would solve little, as there was no guarantee that his successors would sponsor policies that would bring genuine liberty to the people. Moreover, Heinzen recognized the easily demonstrated fact that not only were governments continuing to legally repress and execute citizens under their protection, but the number of victims had risen from century to century. The collapse of the republics that had sprung up in 1848 across Europe, and the savagery with which their supporters were dealt with in the aftermath, convinced him that a specific ruler was not the problem. It was the very system of monarchical legitimacy itself that had to be fought and overthrown with methods of unlimited violence.

To be sure, Heinzen exaggerated and erred in his arguments, stereotyped his categories of analysis, and, most serious of all, provided no alternative for ending the cycle of political violence. Nevertheless, his

---

[41] Grob-Fitzgibbon, "From the Dagger to the Bomb: Karl Heinzen and the Evolution of Political Terror," 104. Also of interest is Heinzen's political imaginary. He sought to plant in newspapers scenes of fictitious terrorist bombings, in the hope of provoking governments into confrontations and bringing out recruits who might actualize these deeds. See Grob-Fitzgibbon's summaries, 106–9. See also Laqueur, "Karl Heinzen and the Origins of Modern Terrorism," 89–99.

[42] For an argument that separates tyrannicide justifications (as the negation of tyranny) from terrorism (as a form of tyranny), see George, "Distinguishing Classical Tyrannicide from Modern Terrorism," 390–419. Oscar Jászi saw a continuum in his *Against the Tyrant*. Grob-Fitzgibbon, "From the Dagger," portrays Heinzen as making the breakthrough conceptually into terrorism.

argument stands at the dawn of the justifications for using insurrection-ary terrorist methods to achieve political objectives that would be reiter-ated in the next century. Though he remained virtually unknown for decades even among radical circles, Johann Most, the radical publicist, rescued Heinzen from obscurity by publishing "Murder" in his news-paper *Freiheit* on the day President McKinley was shot in 1901. Indir-ectly, whether he was aware of it or not, Frantz Fanon's argument linking the necessity of utilizing methods of political violence with the possibility of achieving freedom in the Algerian struggle against France during the late 1950s is a twentieth-century revision of the Heinzen thesis.

With the failure of the republican cause in the revolutions of 1848, an era came to a close in many ways. The problem of defining legitimate and just rule had certainly undergone a transformation as a result of the course of events. For the insurgents, authority was no longer to be understood in terms of whether individual rulers were conducting the affairs of state in a manner that benefitted or abused subjects of the realm. The collapse and revival of the monarchical regimes during the crisis of 1848–9 had shown that despotism was now to be under-stood in systemic terms. For the rulers, the lessons learned had more to do with strengthening the structure of what would soon be known as "the security state." The consequences of this shift in thinking with regard to the future of political violence were to be momentous.

Lastly, at this historical juncture, we can recognize the emer-gence of many of the essential interdependent ingredients of modern political violence. These elements were (1) the initial example of self-proclaimed state terror in Robespierre's Committee of Public Safety within the framework of a democratic republic, (2) the birth of the first insurgent organization, the Carbonari, whose members were dedicated to destroying state authority and reclaiming national territory, and (3) the principal text justifying the role of insurgent violence to bring an end to the terror of the state, as argued in Heinzen's essay. In each instance, the violence was fueled by the growing interrelationship between the police and security forces of the state and the regime's activist opponents, and by the expectations on each side that, ultim-ately, victory and their respective visions of a more perfect future would be theirs. It was left to the Russians to apply this theory and practice in a manner that awakened the world to the frightening realities of the growing menace of this interlocked struggle between agents of terror in government and the underground.

4 NINETEENTH-CENTURY RUSSIAN REVOLUTIONARY AND TSARIST TERRORISMS

As France was the first country in Europe to make the transition from monarchy to republic, Russia was one of the last. Nevertheless, a similar dynamic was at work in Russia's development into a modern nation state. Here as well we find some of the same problems of contested political legitimacy that created the resort to violence that prevailed elsewhere on the continent, although they have their own historically and culturally distinct colorations. For example, the roots of political absolutism lie deeper in Russia, and lasted longer than was the case in Western Europe. Similarly, the forms of political violence made use of by rulers and insurgents in Russia, while entangled with their West European counterparts, assumed their own characteristics as well. The peasantry and its agricultural world continued to play an important role in the evolution of Russian politics, both in court policy and among the opposition factions that challenged it, long after dominating rural influences were integrated into the centralized state systems in France, Prussia and Austria. Assemblies of social elites played a far less significant role in Russia's history, and laws were decreed rather than legislated even into the early twentieth century largely because the legitimacy of autocracy required the absence of any parliament or political parties, unless called into temporary existence by the ruler.

The notion of the state, as it evolved in Western Europe, was confined in Russia for centuries to the concept of *gosudarstvo*, a notion of sovereignty that includes the predominating role of a possessor (*gosudar'*) of the territory and inhabitants "of all Russia." Linked to this idea was the economic reality that the tsar (or Grand Prince earlier, and Emperor later) was sovereign over a domain in which the country was essentially his estate, supported by an expansive network of princes, landowners, soldiers and bureaucrats who served the ruler by fulfilling the assigned professional obligations of their ranks, which came to be referred to as state service. The nationalist concept of a "fatherland" (*otechestvo*), an ancient Slavonic word, began to take on the meaning of the Latin *patria* during the seventeenth century; indeed, Peter the Great in 1721 assumed the title of "father of the fatherland." All of this received sanctified status as a consequence of the historic relationship of the ruler and the church. The Orthodox Church invested the Riurik and Romanov dynastic houses with spiritual legitimacy, creating a bond that lasted for a thousand years until the 1917 revolution.

In Russia, we find neither the tyrannicide nor the republican discourses that were common in Western Europe. Thus, we lack a set of texts that inquire deeply into the criteria for the just ruler and attempt to clarify the justification for opposing, with violence if necessary, the sovereign's despotic abuse. Similarly, we do not have a literature on the collective rights of subjects and citizens rooted in notions of social contracts. In spite of efforts to define the "common good" for which the ruler was responsible, it was always inseparable from ideas of state control.[1]

This does not mean that Russia was devoid of political violence, but rather that it assumed different forms. Nor does it mean that Russia lacks examples of serious inquiries into absolutist theory in defense of the ruling regime against threats to its legitimacy.[2]

Discontent emerged most palpably in two formats: huge rebellions by serfs and Cossacks from below, and "palace coups" arranged by court factions from above. Regarding the former, these revolts raged annually from the sixteenth to the eighteenth centuries, often lasting for months, with enormous devastation on both sides. On the one hand, estates of the landlords were burned to the ground, sometimes accompanied by the killing of the owners and their families, leaving a

---

[1] See the interesting discussion in Kharkhordin, "What is the State? The Russian Concept of *Gosudarstvo* in the European Context," 206–40.

[2] For one example, consult Raeff, "An Early Theorist of Absolutism: Joseph of Volokolamsk," 177–87.

pervasive sense of fear and mistrust seething in relations between landlords and their subjects. On the other hand, the military was ruthless in its repression on each occasion. As for the latter, in the absence of any acceptable law of succession, the death of a ruler frequently led to violent disputes. Especially in the eighteenth century, succession was decided by palace circles, led by alliances of families from the high aristocracy, military leaders and foreign diplomats with their own interests at heart, in which the assassination of disputed and controversial tsars became routinized.[3]

The fears and suspicions of Russia's rulers regarding real or imagined threats to their security, together with catalogs of serious punishments for their opponents engraved in law codes, can be traced back centuries in the written records. The tsars also specialized in establishing police organizations at the court level, at least since the time of Ivan the Terrible's *oprichnina* in the sixteenth century, an official vigilante body that serves as the ancestor of many modern security agencies under state control with authorization to terrorize specified targeted populations. Peter the Great created a special state guard regiment, the *Preobrazhenskii Prikaz*, which was responsible for protecting the tsar, his family and his court. Catherine the Great relied on what she named the Secret Expedition to protect her regime against enemies of the state, headed by her chief prosecutor, Stepan Sheshkovskii, whose reputation for torturing suspects is verifiable in memoir evidence from the 1770s.[4]

To illustrate the violence of her administration, historians have rightly turned to the dramatic events of the huge Pugachev rebellion, that wreaked destruction across the width of the country and almost succeeded in surrounding Moscow in a state of siege in 1774. In her eventual victory, she was without mercy; Pugachev's severed head, removed from his broken body, was paraded around the city in the traditional medieval fashion. Another prominent example that has

---

[3] On the peasantry, see the comparative study by Mousnier, *Peasant Uprisings in Seventeenth-Century France, Russia and China*, Avrich, *Russian Rebels, 1600–1800* and also Mironov and Eklof, *The Social History of Imperial Russia, 1700–1917*, 82–3. For the court violence, see Anisimov, *Five Empresses*. Perhaps the most spectacular of these assassinations was the killing of Peter III in 1762, as orchestrated by his wife and successor, Catherine the Great. The succession of palace murders came to an end in 1801 when Paul I was killed with the involvement, however passive, of his son and successor, Alexander I. Interestingly, no tsarina was ever the targeted object of this trend of court violence.

[4] Efremov, "S. I. Sheshkovskii," 12.

been widely discussed in the literature was Catherine's inflamed response in 1790 to Alexander Radishchev's book, *Journey from St Petersburg to Moscow*. However, historians have paid far less attention to the constant arrests by Catherine's Secret Expedition and the brutality the suspects were subjected to in Sheshkovskii's dungeon cells within the forbidding Schlusselburg fortress throughout her reign.[5]

Soon after coming to power, Alexander I (1801–25) closed down the Secret Expedition but replaced it with his own version of a secret national police force called the Committee of General Security, designed as an intelligence-gathering bureau reporting to the Ministry of the Interior. In 1810, he added a separate Ministry of the Police headed by A. D. Balashov, who led the campaign against the tsar's reforming secretary of state affairs, Michael Speransky. Speransky was charged, falsely, with treasonous activities in connection with the attacking Napoleonic forces, arrested and sent into Siberian exile in 1812.

The role of surveillance and repression in the Russian government advanced to new levels following Nicholas I's (1825–55) accession to the throne in the wake of the Decembrist Affair. In an effort to realize "the dream of a beautiful autocracy," Nicholas set up the Third Section of His Majesty's Imperial Chancellery headed by Lieutenant-General Alexander K. Benckendorff.[6] This iteration of the imperial political police, which was to last for decades, succeeded in creating a mood of fear throughout the circles of educated society as its numerous agents made frequent use of their powers of arrest and censorship as well as their ability to invade the privacy of homes and to destroy the careers of anyone whom they suspected of harboring republican ideas of liberty. An early director of the department, Mikhail von Vock, even attempted to launch a newspaper devoted to principles of autocratic virtue that was to be subsidized and overseen by the police. For Benckendorff, the purpose of the law was to maintain the autocratic order, not to enforce justice in ways that would permit members of society

---

[5] Ruud and Stepanov, *Fontanka 16: The Tsars' Secret Police*, 14–15. Among the many victims of severe interrogations conducted personally by Sheshkovskii was the prominent Enlightenment intellectual Nikolai Novikov in 1792, who was subsequently sentenced to a 15-year prison term for what he had written.

[6] The phrase is taken from Monas, "The Political Police: The Dream of a Beautiful Autocracy," 164–90. See also Squire, *The Third Department*.

to diminish that security of authority. As he memorably stated at one point, "laws are written for subordinates, not for the authorities."[7]

There were contrary voices in the government, with concerns about the escalation of these security measures in the absence of attention to reform policies, however few in number they may have been. As early as 1827, Benckendorff's plan, which was to be implemented together with a modest expansion of public education to instill principles of patriotic enlightenment, was questioned by one of the regime's censors with an awareness of possible violent counter-consequences:

> *Will the people themselves cast off their bonds or will they receive freedom from the government itself? God save us from the former! But this is inevitable if the government merely educates the people without slackening their bonds as national self-awareness awakens. It is important that educational measures go hand in hand with a new civil code.*[8]

Informants were paid to spy on their colleagues in universities and clubs suspected of radicalism in any way. Files containing both censorship reviews and intelligence reports grew to voluminous proportions. As Russian archival repositories have made clear, these extensive reports included material on the poet Alexander Pushkin as well as the members of the nascent critically thinking intelligentsia. Letters were increasingly delivered to their recipients by hand, as the Third Section agents were known to be opening sealed mail sent through the regular post, gathering evidence that gave them the pretext to make an arrest. Many of these letters, incidentally, are documents rich in critical thought, often replete with footnoted references to recent books and articles that were considered dangerous by the authorities.[9] At least in one well-studied case, Peter Chaadaev was found guilty in 1836 of excessive criticism of Russia in a newspaper article, titled "Philosophical Letter," and imprisoned in an asylum, for being not responsible for

---

[7] Quoted in Pipes, *Russia under the Old Regime*, 290.

[8] Nikitenko, *The Diary of a Russian Censor*, 15.

[9] Among many of these collections, one of the most revealing and interesting is the correspondence of the literary editor Vissarion Belinskii, whose network included Alexander Herzen, Michael Bakunin and Ivan Turgenev. See Belinskii, *Izbrannye pis'ma*.

his words by reason of insanity. Thus, mutual fear was the order of the day in matters of politics; the state feared society, and vice versa.

These concerns within the government, even without any overt manifestation of insurgent conspiracies, led to further legislation. The powers of the police were strengthened further in the draconian measures decreed in the 1845 Law Code, which listed a variety of ways in which "direct and clear incitement to rebellion against Sovereign Authority" was to be assessed and punished with sentences of hard labor in exile and execution.[10]

Measures involving surveillance, censorship and arrest soon became far more extreme, in apparent response to resistance from below, which itself grew to more visibly threatening proportions during the decades of the 1860s and beyond. The insecurity of the regime was manifested in the manner in which it persistently relied on the police, whose activities continued to infiltrate daily life. The vital problems with which the intelligentsia became increasingly obsessed – the continuation of the horrors of serfdom affecting three-fifths of the population of the country, and the autocratic nature of the state, which prohibited political parties and representative elective bodies at the central level – were ignored by the government in a manner which suggested either denial or an absence of responsibility.

Instead, the administration became obsessed in its own way with what it saw as the threats from society to its traditional legitimacy. As the rebellious waves of 1848 rolled toward Russia, the security structure was easily ramped up to both locate and provoke opposition groups. As early as February, when the news of the fall of the Orleans dynasty in Paris had barely arrived, the interior minister, L. A. Perovskii, ordered an investigation into the activities of a relatively low-level official in the foreign affairs ministry, M. V. Petrashevskii. The members of his small reading circle were put under surveillance, declared to be a part of a subversive secret society, and condemned to death for treason three months later. Among those in the circle scheduled for execution was a young writer named Fyodor Dostoevsky. Although the sentence was altered at the last minute to terms of exile in Siberia, and granted that the utopian socialist material the circle members were reading and discussing was

---

[10] The harsh terms of the 1845 Law Code can be found in Pipes, *Russia under the Old Regime*, 294.

indeed banned by the state, Nicholas I still was overreacting in imagining a revival of the Decembrists in this affair. The fires of 1848 never got close to St Petersburg or Moscow, even including the disturbances in Budapest, where Nicholas sent troops at the request of the Hapsburg authorities. The tsar's power was never threatened at home or abroad in any serious manner, but what is important is what Nicholas and his officialdom feared could happen. That was the determining motive in shaping state security policies.

The apprehension and mistrust that characterized both sides at this juncture intensified to boiling point during the reign of Alexander II (1855–81). Given the hard lines of unyielding confrontation that the police and the opposition had dug into by this time, it is in some ways surprising that the impending terror did not emerge even earlier than it did. Despite the public reputation for reform that accompanied Alexander II in his first years on the throne, in fact he had approved the repression plan initiated by the new chief of the Third Section, Vasilii A. Dolgorukov.

Dolgorukov was clearly worried about the influence of the exiled socialist theorist Alexander Herzen. From his London residence, Herzen printed illegal Russian language publications that were then smuggled into Russia where they found a wide readership for the extensive reports from Russian correspondents about peasant discontent in the countryside as well as scathing and satirical accounts of court corruption and abuse. Indeed, Dolgorukov increased the number of Third Section agents sent abroad to infiltrate the Russian political émigré opposition, which included one who managed to obtain a position at a bookstore that distributed materials from Herzen's press.[11]

The specific target of Dolgorukov's surveillance within Russia was Nikolai Chernyshevskii, primary editor of the influential literary journal, *The Contemporary* (*Sovremennik*), whom he placed at the top of his list of the 50 most dangerous enemies of the state because of the publication's critical orientation and dedicated readership. The police worked under the assumption that there had to be an association between Herzen's illegal publications abroad and *The Contemporary*, which functioned in St Petersburg. In reality, Chernyshevskii did have a measure of respect for Herzen's radical journalism, but after a visit to

[11] Ruud and Stepanov, *Fontanka 16*, 27.

London to meet the "father of Russian Socialism," he was appalled by Herzen's mansion and aristocratic lifestyle, and dissociated himself from all links to the Herzen press. This the police did not consider of significance. With or without any actual connections to Herzen, Dolgorukov considered Chernyshevskii nothing less than the politically threatening incarnation of the banished Herzen, actively sabotaging the country from within.

Hounded by agents of the Third Section, Chernyshevskii could not escape becoming a victim. As evidence, the police found what they believed to be a direct link to Herzen's illegal press, buried in a long letter to Chernyshevskii, in which Herzen offered to publish sections of *The Contemporary* in London. The most condemnatory evidence for the police, however, were the articles in Chernyshevskii's journal itself, many of which contained, in Aesopian coded language, material clearly considered by the government to be unacceptably critical and indeed even subversive. At the same time, radical broadsheets were appearing on the streets of St Petersburg and Moscow calling for open rebellion and violence against the regime. Chernyshevskii was arrested and exiled for life to Siberia, his journal shut down, and a "White Terror," as Herzen termed it, was instituted for the remainder of the decade of the 1860s.[12]

The tragedy of the escalating tensions was that both sides were convinced of the justness of their cause and the intolerable danger of the other. The police, convinced of their mission to maintain security and order, certainly were involved in contributing to the rising disorder as a consequence of their policies of widespread harassment, censorship, surveillance and arrests. At the same time, the emerging radical underground was equally committed to its own cause, which was formulated as the need to rectify the regime's continued refusal to ameliorate the wretched condition of the peasantry's daily existence, which they found even more glaring after the raised expectations following the 1861 decree abolishing the status of serfdom. The details of how the autocracy's intransigence was to be resisted would soon be enunciated in lurid clarity.

---

[12] An unusually independent-thinking government censor kept extensive notes on the campaign against Chernyshevskii. See Nikitenko, *Dnevnik*, esp. vol. 2. For a representative collection of articles from *The Contemporary* in translation, see Matlaw et al., *Belinsky, Chernyshevsky and Dobroliubov: Selected Criticism*.

If words could kill, Peter G. Zaichnevskii's 1862 manifesto "Young Russia" would have done enormous damage. It was certainly the most chillingly violent document since the Decembrist Pavel Pestel had planned for the assassination of the entire Romanov family in 1825. Zaichnevskii spoke of his admiration for "the great terrorists of [17]92," adding that "we shall not be afraid if we see that to overthrow the present order we will have to shed twice as much blood as did the Jacobins during the [17]90s." He reiterated this point with an ominous prediction: "Soon, soon, the day will arrive when we raise the great Red Banner of the future and, with loud cries of 'Long live the social-democratic republic of Russia,' move on the Winter Palace to exterminate its inhabitants."[13] To find anything so boundary-breaking with regard to the outright proposal to commit regicide and mass political violence, one must go back to Karl Heinzen. While there is no evidence that Zaichnevskii had any knowledge of Heinzen's essay, there is reason to believe that he was imagining himself into a fantasy future in which Russia would erect a regime reviving Robespierre's Reign of Terror.

An even more alarming document followed. A manifesto printed illegally and titled "To the Young Generation" was also distributed at about the same time in various locations in St Petersburg. One of its core passages stated: "if to achieve our goals for the division of land among the people, one must slaughter 100,000 landlords, we would not hesitate, not even for a moment."[14]

Then, on April 4, 1866, Dmitrii V. Karakozov, a member of a small group called Hell (itself a breakaway from a somewhat larger group, Organization), made the first attempt by a revolutionary to actually assassinate the tsar. His shot failed to hit his target, and, moments later, he found himself restrained by peasants in the crowd around him, in whose name he had committed the deed. His act of attempted tyrannicide was, by his own admission, intended to be an act of revolutionary martyrdom:

> It saddened and burdened me that my beloved people is
> perishing like this [i.e., peasants living in conditions of
> poverty and abuse], and thus I decided to annihilate the

---

[13] Quoted in Verhoeven, *The Odd Man Karakozov*, 16.
[14] Quoted in Shlapentokh, *The French Revolution in Russian Intellectual Life*, 126.

tsar-villain and die for my beloved people. If my intention
succeeds, I will die with the idea that my death will be useful
to my dear friend the Russian muzhik. If not, then
I nevertheless believe that there will be people who will take
my path. If I do not succeed, they will. My death will be an
example for them and inspire them.[15]

Karakozov clearly believed that his act would stir a massive rebellion against the regime. As events would soon show, this faith in the potential of assassination that drove Karakozov to act would soon inspire a new generation of Russian revolutionaries to succeed where he had failed.

The late 1860s saw close cooperation between the elite Third Section at the national level and local gendarmes under the supervision of provincial governors-general. The latter were especially concentrated in the European sector of the country where, it was believed, exposure to the radicalism of French revolutionary ideas was most prevalent. However, despite such efforts at enforcing national loyalty and repress all forms of resistance, emotional responses could not be easily contained. Fiery words soon turned into violent deeds as the 1870s progressed.

On November 21, 1869, a student was found murdered in a dormitory of the university in Moscow. An investigation uncovered a serious conspiratorial circle of students and auditors called the People's Vengeance (*Narodnaia Rasprava*), led by Sergei Nechaev, who had not yet attracted attention in the files of the Third Section. This is particularly surprising, given the fact that Nechaev claimed to have at least 80 members in his group and had already made plans for an unprecedented act of violence against the regime – planting a bomb on the railway tracks where the Imperial train was to pass, with the intention of assassinating Alexander II in the process.[16]

Nechaev had been fascinated with Karakozov's attempted regicide in 1866. His terror plans were interrupted not by the police, but as a result of his own miscalculation. At a meeting of his circle at Moscow University, one member, Ivan Ivanov, expressed reluctance to support the assassination plan. Because he knew too much about the circle and its intentions, he was murdered at Nechaev's orders. With the police

[15] Quoted in Verhoeven, *The Odd Man Karakozov*, 130.
[16] See Pomper, "Nechaev and Tsaricide: The Conspiracy within the Conspiracy," 123–38.

investigating what in fact was the first assassination in the history of the university, Nechaev fled abroad and found refuge at the retreat of the aging, legendary Russian anarchist Michael Bakunin in Locarno, Switzerland. There he completed his notorious essay on the tactics of revolutionary violence. Nechaev's "Catechism of a Revolutionary" communicated the sense of collective rage that we have seen in Heinzen's "Murder," but Nechaev went further in literally outlining a comprehensive terrorist hit list as well as portraying the quotidian conditions of living as a permanent underground insurgent. In many respects, his "Catechism" forms the foundation for the theory and practice of modern insurgent terror.

Nechaev's portrait of the genuine revolutionary is of "a doomed man" who "has neither interests, nor affairs, nor feelings, nor attachments, nor property, nor even a name." He must sever all ties to family and loved ones. His identity and consciousness are dominated by one single notion – the total passion for revolution. To accomplish this goal, he must liberate himself first from all connections to the civil order and the state, which he seeks to destroy. His world is solely dedicated to mastering the sciences of physics and chemistry as well as "the living science of people, of their personalities" to construct tools for the cause. Every day he must confront the challenge that he "must be ready to die," to be tortured or to perish in the process of committing anti-state acts that are part of "an implacable life and death struggle."

The manifesto also considers the problem of evaluating the value of a comrade who needs to be rescued. The decision must be based at the moment on a calculation of "the usefulness of the comrade" to the cause. Knowing full well the potential exposure to the extensive surveillance of the police to be faced, Nechaev's organizational structure was planned around a network of cells operating without knowledge of one another, and coordinated by a few trusted individuals. At the same time, the revolutionary must be prepared to "live in society," but in an entirely different manner than in the past. The insurrectionist "must penetrate everywhere, into all strata," from the merchants and the clergy to the bureaucratic officialdom, the Third Section "and even into the Winter Palace."

Nechaev classified the categories of expendable enemies of the movement in a ranking order. Targets, he argued, should be chosen on the basis of determining the extent to which their deaths will "inspire the greatest fear in the government" and "paralyze its power." Others should be chosen as "people who will be permitted to live only provisionally," so that their violent demise, once decided upon, "can drive the people into an inevitable *bunt* [rebellion or uprising]." People of wealth and state connections can be made use of by confusing and exploiting them. In a particularly insightful passage in clause 21, Nechaev recognized the usefulness of trusted women as indispensable allies in the revolutionary cause, a decade before women actually began assuming significant roles in the terrorist underground in Russia.

The goal of all the violence was a massive uprising of the peasantry, "an all shattering revolution of the *narod*." Nechaev claimed that he had no preconceived form of authority that would succeed the collapse of the state, which was to be left to a future generation to work out. The task at hand was to realize the "revolution that will destroy at its roots any kind of statehood and annihilate all state traditions, structures and classes in Russia."[17]

The government meanwhile moved swiftly to ensure that none of Nechaev's cells would survive. At the direction of the minister of justice, K. I. Pahlen, some 200 people identified as connected in some way with "People's Vengeance" were sentenced to various terms of imprisonment and exile. The trials were discussed in the press, with the government hoping that by publicizing the evil intentions of the insurgents, who were presented as both ordinary criminals and dangerous threats to public order, any radicals still at large would be isolated and vulnerable to arrest. Among the many visitors attracted to these trials was the writer Fyodor Dostoevsky, who had become increasingly conservative following his decade of Siberian exile for involvement with the utopian socialist Petrashevskii Circle in 1849. The testimony at these court hearings led him to create his powerful novel about insurrectionary terrorists, *The Devils*, which prophesied much of the violence that Russia was to experience in the coming decade.

In a virtual mirror image imitation of Nechaev's duplicitous plan for revolutionaries to "live in society" to gain information and

---

[17] The complete document of "The Catechism of a Revolutionary" (1869) is included in Pomper, *Sergei Nechaev*, 90–4. This last sentence is Nechaev's most anarchistic passage, and may suggest Bakunin's influence in composing the essay, which remains a matter of some dispute among historians. On this, see Confino, *Violence dans la Violence*.

have proximity to targets, Pahlen also ordered a massive infiltration by the police into the radical circles that developed during the early 1870s, for purposes of intelligence-gathering and facilitating arrests. The objects of the Third Section's attention were small groups of students who mainly in the summers fanned out into the countryside to propagate socialist ideas of liberty and equality and awaken the politically passive peasantry from their bonds of poverty and mistreatment. In general these groups acted peacefully, but their appearance in villages across the European provinces of Russia sent shockwaves of fear through the local gendarmeries. Pahlen made his move during the "mad summer" of 1874, sending squads of agents and police into the villages and arresting over 700 people (of whom 158 were women). 267 were confined on the basis of hard evidence and, during the three years in which their trial was prepared, only 193 would stand trial; the others died, were exiled or, in some cases, went insane from the prison conditions.[18] The government mounted two major public trials in 1877, the "Trial of the 50" and the "Trial of the 193," the latter being the largest political court proceeding in the country's history. In these tribunals, government prosecutors presented what they considered to be irrefutable evidence against the arrested populist revolutionaries that had been gathered from police interrogations. Most were charged with seditious activity in the provinces where they had been attempting to propagandize against state, church and landlord. Very few escaped the guilty verdict.

One day after the convictions, on January 24, 1878, Vera Zasulich, a radical student, arranged an appointment with the military governor of St Petersburg, F. F. Trepov, pulled a gun out of her muff in full view of the officials and guards in the room, and fired at him, wounding him in the shoulder. She claimed she was seeking only to draw attention to the abusive flogging of a fellow student radical in prison. In a sensational trial, again open to the public, she was tried for the criminal charge of attempted murder (rather than the political charge of subversion of the autocracy) and was found innocent by a sympathetic jury who believed her attorney's claim that she was driven

---

[18] The statistics are cited in Ruud and Stepanov, *Fontanka 16*, 39. The main radical organization active in the villages prior to the 1874 arrests called themselves the Great Society of Propaganda. The police provided the name Chaikovskii Circle after one of their early leaders, which has been conventionally adopted in the literature.

only by outrage over the brutal treatment of her jailed comrade.[19] Though she had unintentionally inspired a generation of insurgent terrorists by her daring deed, Zasulich chose to flee to exile in Switzerland, where she included in her political activities a critique of the use of political violence by revolutionary organizations.

The internal campaigns of violence between the police and the revolutionaries intensified to unprecedented levels by the end of the decade as both sides persisted in pursuing their respective grandiose fantasies of realizing either some version of the "beautiful autocracy," or destroying it. There was little time for the tsar and his officialdom to savor what they hoped was the end of the threat from below. Even before the conclusion of the trials, populist activists who had escaped the police dragnet formed a new organization, Land and Liberty (*Zemlia i Volia*), which soon became bitterly divided over whether to continue to propagandize among the peasantry or to turn to the urban terrorism pioneered by Karakozov. Those advocating the latter decided to bolt in 1879 and form their own group, People's Will (*Narodnaia Volia*). From the moment of their inception, they began a series of assassinations against a variety of government officials. They quickly went to the top of the ruling order. In March, they tried to kill the recently appointed chief of the Third Section, General Alexander R. Drentel'n, and on April 2, Alexander Soloviev came very close to ending the life of the tsar himself. He managed to get several shots off from his revolver but missed each time.

People's Will achieved another of Nechaev's goals, in managing to infiltrate the Third Section for the first time. One member of the group's central strategists, Alexander Mikhailov, approached an acquaintance, Nikolai Kletochnikov, and convinced him to spy for the underground from inside the ranks of the police. He succeeded beyond their expectations.[20] Kletochnikov sent classified reports copied from the files of the Third Section to Mikhailov for over a year before he was denounced from within, and sentenced to life imprisonment. Nevertheless, Mikhailov proved that penetration into police intelligence could now take place at high levels by the radical underground, in a mirror imitation of the identical tactics already perfected by the police.

---

[19] See Bergman, *Vera Zasulich*.
[20] Tikhomirov, *Zagovorshchiki i politsiia*, 135–6.

Pushing further, People's Will assigned a new and perhaps bolder task to Stepan Khalturin, who succeeded in getting hired as a Winter Palace repairman. In the course of his daily work, he smuggled a load of dynamite into an area beneath the dining room of the palace, which he set off on February 4, 1880. The blast killed a dozen people, but exploded before the tsar had entered the room. Alexander II immediately brought in Mikhail T. Loris-Melikov to head a revamped security division with virtually limitless authority over the entire police bureaucracy, including the Third Section, to end the revolutionary violence against the regime.

In addition to these events, a number of the revolutionaries affiliated with People's Will who had fled abroad contributed to the expanding involvement with political violence, not by deeds but by words. Specifically, several composed and published essays that dealt with terrorism from the perspective of theory, including the thorny problem of confronting the moral dilemma of justifying assassinations. Nikolai A. Morozov was born in the Yaroslavl province of rural Russia to parents of widely different class backgrounds, though this was far from untypical for the time. His mother was a serf who was bonded to the estate of his landowning father. Morozov was on the police watch list even as a high school student. At that point, he was introduced to the heavy hand of repression as a result of his being expelled for distributing a science journal that had not been approved by the censorship division. His name appears on the Third Section lists for participation in propagandizing the peasantry with anti-regime principles during the "mad summer" of 1874. He also was a member of the Land and Liberty Party and allied with the dissident faction that formed People's Will four years later.[21]

It is not clear whether Morozov's trip abroad in 1880 was intended to enable him to publish on behalf of People's Will, which of course would have been impossible within Russia. Nevertheless, he did compose "The Terrorist Struggle" and had it published in Geneva as a pamphlet before returning to St Petersburg to join his comrades and aid in the distribution of the essay later that year. Morozov's pamphlet is an important document contributing to an understanding of the increased reliance and dependence on violence as a tactical priority in the battle against the autocracy. Indeed, it was among the

---

[21] On Morozov's early career, see his memoir: *Povesti moei zhizni*, esp. vol. 1.

most incriminating pieces of evidence seized by the police in the aftermath of the assassination of Alexander II, and was discussed at the trial of the party's Executive Committee leadership the following year.

The essay's very title signaled the revival of the term "terrorism" with a new twist – instead of using it as an appellation for state violence, as Robespierre had, Morozov unabashedly presents it as a positive tactic in the revolutionary combat against the tsarist regime, reminiscent of Karl Heinzen's earlier manifesto. Because of the imbalance between the overwhelming force of the state and the smaller number of opponents who must operate in secret, Morozov recommended "a new form of struggle," characterized by "a series of individual political assassinations" which, he noted, was already in progress. He proposed renouncing the massive revolutionary movements of the past, whether of peasants or of the intelligentsia, because they were so costly in loss of lives ("where a nation kills off its own children"). This form of rebellion should be replaced by small squads carrying out targeted killings of the possessors of power. In this way, the "reign of violence" of the state can be ended with far fewer casualties and with greater chances for success. Quoting from St-Just at the trial of Louis XVI in 1792, Morozov states that "every man has a right to kill a tyrant and a nation cannot take away this right even from one of its citizens."

Further, Morozov writes that the chief tasks of the contemporary Russian terrorist are "to summarize theoretically and to systemize practically this form of revolutionary struggle ... Political assassinations alone should become an expression of this rich, consistent system." He was convinced that each act of terror would give birth to "new agents of revenge" willing to continue the heroism of the struggle against tyranny. Along with the propagation of socialist principles as an alternative to the existing system, Morozov concluded, the terrorist party seeks to bring about "the final disorganization, demoralization and weakening of government for its actions against freedom."[22]

A companion pamphlet was also printed the same year as Morozov's by another member of People's Will, Gerasim G. Romanenko, who wrote under the *nom de guerre* of G. Tarnovskii. There is evidence of collaboration, since we know that Romanenko wrote to Morozov on

---

[22] Published originally as *Terroristicheskaia bor'ba*, the essay was translated by Felix Gross in *Violence in Politics*, 101–12, and appears most recently abridged in Laqueur, *Voices of Terror*, 86–92.

at least one occasion in which he mentioned "our idea of terror."[23] Written a few months after Morozov's pamphlet appeared in print, Romanenko's essay created a stir of controversy among the Executive Committee of People's Will when it was received and discussed in St Petersburg.[24]

Romanenko's brochure, which he titled "Terrorism and Routine," also embraces the mantle of political violence as a virtuous tactic in the service of ending the despotic tsarist regime. "The terrorist revolution," he writes, "is a pointed manifestation of the abnormalities of social relations in Russia." The application of violence is necessary to abolish the violence of "social slavery" imposed on society by "the crowned vampires" of the regime. It is this system which is criminal, and the terrorists are those who "have decided to strike a blow" against it in "self defense and public defense" in order to establish conditions for the realization of political freedom in a republic.

In addition, Romanenko confronts head-on the charge that revolutionary violence is unethical. He makes the distinction between the tyrannical and brutal legal code of the autocracy, on one hand, which criminalizes the quest for equality, and, on the other, "the natural laws of justice and morality." According to his logic, revolution is the only means of liberating people living under the authority of a brutalizing state. Therefore, it follows that acts of violence committed to achieve this goal are ethical deeds, since the desired outcome is a more morally based social order.

Closely following Morozov's notion of comparing victims in the modes of struggle, Romanenko agrees that far less "blood of the innocent flows in the rivers" in cases of terrorist violence than in traditional mass uprisings. In the latter instances, as both Russian and French history have shown, rulers watch from the safety of their palace windows while the people on the streets are crushed by soldiers and police. The terrorist revolution differs in that it "directs its blows against the real perpetrators of evil."[25]

On March 1, 1881, the plans drawn up by the Executive Committee of People's Will to assassinate Alexander II, finally, and

---

[23] Figner, *Zapechatlennyi trud*, 251.
[24] Valk, "G. G. Romanenko: Iz istorii Narodnoi Voli," 45.
[25] Tarnovski, "Terrorism and Routine," 79–84. The original 1880 Russian version, smuggled from Geneva to Russia in handwritten copies, is a bibliographic rarity. The extant published edition is: Gerasim Grigorevich Romanenko, *Terrorizm i rutina* (Carouge [Geneva]: Elpidine, 1901).

astonishingly, succeeded. In this case, the fantasy of the improbable became a reality. Andrei I. Zheliabov, the acknowledged leader of the party, had been born in 1850 to a provincial serf family in the south of Russia. In addition to growing up amidst the poverty and humiliations of daily life under serfdom, his mother was raped by a local official, which left him with a traumatic emotional scar and, by his own admission, a deep desire for revenge.[26] In the often overlooked examples of upward social mobility in tsarist Russia, Zheliabov was accepted to study at the University of Odessa, where he soon found himself caught up in the student radical movement. He, like Dostoevsky and so many other Russians, was fascinated by the public trial of the students arrested in connection with the Nechaev Affair in Moscow in 1870. He was arrested for his participation in the propaganda efforts in peasant villages during the 1874 "mad summer," but was acquitted for lack of evidence at the Trial of the 193 in 1878. He was invited to the secret 1879 Land and Liberty meeting at Lipetsk, where the revolutionaries argued over whether to resume the tactics of continuing propaganda, or to turn to terror in the manner of Karakozov and Nechaev.

For Zheliabov, the decision was obvious. The path of propaganda was futile because of the lessons learned while exposed to the rural peasantry during that "mad summer" of propaganda and agitation. To Zheliabov, it was clear that, even under the best of conditions in being able to evade the police, it would take many years to wrench the peasantry out of their deeply cherished religiosity and traditional reverence for the tsar. A further hurdle to clear was the fear felt throughout the countryside of the radical ideas presented by the educated outsiders, who came out of a culture remote from their daily lives. But far more important in his mind, as he stated at his trial after the regicide, was the fact that the regime's restrictions left them no alternatives.

> We looked for means of helping the people and the means
> we chose was to take up questions as common working men
> and women with a view to the peaceful propagation of
> socialist ideas. This surely was harmless. What happened?
> Those concerned were imprisoned or sent into exile. An

---

[26] Ivianski, "A Chapter in the History of Individual Terror: Andrei Zheliabov," 87.

entirely peaceful movement, opposed to violence, opposed to revolution, was crushed.[27]

As a result of these experiences, he proclaimed to the court, "I became a revolutionary." He was, in his own words, "forced to turn to violence. I would willingly abandon violence if there were the possibility of serving my ideals by peaceful means."[28]

When he spoke these words at his trial, Zheliabov knew he was headed for execution, and nothing he said could have altered that destiny. Not only was the evidence against him entirely valid, but the mood of the court was well expressed by the acting public prosecutor when he stated that Zheliabov was guilty of "this most appalling of crimes ever committed upon Russian soil."[29] How, with this in mind, are we to understand his motives? Was he suggesting that the whole history of Russia (and perhaps the world) would have been spared the phenomenon of terrorism had the regime permitted political parties, elections to legislative assemblies, and organizations of workers and peasants for the amelioration of their wretched existence? Was he, on the other hand, operating within a mental fantasy in anticipating an autocracy that would permit widespread agitation dedicated to undermining the regime's own legitimate authority, and a Third Section ordering its agents to devote their attention to arresting ordinary criminals instead of political opponents?

On a related note, one of the more unremarked aspects of the People's Will trial was the speech of Nikolai Kibalchich, to which the same questions could be addressed. When his turn came to deliver his defense, he first spoke of the futility of the regime's reliance "entirely on the gallows and the firing squad" as a solution to the enduring problems of inequality and injustice facing the country. Then he added that he had "drafted a project for a flying machine" which he did not wish to fall into the hands of the state after his expected execution. "I wish now to publically declare that my project and sketch are to pass into the hands of my counsel, M. Gerard."[30] Kibalchich, who was the technical expert on weapons for the party, was in fact working on a

---

[27] See Footman, *Red Prelude*, 218–35, for the transcript of the trial proceedings.
[28] Ibid.   [29] Quoted in Footman, *Red Prelude*, 223.
[30] Ibid. Kibalchich was the uncle of Victor Serge, later to become an important revolutionary and novelist involved with terrorism in both France and Russia.

project in which airships would be capable of dispensing dynamite bombs over sites of power in the near future, decades before the Wright brothers' flight experiments.

Finally on this subject, Zheliabov and most of the Executive Committee sought as their goal the creation of an elected constituent assembly to debate and decide on the nature of the future post-monarchic republic. He hoped that this development would end the need for the tactics of insurgent terror. To demonstrate their consistency and commitment to this strategy, the members of the Executive Committee sent a letter to the US Congress on the occasion of the assassination of President Garfield, which they criticized on the grounds that there was no justification for assassinating the head of state in a democratic republic. For People's Will, terrorist actions against the state made sense only when opposing an autocratic regime which deprived, rather than guaranteed, human rights and dignity to its citizens. "Force can be justified," the letter concludes, "only when employed to resist force."[31]

The Executive Committee had also prepared another letter, addressed to Alexander III, dated ten days after they had assassinated his father. It was essentially a plea to the new sovereign to engage in open discussion about the political future of the country and to be willing to realize a comprehensive reform program for the country, that would include amnesty for political prisoners, convocation of an elected assembly to chart the political future, and the introduction of "freedoms of speech, the press, public meetings and electoral addresses." With that agreement, "the Executive Committee will spontaneously suspend its own activities, the forces it has organized will disband, and devote themselves to the fruitful work of civilization, culture, and the welfare of the people."[32]

The police, meanwhile, continued their activities to contain the radical upsurge. In some respects, their modus operandi remained unchanged, but in others, the system of surveillance and repression moved into entirely new tactical territory. The cross-fertilization and mutual exchange of operational intelligence among the European governments that had continued transnationally on the continent since

---

[31] The letter, originally published in *Narodnaia Volia*, no. 6 (October 23,1881), is reproduced in translation in Gross, *Violence in Politics*, 28.
[32] The document is included in Gross, *Violence in Politics*, 117, 118.

the Carlsbad Decrees in 1819 intensified in the last quarter of the nineteenth century. The oscillations of loyalties that we find in the career of Joseph Fouché (1759–1820) became increasingly characteristic of the officials responsible for law and order, and would soon find resonance in Russia. Fouché began as a fervent partisan for the revolution in France in the 1790s, charged at one point with quelling royalist discontent by any means he felt necessary. After the collapse of the Republic, he at first opposed and then supported Napoleon, eventually rising to the position of Chief of Police at the national level. According to those who knew him, his methods were cruel and ruthless, especially when it came to crushing Jacobin or monarchist threats to the security of the Bonapartist Empire. He structured a large network of informers and provocateurs whose commitment to the notion of rights and liberties was far secondary to their mission of abolishing any hint of conspiracy against the regime.[33]

Fouché's most important successor was Louis Andrieux, who was appointed to the same post, Chief of Police, in 1879, with the important difference being that France was at this point a republic once more (to be discussed in the next chapter). Andrieux went beyond his predecessor by closely cooperating with the Russian police authorities during the reign of Alexander III (1881–94). He introduced a number of new techniques, including the use of secret agents at all levels of society (rather than merely at the level of infiltrating revolutionary groups). The one place he found especially effective, which the Russians adopted, was the press. Specifically, Andrieux encouraged, recruited and funded the establishment of newspapers (now more widely read than in earlier decades, due to the increase in literacy and public education) that would essentially be organs of the police. His reporters were often permitted to attend political meetings from which even police spies posing as radical members were at times barred. Andrieux cleverly understood that the police needed to have a direct channel into radical activities in the planning stage, which would allow them to avert bombings and assassinations before they took place. Moreover, he realized that the police could actually plant fears in the press with fictitious events of terror, much in the way that Karl Heinzen had imagined from the other side of

---

[33] For information on Fouché, see the valuable studies by Guyot, *La Police: Etude de Physiologie Sociale*, and de la Hodde, *Histoire des Sociétés Secrètes*.

the conflict.[34] Andrieux's cynical operating code was little concerned with legalities of rights and liberties, an orientation that appealed to his Russian counterparts, who adopted many of his tactics.

However, in spite of all their sophisticated methods of containing the opposition, whether directly imported or not, the agents of the Okhrana (security section of the Department of Police), successors to the Third Section that had been discredited and disbanded after the assassination of Alexander II, were soon to find themselves facing a far more ruthless insurgent terrorist organization. By the end of the nineteenth century the Okhrana operated with at least 20,000 secret agents who claimed through their reports to be infiltrators, spies and *agents provocateurs* throughout the country, with 50,000 officers employed in the bureaucratic chain of command, and another 100,000 police on the payroll at the provincial level. By the time of the 1917 revolution, it was revealed that the Okhrana and its Third Section predecessors had accumulated some 500,000 cards on suspected threats to the country's security.[35] Tens of thousands of these people had already been sentenced to long terms of internal exile, and had experienced the indescribable conditions of being forced to walk, often in freezing conditions, the long distances where transportation to their detention centers was either not provided or not available. At least 45,000 people were sent into administrative exile to the east in 1905–7 alone. Needless to say, the budget for this repressive police program, sanctioned by imperial decrees that amounted to a permanent state of emergency, was a high priority for the government, and shows large increases in these years.[36]

[34] See his own account of these activities in Andrieux, *Souvenirs d'un Préfet de Police*, esp. vol. I. Also consult the useful analysis by Ivianski, "Provocation at the Center," 53–88, and reprinted in *Terrorism: Critical Concepts in Political Science*, 339–68.

[35] The data, gathered from Russian sources, can be found in Ivianski, "Provocation at the Center," 343–4. For further statistics on trials and executions in this period, see Daly, *The Watchful State*, 71–2, and his earlier study, *Autocracy Under Siege: Security Police and Opposition in Russia, 1866–1905*, 35–6.

[36] See Monas, "The Political Police," 173 on the exile data. For the budgets, see Ruud and Stepanov, *Fontanka 16*, 79–80, 288–9. The secret operations units were allotted a budget of 186,877 rubles in 1877, which was doubled in 1881, and rose to 5 million rubles for 1913. The figures decline slightly after that as a result of budgetary priorities for the war. On the camps, the first-hand account by George Kennan still ranks as a deserved classic alongside Mikhail Gernet's multi-volume, exhaustive account. See Kennan, *Siberia and the Exile System*. Both clearly demonstrate the high morbidity and mortality that characterized the hard labor camps.

On occasion, the expenditures seemed to be paying off. Government circles were clearly relieved when the police managed to disrupt a plot, by a small group that remained of the decimated ranks of People's Will, to assassinate Alexander III in 1886. The entire faction was executed after being caught; one of its members was Alexander Ulyanov, older brother of the man later to be known to the world as Vladimir Lenin.[37] That same year, Russian police agents abroad, with cooperation from the Swiss authorities, were able to make arrests and interrupt a number of anti-tsarist operations. Also at this time, Peter Kropotkin, the prominent Russian revolutionary activist and theoretician of anarchism, was arrested in connection with a series of bombings at a mining area near Lyons. Suspicions remain as to whether police provocateurs were responsible, but the Russian court was delighted when Kropotkin, who had made a daring escape from a St Petersburg military hospital in 1876 while awaiting indictment for the Trial of the 193, was sentenced to a prison term in France.[38]

The tsarist security forces had been conducting surveillance on Russian revolutionary emigres in Western Europe for some time, but the regime authorized a higher level of operations, including the employment of violence, under the command of Peter Rachkovskii during this period. Rachkovskii is a stark example of the interplay between the police and the radical underground that was responsible for much of the ongoing terrorist activities. He spent his early years working his way up the ranks of the civil service, largely in the provinces of Russia, until he decided to attend law school courses, which led him to a subordinate position in the Ministry of Justice. Demoted because he was unwilling to take a strong stance in prosecuting captured revolutionaries, he took advantage of the opportunity to declare his intention to actively serve the state during an interrogation by the Third Section in 1879. He was assigned to infiltrate the cells of People's Will, which he did effectively, betraying his new comrades to the police and providing intelligence about their plans to assassinate government officials.

---

[37] The best account of this affair is Pomper, *Lenin's Brother.*
[38] After his release, Kropotkin published one of the first critical comparative studies of penitentiary experiences. See his *In Russian and French Prisons.* His account of his escape in 1876 is vividly described in all the editions of his *Memoirs of a Revolutionary.*

One of the Okhrana's newest operations was the employment of a large number of agents operating abroad to sabotage the activities of the hundreds of Russian revolutionary exiles who were operating printing presses, distributing illegal propaganda inside Russia, and organizing groups that were planning attacks in St Petersburg and Moscow. Alexander III personally sponsored and funded this agency, called the Holy Guard (*Sviashchennaia druzhina*, also translated as Sacred Brotherhood), which was set up soon after the assassination of his father. Beginning with around 700 members, it soon rose to include thousands of agents, operating mainly in Switzerland, Germany and France, with the full permission and active cooperation of those governments. The Russian Embassy in Paris proved to be the largest site of these operations on the continent, with Russian and French agents freely exchanging information from their covert missions. Their activities were limited largely to intelligence-gathering and distributing disinformation to radical circles, but there were a few acts of violence, including bombing bookstores known to have been meeting places for the distribution of literature smuggled into and out of Russia. By 1883, the Holy Guard was transformed into a much larger and permanent body, the Foreign Agency of the Okhrana, which hounded Russian political exiles until the 1917 revolution.[39] Rachkovskii moved with this flow of events, from a volunteer in the Holy Guard to a high position in the Okhrana office in Paris.

As chief spymaster for the Okhrana, Rachkovskii was responsible for numerous projects, many enacted with the cooperation of the French police, to undermine and repress the Russian émigré revolutionaries. In a letter to the chief of the Paris Sûreté, in 1884, Rachkovskii wrote: "I am endeavoring to demoralize [the émigrés] politically, to inject discord among revolutionary forces, to weaken them, and at the same time to suppress every revolutionary act at its source."[40] He was also in continual contact with Gustave Macé, prefect of police in Paris, and Louis Deibler, whose position is listed as

---

[39] Lukashevich, "The Holy Brotherhood, 1881–1883," 491–505. The Russian term for this security service, *Sviashchennaia druzhina* has been translated as Holy Brotherhood or Guard. For a sample of Rachkovskii's reporting to the police at this juncture, see Dedkov, *Politicheskaia politsiia i politicheskii terrorizm v Rossii*, 116–19. Joseph Conrad's *The Secret Agent* (1907) contains a masterful fictional account of the Russian Embassy's violent antirevolutionary activities in London in the person of the sinister Mr Vladimir, who might well have been modeled on Rachkovskii.

[40] Quoted in Butterworth, *The World That Never Was*, 184.

hereditary state executioner. Rachkovskii also received cooperation for his agents to operate in London and Geneva as well. This police alliance succeeded in spreading an atmosphere of pervasive fear among the exiles, forcing them to be particularly vigilant regarding infiltration into their ranks. Leading exiles like Kropotkin, Kravchinskii and Vladimir Burtsev managed to withstand this constant intrusion into their lives of police intimidation and repression, but Lev Tikhomirov, a career activist with the underground, crumbled under the relentless pressure. Rachkovskii managed to threaten and hound him to the extent that Tikhomirov finally agreed to return to Russia in 1887 on condition that he renounce his radicalism and serve the autocracy.[41] His decision stunned the ranks of the émigrés.

The police's spy industry became so intricate that at times it resembled fiction more than fact. Of the many strange cases of double and triple loyalties that came to characterize the warfare between state and society, the tale of Sergei Degaev remains one of the most bizarre. After becoming familiar with some adherents of People's Will, and with knowledge of their planned attacks, Degaev apparently realized he was unable to face the rigors of actual murdering people and confessed to being rather "unheroic" when it came to giving up his own life for the cause. For whatever reasons (and there may well have been deeper psychological issues involved), Degaev decided he could be more useful informing on his comrades to the police. To this end, he was employed by G. P. Sudeikin, who headed the Third Section in 1882 and was responsible for apprehending many of the remaining People's Will members still at large after Emperor Alexander II's assassination. In fact, Degaev was also reporting back to his underground comrades on activities planned by the police, until his arrest in December of 1882.

While in jail, he arranged a deal with Sudeikin, which takes us once more into the realm of fantasies of power. The two were to work together on a joint plan in which Degaev was assigned the task of "escaping" from jail, rejoining the insurgent terrorist party, and informing on their activities directly to Sudeikin. The goal was the autocracy's age-old dream of completely destroying the radical underground; the two key players were both to be rewarded with ministerial posts for their contributions. During the next year, Degaev, following

[41] He explains the transition in his memoir. See Tikhomirov, *Vospominaniia*, as well as the description in Zuckerman, *The Tsarist Secret Police Abroad*, 132–5.

his state-assisted release from prison, worked in deep cover with surviving members of People's Will, providing intelligence secretly to
Sudeikin. The climax came when Degaev was asked to lead the assassination of his own police boss. He complied, and murdered Sudeikin
in December, 1883. Degaev was then spirited out of the country to the
US, where he assumed the identity of a college professor, and quietly
taught undetected in North Dakota until his death.[42]

After Sudeikin's assassination, Viacheslav K. Plehve was
appointed Director of Police and head of the Okhrana. In 1902, he
was appointed Minister of the Interior when the previous minister was
assassinated by Stepan Balmashev, a member of a faction of the Socialist
Revolutionary Party, the insurgent group responsible for an unprecedented number of victims over the next several years. Plehve himself
ended up on that casualty list when he too was assassinated by one of his
own double agents, Evno Azev, who planned the murder and went
through with it to maintain his cover two years later. The treachery on
both sides became infectious as both the police and the SRs grew more
dependent on, if not addicted to, competing over the violence of revenge.

In addition, mention must be made in this context of Sergei
Zubatov, a protégé of Sudeikin's, who also began his career as a
revolutionary until he was attracted to the seductions of the police in
their violent war against insurgent terrorism. He made effective use of
his knowledge of the identities of many radicals after switching sides. In
addition, he is credited with upgrading many of the traditional methods
of repression. One of Zubatov's masterstrokes was to establish labor
unions that were essentially run by the police, as a way of competing
with the influence of the illegal revolutionary parties who were making
inroads with the growing working class.[43]

Surely one of the most unexpected exposures of deception at
the highest levels of the police bureaucracy was the moment when
Arkady M. Harting, the chief of the Okhrana, found his story on the
front pages of the Paris newspapers in 1909. One of his subordinates
had defected to the Russian underground, and provided damaging
information on Harting to Vladimir Burtsev, a prominent Russian

[42] Long available primarily in Russian sources, the details of this extraordinary story can now
be found in Pipes, *The Degaev Affair*.
[43] See Sablinsky, *The Road to Bloody Sunday* and Schneiderman, *Sergei Zubatov and
Revolutionary Marxism*.

exile who ran his own intelligence operation dedicated to revealing the identities of the police spies abroad. Harting, it turned out, was the false name for Abraham Hackelman who, using the pseudonym of Landesen, had earlier been tried and sentenced to five years in prison "as a terrorist provocateur." The outcry went all the way to the office of President Clemenceau, with parliamentary deputies calling for an end to the Russian police spy network in France. Harting was secretly removed by the Okhrana and vanished from public view, ending what the Russian government called his "distinguished career" serving the security of the fatherland.[44]

On occasion, the exposures of agents cooperating with, or provoking, acts of violence against the state ended in self-destructive tragedy. When Boris Savinkov, one of the leading members of the insurgent terrorists in the SR Party, unmasked Ia. F. Berdo in 1910 and exposed another agent working with the SRs, V. M. Kamorskii, a year later, both of them committed suicide.[45]

One further point about the police concerns the significant number of women recruited for work as agents, some of whom are described as working in "deep cover" within the ranks of the SR Party and other insurgent organizations. Some were wives, sisters or mistresses of Okhrana officials who were assigned specific tasks with their own handlers and code names, and were usually placed on separate payroll lists, though none seem to have risen to the officers' level.

One fascinating case involves Zinaida Zhuchenko, a graduate of the elite Smolny Institute and wife of a prominent physician in Moscow, who left her husband in the 1890s and disappeared into the ranks of the Okhrana. Acting under the code name of Francesco (the women often were assigned male names for their field work), Zhuchenko rose in the ranks under the mentorship of Sergei Zubatov. She was sent abroad to work with Harting, who sent her to spy on SR activities in Berlin and Leipzig. She was eventually appointed to head an SR assassination team in 1905 whose plan was to kill General Kurlov, governor of Minsk. Cleverly, she managed to alert her officers, who arranged for her to take the explosive device to an Okhrana safe house where it was exchanged for a dud. In the end, she carried out the attempted killing, but the bomb of course did not go off and she saved

---

[44] Peregudova, *Politicheskii sysk Rossii*, 148–9. See also Fischer, *Okhrana*, 86.
[45] Daly, *The Watchful State*, 103–4.

the life of the general. The ironic finale to this case is that a few years later, General Kurlov somehow was tipped off about an SR agent who was also in the payroll of the Okhrana. An investigation turned up the name of Zhuchenko. The police acted surprised and promised to deal swiftly with the deception. The result was that Zhuchenko was "retired" to a lovely home in the fashionable Berlin suburb of Charlottenburg, with a comfortable pension for support. Her husband finally discovered the fate of his lost wife in 1913 while making "a discreet inquiry" about her at a Moscow police station.[46]

The police had several advantages in their battle with the insurgency. Above all, they had thousands of operatives, whereas the activists in the revolutionary movement who were committed to terrorism usually numbered in the hundreds across the decades. Second, the state had the advantage of the most developed weaponry, operating with budgets that the underground could never begin to approach. Third, the regime possessed a relatively unified ideology. There were differences of opinion among the ministers in the government as to the volume of tactical severity to be employed, but there was an unquestioned consensus that considered nihilists, populists, anarchists and revolutionaries in general to be a mortal threat to the security of the state. Nonetheless, this consensus showed more about the government's will to battle the radical underground than it did about the court's recognition that the insurgency was driven by a number of dire political and moral problems that the regime was not addressing.

By contrast, the radical movements throughout the last half of the nineteenth century in Russia were divided on tactics as well as strategy. Although the focus here is mainly on the exponents of violence, there were far greater numbers of people in Russia who were willing to support reform rather than revolution, and peaceful methods from negotiation to propaganda rather than acts of violence. However, even within the darker corridors of insurgency conspiracies, disagreements reigned from the moment of the inception of the use of violence as a weapon of struggle from below. Dmitrii Karakozov had bolted from his circle when he encountered opposition to his intention to kill the emperor in 1866. The Land and Liberty Party broke apart in 1878 over debates concerning the necessity of turning to reliance on terror.

[46] Kronenbitter, "The Okhrana's Female Agents." For the classified reports on numerous other women working as agents in the Okhrana at this time, see pp. 91–117.

Kropotkin rethought the tactics of propaganda by the deed when he found that too many advocates understood this to mean a blanket justification of insurgent terror. That said, rarely do we find such critical questioning and renunciations of violence among officials of the Okhrana.

For those who wanted to escalate the violence, the division essentially was about whether to choose targets based on revenge or symbolism. In other words, does the revolutionary achieve the desired political objective by killing an official who actually committed a crime as defined by the movement, or is the choice based on what a specific target represents? Kravchinskii claimed he had to murder Mezentsev because the authorities had ordered the execution of Ivan Kovalskii in Odessa, a comrade whom the police claimed was responsible for acts of armed rebellion.[47] It should be added that Kravchinskii was also a believer in political fantasy, which is clearly evidenced in the exaggerated threats he hurled at the regime. In one representative passage, he wrote that though every city and village "is flooded with your spies" and despite the continuation of "merciless executions" of those who oppose tsarism, "you are defenseless and helpless against us ... And know this too, that we possess even more terrible means than those whose force you have already encountered" that will lead to "the elimination of economic inequality, which in our opinion, constitutes the root of all human suffering, as well as to the destruction of the existing economic and political order."[48]

There were also some radical voices warning of the dangers of this unbridled enthusiasm for political violence and martyrdom so celebrated by Kravchinskii. Vera Zasulich, as noted earlier, was critical of the growth of revolutionary terrorism, and took no satisfaction in the fact that she had contributed to it by her own action in 1878. More poignantly, Vera Figner, who was intimately involved with the Executive Committee of People's Will, later wrote in her memoirs that both the state and the insurgents had become demoralized by relying on

---

[47] Kravchinskii, *Smert' za smert': Ubiistvo Mezentseva*, 17. On the debates within Land and Liberty, see Hardy, *Land and Freedom*.

[48] Kravchinskii, *Smert' za smert': Ubiistvo Mezentseva*, 13, 18, 19. In another book, he wrote: "Let them shoot us, kill us in their underground cells. The more fiercely we are dealt with, the greater will be our following. I wish I could make them tear my body to pieces or burn me alive on a slow fire in the market place," an instance of what he called his "positive thirst for martyrdom." See his novel, *Career of a Nihilist* (New York: Harper and Co., 1889), 253, 288.

violence and repression. "From this point of view, the government and the revolutionary party, when they entered into what may be termed a hand-to-hand battle, vied with one another in corrupting everything and everyone around them."[49] And the great writer Joseph Conrad, whose father had fought against the Russian occupation of his native Poland, understood that the rejection of legality by autocratic rule "provokes the no less imbecilic and atrocious answer of a purely Utopian revolutionism encompassing destruction by the first means to hand ... These people are unable to see that all they can effect is merely a change of names."[50]

These divisions led to ever more disastrous consequences with the founding of the Socialist Revolutionary Party in 1901. Like all Russian political parties, the SR Party was organized abroad (in this case, in Germany), since the theory and practice of autocracy did not permit the legalization of any party, across the entire spectrum from monarchists to revolutionaries. Unknown to the inchoate party members, one of the primary organizers, Evno Azev, was already on the payroll of the Okhrana.

From its very inception, the party proclaimed its commitment to violence as one of its major activities. In the summer of 1902, the party theoretician and leader, Victor Chernov, announced the creation of an arm of the SR Party, the Combat Organization, which was to carry out acts of violent "disorganization" against the "unchecked violence of an autocratic arbitrariness that transgresses all limits."[51] The subgroup within the party was allowed virtually complete independence from the party's Central Committee to operate according to its own tactical decisions and to recruit without party ratification.

In addition to Azev, one of the major figures in the Combat Organization was Boris Savinkov who was responsible for some of the most spectacular episodes of SR terrorism against the government. In a pathway similar to that of other converts to the revolutionary movement, Savinkov was arrested for participating in the student demonstrations in the late 1890s in St Petersburg, served a prison term, was rearrested, exiled and, radicalized by these experiences, turned his vengeful rage to acts of violence against the government.

---

[49] Figner, *Memoirs of a Revolutionist*, 120.
[50] Conrad, *Under Western Eyes*, ix-x.
[51] Chernov, "Terroristicheskii element v nashei programme."

The Combat Organization began quickly, assassinating the Minister of the Interior, Dmitrii Sipiagin on April 2, 1902. Heady with success, plans were made for the next action, which landed in the hands of Azev – to kill Sipiagin's successor as Okhrana chief, von Plehve. Azev chose Savinkov to direct the operation, which involved a vast network of participants who were disguised on the street as carriage drivers, news vendors and peddlers.[52] Savinkov also recruited women to the organizations in greater numbers than any previous radical group. One of his recruits, Dora Brilliant, played a key role in planning the murder of Plehve. After several months of abortive attempts, Egor Sazonov managed to place his bomb near enough to the target on July 15, 1904, blowing Plehve to pieces in public view on one of the main thorough-fares of the capital in broad daylight.

This success was followed by discussions about killing Nicholas II, but when division in the group emerged over this, Savinkov proposed assassinating the tsar's uncle, Grand Duke Sergei, who held the post of governor-general of St Petersburg. Choosing the month of February, 1905 as the date for the bombing was important in making a statement. Bloody Sunday, the peaceful march of petitioners and demonstrators that had been fired upon by imperial guards as they approached the Winter Palace, had occurred a month before and proved to be the triggering event that inaugurated this tumultuous year of revolution. Savinkov chose Ivan Kaliaev to carry out this operation. Kaliaev hesitated on his first attempt when he found the Grand Duke's son and wife also in the carriage. However, a week later, he threw his bomb into the window of the slowly passing carriage, destroying his target.[53]

The carnage continued for the next half dozen years until the police repression finally was able to tame the insurgent violence. This was accomplished only when the security forces were able to make effective use of the intelligence received from Azev, as well as further information obtained from other secret operatives posing as members of revolutionary parties, which permitted them to arrest, force into

---

[52] For a recent account of Azev's extraordinary career, see Geifman, *Entangled in Terror.*

[53] These events of violence have been discussed in many accounts but one of the most detailed is by Savinkov himself. See his *Memoirs of a Terrorist*, 71–117 as well as Wedziagolski, *Boris Savinkov: Portrait of a Terrorist*, and B. Spence, *Boris Savinkov: Renegade on the Left*. Kaliaev's hesitation has drawn much attention, including Albert Camus' play, *Les justes* and a section of his enduring analysis of radicalism, *The Rebel*, 133–145.

exile or kill enough SRs to weaken the tide of insurgent violence. The climax of that campaign of SR terror was the assassination of Prime Minister Peter Stolypin. Dmitry Bogrov mortally wounded him with a blast from his hidden revolver on September 1, 1911 in the Kiev Municipal Theater, and he died three days later. As was the case with People's Will when they too finally eliminated their most important target, failure followed success. Stolypin was the last of the leading tsarist officials to die at the hands of this wave of violence from below, but the conditions kindling the joint currents responsible for the acts of terrorism remained in play.

The statistics for this period, though still in dispute, are nonetheless astonishing. By the end of 1907, the total number of officials of the state killed or seriously injured approached 4,500 people. In addition, records indicate that 2,180 people who were not directly working for the government but implicated in its policies were killed by SR violence, with another 2,530 wounded. Government reports list almost 20,000 acts of revolutionary terror in this period, which probably include the widespread tactic of "expropriation," a euphemism for robberies, often with violence, at government banks which were carried out in the cities and in provincial centers by SRs as well as anarchist and Marxist parties. Millions of rubles ended up in the hands of revolutionaries through this method, which were used to replenish weapons and pay non-party agents hired for specific actions.[54] At the same time, the repression by the regime operated at a similar level, bringing over 16,000 suspected revolutionaries to trial for political crimes, of which 3,682 were sentenced to death and most of the rest to long periods of hard labor in Siberia. The total number of political opposition suspects detained in prisons in 1908 surpassed 167,000.[55]

Russia was also witness at this time to another variety of terrorism, which, in spite of its differences with the anarchist and populist forms of insurgent violence that the country experienced, possessed some of the characteristics that link it to those movements. These attacks, rather than being either assaults on government officialdom by insurgents or on the insurgents by the police, were

[54] These data can be found in Geifman, *Thou Shalt Kill*, 21–2, 264.
[55] Ibid., 228, 347. For additional data, see Daly, *The Watchful State*, 40–4. On this period in general, see the rich collection of documents in Bordiugova (ed.), *Politicheskaia politsiia i politicheskii terrorizm v Rossii*, and also Budnitskii, *Terrorizm v Rossiiskom osvoboditel'nom dvizhenii*, esp. 134–217.

inter-communal actions conducted by groups of aroused nationalist vigilantes against Russia's large Jewish population, who created armed self-defense resistance units. The timing of these pogroms is certainly significant. The violence leading up to, and especially during, the 1905 upheaval revealed a powerful insurgency that the government seemed unable to control. There was, as many accounts of the period show, a pervasive sense of unease and vulnerability as the social order weakened under the wave of assaults on government institutions and personnel. Moreover, public transportation, banks, commercial establishments and many local services could no longer be relied upon to function in a timely and reliable manner. For many individuals and groups in urban neighborhoods and rural towns, attention focused on Russia's Jewish community in the quest for a guilty party to blame. These anti-Semitic activists soon found willing partners in government officialdom, at both regional and national levels, to support their plans for violence. Joining forces with the state's personnel undoubtedly created a sense of empowerment for the local participants at a moment of great national and personal uncertainty. The violence became a weapon to help support the regime and contribute to the battle against revolutionaries who were actually seeking to undermine it, since many of the activists behind the pogroms imagined a secret alliance between the Jewish communities and insurgents in the radical parties.

There were reasons to explain the general hostility toward the country's Jews. Some felt threatened by the Jewish community's expansion in numbers, their evolution from a confined status into the secular world where they assumed competitive economic positions and, above all, their involvement in revolutionary groups since the populist movements of the 1870s.[56] No less a figure than Dostoevsky was subject to such fears and anxieties, as his diary entries and numerous characterizations in his celebrated novels clearly demonstrate.

The history of Russia's conflicted attitudes toward Jews goes back at least to the first Partition of Poland in 1772, when Catherine the Great joined with the rulers of the Austrian and Prussian monarchies to divide Polish territory among them and obliterate it from the map of Europe. Since so many Jews had settled in Poland, one of the few places on the continent where they were welcomed after the expulsions from England and Spain, they were absorbed into Russian society as a

[56] Haberer, *Jews and Revolution in Nineteenth Century Russia.*

result of the partition acquisitions. Restrictions existed from the start, but so did some advantages. Though they were confined to mainly rural areas in the western reaches of the Russian Empire (much of which is in what is today Ukraine and Belarus), they were also granted admission to the legal estate (*soslovia*) categories of merchants and townspeople, a significant level above the majority population of serfs and peasants.

Myths born of envy and hostility toward Jews abounded at all levels. Among the more prevalent were the contradictory images of being unproductive as well as excessively productive, parasitical while exploitative, secretive in their religious practices but public in their expanding role in commercial enterprises in the provincial towns. Periodically the Jews were blamed for the wretched condition of the peasantry, a prejudice that was intensified when Jews were identified as members of the revolutionary movement in the 1870s.

Pogroms – assaults on Jewish communities – can be traced back to an outbreak of violence in Odessa in 1821, with episodic repetitions throughout the nineteenth century. A climax seemed to have been reached in 1881, when Jews were widely blamed for the assassination of Alexander II. Only one of the members of the Executive Committee sentenced to death, Gesia Gel'fman, was identified in the press as being Jewish, but this was sufficient proof for the anti-Semitic rage that poured forth at the time.[57]

At this point, most Jews were by law confined to living in the Pale of Settlement, a national ghetto in Western Russia, although there were increasing numbers of Jewish bankers, teachers and businesspersons with "honored guild status" who lived in the major urban centers and were beneficiaries of new opportunities for upward mobility. The worst violence occurred across a wide swath of that territory, with major incidents recorded in Elizavetgrad, Kiev and Odessa. The familiar pattern of past pogroms intensified. The press contributed to the spread of unsubstantiated rumors claiming Jewish involvement in the murder of the tsar, a theme that resonated with the officialdom from the capital to the provincial centers. The Ministry of the Interior left the problem in the hands of local police forces, whose officials did little to restrain the attacks. Only after a year of chaos, with rising numbers of

---

[57] One of the leaders of People's Will, Vera Figner, was also born to Jewish parents, but had no identification with religion as a revolutionary. On the role of Jews in the movement as a whole, see Haberer, *Jews and Revolution in Nineteenth Century Russia*.

victims, did the government order control over the mobs. To be sure, there were examples of police officials who did their best to contain the violence, and some trials were held in the aftermath. However, these instances of "minimal respect for the law" were overshadowed by the more prevalent current of the state's complicity in permitting the anti-Semitic terrorism to run its course before taking decisive action.[58]

The height of this form of political violence occurred in 1903–6 at the very moment when the insurgent terrorism of the SR Combat Organization and the violently oriented anarchist groups began targeting high-ranking officials in the Russian government. It also coincided with the disorders of the 1905 Revolution. Once more, the fusion of anti-Semitic prejudice and myth combined and produced horrible consequences. In 1903–4 alone, there were 45 pogroms, with over 100 deaths and 4,200 severe casualties with many dying subsequently as a result of their injuries. These include the most devastating pogroms in Kishenev and Gomel. During the revolutionary strikes and repression of 1905–6, 657 pogroms were recorded in the Pale of Settlement, with 3,100 deaths and more than 15,000 suffering wounds and injuries to mind and body. This time there were genuine atrocities, with 1,500 children left orphaned when both parents were brutally tortured and killed, together with untold numbers of rapes and cases of bodily dismemberments. The perpetrators of the violence, organized in small bands by local leaders, once more had the passive complicity of the authorities, for whom the violence was seen as part of the patriotic repression of the revolutionary parties, since the pogromists directed their attacks against liberals and radicals as well as Jews.[59]

There was an explicitly political dimension to the violence of the pogroms, centered in the rightist organization called the Black Hundreds. Built out of a national network of provincial cells, the Black Hundreds had an effective and vociferous leader in Vladimir M. Purishkevich. In addition, a number of newspapers propounded virulently anti-Semitic views, as did some political party representatives in the Duma, the national administrative body with highly limited

---

[58] Klier, "Russian Jewry on the Eve of the Pogroms," 56.
[59] Lambroza, "The Pogroms of 1903–6," 218–38 contains the statistics. See also Hoffman and Mendelsohn, *The Revolution of 1905 and Russia's Jews* and also Judge, *Easter in Kishinev: Anatomy of a Pogrom.*

representation, set up in desperation by Nicholas II when faced with a general strike in Moscow in October, 1905. Purishkevich's political party, the Union of the Russian People, received subsidies from Stolypin, chairman of the Council of Ministers, despite opposition to this practice voiced by Finance Minister Sergei Witte.[60] For taking this position, Witte was vilified by the Right in the press and survived two assassination attempts on his life by members of the Union of the Russian People.

Most scholars agree that the role of the state was paramount in contributing to the disturbances. Instead of acting with force, as officialdom did in combating and repressing revolutionary violence, in this situation, the police chose to see the Black Hundreds as volunteer enforcers who were taking matters of defending the regime into their own hands, and thus contributing to the restoration of national security by utilizing tactics of violence. In the town of Orsha, for example, the 1905 pogrom was inspired and led by the district police superintendent. A police station clerk, Tikhon Sinitskii, became the pogrom's chief organizer, proclaiming that "the slaughter of the yids is going on everywhere. We should massacre them and pluck them out until not a single yid remains." At the same time, it should be noted that there were instances of the reverse response, in which some officials actually aided and even rescued Jews from the mob violence.[61]

Adding to the nationalist passions that enflamed many to justify the anti-Semitic attacks were the grotesque political cartoons appearing in the press, which reached a widening readership with their venomous and at times violent caricatures of the alleged danger Jews posed to the country's legitimate authority.[62] In response to this milieu of increasing terror, there were instances of self-defense groups organized by Jews, as well as by workers who were involved with disorders and strikes for purposes of their own economic advancement and who did not directly participate in the concurrent anti-Semitic violence.[63]

---

[60] On Stolypin's role in the pogroms, see Ascher, P. A. Stolypin: The Search for Stability in Late Imperial Russia, 77–8, 105–6.

[61] Surh, "Russia's 1905 Era Pogroms Reexamined," 21–2, 35–6, 38.

[62] See the examples in Weinberg, "The Russian Right Responds to 1905: Visual Depictions of Jews in Postrevolutionary Russia," 55–69.

[63] Surh, "Ekaterinoslav City in 1905: Workers, Jews and Violence," 139–66 and "Jewish Self-Defense and Pogrom Violence in 1905." For another perspective, see Hamm, "Jews and Revolution in Kharkiv: How One Ukrainian City Escaped a Pogrom in 1905," 156–76.

All sides, however, seemed to feel that they were acting in a posture of defensive violence.

Neither the state nor the insurgents could claim victory on the eve of the First World War. The tactics of terrorism used by both the police and revolutionaries had accomplished one result – a huge list of casualties of the dead and the maimed. Each needed the other to designate as the enemy in order to justify the use of violence, but neither was willing to confront the issue of their own dependence on it. For both, the violent means justified the political end, however unreachable those goals had become.

To some extent, the growth of the labor movement in Russia, initiated by the police official Sergei Zubatov, captured much of the drive and passion of the new generation coming of age on the eve of the Great War that might have been attracted to the ranks of the combatants a decade earlier. Also, the opposition parties were fragmented and many members returned to their traditional tactics. Socialist Revolutionaries devoted themselves to spreading anti-regime propaganda among the peasantry, while Marxist Social Democrats sought to recruit the burgeoning factory working class to their cause and liberal-minded Constitutional Democrats placed their hopes on building constitutional assemblies. Outbreaks of strikes throughout this period, culminating in the huge protests following the 1912 Lena Goldfield shooting of workers by soldiers and police, aided in drawing attention away from the tactics of targeted assassination of state officials.

The truly extraordinary aspect of this decades-long combat between the police and the insurgents was the mirror-like quality of their respective modes of operation. Had they been able to look at their reflections from an uninvolved standpoint, it might have been apparent to them how much they resembled each other in their justifications, strategy and tactics. As mentioned above, each believed that the use of violence was absolutely necessary for purposes of defense against the threat of the other. In many cases, they even used the same language to dehumanize the object of their rage. Fear stalked both sides throughout the time period, in part stoked by their own anxieties and insecurities. The government never achieved the stability it sought, and seemed unable to distinguish realistic policy goals to address crucial socio-political problems from unrealizable fantasies achievable by using forces of punishing authority. By imagining that the regime could literally wipe out all resistance before dealing with the critical issues of corruption, poverty, and unjust rule, vacuums of power were left open for the opposition to gain control over. While the officialdom of the state continued to be engaged in a Sisyphean struggle with its enemies, the revolutionaries sought utopian transformations that were far beyond the grasp even of their very destructive tactics of violence. In other words, the ends each side sought were impossible to achieve by the means they chose to employ to get there.[64]

As both the state agents of order and their revolutionary opponents in the illegal underground dug deeper into the varieties of political violence at their disposal, they became more complex and sophisticated in their operations against each other. At the same time, they still followed parallel trajectories in many instances, and indeed, learned certain techniques from each other. As exposures of infiltrators became more frequent, they each intensified their efforts to find new ways to accomplish their secret intelligence gathering. The number of state and party agents working undercover increased dramatically, as did the number of ordinary people working on the streets and in buildings hired by each side as informants to spy on meetings and travel patterns of those targeted for repression, arrest or assassination. Both sides increased their reliance on the use of provocateurs, false papers, bogus passports, and knowledge of the latest chemical discoveries in order to maintain an advantage in their weaponry and explosive devices. National borders were transgressed with great regularity as both the police and the revolutionaries made effective use of terrorism abroad to hunt their prey, with or without the permission of the foreign governments.

Both sides also made use of trials, but only to punish and expose their respective enemies. Both also sought to utilize the press to further their own ideological or nationalist goals whenever possible. Although the state appeared to have had the clear advantage in this domain, since it controlled so many newspapers either through ownership or censorship, we should nevertheless not discount the impact of the growing opposition press. To be sure, the radical publications still had to be smuggled illegally, as they had since Herzen's initial

---

[64] The eminent writer Leo Tolstoy had his own idealistic hopes for the aftermath of 1905, which were rooted in his conviction and faith in the tactics of passive resistance, non-violence and Christian anarchism. See his "The Meaning of the Russian Revolution," Raeff, *Russian Intellectual History: An Anthology*, 323–63 and Medzhibovskaya, "Tolstoi's Response to Terror and Revolutionary Violence," 505–31.

experiment, but the appearance of legal liberal newspapers, particularly after 1905, added voices of reform to the arena of criticism and change, and in this way, competed with both the mainstream and the radical media for the attention of educated society. In a related development, book publishing became crucial in the battle over the control of words as well as weapons in 1905. In that revolutionary year, as the regime found itself temporarily paralyzed by the chaos in the streets, censorship virtually disappeared and a flood of previously forbidden books was published on presses taken over by opposition factions and sold openly in bookstores. These imprints included books by some of the most feared revolutionaries, including Herzen, Bakunin, and Kropotkin.

Apart from these general trends, there were quite a few specific comparative examples that exemplify these "mirrors." Loris-Melikov, who was one of the closest persons to Alexander II among his ministers in 1880, was working on a proposal for a constitutional structure that would introduce some level of representation from society while not significantly reducing the authority of the monarch. At the same moment, the Executive Committee of People's Will was drafting plans for a constitutional convention that would be responsible for establishing a post-autocratic republic in Russia. Despite the wide differences in the specific clauses of these documents, the importance here lies in the fact that they were being drafted simultaneously by two sides in mortal combat without either seriously considering the details of the other's planning. Even the rhetoric on each side reflected the other's terminology. One cabinet minister, speaking for many who mourned the death of Alexander II, referred to him as "our martyred Emperor," which was exactly the imagery used by Stepniak and the radical camp in referring to their fallen comrades.[65]

Savinkov was devoted to his work with the efficiency and goal orientation of his counterparts in the state administration. Plehve and Stolypin described in internal policy memoranda codes of conduct and methods of operation for the police subordinates and field agents to follow which strikingly resembled Savinkov's operational commands issued to the Combat Organization's rank and file members. Indeed, the terrorists from below often found themselves caught up in webs of

---

[65] Quoted in Footman, *Red Prelude*, 224; Stepniak-Kravchinskii uses this term frequently in *Underground Russia* as well as elsewhere in his writings.

bureaucratic hierarchies not unlike similar situations confronting the police. On more than one occasion, Savinkov decided to order assassinations without even consulting the opinion of the SR Party's Central Committee, just as Rachkovskii often made such independent decisions for the Okhrana in the Paris office without informing or getting permission from the ministries in St Petersburg.[66]

Azev and Savinkov sought to inculcate what they called "revolutionary discipline" into the Combat Organization's operations that in fact strongly resembled forms of military discipline practiced by the police according to their instructional training manuals.[67] The qualities of bravery, honor, devotion to the cause and the virtues of service and dying for country can be found as codes of conduct for both the police and the revolutionaries. Each accepted without question the moral justification of the use of violence to achieve their ends.[68] Perhaps the most striking aspect of the grandiosity and unreality of both sides was the common assumption that violence was the ultimate form of redemption in their work. At the same time, in what was perhaps the regime's ultimate exercise in the fantasy of power at this historical juncture, Nicholas II ordered the construction of a new palace, Livadia, to be located on a bluff in the Crimea overlooking the Black Sea.[69]

---

[66] McDaniel, "Political Assassination and Mass Execution: Terrorism in Revolutionary Russia, 1878–1938," 128–32, 136.

[67] Ibid., 185, 186.   [68] Ibid., 192.   [69] Gelardi, *From Splendor to Revolution*, 300.

5 EUROPEAN NATION STATE TERRORISM AND ITS ANTAGONISTS, AT HOME AND ABROAD, 1848-1914

Considering that the police and the revolutionaries in Russia were locked together in a violent dispute over political authority, it should not be surprising to find a similar trend in Western Europe during the same time period. Tsarist Russia was in many ways a part of Europe throughout the nineteenth century, yet also, in more significant aspects, apart from it. Thus, though the structural conflicts over state legitimacy and citizen participation in the political process bore strong resemblances, the specific situations in Western Europe require a separate discussion of these separate campaigns of terrorism. Russia's governance remained committed to medieval justifications of authority via divine right and the exclusion of any wider political involvement of the general population in decision-making. These circumstances explain the emergence of social groups there, such as an influential literary intelligentsia willing to engage in political challenges to the regime's authority, and powerful insurgent groups, forced underground to play a more extreme role in confronting the Romanov administrations and their enforcers, particularly during the second half of the century. Western European countries, by contrast, permitted far more dissonance within the boundaries of legality for the conflicts over state legitimacy to be contested, as witnessed by the gradual introduction of representational institutions, however limited they were, in response to demands from below. Nonetheless, the governing officialdom and their opponents were unable to avoid a continuing resort to violence in order to resolve the issues that divided them.

The flames of 1848 had been dampened but not extinguished, as the traditional regimes resumed their places in the aftermath. Every republic established during that revolutionary year was crushed by the revived monarchical armies, but the resort to policies of terror continued without interruption in the post-revolutionary period, as governments once more sought to legitimize their regimes using enforcement policies when deemed necessary. The forces of repression and resistance continued to grapple all the more desperately, as the violence escalated even beyond their collective imaginaries.

The motivation behind this ongoing clash remained the need to resolve the central political question of the age: the foundations for the legitimacy of the state and its responsibilities for the welfare of its citizens and subjects. In the era of monarchical absolutism and religious hegemony, men of the pen in power framed policies for a future in which resistance from below would be punished with severity and brutality if necessary. Those who sought power, or refused to accept the status quo, wrote treatises to establish criteria to distinguish legitimate rulers from tyrants who either abused or unlawfully seized power and proceeded to misuse it on their subjects. In certain cases, when all other means of change were exhausted or prevented, violence in the form of tyrannicide was justified. And there was no shortage of men of deeds who were more than willing to carry out acts of terror to realize their counter-proposals.

This resort to violence in order to resolve the question of governmental legitimacy, however, was now far more complicated than it had been prior to 1848. Instead of the hegemonic monarchic polity of the past, there were now a number of potential bases for legitimizing state authority, with advocates contesting against one another. As nation states evolved through stages of constitutional representation, bringing greater numbers of citizens into the governing process, the alternatives to monarchism increased. This situation produced further political divisions among the competing antagonists, as well as a continuing barrier between the central administrations and their opponents. The state remained the central focus in the theory and practice of political authority, but assemblies of enfranchised citizens also grew in stature and worked in consort with the royal authorities, despite the limitations imposed by the regimes. Governance became the potential responsibility of greater segments of society with the expansion of political suffrage, civil and judicial rights, economic advancement and educational opportunities during the nineteenth century. However, for those frustrated by being excluded from these changes, such as the emerging labor organizations, activist student groups in public universities, and political parties denied access to the continental parliaments of the monarchical states, a different mission was in preparation. Within these ranks, the perception was that if state authorities sought to restrict participation to privileged sectors of society, or to coercively impose their notions of political legitimacy, antagonists would take up the cause of signaling state despotism and seeking solutions. For some, this meant turning to violence.

In the aftermath of the 1848 uprisings, widespread anxiety pervaded society as competing factions vied for power, all but paralyzing the legislative process. Traditional monarchists sought to limit the influence of socialists, nationalists and liberals in seeking a political consensus. When the National Assembly in France rejected the request of Louis Napoleon Bonaparte to revise the constitution so that he could run for a second term as president, he seized power on December 2, 1851 in a *coup d'état*, which brought an end to the republic and established the Second Empire in a facsimile imitation of the first Napoleon's regime a half century earlier. Once in control as emperor, he instituted a wave of repressive measures that included press censorship, the banning of trade unions and public assemblies until the end of the 1860s, making illegal the anthem of the republic, "the Marseillaise," and the purging of universities. The central authorities in Paris now appointed many local officials, whereas previously they gained office through elections. The police were relentless in these years as enforcers of state policy.[1]

The line between, on the one hand, what governments claimed were harsh but necessary policies called forth in response to threats to the legal order and, on the other, state actions that in fact kindled or even provoked the feared disorders, continued to be a blurred boundary. With the rise in executions, states of siege, and extraordinary measures enacted by governments to prevent any revivals of 1848, those seeking to resist and oppose the government became political outlaws.

---

[1] The role of the police is meticulously described by one of its own in Guyot, *La Police*, 173–83. See also Goldstein, *Political Repression in Nineteenth Century Europe*, 200–15 for similarities across Europe.

Reactions were not long in coming. Napoleon III (as Louis Napoleon crowned himself) was the target of several assassination attempts in the early 1850s, and other insurgents made attempts on the lives of Emperor Franz Joseph of Austria in 1850 and Frederick William IV of Prussia in 1853. The most publicized assassination attempt was undoubtedly the attack planned by the Italian nationalist Felice Orsini in 1856. Stirred by Mazzini's calls for national unification, and enraged by the continued occupation of Italian territory by the French, Orsini, with the aid of a small group of conspirators, tried to kill the Emperor by detonating a bomb near his carriage as it approached the Paris Opera House on January 14. The Emperor escaped unharmed, but eight people were killed and 156 others wounded, some very seriously. Orsini was captured, quickly tried and executed for his deed, but his act created a sensation; it would be repeated in coming decades under a new ideological banner and with unexpected success.[2]

There is ample evidence that Napoleon III was driven by illusions of political grandeur, convinced of his ability to follow in the imperial footsteps of his renowned ancestor by realizing his vision of French triumphalism. To accomplish this and solidify his legitimacy as ruler, he made full use of the repressive forces of the police, in some instances continuing the methods developed by Joseph Fouché during the Restoration years before 1848 and, in others, moving into more sophisticated techniques of surveillance and terror.[3] Although he made far less use of the death penalty than his predecessors, Napoleon III made liberal use of punishment by exile. He began by banishing 88 members of the former National Assembly and then enlisted the aid of public officials, from judges to inspectors across the country, to uncover opposition groups. Once arrested, suspects were deported by the thousands to live in dreadful conditions in camps in remote New Caledonia and Guiana. Newspaper editors and their leading reporters were subjected to rigid state censorship policies and sent to the courts for sentencing when disobedient.[4] Meanwhile the government set up its

---

[2] Packe, *Orsini*. Orsini had assembled a small international cell which included Simon Bernard in Paris, Joseph Taylor in London, and three fellow Italians in Paris. Had he succeeded, he may well have gone on with this group to plan further acts of insurgent terror against the French authorities to end their occupation in Italy.

[3] On Fouché, see Mazower, *The Policing of Politics in the 20th Century*, 5.

[4] Plessis, *The Rise and Fall of the Second Empire, 1852–1871*, 15, 132–5.

own Cahot news agency that set standards for all to follow, and took control of the coverage of over 300 newspapers nationwide. Economic data from the era of the Second Empire show an increasing cleavage between the new "business aristocracy," whose material condition improved, and the poorer classes, for whom crowded living quarters, exhausting hours of labor and hungry children were the norm.[5]

In tandem with these trends, a special bureau, the *cabinet noir*, was created with the specific task of unsealing letters to obtain intelligence on regime opponents. The role of *agents provocateurs* was upgraded as well. They were sent to infiltrate factories not only in order to spy on labor organizers, but also to propose actions against the government, that were then used against the group supposedly responsible for the planned acts of sedition. They even arranged for several riots and fictitious attempts on the Emperor's life that were called off prior to their being executed, but which provided the kind of evidence needed to make arrests.[6] Once again, we find an example of the mirror-behavior present in the Russian case. The opposition developed what they referred to as a "revolutionary counter-police," led by Raoul Rigault and Théophile Ferré, who constructed a network of their own to conduct surveillance on the national political police.[7]

The ongoing tension came to a climax in 1871 with France's defeat in the Franco-Prussian War. This military conflict not only brought an end to the Second Empire after two decades of rule, but also created the conditions for the unification of the German states into an empire under the leadership of Prussia. These results were certainly calculated by Bismarck and his general staff, but neither they nor the French authorities foresaw the reaction in France to the admission of defeat, which brought forth the most violent and murderous political event, short of actual warfare, in modern European history – the destruction of the Commune of Paris. This was a moment of unbridled state terror, with consequences that would, in combination with other political discontents, inspire acts of violent revenge for decades. More

---

[5] For the statistics and the impact, see ibid., 116–28.
[6] Payne, *The Police State of Louis Napoleon Bonaparte, 1851–1860*, 269–72; see also Guyot, *La Police*, 156–69 on "mouchards et agents provocateurs" and pp. 170–83 on police-organized conspiracies and riots at this time, written by a former gendarme official from the perspective of the police.
[7] On these developments, see Bramstedt, *Dictatorship and Political Police*, 35–49 and Jellinek, *The Paris Commune of 1871*, 22–3. Interestingly, Blanqui condemned this exercise in police imitation. See his *Critique sociale*.

specifically, the carnage of the Commune contributed to the spread of the ideology of anarchism, which became the predominant justification for vengeful attacks on the state in Western Europe until the violence of the First World War overtook its momentum.

The immediate origins of these developments lie in a growing diplomatic crisis in which Prussia, the rising power in central Europe, challenged France over the question of succession to the vacated throne of Spain in 1868. Two years later, Napoleon III, for the last time displaying his characteristic delusions of authority, essentially provoked a willing Prussia into war. The battles turned against the French from the outset and by October, 1870, Paris found itself under siege and bombardment. Holding out for several months, the city was the scene of competing local political organizations – military and civil, monarchist and republican – vying for prominence. The most serious schism was over the issue of whether to continue the war or concede defeat and sue for favorable terms. In February 1871, the National Assembly elections produced a monarchist majority favoring the latter option, which was vigorously opposed by many provincial assemblies as well as the array of socialist and republican groups in Paris. When a spirited faction of Parisians proclaimed their intention to fight on and took possession of both the City Hall (Hôtel de Ville) and a huge depot of cannons, Adolphe Thiers, the last prime minister to serve Napoleon III (and soon to be provisional President of France) moved his national administration out of Paris to the presumably safer grounds of suburban Versailles and prepared to negotiate with Bismarck's victorious Prussian representatives.

The Commune of Paris officially formed as a result of elections held in the city on March 26 under these complex circumstances, and moved quickly to fill the power vacuum in Paris and press their own agenda. Rumor moved more quickly than fact, producing fear and uncertainty across the city. Adding to the confusion, communications between Paris and Versailles were inept at best, with the result that mutual mistrust and elements of political paranoia pervaded through the stalemate. As tensions mounted, the Prussian command released some 40,000 French prisoners of war from military detention centers at the request of the Versailles administration, who were mobilized to restore the state's authority in Paris. In the city, the National Guard and a variety of political militias collected and distributed arms to defend the Commune against the expected assault.

An insurrectionary mood took hold in the Commune's administration, with the more radical elements gradually gaining leadership. Brutal acts soon erupted on both sides. When Communards captured by the advancing French forces were executed, the militants defending the Commune began seizing hostages. At one point, the Commune's Central Committee sought to negotiate an exchange with Thiers in Versailles, in which the Communards would release the Archbishop of Paris, whom they had captured, if Thiers would free the imprisoned legendary revolutionary, Louis Auguste Blanqui. The proposal was rejected. In another instance, General Claude Martin Lecomte was rumored to have ordered the troops under his command to fire on Communards and unarmed citizens; in the resulting melee, he was pulled off his horse by an angry crowd and shot to death. As supplies in the city dwindled, reports spread that some Communard supporters had raided the Paris zoo to steal animals for food. As the climax neared during the week of May 22, with the Versailles divisions marching toward the center of the city, the Communards executed 56 hostages, including the Archbishop, and set fire to some of the main government buildings in the heart of Paris. Although there is evidence that the worst fires were the result of shelling by the invaders, the blame was placed entirely on the Commune for the enormous damage.[8]

With all of this in mind, still, nothing prepares an objective observer for the level of the ensuing violence adopted by the Versailles troops. During a "week of blood" (*semaine sanglante*) in June, the government essentially declared central Paris a battlefield. The Commune had in the meanwhile established committees in the manner of an alternative government, which some of its members considered it to be. Among the most active were the Central Committee, responsible for overall policy, and the Committee on Public Safety, which was responsible for security and discipline. Charles Delescluze, the Commune's Delegate of War, and his associates organized defense strategy of calling the citizenry to arms with instructions to erect cobblestone street barricades, and to resist the invasion by any means. The Commune's intention, as Delescluze put it, was to prevent the city from "falling into

---

[8] Jellinek, *The Paris Commune of 1871*, 328–9. Partisan support for the Commune was broadly based, extending, e.g., from the artist Gustave Courbet to a variety of radical figures including both Marx and Bakunin, all of whom had their own interpretations of its significance.

the hands of the reactionaries and clericals of Versailles, those scoundrels who deliberately handed over France to the Prussians and are making us pay the ransom of their treachery."[9]

The efforts were futile against the vastly superior forces of the state. When the carnage ended, at least 25,000 Parisians had been shot to death, some of whose bodies were found bearing no weapons. This was a larger number of casualties than those executed in Paris during the entire Reign of Terror in 1793-4, and more than were lost in any single battle of the Franco-Prussian War. In one jail housing captured Communards, 1,000 prisoners were shot in a two-day period during that bloody week. Bodies were piled up at the Trocadero and the Ecole Polytechnique numbering in the thousands, rising to a height above the level of the officers patrolling the areas. The smell of death lingered in the city for weeks while mass arrests and hastily arranged trials with summary sentences of imprisonment and exile took place. 28,000 prisoners were shipped off to the coastal fortresses of northern France, and several thousand more of the convicted were sent to the barren wasteland of New Caledonia in the South Pacific. A few of the fortunate escaped, but many more went mad from the horrid conditions either en route while in cages or in the labor camps where they were later interned.[10]

Fears of further terror continued to be stoked by the governments of Europe after the massacre. The press fed anxieties about the alleged influence on the Communards of the subversive activities of the International Workers Association, which had been founded by Marx, Bakunin and other socialists in the early 1860s. A French diplomat called the organization "an agent of destruction aimed at all nations," which had to be combated and defeated. A German newspaper, echoing the new Imperial government's perspective, called for a European alliance to withstand the threat of the International, which was seen as "the only possible means of saving the state, church, culture, in a word, everything which makes up the life of European states." One of

---

[9] Proclamation by Charles Delescluze, 21 May 1871 in Edwards, *The Communards of Paris, 1871*, 160-1.

[10] See the following references: Shafer, *The Paris Commune*, 86-109, which includes graphic images of visual evidence; Tombs, *The Paris Commune*, 151-83; Christiansen, *Paris Babylon*, 341-69, 373-7 and the documentary photographs following p. 308; Edwards, *The Paris Commune, 1871*, 346-8; Goldstein, *Political Repression*, 249-50; Simpson, *Louis Napoleon and the Recovery of France*, 187-8.

the most important diplomatic alliances of the time, the so-called "Three Emperors League" signed in Berlin in 1873, agreed to combine forces to seek "the repression of the revolutionary movement in Europe." This clearly was a reference to continuing fears of both partisans of the International and the political exiles in Switzerland, who had escaped the French dragnet and who, in the view of the government officials, were engaged in spreading false information about the heroic resistance of the Commune experience.[11] However, the exaggerated nature of such claims can be seen from the facts that the International imploded from its own internal divisions and disappeared three years later, in 1876, and nothing resembling a Commune uprising appeared anywhere on the continent.[12]

The militant who consistently antagonized the authorities and perhaps best represents the bridge between the legacy of the Commune and the appearance of the anarchist-inspired terrorism of the next decade was Louise Michel. Beginning as an ambulance driver for the National Guard, Michel became deeply committed to the radical ideology espoused by the leaders of the Commune in the spring of 1871. She was among the Communard fighters at the last stand in Montmartre before they were crushed entirely by the government's troops during the "week of bloodshed." She was charged at her trial with sedition and seeking to overthrow the government. Her sentence was prison for a year and a half, before being deported to New Caledonia. There she converted to anarchism and after the 1880 amnesty, returned to France where she became a prominent writer and public speaker on behalf of the cause of the Commune and anarchist principles. Emma Goldman was one of the many nascent anarchists Michel inspired.[13]

Despite the endemic fear that the Paris Commune experience generated, which went largely unchallenged in the mainstream European media, the most savage violence in this case was clearly committed not by the insurgents but by the state. Moreover, it was ordered not by an authoritarian monarchy but by a regime that was in the process

---

[11] For this evidence, see Goldstein, *Political Repression*, 250–1. On the Communards in Swiss exile, see Vincent, *Between Marxism and Anarchism*.

[12] The last meeting of the First International was in 1876 in Philadelphia. A revival did not take place until the formation of the Second International during the 1890s.

[13] Michel et al., *The Red Virgin*; Shafer, *The Paris Commune*, 146–8. There has never been a scholarly biography of Michel in English.

of constructing a new democratic republic in France. As for the matter of the actual influence of the Commune and the atrocities associated with its demise, there were indeed people who were inspired by the courage, purpose and martyrdom manifested during its brief existence, though not where European governments were suspecting. One central point of influence was the growing revolutionary movement in Russia, where its mythology was adopted by both populists during the 1870s, and later, Marxists in the 1890s. The narrative they chose to revere was a partisan portrait that celebrated the heroic efforts of outnumbered and outgunned socialist communards in a bitter struggle against the state's reactionary policies.[14] Further afield, echoes of the combat over the Commune were felt in the US, in the ranks of the emerging labor movement.[15]

The violence of the Paris Commune has also generated interest as a subject of national memory and trauma.[16] The impact of the massacre at the moment of the denouement left in its wake a welter of confusion and rage that played itself out in a variety of ways in the following decades. For those sympathetic to the communards, the event revived the utopian hopes of realizing ideals of liberty and equality that were aroused and fought over in 1789 and 1848. For most citizens, however, the Commune was the symbol of fear of precisely those ideals. Freedom for masses of people with little experience in the complexities of political responsibility was perhaps only marginally more frightening to those who governed, than the prospect of the blurring of social class distinctions that equality promised to bring. It was a moment of societal vulnerability, revealed in raw relief, during an extraordinary transition from empire to republic, of national defeat, and unstable authority as competing forces sought control in Paris over the shape of the responsibilities of the modern nation state.

The larger issue of the use of the power of the new governments, particularly in Germany, France and Italy, merged together with the unresolved questions over state legitimacy that had been one of the chief motives in the continuing resort to political violence for answers. France managed to establish (or re-establish) its national identity as a

---

[14] See Itenberg, *Rossiia i parizhskaia kommuna*. Radicals of all stripes continued to discuss the Commune as a precedent for a socialist administration of the future. See also the collection of documents in Schulkind, *The Paris Commune of 1871*.
[15] This is discussed in detail in Katz, *From Appomatox to Montmartre*.
[16] See the analysis focusing on these themes using literary evidence from the novels of Flaubert, Hugo and Zola in Starr, *Commemorating Trauma*.

republic, with commitments inherent to respect the legal rights of a loyal citizenry. United Germany, the newest and strongest member within the European nation states system, represented the more prevalent European polity, that of a constitutional monarchy, though parliamentary representation and political parties would now play a more important role than had been the case in the past. In both models of governance, the effort to balance the interests of the state with those of society remained precarious and unresolved. The wave of violent assaults on the rulers of Europe soon to erupt in the name of anarchism was, to a large extent, the result of conflicting forces which sought to bring clarity to the confused political situation by either defending the security of the state, or undermining it. The Germans had achieved national unification through wars against Austria in 1866 and France in 1870–1; the French had created their Third Republic by crushing, with unbridled brutality, the Paris Commune. In both cases, however different the governing systems might appear to be, it was undeniable that state violence was the decisive factor.

The role of the police, particularly in France where the new Third Republic was in the process of establishing its legitimacy after the repression of the Commune, remained a subject of intense discussion. With the presence of so many antagonistic political parties and factions, the stability of the new administration was of paramount importance. Expectations of a new and innovative security force that would cast off the imagery of both monarchic and Bonapartist authoritarianism were quickly dashed. Not only were many of the old personnel reappointed, at all levels of rank, but the tactics and strategy of the preceding systems were recast in even more comprehensive forms. Indeed, its critics frequently referred to the police and the security forces as "a state within a state" during the 1880s and 1890s.

There were good reasons to fear the security services, even though they were often enunciated in exaggerated terms. According to one analysis of the period, "when a prominent revolutionary syndicalist, a militant socialist or a key right wing agitator traveled about the country, he was escorted to the train by his clandestine observers and met at his destination by a *commissaire spécial* or his aide, if indeed an agent did not accompany him on his journey." Voluminous telegrams and reports from the field in the police files testify to these procedures, which were conducted both by the Paris Prefecture of Police and the national Sûreté Générale, and which involved hundreds of informers (*mouchards*). A number of these informers were convicted criminals who were offered lesser sentences or reduced jail time for providing intelligence as spies to their handlers.[17] A smaller but still significant number of the *mouchards* and *agents provocateurs* were tasked with the job of fomenting violence by militants at demonstrations and creating dissent at secret meetings, so that the police could take appropriate measures. There were criticisms of the repressive tactics of the security forces in the mainstream press, but evidence shows that the Minister of the Interior and the police not only largely ignored the charges in these articles, but made regular financial contributions to major newspapers in return for favorable coverage of their activities.[18]

In order to deal more effectively with the increasing number of strikes at mines in France and the rise of both the labor union movement under the aegis of the General Confederation of Labor (CGT) and the more radical syndicalist and anarcho-syndicalist movements, the government appointed Louis Lépine as chief of the Police Prefecture in 1893. He served in that position for 17 years, the longest in French history. In addition to reorganizing the police bureaucracy, Lépine also issued directives on the use of violence against agitators who represented a threat to public security. During these years, the violence escalated as the strikes attracted larger numbers of workers and required similarly expanded numbers of security forces to contain them. One of the guaranteed sites of confrontations was the annual commemoration of the slaughter of the 1871 Communards at the end of May, which traditionally brought out as many as 150,000 demonstrators to face down not only the police but also military troops called in to maintain order.

As the combat between militants and the security forces intensified with the rash of strikes that threatened to cripple the country, the government feared above all that a national crisis could emerge if a general strike, as theorized by Georges Sorel in his influential book, *Reflections on Violence* (1908), actually became a reality. At a strike of miners in Chalon-sur-Saône, soldiers savagely beat the demonstrators, killing three, after a stone-throwing

---

[17] Calhoun, "The Politics of Internal Order," 123–5. I am grateful to K. Steven Vincent for alerting me to this valuable study.
[18] Ibid., 129.

incident.[19] By 1905, under the premiership of Georges Clemenceau, the government assigned 70,000 troops specifically to aid local police throughout the entire country. He also issued directives on how the security forces were to act at strikes and demonstrations. On the one hand, he noted that respect had to be paid to the legitimate right to strike while, on the other, violent measures could be undertaken against demonstrators after issuing proper warnings. First, police and troops were instructed to use the butts of their rifles to restore order, then their bayonets and, only in "desperate cases" could they then fire directly into the crowd. The degree to which the two sides were locked together in a dependent relationship is visible in one of Clemenceau's notes to the leaders of the CGT in the spring of 1906: "You are behind a barricade; I am in front of it. Your means of action is disorder. My duty is to maintain order. My role is thus to counteract your efforts. The best thing is for each of us to play his part."[20]

These developments may help explain the timing if not the content of the other wave of violence that swept across the continent and beyond for the coming decades. For this generation of insurgents, violent action was frequently justified in the name of anarchism, the philosophy that saw the authority of the state as an unmitigated evil and as inherently despotic. While the theory of anarchism had been discussed for decades in France largely as a result of the influence of Proudhon's writings, activism inspired by his ideas only now emerged. In a sense, the assassinations and bombings of this era also seemed to begin as a secular revival of the pre-modern rationales for committing acts of tyrannicide. However, the attacks soon expanded to include a wider number of targets in society as well as government, embodying Heinzen's conceptualization of a "barbarian party" with complicit allies in society as legitimate targets. At the same time, the police bureaux of France, Germany, Russia and much of the rest of Europe were deeply engaged in their own acts of repressive violence, which they referred to as "counter-terror" or "counter-insurgency."[21] The state was assumed to be under assault and in need of vigorous defense. For the insurgents, such policies were understood as aggressive

---

[19] Ibid., 223–4.   [20] Ibid., 300.
[21] See de la Hodde, *The Cradle of Rebellions* for the police narrative. De la Hodde comments on the need for the police to devote attention to repressing elements of "anarchy" (p. 468) in the radical underground, an early usage of this term well before it became a common designation to characterize the anti-state opposition three decades later.

components utilized by government rulers and ministers as routine in defense not of their citizenry but their own power.

In 1878, shots rang out in Berlin announcing a strategy of war against the state. On two occasions only months apart, the German emperor escaped assassination attempts by men who shouted the battle cry of anarchism as they were arrested. For the following 20 years, politically motivated bombings and shootings intensified across all the borders of Europe. The founders of anarchist theory, Proudhon, Bakunin and Kropotkin, had sought to demonstrate that the state was a mechanism of oppression and violence against its own citizenry. To many, it seemed that Germany and France in 1871 had brought this perspective into focus with extraordinary clarity. It mattered little to the new militants whether the government was a constitutional monarchy or a republic; so long as there was a central government of any kind, it would of necessity and by definition act in an authoritarian and violent manner against its own subjects and citizens.

Inspired by the 1880 formulations at the London congress of the Anarchist International, adherents believed they were carrying out acts of "propaganda by the deed" as they struck their violent blows against the political administrations of the world.[22] The attacks took various forms. One was the direct assassination of the ruler, regardless of title or the nature of the government involved. The list of those successfully killed includes President Sadi Carnot of France in 1894, Prime Minister Antonio Canovas of Spain in 1897, Empress Elizabeth of Austria in 1898, King Umberto of Italy in 1900, and President William McKinley of the US in 1901. The assassination of Archduke Franz Ferdinand of Austria-Hungary by the Serbian Black Hand in August 1914, the immediate prelude to the Great War, was nationalist rather than anarchist in terms of its ideological motives, but was very much in synch with the previous *attentats* driven by the tactics of propaganda by the deed.[23]

Another part of this particular landscape of fear raised by insurgent terror in this period was the activity of the Fenian Brotherhood, a movement in support of Irish independence, which made

---

[22] Stafford, *From Anarchism to Reformism*. Though Kropotkin is often credited with the original formulation of "propaganda by deed," the evidence points more conclusively to Brousse.

[23] For a recent study of the Black Hand and the assassin of the archduke, see Fabijancic, *Bosnia: In the Footsteps of Gavrilo Princip*, 143–88.

frequent use of violence and targeted primarily British military and government officials. The Fenians operated in the US as well as Ireland and England, but their most spectacular act of violence was probably the assassination in Dublin's Phoenix Park of Lord Frederick Cavendish and Thomas Henry Burke, the highest-ranking officials in Ireland, on May 6, 1882. Their bodies were found fatally slashed and bleeding, a crime allegedly committed by nine Fenians who were observed racing from the scene. They had little to do with anarchism, being involved in what can better be termed nationalist terror since their intention was to expel the British and establish a republican state of their own. Nevertheless, the violence they perpetrated against the "occupying officials" was an attack on the British crown and played a role in encouraging the constabulary to develop more repressive measures in Ireland.[24]

The second type of attack was the bombing of "innocents" in society, who, because of their privilege and wealth, were considered as conspiring with the state to improve their own status at the expense of the impoverished masses. Thus, bombs were hurled with frightening regularity in public spaces, breaching a previously respected boundary. Until this era, almost all of the violent political actions committed by revolutionaries had tended to target rulers and members of their immediate subordinate officialdom. The bombings of the 1880s and 1890s expanded the targets to include not only government sites but also cafes and department stores packed with ordinary shoppers, *flâneurs*, and random citizens. In Russia, where the number of victims was so much greater than in Europe, both People's Will and the SR Combat Organization made every effort possible to kill people who worked directly for the state or who were symbolically representatives of its authority. The anarchist-inspired terror stands out as the moment when the line between society and the state was completely elided. As the theorists of all forms of socialism, including anarchism, had long pointed out, the privileged members of the social order were conspirators with the state in prolonging the injustice and poverty that afflicted the majority of every nation state. This was even more the case in a republic, where the privileged elite actually participated in the

[24] On the Cavendish assassination, see Ford, *Political Murder*, 230–3. On the police, see Porter, *The Origins of the Vigilant State*. For another case involving Fenian violence, see Jenkins, "1867 All Over Again?," 81–97.

election of the state's officialdom, thereby imprinting their sanction on the repression and violence enacted by their chosen representatives.[25]

Anarchist ideas spread widely from the 1860s onward in much of Europe, especially in rural areas where agricultural economies predominated. In Italy, Carlo Cafieri, Andrea Costa and Errico Malatesta were among the pioneer proponents of the Bakuninist alternative to Marxist social democracy, which was oriented much more toward the rapidly expanding working classes in urban areas and factory towns. For peasants in the countryside, the local administrations and landlords were the perceived representatives of the state, and were therefore seen as being responsible for local deprivations of liberty and income. In 1877, peasant mobs attacked, burned and sacked municipal office buildings in Benevento and Letino. The police, aided by thousands of soldiers, made a huge number of arrests. Among the detained were ideologically committed Bakuninists who were armed not only with torches but also with pamphlets and broadsides proclaiming the arrival of the era of "propaganda by the deed" and the necessity of joining the rebellion "in the name of the social revolution."[26] In Spain, Giuseppe Fanelli, a career revolutionary from Italy who had fought with Garibaldi in his homeland in 1848 and with the Poles during their 1863 rebellion, spent years travelling through peasant villages in Spain spreading the ideas behind Bakunin's critique of the state in the 1860s and 1870s.[27]

The element of violence had always been present in Bakunin's writings and was interpreted in various ways by his followers. We may never know to what extent his words were responsible for motivating the shift to acts of terror, but the anarchist cause was now in the public domain as a kindling spark for the discontented. In 1878, the same year that Zasulich shot Trepov in St Petersburg, Max Hoedel and Karl Nobiling made their unsuccessful efforts to kill the German emperor. Following those acts, Juan Oliva Moncasi, a member of an outlawed Spanish anarchist-oriented labor organization, fired shots at a royal procession in Madrid in an attempt to kill King Alfonso XII. All of the

---

[25] See Miller, "The Intellectual Origins of Modern Terrorism in Europe," 27–62.

[26] Chaliand and Blin, *The History of Terrorism*, 117. Bakunin's influence in much of Italy in the early 1870s had much to do with his presence there as well as his radical publications. See Leier, *Bakunin: The Creative Passion*, 170–2.

[27] Pernicone, *Italian Anarchism, 1864–1892* and Corbin, *The Anarchist Passion*.

assailants proclaimed their dedication to the anarchist ideal of ridding the world of state tyrants.[28]

One of the worst incidents of insurgent violence in these years was the bombing of the Barcelona Liceu opera house on November 7, 1893 by the anarchist Santiago Salvador where at least 30 people were killed. He claimed to be acting to avenge the regime's execution of Paulino Pallas, the assassin of the notorious military commander, General Arsenio Martinez Campos. The government responded by intensifying its repression of the radical underground after the Liceu incident. It was now undeniably clear that militants had shifted their targets from primarily the representatives of the government to the heart of ordinary society. Matters were soon to worsen further.

In France, an even more intense campaign of insurgent terror was played out. The damage done by the violent suppression of the Paris Commune continued to loom large in the politics of the Third Republic. Requests for amnesty for the imprisoned Communards were raised frequently in the 1870s, including by the noted writer Victor Hugo and the Communard partisan Louise Michel after her release from prison. Even when the republic did issue a limited amnesty in 1880, it admitted no responsibility for the excessive killings of Communards by its forces.

At the same time, France, now the continent's paramount democratic republic, reorganized its security forces in Paris and local gendarmeries around the country to ensure that socialists at home and Communard exiles still at large abroad were under strict surveillance. To this end, contacts were made with counterparts in Belgium, Switzerland, Germany, Italy and Russia for the sharing of intelligence and the processing of arrests and extradition requests. Mistrust and suspicion among the rival governments were rampant. Nevertheless, there were also proposals for grand schemes of European-wide security against alleged common dangers from the left. Anarchists were described as lurking all over the continent, plotting violence at secret meetings that were infiltrated and reported on by the ubiquitous police spies. In one of the more spectacular examples of police cooperation, the French Sûreté permitted the Russian Okhrana to operate in its own

---

[28] King Alfonso XIII was the target of assassination attempts in 1902 and again in 1905 among others. See Eisenwein, *Anarchist Ideology and the Working Class Movement in Spain, 1868–1898*, esp. 65–6.

office building in Paris virtually without obstruction or supervision, so long as copies of the reports sent to St Petersburg were duplicated for the Foreign Ministry at the Quai d'Orsay. Surveillance and repression were sufficiently comprehensive that the prominent expatriate writer Ivan Turgenev, believed to be "the father of Russian nihilism" according to the police, was watched day and night for years.[29]

New acts of violence emerged amidst news of the assassination of Emperor Alexander II of Russia, a startling event that was widely reported in the press. Several attacks against factory officials, associated with the labor strikes, occurred in the early 1880s in French mining areas including Roanne, Decazeville and Aveyron. Two political figures, Jules Ferry and Léon Gambetta, were shot at in the same time period, but survived unharmed. For France, an act showing that terror from below had transgressed the previously respected boundaries of combat occurred on March 5, 1886 when Charles Gallo, a mid-level finance official, tossed a bottle of vitriol and fired shots from his revolver from the balcony of the Paris Bourse onto the trading floor below. There were no fatalities, but Gallo was apprehended and brought to court where he was sentenced to spend the rest of his life in a penal colony. At his trial, he made it clear that he had committed an act of propaganda by deed against one of the pillars of support for the corrupt and unjust government, namely its central financial institution.

Meanwhile, a young militant who took the name of Ravachol (François-Claudius Koenigstein) had identified another category of targets. He claimed he was driven to avenge two events that took place on May Day, 1891. One was the brutal assault by the police in the town of Fourmies at a demonstration by workers seeking to limit their workday to eight hours. Particularly disturbing was the shooting dead by the police of several women and children, among the nine fatalities. The other was the arrest of three anarchists at a similar demonstration in Clichy, who were beaten and tortured in police custody before being sentenced to prison terms by Judge Zephirin Benoit. Ravachol believed that if there was a crime committed on May Day, it was the behavior of the police, not the demonstrators.

[29] For excerpts from the archival files of the police reports and an analysis, see Liang, *The Rise of Modern Police and the European State System from Metternich to the Second World War*, 83–150.

His response was to explode two crude but powerful bombs at the apartment buildings of Benoit and his state-appointed prosecutor. There were no deaths from the bombings, but Ravachol was apprehended and charged with two other public bombings. Although the evidence was inconclusive, he was sent to the guillotine on July 11, 1892. He was quickly avenged by a militant, Théodule Meunier, who had earlier bombed one of the military sites where hundreds of Communards had been shot to death by French troops in 1871 during the "week of blood." Meunier's explosion destroyed the restaurant where Ravachol had been arrested. This time there were two deaths.[30]

This was followed by the bombing of the Chamber of Deputies by Auguste Vaillant, an anarchist also seeking to avenge Ravachol whom the police identified as a member of an anarchist group, *Les Révoltés*, on December 9, 1893. Only one person was wounded, but Vaillant was nevertheless sentenced to death. At his trial later that month, he spoke proudly of "having wounded this cursed society" by his act. "I carried this bomb to those who are primarily responsible for social misery," he concluded.[31]

The range of blame and fear was expanding. On the one side, the police increased their surveillance and repression of larger numbers of activists, who increasingly were referred to as "nihilists" as well as anarchists. On the other side, insurrectionists widened their list of targets to include the economically privileged sectors of society working in legislative bodies and business establishments, especially in wealthier neighborhoods, whom they considered responsible for the unending suffering of ordinary people.

Perhaps the most startling incident was Emile Henry's decision to blow up the Café Terminus, a fashionable restaurant near the busy Gare St-Lazare train station on February 12, 1894, during the middle of the day when wives and children were seeing off their husbands and fathers. Miraculously, only one person died, although 20 others were harmed, some quite seriously. Henry was apprehended shortly after the bombing and brought rapidly to trial. There, in front of some of the survivors of the attack in the courtroom, he made a stirring speech proclaiming his cherished political principles. Declaring his loyalty

[30] Lippman, "Ravachol, King of the Anarchists." For a full account of his career, see Maitron, *Ravachol et les anarchistes*.
[31] Chaliand and Blin, *The History of Terrorism*, 128.

only to the abolition of the state and to the tactics of propaganda by deed, he noted that he acted to avenge the martyrdom of Ravachol and Vaillant, who were, in his view, killed by the state and its "bourgeois supporters."

> [We will] spare neither women nor children because the women and children we love have not been spared. Are they not innocent victims, these children, who in the faubourgs slowly die of anemia, because bread is rare at home; these women who in your workshops suffer exhaustion and are worn out in order to earn forty cents a day, happy that misery has not yet forced them into prostitution; these old men whom you have turned into machines so that they can produce their entire lives and whom you throw out into the street when they have been completely depleted? ... You will add other names to the bloody lists of our dead. You have hanged us in Chicago, decapitated us in Germany, garroted us in Xerez, shot us in Barcelona, guillotined us in Montbrison and in Paris, but what you can never destroy is anarchy. Its roots are too deep; born in a poisonous society that is falling apart, it is a violent reaction against the established order. It represents the egalitarian and libertarian aspirations that are opening a breach in contemporary authority. It is everywhere, which makes anarchy elusive. It will finish by killing you.[32]

The verdict was never in doubt. The sentence announced was death by the guillotine. In addition to his ideological justifications, Henry may have been influenced by a more personal compulsion. At the moment the judge read out the verdict, Henry's mother shouted from her seat in the courtroom that her son had achieved revenge for his father's brutal treatment at the Paris Commune, where he had fought against the Versailles troops and been driven into exile.[33] Emile Henry's execution took place on May 21, 1894.

Events moved inexorably forward, with victory remaining elusive for both sides. To suppress the anarchist threat once and for all, in

---

[32] Quoted in Merriman, The Dynamite Club, 187.
[33] See Sonn, Anarchism and Cultural Politics in Fin de Siecle France, 245–6.

1893 and 1894 the French government issued the severe *lois scélérates*, or laws of iniquity, which rigidly censored the anarchist press and effectively made anarchist activities a criminal offense. The response was not long in arriving. On June 24, 1894, an Italian anarchist, Sante Geronimo Caserio stabbed Sadi Carnot, the President of the French republic, at a public banquet in Lyons. He died the following evening from the mortal wound. At his trial, Caserio proclaimed that he had acted in the name of anarchism. He was executed on August 14.[34]

A similar surge in anarchist theory and practice developed also in the US in this general time period. The German exile Johann Most played a key role in the transmission across the Atlantic of both European anarchist ideas and the tactics of propaganda by deed. Forced out of Berlin in 1878 by Bismarck's severe anti-socialist laws, he moved to London where he published his anarchist journal *Freiheit*. In 1881, he wrote approvingly of the assassination of Tsar Alexander II, and celebrated the exploits of People's Will as justified tyrannicide. The following year, he went beyond tolerable limits with his reporting on the Phoenix Park assassinations, which, in his view, were a heroic act for Irish liberty. The British Home Office took advantage of an outraged public reaction, declaring his reporting libelous and criminal. Not only was he arrested and threatened with a lengthy term of imprisonment, but the offices of *Freiheit* were raided, and the police impounded most of the paper's publishing equipment.[35]

Most chose exile once more, this time to the US. His first years were spent quietly working in a munitions factory in New Jersey, where he pilfered enough quantities of explosive materials to offer bomb kits to readers of *Freiheit*, which had resumed publication under looser American publishing conditions. During the 1880s, Most republished Nechaev's "Revolutionary Catechism" and Heinzen's "Murder" in his journal, introducing these terrorist texts to a new generation of recruits to the anarchist cause. His most widely distributed work was *The Science of Revolutionary Warfare* (1885) in which he both argued for anti-state violence and presented instructions on "the use and preparation of nitroglycerine." Indeed, he included advertisements for

---

[34] The Carnot assassination was described in the *New York Times*, August 16, 1894, and was the cover story in *Le Petit Journal*, July 3, 1894, among many transatlantic newspapers that featured the events.

[35] Burleigh, *Blood and Rage*, 72.

bomb-making kits with assembly instructions in the back pages of *Freiheit*, which was one of the many German language papers popular among the increasingly large immigrant working class population in the major urban centers of the US.

The arrival of the anarchist moment for many Americans was the day they read the newspaper accounts of the 1886 Haymarket Affair in Chicago, which has been characterized as "the first outbreak of terrorist violence on American soil."[36] There had certainly been instances of violence leading up to this event, but these had frequently taken the form of labor conflicts. Working conditions in Chicago were notoriously shameful. Factory owners were subject to little outside oversight and were protected by local police when enforcing their harsh standards of productivity and obedience. The city was also the home of two of the country's main anarchist papers, which rivaled Most's *Freiheit* in Chicago. One was the *Alarm*, edited by Albert Parsons, and the other was *Arbeiter Zeitung*, run by August Spies.

On May 1, 1886, workers at the McCormick Reaper plant went on strike to achieve better working conditions. The factory management called in the police, who went beyond their usual brutal tactics of crowd control by shooting at the demonstrators, two of whom died. Two days later, at Haymarket Square on the near North Side of the city, a protest was organized on behalf of the striking workers, sponsored and publicized by the anarchist newspapers. The chief of police, John Bonfield, antagonized by the incendiary speeches, decided to end the public meeting and ordered the police to take action. As they pushed bystanders out of the center of the speaking platform, someone threw a small bomb into the police ranks, leaving seven officers dead. The police responded by firing wildly into the crowd. The exact number of casualties still remains in dispute. The mainstream newspaper coverage was sensationalized, demonizing the foreign workforce as dangerous, and dominated by vitriolic propaganda from the anarchist press. The police were portrayed as noble warriors defending the public sphere against an irrational mob. As a result of this media campaign, the outcome was not surprising. Although the evidence was very murky at best, eight anarchists were indicted for acts of murder and conspiracy, to calm the furies of public demands for vengeance that had been

---

[36] Clymer, *America's Culture of Terrorism*, 29. The Haymarket Affair is analyzed in detail, pp. 33–68.

stirred up in the press. Three were sentenced to life in prison, one committed suicide, and four were executed by hanging on November 11, 1887, including Parsons and Spies. There were no investigations of the police to learn who was responsible for the numerous civilian victims.[37]

To their followers, *Alarm* editor Albert Parsons and his comrades were innocent martyrs; to the government, they were dangerous threats to public security. Behind the scenes, the real terrorism had taken place before the Haymarket tragedy occurred. The editors of the *Alarm* did print articles denouncing the captains of industry for mistreatment of their workers, and did indeed advocate violence as a strategy of defense against the brutality of labor conditions. Meanwhile, the police were active in spreading fear of the anarchist peril. According to the authoritative police account of the period, spies were hired who posed as radicals to conduct surveillance and provoke actions that allowed the police to conduct raids on anarchist organizations and make numerous arrests. Prominent business leaders, including Marshall Field and George Pullman, raised $100,000 that they gave to the Chicago police department to support the struggle against anarchism.[38] A prominent scholar of the affair has called the acts surrounding and including the Haymarket incident an American form of "police terrorism."[39]

The second event that further imprinted the association of anarchism with political violence in America was the shooting of Henry

[37] Among the many studies on the Haymarket Affair, see Avrich, *The Haymarket Tragedy*. For a recent general account, consult Carr, *The Infernal Machine*, 43–6. Frank Harris' novel, *The Bomb* remains a vivid fictional account based on the actual events. In the aftermath of the violent event, the Illinois governor, John Peter Altgeld in 1893 pardoned the three anarchists still in prison, and conducted a full-scale inquiry. He concluded that Bonfield, the police chief, was responsible for the violence and deaths, including of his own police officers, which provoked a huge and threatening backlash that ended Altgeld's political career.

[38] Schaack, *Anarchy and Anarchists*. Schaack was a captain in the Chicago police department. His 698-page book, its open partisanship notwithstanding, is undoubtedly the most comprehensive coverage of the Haymarket Affair, vividly conveying the fear and paranoia of the moment, and was a deliberate call to arms in the war against anarchism. See esp. pp. 682–90.

[39] Quoted in Avrich, *The Haymarket Tragedy*, 222. For a more recent scholarly account of the affair and its larger context, see Fellman, *In the Name of God and Country*, 143–65. Fellman includes reprints (pp. 171–4) of Thomas Nash's contemporary, influential lithographs published in *Harper's Magazine* and many newspapers, which contributed to the public hostility against workers and anarchists.

Clay Frick, the chairman of the Carnegie Steel Corporation, by Alexander Berkman in 1892 at the site of a factory strike in Homestead, Pennsylvania. Berkman was the political comrade and personal partner of Emma Goldman, one of the most prominent anarchist writers and activists in the US. He decided to kill Frick in a symbolic act to avenge the Haymarket executions and protest the brutal repression of the strikers by the private police forces of the Pinkerton Agency, hired by Frick to maintain order at the factory. He only wounded Frick, was captured, and sentenced to 14 years in prison.[40] Anarchist violence returned to the front pages once more when Leon Czolgosz, a fringe figure claiming anarchism as his cause, assassinated President McKinley in 1901. Once more the press whipped up a relentless campaign of fear in which immigrants, minorities and the entire spectrum of socialist factions were labeled as dangerous nihilists susceptible to anarchist ideas that threatened Americans within their very gates.

To keep matters in perspective, with all this violence, during the entire period of two decades, about 160 people were actually killed and some 500 injured by individuals associated in some way with anarchism.[41] Tragic though it was, this total pales beside the thousands killed by the SR terrorists in Russia, despite earlier calculations by Morozov and Romanenko that a "terrorist revolution" with targeted victims caused far fewer casualties than open revolutionary warfare. However, it was not the relatively small number of victims generating the public's fears in Europe and America that explains their willingness to permit governments to use violent methods in defense; rather, it was the prominence of the insurgents' chosen targets, their astonishing success in carrying out the planned *attentats*, the unpredictability of the attacks, and the transgression of previously respected social boundaries that caused such alarm.

Certainly the discovery of dynamite in 1866 by the Swedish scientist Alfred Nobel played an important part in the rising incidence of victims of terrorist acts, as did his later 1875 invention of a more powerful application in a gelatin format. Dynamite was quickly processed for use in blasting through mountain terrains to create new

[40] Krause, *The Battle for Homestead, 1880–1892*. Berkman's side of the story is told in his *Prison Memoirs of an Anarchist*.
[41] Jensen, "The International Campaign against Anarchist Terrorism, 1880–1930s," 90. Jensen and other scholars have raised doubts about some of the assassins' actual commitment to, or involvement with, the anarchist movement.

railways, roads and sites for industrial production. It had even greater potential as weaponry, but governments were unable to contain the spread of dynamite formulas and its chemical components, which ultimately were obtained by revolutionary groups for their own purposes. People's Will, for example, made very effective use of gelatin dynamite in their campaign of assassinations, including the killing of the Emperor in 1881.[42]

Anxieties over the control of their power led officials in both government and the police to vastly exaggerate the threat posed by anarchism. These fears were replicated in the press and passed along in daily columns and bulletins in newspapers. To be sure, the outrages committed by insurgents who were (or claimed to be) inspired by the anti-state ideology of Bakunin and Kropotkin had to be taken seriously and did constitute crimes. Nevertheless, the combatants on both sides of the violent divide operated with unyielding hostility toward one another. The police and the insurgents appeared to believe that they could actually destroy one another with the application of sufficient force. Moreover, there seems to have been a concomitant unwillingness by both to understand the very real problems that lay beneath the violence that each was willing to commit against the other. The poverty of the underclasses had not been substantially reduced in spite of the growing material wealth of the new bourgeoisie in privileged neighborhoods of urban Europe and America. The liberties and rights promised to citizens of the nation state since the democratic revolutions in the US and France had been granted mainly to the educated and wealthy elites. Political power remained in the hands of rulers who governed with the consent of parliaments that largely excluded the concerns of the laboring classes.

The insurgents professed as an article of faith that they could fatally damage the operations of the state by killing off its mechanics, while the government was equally convinced it could win the internal war against its declared and undeclared enemies. Visions of past revolts from 1789 to 1871 frightened rulers and inspired insurgents. Victory meant nothing less than a full vindication of methods of violence that were necessary to achieve the desired outcome.

---

[42] Jensen, "Daggers, Rifles and Dynamite," 134. For a more general treatment, see Ghosh, *Science and Technology of Terrorism and Counterterrorism*, 22–8.

The bombings of theaters, stock exchanges, parliaments and government buildings, chosen for symbolic purposes, led to an unprecedented effort to contain and destroy what was believed to be a coordinated strategy of terror from below, organized by a clandestine anarchist network. Stringent laws were enacted across the continent permitting punishments for the unauthorized use of explosives and arrests on the grounds merely of suspicion of having anarchist affiliations.[43] Police cooperation on the sharing of intelligence, including permissions for extradition and exile, across national borders increased as government leaders perceived a common enemy. This attempt to crush the anarchist peril reached its highest diplomatic levels in 1898 when the Great Powers convened an international conference in Rome to seek agreement on methods to rid Europe of anarchist violence.[44] A second meeting was held in St Petersburg in 1904 amidst the rise of SR terrorism against Russian officials and following the assassinations of King Umberto of Italy and US President McKinley. Much effort went into enhancing the powers of security forces at the national level, including the formation of a secret service in Washington and another organization in the Department of Justice that would soon be enduringly known as the Federal Bureau of Investigation.[45]

Although these international conferences were hampered by foreign policy differences over a range of issues that would soon solidify into opposing alliances, the governments were clearly alarmed by the assassinations. The Austro-Hungarian ambassador to France, writing in a confidential note at this time, was convinced that the pernicious ideas spread by the theoreticians of anarchism in their numerous publications were responsible for "the anarchist criminal actions, arousing partisans to commit 'propaganda by the deed.'"

[43] The acts of legislation are cited in Jensen, "The International Campaign Against Anarchist Terrorism," 91–2.

[44] For the protocols of the Rome congress, see "Propositions arrestées par la Conférence internationale réunie à Rome," in Kinna, *Early Writings on Terrorism* III, 326–9. See also Jensen, "The International Anti-Anarchist Conference of 1898 and the Origins of Interpol," 323–47. Further information on the international effort to coordinate the repression of anarchism can be found in Liang, *The Rise of the Modern Police and the European State System from Metternich to the Second World War*, 155–74.

[45] Jensen, "The United States, International Policing and the War against Anarchist Terrorism, 1900–1914," 15–46, and Deflem, "'Wild Beasts Without Nationality': The Uncertain Origins of Interpol, 1898–1910," 274–85.

He urged a concerted effort by the European powers to shut down the spread of these dangerously provocative newspapers and journals.[46]

One of the most comprehensive statements on the part of the governments in the war on anarchism, written by the Spanish envoy to the US, the Duke of Arcos, appeared soon after the assassinations of presidents Carnot of France and McKinley. Reviewing in detail the growth of the anarchist movement and the chain of killings of major state leaders during the previous decade, the author described possible ways that governments might deal with this crisis. One proposal that had come up at their ambassadorial meeting was to wipe out "these wild animals," which would involve classifying "all anarchists as lunatics and treated accordingly." For the protection of society, these "lunatics" who threatened public safety "should be confined in asylums until cured ... of their mania."[47] The author further pointed out that anarchist targets, unlike those of the Irish and other rebellious groups, involve not only state officials, but innocent, ordinary citizens attending concerts or cafes.

As a result, speaking on behalf of Spain, the report stated that "the nation by this time had grown desperate and demanded summary vengeance on every one who was tainted in the slightest degree with anarchy." Hundreds of Spanish suspects were being arrested, tried, sentenced, and, when warranted, executed. Though justice was swiftly meted out, the attacks were continuing with ever-greater violence. The government of Spain, the report continued, now sought "to destroy the evil, root and branch." Far-reaching repressive measures had been taken, including killing the major instigators of these assaults on "the integrity of the state." The article concluded with an appeal to all governments to join together to extend police powers, shut down safe havens when anarchists seek refuge beyond their national borders and crush domestic anarchist publications and their transnational distribution.[48] There is no mention in the article of any responsibility on the part of the state for the political, economic and social problems raised

---

[46] Kinna, *Early Writings on Terrorism*, III, 332–3.
[47] The Duke of Arcos, "International Control of Anarchists," 348.
[48] Ibid., 354–6. A similar mood of heightened fear was a factor in the trial and execution of Mary Surratt in 1865 for her alleged involvement in the John Wilkes Booth conspiracy to assassinate President Lincoln and members of his cabinet. Surratt was the first woman ever to be executed by the US government. Her guilt remains a subject of debate. See Larson, *The Assassin's Accomplice*.

by the perpetrators of the insurgent violence. The government stands as the virtuous defender of state and society against what it perceives to be a mortal threat to both.

The assassination of President McKinley had the effect internationally of permitting European heads of state to view the US as a crucial ally in the campaign against worldwide anarchism. At home, the impact was more direct. Anarchism in any form was portrayed as a growing bacillus menacing the entire body politic. A number of states, especially those with large urban areas where immigrants arrived to find themselves suspected of radicalism and subversion, rapidly passed laws specifically designed to criminalize anarchism. In New York State, for example, a law was passed in January 1902, defining anarchy as a crime because of its presumed ideological commitment to the revolutionary overthrow of governments and its adherents' responsibility for the killing of state officials. "The advocacy of such doctrine either by word of mouth or writing is a felony" punishable by the full extent of the law. Further clauses detail numerous examples of such criminal activity, which might take place in any public assembly or in any form of print media. Further, "whenever two or more persons assemble for the purpose of advocating or teaching the doctrines of criminal anarchy, such an assembly is unlawful," and every participant is thus "guilty of a felony and punishable by imprisonment." Lastly, anyone who knowingly permits such acts (a building owner or a newspaper publisher, e.g.) was now to be considered guilty of a misdemeanor, which was punishable by a term of imprisonment. The act was to take effect immediately.[49]

The McKinley *attentat* also generated renewed interest in presidential security. In the late nineteenth century, before the existence of the FBI and CIA, the Pinkerton Detective Agency filled many of the roles these organizations later assumed. Allan Pinkerton, a Scottish immigrant who had been associated with the English Chartist movement there, established a private detective agency in 1850 in Chicago. Pinkerton was able to build a large organization as a result of his willingness to provide protection and security for the expanding

---

[49] *Laws of the State of New York*, II, 958–60. Henry Tutus, the police official who headed the division in Paterson, NJ, openly encouraged a mob to avenge the death of the president by taking matters into their own hands: "The only proper way for the police to deal with these [anarchists] is to go to their meeting's armed with a sawed off gun and shoot for the speakers when they begin to rant." Quoted in Thorup, "The Anarchist and the Partisan," 337.

railway system. The agency's growing prominence was highlighted by Pinkerton's involvement with surveillance and repression, from Western outlaws to factory labor strikes. After his death, he was succeeded by his son Robert, who brought the agency to national prominence. In the last decades of the nineteenth century, industrialists and state governments came to rely on the Pinkertons as a private armed force available to suppress any public disturbance. One of the most notorious examples was the 1892 Homestead strike when Carnegie steel factory owner Henry Clay Frick called in the Pinkertons, who violently ended the workers' protest, killing at least nine people and severely injuring scores more. For Allan Pinkerton, repression was justified and necessary, given the threat posed by the enemy within. "Every trades-union has for its vital principle, whatever is professed, the concentration of brute force to gain certain ends. Then the deadly spirit of communism steals in and further embitters the working man against that from which his very livelihood is secured; and gradually makes him an enemy of all law, order and good society." The violent danger lurked in shadows, he argued. "It was everywhere; it was nowhere."[50]

The agency, which by 1901 had already served several presidents, was called into action again at the time of the McKinley shooting. Robert Pinkerton, after familiarizing himself with the anarchist movement to his satisfaction, wrote a detailed analysis that was published in a prominent American journal and which sheds light on the government's perception of the threat posed by anarchist violence that led to the president's death in Buffalo.

His essay reveals the conflict within government circles over security priorities. Pinkerton's argument is that had his agency, composed of trained professionals, been in charge of protecting the president, instead of the politically appointed secret service, the assassination would have been thwarted. He argued that his personnel's superior surveillance techniques of analyzing dangerous individuals buried in crowds assembling around heads of state would have been better placed to avert the tragedy. Czolgosz, the assassin of McKinley, could have been apprehended before his deed had the agency been permitted to conduct proper spying on him prior to the shooting. According to the Pinkerton files, Czolgosz was clearly influenced by "the Reds," a dangerous grouping that included the executed

---

[50] Pinkerton, *Strikers, Tramps and Detectives* no, 40–1.

Haymarket conspirators as well as Emma Goldman, who "openly preach violence and murder." Such people understand only one argument, "and that is the argument of brute force."

Pinkerton had concrete proposals to offer. First, a law should be passed by Congress to permit "the deportation of every man and woman who preaches the overthrow of government and the principles of anarchy." Second, the government should establish a colony in the Philippines for all anarchists who wish to "govern themselves" rather than submit to American law. They should be left to determine their own system, but "a system of patrol boats" should keep close watch on their activities. "There we could send our Goldmans and our Mosts and our Parsons, and all the other ranters who are constantly striving to tear down what has been so laboriously built up, and who, in doing so, are raising up a constantly growing army of danger-breeding converts." Finally, in a particularly chilling passage, the author recommends that all suspected "Reds" should be "marked for constant surveillance and on the slightest excuse be made harmless."[51] Pinkerton and the Spanish ambassador to the US were convinced that governments had to legislate with severity in order to contain and ultimately abolish the anarchist peril.

This expression of the need to create the legal authority to move decisively, swiftly and, when necessary, violently against the terror from below had other interpretations as well. In one cry from the heart by a sympathetic observer with no anarchist connections, the writer Marie Louise de la Ramée published an article at this time in which she described the rash of laws and decrees against the anarchist terror as "the legislation of fear." For her, the anarchists were not ordinary criminals and should not routinely be "sent to the scaffold." Anarchists, she argued, have "great qualities allied to great cruelties." In the absence of "seismographic instruments in the political world" to fathom the motives for the violence, we rely on "the clumsy machinery of tribunals and police offices" who have recourse only to torture in prisons or capital punishment. In conditions of brutality in solitary confinement, those who are lucky enough to emerge are turned into "a second Caserio, a second Vaillant." Crimes are proclaimed when a

---

[51] Pinkerton, "Detective Surveillance of Anarchists," 338–46. It is probable that Pinkerton's notion of the remote site to exile anarchists described here was modeled on his knowledge of Britain's earlier penal colony in Australia.

state official is brought down but no one notices the countless daily cases of injustice and violence committed against those who have walked peacefully in a demonstration, not to mention the frequent murder of ordinary men and women by police bayonets and bullets in the name of the law by this system of "military despotism." Press laws have grown so severe that "the assassination of opinion is a greater crime than the assassination of a man." When legislation is motivated by fear, there can be no justice. In the essay's final line, de la Ramée writes: "[French President] Carnot lies dead in the Pantheon, and Liberty lies dying in the world. His tender and unselfish heart would have ached with an impersonal sorrow, greater even than his grief for those he loved, could he have known that his death would have been made an excuse for intemperate authority and pusillanimous power to gag the lips and chain the strength of nations."[52]

As international tensions leading to war in 1914 intensified, the combat between anarchist militants and the security forces of the transatlantic powers declined. Anxieties over the greater problem of national and imperial defense took attention away from the authorities' war against anarchism. At the same time, the critical narrative on the street also changed, as the rise of labor movements, new political parties stridently arguing their causes, and the creation of legal unions for workers to bargain collectively and to strike when demands were not met, overtook the attraction to anarchist causes.[53] The world was about to be transformed by government appeals to national pride, loyalty and defense, which would soon usher in their own forms of political violence. However shocking the politically motivated bombings and killings had been up to this time, the twentieth century that lay ahead would prove to be infinitely more violent, with more casualties from state and insurgent terrorisms than all previous centuries combined for which we have data.[54]

There was one other important category of political violence in the period leading up to the Great War that can be linked to the contemporary anarchist conception of the uncontrolled and brutal nature of state power, despite the fact that most of the Western world

---

[52] Ouida, "The Legislation of Fear," 265–74.
[53] Jean Maitron has made a convincing case for this trend. See his masterful *Histoire du mouvement anarchiste*, II, 440–81.
[54] Rummel, *Death by Government*; Naimark, *Fires of Hatred*.

understood it in terms of a "civilizing mission of the higher civilizations." This "mission" involved the colonization of the continent of Africa by European states, but its reach extended to the Philippines and Cuba, where the US staked its imperial claims. To be sure, there has been no lack of attention in the scholarly literature in documenting "the scramble for Africa." However, for generations this imperialist phenomenon was largely interpreted through the patriotic lenses of what was understood to be the necessary competition among the great powers for vital economic resources along with the benign work of missionaries converting and educating natives in the Christian faith. We now possess a more complex portrait of these endeavors, thanks to recent work that has uncovered important elements of political violence directed by these very governments and their officials in the field.

Late nineteenth- and early twentieth-century accounts of the colonization process in mainstream newspapers made occasional references to casualties and victims, but usually only as minor themes. The most critical attention paid to the colonial experience at the time was to be found mainly in socialist publications and far less widely read works of anarchist and Marxist research, such as Kropotkin's *The Conquest of Bread* (1892) and Lenin's *Imperialism, the Highest State of Capitalism* (1916). Lenin was, as he admitted, deeply influenced by the pioneering work in this field by the British political economist John A. Hobson, in his book *Imperialism* (1902). Even the anarchists of this era, with their consistent portrayal of the repressive capacities of the state, were either uninterested in, or unable to imagine, the entire scope of the savage and unrestrained violence of the agents of imperialist powers in Africa.

Europeans had been exploring in Africa long before King Leopold II of Belgium became involved, mainly in search of young men sold into the lucrative slave trade, and fabled sources of wealth. In 1878, Henry Morton Stanley, the prominent English explorer, was commissioned by Leopold to realize a fantastic scheme of gaining control over a huge swath of the center of Africa in order to establish the continent's largest European colony along the 1,500 miles of the Congo River for his country's prestige and development. By 1884, Stanley had completed his task. Leopold reigned over his cynically named Congo Free State for decades, respected around the world as a philanthropic monarch until 1898 when an obscure customs official working in the shipping docks of Liverpool, Edmond Morel, noticed a strange and unexplained disparity in the import and export papers from the colony. The problem was that instead of trade in products, as the paperwork indicated was the case, Morel found that in exchange for the ivory and rubber being imported from the Congo, guns and ammunition earmarked for the Belgian local officials were in the returning crates.

Further inquiries by Morel led to his uncovering of a highly guarded state secret, namely that Leopold's success was the result, in large measure, of a vast system of African slave labor that had the authentic characteristics of a regime of terror. This discovery in turn led to a crusade on Morel's part to expose the problem and uncover its consequences, a process which led to questions, protests and criticism in the British Foreign Office, the French government and the administration of President Theodore Roosevelt in Washington. Two Americans, the journalist George Washington Williams and the clergyman William Sheppard, played salient roles by publishing articles describing in vivid detail aspects of the violence in the Congo.[55]

The statistics on the victims portray a genuine reign of imperialist state terror, ranking with the worst mass atrocities of the modern period. When villagers were unable to supply the established quotas of rubber, or if they dared to resist and fight back, the Belgian *Force Publique* retaliated by shooting the villagers responsible. There are surviving graphic photographs of piles of skeletons, and natives with severed limbs, taken in the aftermath for souvenirs by the soldiers. In addition to the body count, other evidence is available in the official records of requests made for enormous amounts of weaponry and ammunition. Villages were routinely burned down after the atrocities were completed, leaving untold numbers of women and children homeless. Calculating from census data as well as from the Belgian records, estimates of fatalities have been made that reach into the millions.[56]

Another witness to the atrocities in the Congo who corresponded with Morel, the British consul Roger Casement, also became involved

[55] Edmond Dene Morel later became a well-known journalist, writer and Labour Party member in England. His books include *Red Rubber* (1906), his first extensive account of the Belgian Congo's system of forced labor, and an elaboration in *The Black Man's Burden* (1920). Morel also established the Congo Reform Association in 1904. His papers are deposited in the Archives Division at the London School of Economics.

[56] Much of this information can be found in Hochschild, *King Leopold's Ghost*. For the data, see pp. 225–34.

with a separate episode of imperial state terrorism. In one of his letters to Morel, he confided that European colonialism had come at a terrible price for the natives. "What has civilization itself been to them? A thing of horror – of smoking rifles and pillaged homes – of murdered fathers, violated mothers and enslaved children." Casement's Foreign Office posting in South America brought him face to face with the brutalities of the Peruvian Amazon Company and its ruthless head, Julio Cesar Arana.

The public scandal of this previously secretive endeavor broke on July 15, 1912, when an article appeared in *The Times* with the headline, "The Putamayo Atrocities: A South American Congo: Sir Roger Casement's Report Published." In his report, Casement had evidence from villagers in the Amazon who were ordered to carry out "heinous acts against the Indians" in a campaign of "systematic slavery reinforced by the lash and the bullet." Casement estimated that the victimized population had declined from 50,000 to 8,000 between 1906 and 1911. The report made clear that the responsibility for the violence was in the hands of the Peruvian government, since they were the chief sponsors of Arana's company. In a separate report also largely written by Casement, called the Blue Book on the "Treatment of Native Indians in the Putamayo District," details of the atrocities and photographs were more extensively presented. Newspapers and journals internationally picked up the story in articles and essays, often with titles like "wholesale murder in the Amazon."[57]

In spite of all the evidence and its widespread distribution, little was done to stop the violence which ensued from the Peruvian state's support of Arana's brutal control of the eastern Amazon territories. In a truly unexpected twist, Roger Casement ended up being brought to trial in 1916 in London on charges of treason for his support of Irish independence, and for having committed sodomy in a homosexual relationship, which, though having nothing to do with his crusade for justice in the Amazon, for many readers probably tarnished his name enough to throw suspicion on the validity of his reporting. He was found guilty and executed on August 3. Arana, meanwhile, went on exploiting and profiting from his Amazon venture, although there were some rebellions reported by Indian resisters.[58]

[57] Goodman, *The Devil and Mr. Casement*, 73, 165–9.
[58] Ibid., 235–7. There is also an interesting account of Casement's embattled career in Sebald, *The Rings of Saturn*, 127–34.

Yet another example of this colonizing state terror involves the French. This story, like those of Morel and Casement, was buried for many years in part due to its reinterpretation in the government's interest, and the fact that the events never managed to seep their way into the collective memory of the country. Perhaps another reason has to do with the historical moment in which this scandal broke, which was at the time when France was preoccupied with the emotional shocks of the Dreyfus Affair and the anarchist bombings and trials that spread so much domestic fear and garnered lurid newspaper reportage.[59]

In 1898, General Arsène Klobb was ordered by the French military to travel to Africa and restrain a mission led by two captains, Paul Voulet and Charles Chanoine. This was a reversal of policy, in that the mission had earlier been approved by the government's Ministry of Colonies, and both Voulet and Chanoine were celebrated military figures in France. Although it started as an effort by the French Third Republic to establish its own beachhead in Africa along with the other European powers, Voulet had a plan far more extensive than his government's. He fantasized about the creation of control across virtually the entire swath of the central equatorial African continent. Joined by Chanoine, he requested and received huge quantities of the most advanced weapons, including the new repeating machine gun, which he then used to slaughter whole villages as he cut his path across the land. With around 600 soldiers, supported by some 800 "porters" who were forced to carry the arms on foot, Voulet carried out these massacres that claimed many thousands of victims. A soldier who came upon an example of Voulet's violence described the devastation he witnessed: "A long walk in the bush. Arrived in a small village, burnt down, full of corpses. Two little girls hanged from a branch. The smell is unbearable. The wells do not provide enough water for the men. The animals do not drink; the water is corrupted by the corpses."[60]

By the summer of 1899, Klobb's forces caught up with Voulet, but Klobb was killed in an ambush by Voulet's guards. Learning of the government's official rejection of his mission, Voulet announced his status as a renegade outlaw along with his fantasy of power: "I do not

[59] Two recent studies on the impact of the Dreyfus Affair are Read, *The Dreyfus Affair* and Begly, *Why The Dreyfus Affair Matters*.
[60] Taithe, *The Killer Trail*, 29.

regret anything of what I have done. Now I am an outlaw, I disavow my family, my country, I am not French anymore ... We will create an empire that I will surround with deserted bush; to seize me you will need 10,000 men and 20 million francs ... What I have done is nothing but a coup. If I were in Paris, I would be the master of France."[61] Several days later, on July 15, Voulet and Chanoine were both shot dead by a sentry in a village that they thought was under their control. The next year, 1899, saw an uncanny reflection of this reality with the publication of Conrad's *Heart of Darkness*. However, the campaign of sadistic savagery and truly grotesque reign of terror established by Voulet and Chanoine vanished from all official military accounts and never received adequate press coverage. With their violent deeds in fulfilling a mission originally conceived at the highest levels of the republic, Voulet and Chanoine have more recently been characterized as having embodied "the ordinary cruelty of the servants of the modern state" and who justify their acts as "crimes of obedience" in a context in which "civilization becomes the bloodiest of ironies."[62]

One last episode that formed an important part of the widening reach of imperialist state violence at the turn of the century, and which reflected another example of the widespread efforts of the Great Powers to violently repress contesting insurgencies from below, took place in the Philippines. After its victory over Spain in 1898 in what Secretary of State John Hay called "a splendid little war," the United States claimed control of a territory of islands which included a Filipino nationalist organization that had a structure of governmental authority in place and which was willing to engage in a guerrilla campaign to resist the American occupation in favor of independence.

---

[61] Ibid., 31. Graphic illustrative evidence of the violence follows p. 180.

[62] Ibid., 253–4. See also the interesting meditation on European imperialist state violence in Africa in Lindqvist, *Exterminate All the Brutes*, which emphasizes the racist themes of terror in the colonial era. See especially the discussion in which the author shows that the Germans joined "the Americans, British and other Europeans" in mastering "the art of hastening the extermination of a people of 'inferior culture'" in their control of the Herero people in German South-West Africa (149–60). For more on the German case, which was particularly violent, see Perraudin and Zimmerer, *German Colonialism and National Identity* and Sebastian Conrad, *German Colonialism*, esp. 79–87. Conrad notes that Kaiser Wilhelm, in a public speech on July 27, 1900, openly called for Germans in South-West Africa to use brutally repressive tactics to crush any resistance (p. 83). At least 80,000 Herero were killed prior to the Great War in German colonial territories. In spite of efforts by administrators to build roads and provide some educational facilities, resistance continued. German colonial legitimacy was never successfully established.

Although formally committed to a policy of "benevolent assimilation" in the Philippines, the army, once encountering local armed resistance, resorted to harsh measures encoded in General Order 100. Titled "Instructions for the Government of Armies of the United States in the Field," GO 100 had been written in 1863 as a Civil War field manual for the conduct of Union troops occupying areas of the Confederacy. Apart from the clauses dealing with the lofty standards expected of troops in control of hostile territory, the document also describes punitive measures permitted when necessary in the face of resistance. This section was applied as a general policy of repression in the Philippines, which meant the American forces could "deport insurgents, destroy the property of sympathizers, and summarily execute offenders."[63] To put the matter in more contemporary terms, the army was permitted, if not encouraged, to make use of acts of terrorism to ensure control as an imperial power over a conquered colony. It was also a case of brutal warfare against civilians, not an enemy army.

For Vice-President Theodore Roosevelt, as well as some senior officers who had combat experience with Native American resistance to US treaty violations, the Filipinos were a "jumble of savage tribes" similar to the Apache "savages" they had fought earlier. Senator Albert Beveridge from Indiana, among his many eloquent speeches to the Congress, spoke passionately of the righteousness of using all methods necessary to subdue the Filipino resistance to American control of the islands. While admitting that "our conduct of the war has been cruel," he nevertheless felt it to be justified because "we are not dealing with Americans or Europeans [but] with Orientals [who] mistake kindness for weakness, forbearance for fear." Such people were also anarchic in that they "are not capable of 'consenting' to any form of self-government" and therefore "must be governed" by force under the circumstances.[64]

The outcome was a violent and tragic two-year struggle in which atrocities were committed by both sides. The American troops were ultimately victorious because they had the advantage of lethal force in both numbers of combatants and weapons technology. The appalling atrocities committed by Americans were not mentioned in the press coverage at the time. However, military records clearly indicate

[63] Coats, "Half Devil and Half Child," 180–3.
[64] Fellman, In the Name of God and Country, 193–4.

that slaughters of entire villages were not uncommon. Concentration camps were set up for captured insurgents who survived, where torture was not uncommon. Troops were under orders to ensure "the complete clearing out of every vestige of animal life and every particle of food supply" in addition to burning houses and killing the inhabitants of areas suspected of insurgent support. Filipino guerrillas also used similar tactics of brutality, both against villages where loyalty was suspect, and against the Americans when they succeeded in ambushing and capturing soldiers. Estimates of the civilian casualties of the violence have been estimated as high as between 25 and 40 percent of the island population as a whole.[65] Embers from the flames of this terror remain in the twenty-first century, with the insurgency of the Moro National Liberation Front and its affiliates, with whom the Philippine state is locked in violent combat.

Such episodes of state terrorism ordered and directed by governments in Brussels, Paris and Washington in the decades before the Great War can be seen as an extension of the battleground that had emerged mainly in Europe and the US that focused on the problem of defining nation state power. The violence of this period was driven largely by the entangled and competing agendas of governments and their oppositions. Rulers of these nations, who had acquired significant power during the nineteenth century, were held responsible for the well-being of their citizens and subjects. Indeed, it was a government that established the European continent's first modern republic that based its legitimacy on a declaration proclaiming human and civil rights in France in 1789. Oppositions, however, considered it their responsibility to ensure that the promises of liberty and equality for all would be realized. Throughout the century, even during the repressive Restoration years, while making some progress in ameliorating the condition of its impoverished and politically excluded underclasses, state administrations were confronted by increasing numbers of political factions, from nationalists to anarchists, who deplored the pace of change, questioned the degree of commitment on the part of the state, and were willing to find their own pathways, even if this meant accepting violence as an option.

After the failure of the insurgencies of 1848, governments in Europe and the US moved against elements of dissent with expanded

[65] Ibid., 229–30. See also Hofstadter and Wallace, "Brutalities in the Philippines," 283–91.

powers of police repression, judicial discrimination in favor of the privileged, and a refusal to confront the plight of the economic exploitation of the impoverished majority. For the opposition, a bitter and unresolved dilemma remained: if governments were proving incapable of responding to the economic and political demands of their constituencies and were willing to rely on violence to enforce their authority, what was the legitimate basis of their authority?

The anarchist response to this question was clear. There was no basis. Moreover, according to its major theorists, states were inherently authoritarian and repressive. Violence was an inherent part of national policy, regardless of which monarch, president or political party happened to be in power. For a minority of those who accepted this thesis in the anarchist camp, the turn to violence was a natural response to the violence of the state, as Emma Goldman argued so eloquently in one of her essays.[66] As the violence between the insurgents and state security forces spread globally across national borders, governments were embarking on the exporting of policies of terror to Africa and Latin America in the continuing search for resources to enforce their own authority at home and defend it against competing international interests abroad. Administrations still made public statements that they were acting on behalf of their citizens as part of their claim to legitimate authority, but the fantasies that compelled them to overreach at home and beyond their borders would soon lead to their own downfall. The problems that engendered the terrorisms of this era were, however, not confronted, and the mentalities that were in such dialectical conflict maintained their positions, more hardened than ever, as the parallel drama at work within the US was to show.

[66] Goldman, "The Psychology of Political Violence," 79–108. The essay was originally published in 1910.

6 TERRORISM IN A DEMOCRACY: THE UNITED STATES

Episodes of political violence in the US such as the 1886 Haymarket riot in Chicago, the Homestead labor casualties in Pennsylvania in 1894, the 1901 assassination of President McKinley, and the Wall Street bombing in 1920, are among many other such moments that could be cited. The distinguishing and prevalent explanation of these events, as presented relentlessly in newspapers across the country, was that the people responsible for the violence were politicized immigrants from Germany, Italy, Russia and elsewhere in Europe, acting under the nefarious influence of anarchist and socialist ideologies. The corresponding understanding was that, with the aid of the authorities charged with public security, whether private forces like the Pinkertons or the local police, the danger posed by these aliens to ordinary American citizens could be eliminated.

There was, however, a far deeper current of American terrorism that, rather than occurring episodically, persisted over many decades throughout the nineteenth and into the twentieth centuries. Moreover, the problems that undergirded the violence were longstanding domestic issues traceable to unresolved conflicts that emerged as far back as the establishment of the republic. Because the US had been a democratic republic from its inception in 1776, operating under a constitutional legal system without monarchical authority, concerns about state legitimacy and public security evolved in ways that differed from the established European patterns of nation state development. Moreover, widening the lens in this way presents us with evidence showing that there are, in certain contexts, situations of multiple currents of terrorism functioning simultaneously within a single country that may operate independently of one another from below, but are confronted by the same authority from above.

Precisely because of this democratic and constitutional foundation, the relationship between political violence and the legal system is a critical variable in analyzing the role of political violence in the US. Indeed, the American judicial process justified acts of terror at both the national and local levels in many instances. Furthermore, because of the constitutional commitment to decentralized federalism, American violence frequently entangled authorities and citizens in a common cause that operated within that acceptable legal space. In addition, in striking distinction from European legal standards, American "militias" were permitted to bear arms under the Second Amendment of the Constitution. This right came to be widely interpreted as applying to groups and even individual citizens. As a result, Americans became the most heavily armed citizenry in the Western world. Given these circumstances, it should not be surprising that this privately held arsenal would be used against non-citizens considered to be dangerous threats or political competitors in contested areas, and who were entirely vulnerable to being terrorized precisely because they were unprotected by the legal system. These variables lie at the heart of the reality of the particular features of political violence in a democracy, which include instances of terrorism by the federal government as well as violence carried out by legally armed citizens either in the name of the law, or by "taking the law into their own hands" with the tacit or overt consent of the political and judicial authorities.

The assault on Native Americans

The manner in which the "Indian problem" was resolved in the US is an illustration of the ways in which the violent aspects of this history were elided in traditional accounts. The extraordinary outpouring of new material in recent years has permitted us to document this important and neglected aspect of the story. The earlier textbook version offered a portrait of embattled pioneers settling on agriculturally rich land and taking defensive action to secure a peaceful existence against unwarranted attacks by Indian "savages." The actual story is far more complex, and involves the ways in which the American legal system could be interpreted to justify terrorism in order to carry out the settlement process.

Most of the tribes along the Eastern coast had had commercial and military contacts with British, French and Spanish explorers long before the American War of Independence. To take one prominent tribe, the Cherokee were largely allies of the British during that war, since they had agreements with them and perceived the American armies as hostile interlopers. At the conclusion of the war, the Peace of Paris essentially handed over to the victors the lands of the defeated colonial power, which included a huge swath of tribal territory. Conflict broke out almost immediately after the founding of the new American republic. Congress considered the Indian lands to be "conquered territory" and permitted state legislatures to transfer acres in the form of land grants to families willing to settle there. Resistance was strong, especially in southern states, and violent hostilities thus became part of the price to be paid for settling in these territories.

The federal government attempted to address these problems by peaceful means. On November 28, 1785, the Treaty of Hopewell was signed with the Cherokee leadership. Its purpose was to delineate the boundaries of tribal lands and slow the growth of settlement favored by the state legislatures, whose elected delegates were seeking to expand their own boundaries for political, economic and security reasons. In practice, little attention was paid by the states to the Treaty of Hopewell and they continued to sponsor the march westward. Indeed, there were 23 reported invasions of Cherokee territory between 1776 and 1794 in an overt effort to drive out the native inhabitants using full military force.[1]

In response, Henry Knox, President Washington's Secretary of War, attempted, with the cooperation of the Congress, to respect the rights of tribal authorities within agreed territories as codified in the Treaty of Hopewell.[2] A new set of demands on the Indian tribes accompanied the treaty, the centerpiece of which was a "civilization program" that included provisions for the encouragement of settled (rather than nomadic) tribal farming, granting of property rights and the establishment of schools. These measures were designed to integrate Indians into the mainstream of American culture and to reduce

---

[1] Boulware, *Deconstructing the Cherokee Nation*, 162–3.
[2] Ibid., 164, 168, 179–80.

conflicting interests between the tribes and the states that had led to violence in the past. Further efforts were made to Christianize tribes, with missionaries tasked to set up church services. There was some intermarriage between Indians and Americans, and attempts were made to inspire an Indian-American nationalism by encouraging the development of tribal written languages; in the 1820s, a Cherokee dictionary and a newspaper, *The Cherokee Phoenix*, were published.

By the time Andrew Jackson became president in 1828, most of the earlier attempts to resolve the conflicts between settlers and tribes had proven unworkable. On the one hand, the tribes demanded more land than the areas eventually allotted to them; from their perspective, they were seeking to hold on to as much as possible of what they considered their ancestral possessions. On the other, an emerging and powerful plantation culture viewed the Indians as racial inferiors and as obstacles to the further expansion of the burgeoning cotton industry. Jackson was strongly supported by this southern elite, and included in his campaign platform a promise that he would use the authority of the federal government to remove the Indians from their lands to satisfy the demands of his constituency. Despite some congressional opposition, the Indian Removal Act was passed into law on May 28, 1830. Its clauses "created the machinery that expelled to a distant territory some one hundred thousand Indians, including sixteen thousand Cherokees."[3]

As the previous efforts at developing conditions designed to move the tribes into pathways leading toward citizenship and peaceful relations with the states continued to fail, violence became the tactic of choice for both aggressors and resistors. Efforts by John Ross, a Cherokee chief who was an educated example of the "civilizing policy" introduced by Knox earlier, to negotiate favorable terms for his tribe with the administrative and congressional representatives all disintegrated, mainly because of non-compliance on the part of the states. Georgia, for instance, simply disregarded a Supreme Court ruling in favor of tribal lands; in the absence of federal enforcement, the state acted without concern for penalties.

Another effort at negotiation was made at the signing of the Treaty of New Echota in 1835. In this instance, the conciliatory tribal representatives who participated went against the wishes of John Ross

---

[3] Perdue and Green, *The Cherokee Removal*, 19.

and ignored the opposition of the great majority of the Cherokee people. Article I states that "the Cherokee Nation hereby cede, relinquish and convey to the United States all the lands owned, claimed or possessed by them east of the Mississippi River, and hereby release all their claims upon the United States for spoliations of every kind." In return, the tribe was to be paid "a sum not to exceed 5 million dollars." The government in turn was obliged to provide transport west "to remove them comfortably." The treaty also called for the presence of "a physician well supplied with medicines" to care for the sick. The treaty further stipulated that "the United States shall protect and defend [the tribe] in their possessions and property."[4]

Reality proved to be far more violent than the benign terms of the treaty would suggest. The extraordinary existential threat that the Cherokee found themselves facing was well described by Elias Boudinot, a prominent member of the Cherokee delegation to Echota and one of its signers. Boudinot tried to explain why he felt he had no choice but to agree to the terms of the treaty, while being fully aware of the utterly painful impact the decision would have. "Instead of contending uselessly against superior power, the only course left was to yield to circumstances over which [we, the Cherokee people] had no control." Yet, at the same time, Boudinot recognized that "to advocate a treaty was to declare war against the established habits of thinking" particular to his tribe, and meant renouncing "the deep rooted attachment for the soil of our forefathers."

He also knew the truths that could only be whispered. He explicitly made reference to the fact that Indians had been introduced to the addiction of alcohol as part of the "civilizing" program with Americans. He admitted he was appalled by the consequent "debasing character of that vice to our people," that the Cherokee were suffering "its cruel effects in the bloody tragedies that are occurring," which include "frequent convictions and executions" for crimes committed under the influence. For the masses of the population, their condition had been reduced to homelessness in their own lands along with hunger and poverty without solution. The most difficult consequence of accepting the world of the white man was the "insinuation of the lower vices into our female population," a clear admission of the cases of rape

---

[4] Ibid., 147–53 contains an abridged version of the treaty. For the complete text of this treaty and all others negotiated with the Indian tribes, see Kappler, *Indian Affairs*.

of Cherokee women by white settlers that were taking place. Boudi-not's conclusion was tragic: the choice was, on the one hand, extinction either by having "merged with another race" or dying by resisting US authority, or, on the other, signing and renouncing any future hope of retaining their ancestral territory.[5]

In the end, his reputation was sealed by the fact that he had signed off on the treaty, in spite of his awareness of the agonizing moral dilemma of his people. Shortly after arriving in the West following the exodus of the Cherokee from their lands, in 1839, Boudinot and John Ridge, the other principal signer for the Indian delegation at Echota, were assassinated by a group of fellow Cherokee who considered them traitors.[6]

The removal was an experience of brutality and terror in a climate of unrelieved fear. Cherokee were requested and ordered to leave their homes. When they refused or resisted, they were forced out. In addition, they endured repeated acts of harassment from local settlers as well as efforts to assume possession of their homes and land. By the spring of 1838, only a few thousand Cherokee had actually left their territory in Georgia and Tennessee.[7] That summer, troops were ordered into the areas to forcibly remove all remaining Cherokee from their homes and place them in makeshift prisons until they could be organized into large groups under the surveillance of armed federal and state officers for the trek west. The groups arrived in what was called the Western Cherokee Nation during the first months of 1839. This Trail of Tears, which has been frequently recounted and memorialized in all its horror, was a forced march through hostile land in extreme conditions of heat and cold, which claimed the lives of anywhere between four and eight thousand people of all ages.

The person selected by President Jackson to head the "enrol-ling" of the Cherokee for the deportation process was Benjamin F. Currey, whose personal interpretation of his responsibilities was stated as making "the situation of the Indians so miserable as to drive them into a treaty or an abandonment of their country." Documents attest to his personal interventions in instances in which resistant

---

[5] Perdue and Green, *The Cherokee Removal,* 161–6.
[6] On Boudinot and Ridge, see the account and documents in Anderson, *Cherokee Removal: Before and After.*
[7] On the situation in Georgia at this time, see Young, "The Exercise of Sovereignty in Cherokee Georgia," 43–63.

families were to be separated and sent to different locations, or to be punished by spending several nights in frigid conditions of detention without food or heat. He freely permitted the use of armed force to move the Cherokee to the stockades while awaiting departure.

Once en route, the situation was unbearable. Although there were wagons for some of the aged, infirm and children, most of the tribe was compelled to walk the thousands of miles to the Oklahoma territory through extreme heat in the summer and daunting cold in the winter. Missionaries who accompanied the walk west described the ice floes and almost impassable conditions of the roads that delayed the crossing for days, while enduring harsh nights. A Baptist missionary counted 1,250 people in his group when they left; after almost four months of surviving the Trail of Tears, 71 people are known to have died along the way, not counting those who fell ill from the walk and died later. Other memoirs mention how so many of the Indians were reduced to conditions of utter inhumanity, stripped of their possessions at gunpoint by ravenous mobs as they were coerced out of their homes and treated like ordinary prisoners once under the command of the army throughout the march to the West. In the apt words of one missionary, "they are prisoners without a crime to justify the fact."[8]

"It is possible," according to one scholar, "that no other factor has exercised a more brutalizing influence on the American character than the Indian wars." The violence was horrific on both sides as the white settlers relentlessly advanced deeper into Indian country, to find continuing tribal resistance. Distinctions between the "defenseless" and the armed combatants disappeared in the face of massacres, rapes and the wholesale destruction of property.[9] For over a century, with treaties signed and broken, the violence went on across a wide swath of the country from the East Coast to Texas and beyond. In Texas, a frontier battalion was organized along with a number of volunteer vigilante groups, conducting campaigns of terror across the state in the 1870s against the Comanche tribes. The Comanche, for a time at least, held their own largely by conducting surprise night raids in which they often kidnapped the wives and daughters of their victims. The evidence

---

[8] For a selection of these documents, see Perdue and Green, *The Cherokee Removal*, 165–79. For further evidence on the atmosphere of terror and the acts of violence committed by settlers and soldiers during the expulsion and exile, see Smith, *An American Betrayal*, 187–240.

[9] Brown, *Strain of Violence*, 26.

makes clear that Comanche terrorism was extensive and horrific, as reports indicate numerous instances of serial rape, torture, scalping and disembowelment.[10]

The strategy of both settlers and the US cavalry forces, which they understood as a defense against Indian aggression, was to create an agricultural wasteland by slaughtering the buffalo herds that sustained the tribes, forcing them into devastating conditions in which they could no longer generate resistance to the American assaults. Facing defeat, the Comanches turned toward an embrace of "eschatological visions" to avoid a total cultural collapse, with an intertribal Sun Dance in the winter of 1873–4. Nevertheless, by the summer and fall of 1874, US forces had all but wiped them out. Population figures from the area show that Comanches declined from nearly 5,000 in 1870 to around 1,500 by 1875.[11] These triumphs, rather than solving a problem, encouraged a desire to push further to eliminate all remaining resistance to the establishment of a "western empire" in an effort to complete the American domination of the continent.[12]

In some cases, this terrorizing phenomenon was complicated by the involvement of multiple players. One of the more glaring and tragic examples of this was the pre-dawn massacre of nearly 150 Apache while they slept in the Aravaipa canyon on April 30, 1871, near Camp Grant in the southern Arizona territory. The terrorists in this case were "an informal army of Arizona civilians" composed of a mixture of Hispanics, Anglo-Americans and Papago (O'odham) Indians, all of whom fought for control of the area against the Apaches who resided there. Each group had its own intentions and its own justification for the violence. As a historian of the event has written, in this instance, we cannot confine ourselves to any single narrative "without enacting yet another form of historical violence: the suppression of the past's multiple meanings."[13]

The devastation suffered by the Native American tribes in the aftermath of the futile struggle to maintain their political independence

---

[10] Ibid., 244–5. More information can be found in Gwynne, *Empire of the Summer Moon.*
[11] Hamalainen, *The Comanche Empire*, 337–40.
[12] Fehrenbach, *Commanches: The Destruction of a People*, 387.
[13] Jacoby, *Shadows at Dawn*, xv, 278. Jacoby effectively presents each of the narratives in separate chapters. Similar acts of politically motivated violence against the Western tribes took place at Bear River in 1863 and at Wounded Knee in 1890, among others. For more evidence of the acts of terrorism committed by and against Native Americans in this period, see Blackhawk, *Violence Over the Land*, esp. 295–7.

and ancestral lands has been poignantly described by the last of the Crow leaders, Chief Plenty-Coups. Not long before his death, when he was around 80, Plenty-Coups recounted his life story in the historical context of his tribe's demise as a vibrant culture, to a trusted friend, Frank Linderman, who had come to the West decades earlier to live with the Crow. After the surrender to American forces and renunciation of their lands to white settlers, there was one last symbol of defeat – the slaughter of the buffalo, whose bodies were "left to decay on the plains by skin-hunting white men." This devastation abolished the food supply for the tribe, as well as depriving the Crow of hides for clothing and shelter. Confined to reservations often run by hostile officials, stripped of all meaning in their lives, and rendered completely dependent on American authority for survival, the tribe sank into poverty, illness and alcoholism. In his despair, Plenty-Coups told Linderman: "After this, nothing happened."[14]

More recently, this sentence so profoundly affected Jonathan Lear, a scholar at the University of Chicago, that he decided to engage in an entire research project devoted to trying to understand what Chief Plenty-Coups meant when he made this statement to Linderman. The result is an engaging meditation on the consequences of the losses suffered by the Crow in their defeat. Lear was particularly struck by the widespread nature of the targets selected by the American settlers and local officials as well as the federal government. The Crow lost not only untold numbers of the tribe, as did the Cherokee and every other tribe that resisted, but the sources of their ability to sustain themselves. In addition to the tactic of slaughtering the buffalo, mentioned above, a Native American historian, Joseph Medicine Crow, has described how the US government, after requests by settlers, pursued a policy of destroying all of the wild horses on Crow lands, thereby depriving them of all mobility and leaving them starved and vulnerable to conquest. The estimates cited by the Crow who counted carcasses numbered at least 40,000 horses that had been "exterminated" by 1930. "To say the least," the historian wrote, this was a traumatic and tragic experience for a proud horse-oriented tribe; it was worse than the actual military defeat, which some Plains tribes sustained. This policy, Lear concludes, led to "the destruction of the traditional way of Crow life" and created an extraordinary sense of pain that

---

[14] Linderman, *Plenty-Coups, Chief of the Crows*, 311–12.

accompanied the ensuing void. Without buffalo and horses, the nomadic warrior culture that defined the Crow was wiped out by this terrorizing policy.[15]

As is the case in all situations of terrorism, there were two sides engaged in the violence here as well. Including the instances of violent acts by Indians against civilian settlers as well as soldiers and armed militias, whether as aggression or as defensive resistance, is a crucial ingredient to our having a full picture of the terror. Survivors of Indian raids have recorded witnessing numerous atrocities. Some appear to have been traumatized by having watched not only killings, but also the staking out and burning of eyes, tongues and genitals, women and children being impaled on fences, and the burying of disemboweled or decapitated infants.[16] For the pioneers and settlers, the Indians represented an unrelentingly brutal culture capable of the most horrific crimes against the innocent. Because the American government provided inadequate protection, the brave frontiersmen believed that they had no choice but to take matters into their own hands. The only response to such terror, they argued, was counter-violence in self-defense.[17]

Violence against African Americans

If the most critical domestic problems in the histories of France, Russia and the rest of Europe have been the injustices caused by social class hierarchies, the American counterpart of this would have to be the impact of the hierarchies of racial differences. In spite of the obvious irony involved, the fact is that the US has been, since its very inception, a nation founded by and composed of immigrants of varied ethnicities, and yet, it has often acted as if the imagined homogenous society was under constant assault from alien portions of itself. The predominant trope has centered on the fears experienced by the white majority of being threatened, politically, economically and sexually by dark masses from elsewhere, which in turn has produced a climate of terror over the

---

[15] Lear, *Radical Hope*, 58, 136, 140.   [16] Fehrenbach, *Commanches*, 270.
[17] See the documents assembled in Wilbarger, *Indian Depredations in Texas*. This book must be the single largest collection of material presuming to document the atrocities committed by Native Americans during the period from 1838 to the Civil War. Corroboration of the many memoirs narrated in this 672-page book, however, is lacking, since no sources are cited.

last two centuries to contain the threat. The Indians were from "elsewhere" because they were regarded as remnants of some ancient migrating primitive culture standing in the way of state legitimacy and national development. Those who came to American shores from Italy, Poland and Russia in the second half of the nineteenth century before strict immigration laws were enforced were particularly subjected to prejudice, abuse and, ultimately, violence if they dared to act collectively to gain access to advertised liberties and economic advancement.

As the decades prior to the Civil War focused on the violence between the white majority and the Native American minority, the decades following the war brought forth an antagonism between the country's white majority and its black minority. In the latter case, the origins of the targeted threat were different. Whereas the Indian tribes lived on the American continent long before the British colonies were formed, blacks were coercively imported as captive slaves from Africa to a democratic republic founded on the principles of liberty and equality for all. The cruel irony, however, was that this slave labor population was to be the exception to those principles. There were to be neither treaties nor negotiations with this population, and no acceptance of them other than as stateless laborers who were essentially items of property, along with agricultural implements and animals required for the functioning of a plantation economy. None of these efforts at containment prevented the violence that was to emerge as a result of the unresolvable political problems inherent in seeking to maintain a relationship between masters and slaves in a democracy.

The tactic of violence utilized most frequently to realize the fantasy of total white hegemony over any form of black resistance was the practice of lynching. There were some early efforts to try to document and understand this rather American phenomenon, which not only killed many people, often in public places in the full light of day, but truly terrorized an entire population. One of the pioneering studies, written by historian James Elbert Cutler and published in 1905, was a comprehensive inquiry into the history of lynching in the US, and included an analysis of motivation, statistics and efforts by states to pass laws dealing with these mob executions. Taking data largely from the *Chicago Tribune* and other public sources, Cutler calculated that between 1882 and 1903, a total of 3,337 black persons were lynched across the country, the great majority of lynchings occurring in southern states.[18] Another early study, conducted by James Chadbourn, was able to document 3,753 lynchings between 1889 and 1932. He also opened up a new avenue in his discussion of the enabling role played by local officials in the vigilante killings. In addition, he included the actual texts of existing state legislation that described specific judicial punishment for injury or death to persons conducted by "assemblies" outside of the legal process.[19] It remains a bone of contention among scholars as to whether lynching should be considered an aspect of the legal system in historical context, or whether it has always been an example of "extralegal violence" that stands outside the law but was permitted for specific reasons by judiciaries and law enforcement authorities in certain states and defined time periods.

The term appears to come from Charles Lynch, a judicial official in Bedford County, Virginia, and later a colonel in the American army which fought the British in the 1770s. In the absence of courts in daily session amidst the atmosphere of war, Lynch decided to take his own measures to end the prevalence of horse-stealing by Tories sympathetic to the British. He ordered captured thieves to be brought to his home, where he convened a court of his choosing, with trials often resulting in torturous punishments. In a number of instances, prisoners were hung by their thumbs from nearby trees until they renounced their misdeeds and allegiances to the invading British forces. This form of summary justice in later decades came to be known as Lynch's Law, despite the fact that this private form of justice went unrecognized at the time by Thomas Jefferson, the governor of Virginia.[20]

Interestingly, this first appearance of what was to be known as lynching conducted by private citizens acting outside the state court system does not seem to have made use of death as a penalty and had little to do with racial matters. The shift toward applying lynching to race is revealed initially in instances involving abolitionists in the South prior to the Civil War. There are also cases in the 1850s in which blacks were put to death in summary executions by mobs, but these appear to

[18] Cutler, *Lynch-Law*, 101. Cutler breaks down his data in detail on pp. 155–92. On the many state laws passed to limit the practice, see pp. 228–45. Most were ineffective, for reasons to be explored below.
[19] Chardbourn, *Lynching and the Law*, 1, 120–38, 149–214.
[20] For the most exhaustive study of the origins of the term, see Cutler, *Lynch-Law*, esp. 13–40.

be rooted in actual rebellions or resistance, such as the Nat Turner or John Brown affairs, and others far less well known.[21]

Although it is difficult to determine to what extent these instances of slave violence directed against landowners influenced the rising prevalence of lynching, they did occur with sufficient frequency to alarm the white majority. In 1800, a group of slaves near Richmond were apprehended prior to initiating a violent rebellion against the plantation system. Fantasies dominated this plot as the leader, Gabriel, believed he had thousands of followers who were about to join with the Catawba tribe to destroy white rule in the area. At least 25 blacks were arrested, tried and executed as a result of the plot. In 1822, an insurrection allegedly planned by a Caribbean slave, Denmark Vesey, was designed to liberate the city of Charleston. Authorities uncovered the conspiracy before it was put into action, and again, white fears of slave rebellions were aroused as Vesey and his followers were arrested and sentenced to death.[22]

To combat both the fantasy and reality of the black threat, the most frequently chosen format was the emerging pattern of summary executions of blacks that took place in prominent public sites, often during the day, with a local white audience present for the hangings and burnings. The newspapers recorded the event with approval, with statements such as this one from a Georgia article in 1856: "we should be glad to see our citizens rise en masse and avail themselves of Lynch law, and hang the rascal without court or jury."[23]

The escalation of violent assaults on the black minority population in the US developed rapidly following the conclusion of the Civil War. This period, known as Reconstruction, lasted until 1877 and established in an indelible manner the political motivation of communities using lynching as summary justice. Once more we see the role played by collective fears, anxieties and fantasies in establishing the tactic of terror as a justified mechanism designed to resolve, in this case, an imagined political crisis posed by a free black population. The nightmarish specter was how to cope with the behavior of former slaves elevated by victors' justice in war to the level of citizens with rights equal to those of their former masters. Would the newly

[21] Ibid., 121–36. See also McGlone, *John Brown's War Against Slavery*.
[22] See Kolchin, *American Slavery*; Foner, *Give Me Liberty*; Egerton, *Gabriel's Rebellion*; and Caroll, *Slave Insurrections in the United States*.
[23] Cutler, *Lynch-Law*, 128.

empowered black citizens, driven by bitterness and resentment over their antebellum treatment by former white superiors, seek revenge for a century of bondage?

Thus, the struggle of this period focused on the contested nature of two conflicting currents. On the one hand, federal efforts were in process to create the kind of inclusive national citizenship that had been propounded by abolitionists for decades. On the other, constituents of the former Confederacy were asserting passionate claims for states' rights priorities.

The mechanisms of Reconstruction were put into place quickly. A number of acts were passed intended to set up the institutional structure for bringing former slaves into the mainstream political and economic cultures from which they had been excluded. One of the most important offices created at this time was the Freedmen's Bureau. Among its many responsibilities was organizing the procedures to ensure that the newly enfranchised black population would receive land with property rights as well as access to hospital care, secondary schools and colleges. In addition, banks were to support the development of minority enterprises, and regulations were put in place to guarantee voting privileges to blacks in local and national elections.[24]

The reaction was swift. Southerners began isolated attacks on blacks that became increasingly savage. In the first months after the conclusion of the Civil War, there were already reports filed with the Freedmen's Bureau of the emerging terrorism. Hospitals admitted blacks who had suffered attacks that resulted in their ears being cut off, heads carefully scalped on one side, gunshot wounds, and cut throats. In several counties in Alabama, blacks were first tortured by being chained to trees and then were burned to death, after which their decapitated bodies were left to rot in rivers.[25]

It was not long before the rage was institutionalized into a movement. A judicial official in the town of Pulaski, Tennessee, Thomas M. Jones, called a meeting in his office in June, 1866 to which he invited five Confederate veterans and the editor of the local newspaper to deal with the terms of the Reconstruction Act (enacted the

---

[24] The full name was the Bureau of Refugees, Freedmen and Abandoned Lands, instituted into law by Congress in March, 1865.

[25] These descriptions, taken from the archives of the Freedmen's Bureau in the Library of Congress, are included in Dray, *At the Hands of Persons Unknown*, 36–7.

next year but in public debate at this point). Among the terms most invasive and unacceptable to Jones and his group was the requirement that all states in the South organize new governments at the state and local levels with constitutions consented to by both races. Jones kept his group's work secret but they were actively organizing meetings that spread fear among an already anxious community and urged immediate action to stop the black threat to their political hierarchy being imposed from Washington.

They named their secret society "Kuklos" (after the Greek word for group, circle or band) and were actively recruiting others in the community to form collective bodies willing to take action to prevent this stipulation from becoming a political reality. By early in 1868, "riots" by groups attacking blacks in and around Pulaski were reported in a Nashville newspaper, using the enduring and notorious name that the entire nation would soon know, Ku Klux Klan. The tactic used was beating "in a terrible manner with beach goads," which in some cases involved whipping their victims into unconsciousness "with not less than 100 lashes." The report further mentions that the members of the Klan gang wore masks, "were commanded by a major and a lieutenant" and were armed with military distributed revolvers.[26]

Although the motive of alleged sexual threats to white women was often used as the justification for the attacks on blacks, the hostility was, at its core, political in nature. This was made abundantly clear in the 1871 reports of Hiram C. Whitley, a detective sent by the Justice Department to ascertain the objectives of the Klan in the South. At a Klan meeting that Whitley attended undercover in South Carolina that year, one local member told him that they had murdered a black man "because he'd declared his intention to vote." In Louisiana, he reported that the Knights of White Camelia had massacred at least 200 black plantation workers in a single day to prevent them from becoming citizens. In 1875, George K. Chase was appointed by Attorney General Edward Pierrepont to lead a squad of detectives to Mississippi with the mandate to ensure fair voting procedures for blacks. He indicated, however, that he was quite willing to collaborate with local Democrats to ensure "the nigger did not rule the Anglo-Saxon."[27]

The violence sponsored or condoned by the Klan continued unabated in subsequent years. In North Carolina, the movement

[26] Waldrep, *Lynching in America*, 99–100.   [27] Jeffreys-Jones, *The FBI*, 17–18, 22, 34.

inspired by the Klan operated under a variety of other names, such as the Constitutional Union Guard, but the atrocities were imitated repeatedly from group to group. Anyone who was black, a Republican, or involved with Freedmen's Bureau activities was a target. There are numerous newspaper accounts of beatings, burnings and hangings in Lenoir and Chatham counties, with tales of children forced to watch their parents mutilated and kicked to death, as well as parents humiliated before their children, who were also senselessly killed.[28] The assaults escalated especially around the time of elections, which were moments when white citizens felt most vulnerable to the threat posed by newly enfranchised black voters. Many instances of intimidation by terror, for example, appeared soon after the narrow victory of Ulysses S. Grant in the 1869 presidential election, a candidate whom southerners detested both for his Republican politics and his role as commanding general for the Union in the Civil War.[29]

There were efforts at resistance to the Klan at the federal level. Indeed, it was President Grant who sponsored the Reinforcement Act of 1871 that permitted the establishing of martial law if needed in states threatened by Klan violence. There were arrests and trials in the early 1870s of Klansmen, some of whom were convicted and sent to prison. A joint committee held hearings in the capital in 1871–2 and produced a 13-volume report, which has been assessed as "one of the most extensive ever made by Congress ... for the sheer quantity of compelling testimony it provides on Klan terrorism." Considering the disturbing snapshot it offers of Reconstruction politics at ground level in the rural South, one study of this period has called it "a singular document in US history."[30] Although its impact was far from decisive, the report may have inspired a number of state laws intended to lessen the violence against blacks. The legislation, often fought over by divided representatives, called for the indemnification of property damaged by mob attacks and the bringing to trial of persons conspiring to kill or injure prisoners in jails, and

[28] See the description in Trelease, *White Terror*, 189–207.
[29] Other groups with similar intentions operated openly in the 1870s. Among the most feared by post-Emancipation blacks were the Redeemers and the White Line Party in Mississippi, who used violent tactics repeatedly in their effort to overthrow local Republican administrations. See Fellman, *In the Name of God and Country*, 99–103. Their fantasy of power was to confine blacks in work camps to ensure white political supremacy.
[30] Dray, *At the Hands of Persons Unknown*, 46.

recommended mandating acts designed to "punish sheriffs who permit prisoners in their custody to be put to death by violence."[31]

However, these efforts to reduce the victimization of blacks, were, more often than not, failures in practice. In addition to the fact that local law enforcement officials were often completely sympathetic to the strategy, if not always the tactics, of the Klan's terrorism, the court system also found its way around the federal government's legislation. As one historian has put it, decisions in the courts were simply ignored, "rendering toothless one judicial command after another on behalf of racial justice." As a result, cases that were supposed to limit mob injustice frequently ended up enabling it, permitting not only the continuation of one-way kangaroo courts at the state and county levels where all-white juries convicted black defendants who actually had often been their victims, but also the practice of white sheriffs allowing the extralegal torturing and murdering by mobs of blacks suspected of political and sexual offenses.[32]

The Supreme Court played its own role in permitting the continuing political violence against blacks. Among a number of decisions issued between 1857 and 1883, the court repealed the 1875 Civil Rights Law and turned over to the states responsibility for the protection of rights and citizenship. In US v. Cruikshank, the court's ruling in favor of states' rights opened the door to the exoneration of three men convicted in the 1873 Colfax Massacre in which over 100 blacks were murdered by a white mob breaking up a political meeting. In another ruling, the court decided in Reese v. US in 1876 to make a distinction between its ability to grant suffrage (which was constitutionally valid) and its authority to prohibit the exclusion of voters on racial grounds (which it ruled invalid). This essentially established a federal legal precedent for southern state legislatures and assemblies to exclude blacks from voting lists by requiring literacy tests, property possession requirements such as an expensive poll tax, and other rules that had the obvious intention of excluding blacks from influencing the existing structure of political authority.[33]

On another front, the heroic efforts made by black reformers like Ida B. Wells and Frederick Douglass to awaken the nation to the

---

[31] For the documents, see Waldrep, Lynching in America, 135.
[32] Ibid., xix. See also Brundage, Lynching in the New South.
[33] Dray, At the Hands of Persons Unknown, 109–110.

horrors of lynching encountered insurmountable opposition throughout the decades of their battles.[34] They quickly learned that they could
not rely on the promises of the 14th and 15th Amendments, which
supposedly guaranteed African Americans equal protection under the
law, and the right of all black male citizens to go to the polls on election
day and vote.

A truly remarkable moment in the trajectory of political violence against blacks in the US was the Wilmington, NC race riot in
1898. Indeed, so serious was the event that it has been called the only
coup d'état in the nation's history in which a municipal administration
was overthrown. Wilmington was at the time the largest city in the
state, with a black majority population. It was in many respects a
fulfillment of the ideals of Reconstruction, in that blacks occupied
many positions in the local government. These included the offices of
the county treasurer, an assistant sheriff and members of the elected
municipal assembly. In addition, the editor of North Carolina's sole
black-owned newspaper resided in Wilmington, black citizens there
occupied leading roles in a number of law firms, and others had
managed to become successful business owners with significant property holdings.

Violence emerged when the combustible mixture of sexual and
political fears surfaced simultaneously. In the aftermath of the 1896
election in which a Republican candidate, Daniel L. Russell, won the
governorship, white Democrats in Wilmington, led by a former con-
gressman, Alfred Waddell, began to challenge the controlling political
interests of blacks in the city. Waddell was quoted as saying that
"nigger lawyers are sassing white men in our courts. We will not live
under these intolerable conditions. No society can stand it. We intend
to change it, if we have to choke the current of the Cape Fear River
with negro carcasses."[35]

Other forces played crucial roles in the unfolding drama. White
gangs tried to prevent blacks from voting in the 1898 municipal elections, threatening them with violence if they dared to cast ballots.
Newspaper coverage, even beyond the borders of North Carolina,
was also a significant factor. One instance revealed the region's wide
sympathy for what was portrayed as the embattled white community in

---

[34] See, most recently, Giddings, *Ida: A Sword Among Lions.*
[35] Dray, *At the Hands of Persons Unknown*, 123.

Wilmington. A column in a Georgia newspaper written by a member of a prominent Democratic family, Rebecca Felton, argued that white farm women needed greater security to be protected from the threat of black rapists. "If it takes lynching to protect women's dearest possession from drunken, ravening human beasts," she was quoted as saying, "then I say lynch a thousand a week if it becomes necessary." The article was picked up by the Wilmington press, provoking a response in the Wilmington *Daily Record* by its editor, Alex Manley, who directly challenged the Felton charges by arguing that the real problem was the widespread and unpunished practice of white men violating helpless black women in their employ.

The climax to the crisis came when Waddell led a mob of over 400 whites into the black community's side of town on November 10 and destroyed the entire building that housed the offices of Manley's newspaper. They then marauded their way through one black neighborhood after another, shooting, beating and lynching anyone they could find. The official casualty list numbers 25, but the actual total has also been cited at over 100. Literally thousands of black families, grabbing what they could from their homes, fled for safety into the forest surrounding the city. Governor Russell appealed to black officials to resign their posts in an effort to bring peace to the city, but they had already been driven out of town. Waddell became the self-appointed mayor and immediately annulled the previous, elected city council. In its place, an entirely new city council was hastily elected by the virtually all-white electorate and took office the same day. The success of the insurrection was made permanent in the election of 1900 when the Democratic Party won by a huge margin; no blacks were on the ticket and none were returned to office.[36]

Political terrorism leveled against blacks continued unabated throughout the first decades of the twentieth century, and was not confined entirely to the South. The most virulent trend was the increase in what were to be called "race riots" in metropolitan areas throughout the country. Though it began as a largely rural phenomenon occurring primarily in the South, the pattern of violence

[36] For a complete analysis of this event, see Tyson, *Democracy Betrayed*. The Wilmington terrorism has also been portrayed in John Sayles' novel, *Moment in the Sun* in Book Two, 293–495. Waddell's inflammatory speech, "The White Declaration of Independence," is quoted verbatim, including the statement that "we will no longer be ruled, and never will again be ruled, by men of African origin" (p. 464).

followed the migration of blacks to the North and West. Massive mob assaults were made on black neighborhoods in New York in 1900, Philadelphia in 1917, Chicago in 1919, and Tulsa in 1921, to name only a few of the most virulent of these attacks. As urban areas expanded in the South and more blacks moved there from towns and farms, similar destruction was visited on their homes and businesses; two of the most deadly of these riots took place in New Orleans in 1900 and in Atlanta in 1906. The number of victims, including those who were tortured and lynched on the street in full public view may never be accurately known.

One of the worst of these mob onslaughts took place in Springfield, Illinois in August 1908. Examining this event helps to understand the motives at work elsewhere as well as at this site. Once again, the volatile mix of reports of blacks raping several white women and the fears generated by an increasingly prosperous and politically significant sector of the black population of the city brought whites out into the streets to take action against the perceived threat. Led by a female lodging house proprietor, the alarmed crowd stormed into black-owned stores and homes, burning and killing as they went, block by block. One brave black man, a local barber named Scott Burton, attempted to defend himself and his family with a rifle, but he was overwhelmed. The mob, estimated in newspaper accounts at a thousand people at its height, slashed his flesh and then hung his bleeding body from a tree. So many whites, including women and children, came later to take souvenir pieces of bark from the lynching tree that there was little left of the tree itself by day's end.

There were trials and a few people were sent off to prison, but blacks ended up paying a large price. In addition to their damaged property and wounded family members, at least 50 blacks were summarily dismissed by the mayor from their jobs in the local administration, from county clerks to policemen and firemen. The state militia was called in to keep the peace, but after it left a few weeks later, gangs of whites resumed their rampage, seeking to realize the fantasy of cleansing Springfield of every remaining black person.[37] The effort did not succeed, but came narrowly close.

Burnings, mutilations and lynchings continued to spread like a contagion across the country at this time. The savagery of these

[37] The Springfield race riot is described in Rasenberger, *America, 1908*, 173–84.

outrages in East St Louis in 1917 as well as in communities in Texas, Georgia and South Carolina in particular in 1918 have been compared to the worst horrors of the Belgian Congo.[38] The threat that whites felt so viscerally was evident on a number of levels. Black-owned newspapers and magazines were expanding across the country. The *Chicago Defender* and *The Crisis* alone claimed some 250,000 subscribers combined. More importantly, these publications presented a very different interpretation of race relations than the perspectives available in the mainstream press. In 1919, there were articles in the *Defender* reporting on the rise of black self-defense groups in rural southern areas, some with bravado appeals for an end to the "lynch law" and, on occasion, calls to recognize the need to arm "to the teeth, and kill every white scoundrel who approaches."[39]

Another episode in this unbroken chain of racial terrorism in the US was the Hoop Spur massacre in Arkansas during the "red summer" of 1919. In Helena, Arkansas, the threat to whites posed by black cotton workers forming a union to bargain collectively with their landowners and factory managers brought these fears to a climax. On the night of September 30, a car full of aroused white residents drove to a church in nearby Hoop Spur where a union meeting was taking place, and opened fire. A guard was able to respond and managed to kill one of the assailants. With local papers asserting that "the colored will never be permitted to administer affairs," a vigilante mob set off the next day to end the "negro rebellion." The group rampaged through the area, killing blacks in their houses as well as sharecroppers whom they passed working in the fields, leaving the bodies to rot. A contingent from Mississippi joined them, indiscriminately hunting down and murdering blacks wherever they could be found in the area. Over 100 were reported killed but the actual total remains in dispute and may never be known with certainty.

Newspaper headlines depicted the manner in which the story was told at the time. One mentioned a farmer who was "charged with inciting blacks" to rebel against the whites of Helena. Another claimed "Negroes had plot to rise Against Whites" and was accompanied by these sub-headlines: "All Negroes Said to have been Armed" and

---

[38] Whitaker, *On the Laps of Gods*, 38. The comparison with the Congo atrocities references Hochschild's *King Leopold's Ghost*.
[39] Whitaker, *On the Laps of Gods*, 49.

"Propaganda led Negroes to Secretly Organize." The *Arkansas Democrat* on October 4, 1919, stated that "vicious blacks were planning a great uprising." Two days later, the *New York Times* published an article on the Helena affair, which reported that blacks had been "seized in Arkansas Riots" and had confessed "to a widespread plot among them, including a password for the rising, identified as 'Paul Revere'." Indeed, so powerful were these unfounded rumors that 12 blacks were charged with rebellion and condemned to death, though the sentence was commuted five years later after a huge campaign on their behalf.[40]

Instances of lynchings of blacks continued unabated well into the 1930s.[41] In many instances, the authorities were complicit, either actively or passively, as the legal system was processed in a way which legitimized these killings as acceptable acts of punishment sanctioned by one race against another. At the same time, the media participated prominently by narrating and advertising the atrocities, thereby normalizing and justifying the crimes. In addition, varieties of the Klan and groups it inspired went on provoking and sponsoring the bloody rituals. The lynchings were still largely public events, spectacles uniting the collective body politic and designed to calm the insecurity of white communities who felt threatened by the political consequences of dealing with former slaves as equals, thereby justifying these acts of terrorism as both necessary and ordinary.

White resistance to black empowerment extended from the imposition of voting restrictions, to outright acts of collective terror. One instance where the evidence is blindingly clear is the case of Marsh Cook, a white Republican who was shot to death in July, 1890, after winning office with the support of blacks in Mississippi. Another was that of S. S. Mincey, a member of the Republican Party in Georgia who was beaten to death by a Klan mob in the summer of 1930 after he refused to renounce a political post he had won in an election.[42]

The violence reached its zenith in the years when whites felt most insecure about losing their traditional status in the racial hierarchy. For as long as they could, they carried out the acts of violence with the expansive support network of local politicians, judges and law enforcement officials and in the absence of opposing outside forces,

[40] Ibid., esp. 72–98, 302–4, 327–9. [41] See Ifill, *On the Courthouse Lawn.*
[42] Tolnay and Beck, *A Festival of Violence,* 66–7.

including, in particular, the federal government. The recurring fantasy on the part of white activists was that blacks could in fact be prevented from voting and holding political positions by both mandates and violence, and that a return to the racially exclusionary past was a realistic possibility.

The community lynching spectacles of mutilation, torture and killing of blacks that took place mainly (though certainly not exclusively) in so many rural areas of the South finally declined in the years after the First World War.[43] The racial terror, however, did not. Indeed, the major change was that of the sites where violence occurred, not an end to the phenomenon itself. The political violence against blacks shifted to the cities, following the migration patterns of blacks who fled the South and relocated in urban areas from Tulsa to Chicago, Boston and New York. As already noted, all of these areas experienced an outbreak of vicious "race wars" in which entire sections of cities, where blacks had been largely confined as a result of restrictive real estate policies, were assaulted. To be sure, there were other factors involved, such as economic competition, sexual myths, and pure racism in encouraging so many white citizens to commit such outrageous acts of violence.[44] Nevertheless, the phenomenon of white terrorism remains primarily a tale of overwhelming political fear and anxiety.

The government was hardly unaware of the cruelties of this political racism. A number of bills were proposed in Congress over the course of several decades that brought the evidence to public scrutiny and also underscored the deep divisions in American society in response to the problem. One of the earliest attempts to establish a federal anti-lynch law was made in 1922 by Leonidas C. Dyer, a Missouri Republican in the House of Representatives. His bill defined lynching broadly as a criminal act in which three or more persons act to deprive any person in the US of life without the authority of the law. It was actually passed by the House but blocked in the Senate by southern Democrats. In 1935, Robert Wagner and Edward P. Costigian sponsored a bill designed to become a federal anti-lynch

---

[43] Declined, but by no means ended. See the disturbing description of a contemporary lynching festival in Fayette County, Tennessee complete with professional photographers creating on-the-scene postcard snapshops of white celebrants in front of the dangled corpse as quoted in Litwack, *How Free is Free?*, 23.

[44] See Tolnay and Beck, *A Festival of Violence*, 198–9, 256–7.

law, but President Roosevelt refused to support it for fear of losing southern votes in the upcoming election.

The most serious attempt was made in January 1948, when Senator Albert Hawkes of New Jersey introduced his bill at hearings of a Judiciary Subcommittee of the Senate on the "crisis of lynching." The purpose of this bill was to define the act of lynching with sufficient evidence, to declare it outside the law, and to provide clear punishment for both the perpetrators and those in public office who permit such criminal activities to take place. The evidence presented at the hearing was overpowering in its graphic content and comprehensive in its scope. Although the annual incidence of lynching had declined in recent years, there were at least six persons in the US lynched as recently as 1946, "all of whom were Negroes." There was only one trial, which ended with an acquittal. According to evidence submitted by the Tuskegee Institute, between 1936 and 1946 there were "at least 43" recorded cases of lynchings, one of which included the shooting of a victim 60 times. Hawkes concluded from the evidence that the "threat of lynching hangs over the heads of all Negroes," since the mobs who commit these racial crimes are essentially immune from justice. "As a terrorist device," Hawkes said, "it reinforces all the other disabilities placed upon [the Negro]."[45]

The following day at the second hearing, Senator Wayne Morse of Oregon testified that he had accumulated evidence (also from the Tuskegee Institute) proving that "during the past 50 years, approximately 5,000 persons were known to have been lynched" in the US. He submitted into the record tables and charts showing how widespread the practice had been, and asked rhetorically, "How long can we as a nation countenance these atrocities?" He also documented the complicity of law enforcement officials in most of the lynchings, which showed clearly that either they actively participated in the murders or "refused to interfere to prevent the lynching ... or later to punish the lynchers." This "sickness" which has "flowed through every section of the country and in nearly every state," he concluded, must be declared unlawful at the federal level in order to prevent the practice where "the mob becomes the court." In spite of his eloquence and his evidence, which included submissions from a wide variety of sources nationally, the Hawkes bill was prevented from being sent to the Senate floor for

---

[45] *Crime of Lynching*, 7–22. The hearings were held on January 19–20.

a vote, largely due to the objections by Mississippi Senators James Eastland and John Stennis, and the Attorneys General of Tennessee and Florida on behalf of a strict interpretation of state sovereignty embedded in the Constitution.[46] The consequences of this and every subsequent attempt to render lynching illegal was that no bill seeking to outlaw lynching ever became federal law, nor did the Supreme Court ever consider the issue.

In 1948, in the aftermath of the Second World War, Clinton Rossiter wrote an interesting analysis of the problems facing a democratic republic in the midst of a crisis. More specifically, he was inquiring into the degree to which a republic could assume certain dictatorial powers, within its legal constitutional limits, in order to defend the system of democracy from threats, and still remain a democracy. He called this situation a "constitutional dictatorship," and defined its conditions. For a democracy to survive a national crisis, it "must be temporarily altered to whatever degree is necessary to overcome the peril and restore normal conditions." In such times, "government will have more power and the people fewer rights."[47]

When he wrote his book, Rossiter had in mind wars, like the Civil War and the two world wars, in which the US was in danger of having its democratic system altered had the outcomes been different. His point is that in such instances of crisis, democracies cannot survive unless they become dictatorial, but he was careful to note that the period of time for such emergency measures was to be clearly limited, and that certain critical factors defining the American democratic system, such as the separation of powers, were not to be altered. He certainly was not thinking of the impact of the Native American Removal or the Jim Crow laws as examples of a national crisis justifying authoritarian rule.

Nevertheless, the terrorism experienced by many blacks and Native Americans may well have felt like constitutional dictatorship, complete with majority citizen support. They were indeed denied rights, and lived under administrative rule as captives rather than as citizens, with policies of violence seemingly justified in a democratic republic. For the white majority, perceptions of danger and threat did

---

[46] Ibid., 29–42. Morse also cited Arthur Raper's pathbreaking book, *The Tragedy of Lynching* and Gunnar Myrdal's *American Dilemma*.

[47] Rossiter, *Constitutional Dictatorship*, 5.

drive their actions, because it did seem to be a crisis situation. Native Americans were violently opposed to white settlers, who felt it necessary to develop land in what, for them, was a legitimate part of their state's territory, not sacred tribal ancestral lands. Similarly, whites, especially in the South, experienced the freed slave as a threat to their political position and power in crisis terms, and reacted accordingly. Regardless of social class identification, whites were protected constitutionally in their violent endeavors; the majorities of the two minorities, blacks and Native Americans, lived under conditions of terrorism within the same legal system.

7 COMMUNIST AND FASCIST AUTHORITARIAN TERROR

Wars by definition are violent. While this fact may make warfare unhelpful when identifying political violence in the civil order, wars nonetheless have always had a close correlation with some of the most significant moments of domestic political violence since the formation of the modern nation state. France's Reign of Terror, conducted by the government in 1793–4, was carried out within the fearful framework of potential invasion by monarchical armies from almost any site around the entire border of the country. The first outbreak of political violence from below in the modern era was initiated by the Carbonari as a form of national resistance by Italians seeking to end the Napoleonic occupation of the peninsula. Russia's entrance into the world of insurgent terror began with the Decembrists in the aftermath of the Napoleonic war. Later, in the 1860s and 1870s, radicalism and terrorism from below reappeared in the aftermath of the country's demoralizing defeat in the Crimean War. The creation of the Paris Commune and the extreme violence utilized to crush it in the summer of 1871 were consequences of the French surrender in the Franco-Prussian War. Nowhere perhaps was this association of national war and civil terror more pronounced than in Weimar Germany and Soviet Russia, two newly proclaimed post-Great War republics which replaced monarchical regimes in territories where rulers had been at best only grudgingly responsive to competing political parties, representative assemblies of the people, and independent judiciaries. Although the specific characteristics in each situation differed enormously, both ultimately were transformed into authoritarian state formations in which political violence would play a prominent role.

In Russia, the tsarist government collapsed in February 1917, after decades of resistance and repression combined with the more immediate enormous losses of both human life and political credibility during the war years. The unelected administration that succeeded the monarchy assumed the name of Provisional Government.[1] The stated intention of its multiparty leadership was to hold elections, form a constituent assembly and draw up a constitution, but only once the war was over. Operating with a cabinet of ministers but in the absence of a parliament, the administration managed to issue an historic proclamation of general amnesty to all incarcerated political prisoners and revolutionary exiles in Europe. The leaders also committed themselves to work out a framework for an equitable distribution of land to the impoverished peasantry, fulfilling a demand made by generations of radical parties. This expectation, along with many others, was never realized, as the government fell in an overnight seizure of power organized by the Bolshevik faction of the Russian Social Democratic Labor Party in November. Within a single year, Russia evolved through all three of the primary forms of political rule in the Western world, from a monarchy legitimized by divine right, to a republic claiming popular sovereignty, and finally to a new nation state founded on the principles of Marxism.

The constituency of the leadership of the new ruling party in Russia was composed largely of revolutionaries who for decades had lived the lives of political outlaws in exile, mainly in the capital cities of Western Europe. They had had little direct experience of their homeland in these years, and their daily experiences were shaped by sectarian political combat on a variety of levels. They wrote articles and books based on the Marxist principles to which they had committed themselves, predicting and justifying the onset of a worldwide revolutionary tide in which political ideologues in their own image would command the loyalties of vast armies of humiliated and exploited workers and peasants in realizing the communist utopian vision of a historically unprecedented egalitarian social order. They thrashed out their plans in innumerable meetings and congresses, constantly seeking to attract hearts and minds to their cause while always seeking to defeat all opposing and competing perspectives.

---

[1] The Russian word "vremennoe" also carries the meaning of "temporary."

We may never know to what degree Lenin, Trotsky and their comrades actually ever really expected to rise from the diasporic underground in Europe to the heights of power in the largest country in the world. We do know that from the moment they received the news of the abdication of Nicholas II, they began to make serious plans to move from arcane party debates to the creation of the world's first socialist state. Once in power, the mentality of war informed much of the initial decision-making on the part of the early Bolshevik leadership elite.

Red Terror in Soviet Russia

Aside from Lenin himself, it was Trotsky who left the most indelible imprint on the reins of the state, as the new regime sought legitimacy and the means to consolidate its authority. No sooner had Trotsky negotiated a separate peace with the German high command (to which he was personally opposed, but he accepted Lenin's strategy on withdrawal from fighting an "imperialist war") than he confronted the threat of the combined forces opposing Bolshevik rule that triggered a full-scale civil war in 1918. Trotsky was asked to head the newly formed Red Army, in spite of the fact that he had no military experience. Against all odds, he led his forces to victory within two years over the White Army of Russian monarchists, conservatives, liberals and assorted moderate socialists supported by US and British expeditionary forces, all of whom shared little in common beyond hostility to the Bolsheviks. Trotsky also instituted a daring socialist economic policy he called War Communism, which mandated a rapid program of nationalizing industry, banking and hospitals across the country.[2]

Most importantly for our purposes, Trotsky inaugurated his policy of Red Terror, which he publically defended both in the party press within the country and in debates with prominent Marxists abroad who disagreed with its coercive and repressive nature.[3] Although the term "terror" had long been used in a positive context by radical theorists such as Karl Heinzen in Germany and Nikolai Morozov in Russia, one must reach back over a century to the French Reign of Terror of 1793–4 to find a similar policy of justified political violence at the state level.

[2] See the essays in Trotsky, *Military Writings* for insight into his strategy and tactics.
[3] Miller, "Exile's Vengeance: Trotsky and the Morality of Terrorism," esp. 214–19.

Making use of the military strategy that he developed in his essays about the purposes of the Red Army during the Civil War, Trotsky launched a vigorous defense of the necessity for state violence as a requirement for the success of what the party unanimously referred to as "the revolution." Moreover, his interpretation blurs the distinction between what were conventionally understood as separate military and civilian zones of combat. There were, he argued, numerous opponents to the Bolshevik experiment that he referred to as "enemies," consciously using the term that Robespierre and St-Just formulated during the Reign of Terror. To permit them access to the media so they could advocate their "reactionary politics" was both dangerous and unproductive, and therefore could not be allowed. But Trotsky went much further. Since revolutions were by their very nature a form of civil warfare involving violence, the new regime had to assume the responsibility of defending its authority to protect the Russian people, in whose name the revolution had been made.

Trotsky's purpose was not only an exercise in Marxist dialectics and praxis. He was also seeking to mobilize Soviet society in the effort to consolidate the revolutionary regime by denouncing and uncovering the threatening "enemies" within. The fantasy of power at work behind the Bolshevik leadership's ideology in the battles against their political opponents was in fact an extraordinary utopian vision of a future political order that was only vaguely in focus but was charismatically inspiring in its promises of a classless society and an end to the wretched existence of the poor.

Violence was to be an integral ingredient of this program of change. The enemies turned out to be many of the familiar members of the competing political parties. The liberal Kadet Party and the Socialist Revolutionary (SR) Party were identified and fell first. Much of this campaign was conducted in full public view, for maximum impact. Dziga Vertov, an aspiring and innovative film director, made several documentaries of the SRs seated in the dock during their trials that were shown in Moscow theaters.[4] Articles in the Bolshevik Party newspaper *Pravda* and the government's official paper *Izvestia* carried accounts of the trials against the accused, most of whom were ultimately sentenced to prison, exile or execution. In one particularly

[4] Vertov's newsreels of the trials were part of his experimental KinoEye documentaries at this time.

striking case, Lenin ordered the arrest of a number of prominent intellectuals, sending them into exile in order to rid the country of their potentially harmful influence, which had involved questioning, more than actually opposing, the regime's principles.[5]

A decisive moment sealed the fate of the tsar as well. Learning that forces allied with the White Army were advancing toward the town of Yekaterinburg, where Nicholas II was held with his wife and children, Lenin decided to accept the recommendation of the Ural regional soviet to kill the entire family. The decision was carried out on the night of July 16, 1918. The public was informed in an understated manner when days later, the state newspapers carried an announcement that the former emperor had been executed to prevent his possible escape with the opposition army. The understood assumption was that once liberated from detention, he could have become a symbol of popular support for armed resistance against the state. Unlike the decision Robespierre made to put the deposed monarch Louis XVI on trial during the French Revolution, Lenin chose summary assassination instead.

There were legitimate reasons for Bolshevik fears of regime insecurity. The political atmosphere turned increasingly confrontational and violent in 1919, following the assassinations of the Petrograd Bolshevik police official Mikhail Uritskii and V. Volodarskii (a member of the Executive Committee of the governing Presidium in the capital), and the subsequent attempted killing of Lenin by an SR member, Fanya Kaplan.[6] Trotsky saw this as an opportunity for reprisals on a massive scale. The newly constituted national secret political police force, the Cheka, rooted strongly on the model of the detested tsarist Okrana, and under the command of Felix Dzerzhinskii, expanded the number of political victims as the cells of their headquarters in the notorious and forbidding Lubianka building were soon filled to capacity. Decrees on state terror as government policy under the aegis of the Cheka were issued even before the first anniversary of the revolution. On September 5, 1918, to take one example, Dzerzhinskii

---

[5] Chamberlain, *The Philosophy Steamer.*
[6] Volodarskii's first name is not known but his original name was Moisei Markovich Goldshtein. It was very common for Russian revolutionaries to choose a *nom de guerre*, as did Lenin, Trotsky, and Stalin. Volodarskii was fatally shot on June 20, 1918 by Grigory Semyonov, an SR from a faction different than Kaplan's. As Volodarskii had both editorial and censorship posts, he was therefore a symbolically significant target. His comrade Anatoly Lunacharskii in his memoirs referred to him as "a terrorist."

stated it was "imperative that the country be made secure by means of terror" and further, that opponents of the revolution "associated with plots and uprisings shall be shot, and the names of all those executed as well as the reasons for the application of the measure, shall be published."[7] Thus, the terror of the state was functioning in full force already in the initial years of Bolshevik power, alongside the campaigns to improve housing, literacy and health care, which were certainly of greater concern to the citizens of the new socialist republic.

The problem of identifying the "enemies of the state" would remain a constant throughout the history of the Soviet Union. Many were authentic opponents of the Bolsheviks who in fact were willing to engage in acts of anti-state violence, such as some members of the SRs and anarchists still at large. Most, however, were concoctions of the Bolshevik imagination, and their potential to disrupt the stability of the regime was minimal if not entirely non-existent. The issue was more one of assuring control of the government in the conditions of questionable legitimacy that Lenin and his associates had established. Having literally seized power from the Provisional Government in October 1917, and having rejected all previous forms of political legitimacy, the Bolshevik Party leaders chose to commit themselves feverishly and intolerantly to fashion an entirely new kind of state justification based on the ideological foundations of Marxism as interpreted in the specific conditions of Russian national development.

Though no one in the ruling party could admit it, they were in fact operating in a situation of extreme vulnerability and instability. The machinery of propaganda that the party organs churned out like excessive factory fumes over the following years was designed to establish a belief in the opposite of this reality, namely, that the new state was powerful, secure and transformative. Secure states, however, do not fear poets and artists, and usually do not find it necessary to conjure up massive lists of "wreckers" and "saboteurs" on a permanent basis, decade after decade, who allegedly pose such an existential, subversive threat that they require violent repression, as was the case with the leadership of the Soviet Union. Precisely because the Bolsheviks lacked the framework of legitimacy and voluntary support

---

[7] Dzerzhinskii, "Decree of September 5, 1918," 103. This volume also contains numerous documents concerning the formation of the legal system in the USSR, including the justification of terror as state policy. See especially pp. 99–109, 287–309.

from below, such enemies, real or imagined, and their repression by terror, were necessary for the regime's survival.

The Red Scare in the US

Some of the most effective consequences of the Bolshevik ideological narrative were to be found thousands of miles away, in the US. The concept of "the Bolshevik menace" replaced the image of the savage Hun of the Great War, portrayed in lurid posters as King Kong-like gorillas emerging from the jungles to threaten civilization. In many respects, the postwar image of the Bolshevik was similarly violent, primitive and threatening. There was certainly no actual danger of Marxist-inspired armies invading American shores, but there were very palpable fears of the enemy that lurked within. The threat was perceived as treacherous subversive cells of communists already embedded in the American social fabric, making plans to indoctrinate workers and intellectuals to lead an insurrection designed to bring down the federal government and replace it with a socialist regime modeled on the Soviet example in Moscow. "Every day," the *New York Times* announced, "many people are ready to declare that the United States will be the next victim of this dangerous malady" – the Red Terror.[8]

There were many reasons for the sudden pervasiveness of this atmosphere of fear and anxiety. Some of the most significant were economic in nature. With the end of the First World War, the country was forced to confront the mass demobilization of some four million troops at a moment when the national economy had to be transformed from the heightened demands of wartime productivity to the far slower pace of growth expected in peacetime. As a result, rates of joblessness rose dramatically as factories conditioned to fulfilling the challenging needs of war were either reduced in capacity or shut down completely. At the same time, prices soared at the close of the war, as supplies of goods and services lessened. Nevertheless, as one student of this era put it, "these statistics do not record the psychological torment and confusion experienced by those who

[8] Ratshesky, "Americanization is Cure for Bolshevism," 1.

were so suddenly left jobless and who were forced to readjust their own and their families' lives."[9]

In addition, the period witnessed a surge in the formation of labor unions, from the mainstream American Federation of Labor to the far more radical International Workers of the World (IWW, aka Wobblies). As the unions grew larger and more confident in asserting their demands for improved working conditions, strikes were called with greater frequency than they had been in the past, producing both support and vigorous opposition in government and society. Shutdowns and lockouts led to violence in many cases.[10]

One other telling result of these forces was the rise of patriotic organizations that played a key role in mobilizing Americans to confront the dangers of Bolshevism, immigrant labor radicalism, and the threat of further political enfranchisement of the country's black population. This heated atmosphere also contributed to the rebirth of the Ku Klux Klan in the early 1920s. Stridently posing as American ultra-nationalists, the Klan contributed to the continued popularity of Thomas Dixon's violently racist novel, *The Clansman*, originally published in 1905. It made further inroads at this time as a result of the success of D. W. Griffith's monumental 1915 film, *Birth of a Nation*, which was based explicitly on Dixon's novel. Though it is difficult to feel its emotional impact upon viewing it now, at the time, it effectively portrayed white American society gripped by a palpable threat from black insurgent terrorism, and the triumphant reaction in defense of national honor and security. The film, still shown in theaters during the 1920s, was given a personal recommendation by President Wilson, who had been Dixon's roommate in college, after a private screening at the White House to which the Supreme Court was invited.[11] The impulses to link this presumed domestic danger with the international menace posed by the Bolshevik regime in Moscow were not long in coming.

[9] Murray, *Red Scare*, 6.
[10] These strikes and their impact have been studied most recently by Rebecca Hill, *Men, Mobs and Law*, 112–61 and more comprehensively in Goldstein, *Political Repression in Modern America*.
[11] See the useful introduction by Cary D. Wintz to the republication of the book in Dixon, *The Clansman*. Book Three of the novel is titled "The Reign of Terror." Wilson was also sympathetic to Dixon's politics, as evidenced by his policy of removing black officials from their government posts and his refusal to sponsor minority appointments in his administration. See also the insightful analysis of Dixon's novel in Clymer, "Propaganda by the Deed," 194–237.

Also of significance at this time was another serious problem that emerged from the White House. Following his return from Paris in the fall of 1919 after his exhausting participation in the postwar treaty negotiations and his cross-country campaigns on behalf of the League of Nations, President Wilson suffered a massive stroke, which left him severely paralyzed, partially blind and victimized by frequent, disabling migraine headaches. Though the frail nature of his health was kept from public notice, he was nevertheless largely confined to quarters in Washington under the constant supervision of his doctors until the end of his term in 1921, leaving the country without a forceful leader when such a presence was greatly needed.

The events of the period reflect the now familiar interrelationship in America between violence conducted from above and below. Journalists and publicists insisted on the association of the dangerous ideology of socialism, regardless of its particular orientation, with recent immigrants to the US. Insurgent attacks seemed to confirm the linkage. The spectacular bombings that took place in 1919 and 1920 heightened these nativist suspicions of the dangers posed by politically active immigrants. Led by the charismatic Luigi Galleani, a small group of anarchists sent out some 30 explosive devices in small packages addressed to a wide variety of officials and business tycoons at both the federal and local levels between April and June 1919. Those targeted included the Attorney General, A. Mitchell Palmer, the Supreme Court Justice Oliver Wendell Holmes, John D. Rockefeller, J. P. Morgan, several cabinet secretaries in Washington, as well as a number of governors and mayors from coast to coast. Though little damage was done (most were discovered before delivery, after one package ignited while being opened), a virulent backlash against anarchists followed.

Far more serious was the Wall Street explosion the following year, in which 38 people died and over 400 were wounded.[12] This was the most deadly assault of insurgent political violence in the country to date, topping the casualty list of the October 1910 bombing of the Los Angeles Times building in which 21 people had died and at least 100 others ended up in local hospitals with injuries from the blast. While that tragedy was the result of a harsh

---

[12] For an exhaustive account, see Gage, *The Day Wall Street Exploded*.

labor dispute between workers and the Times management, and was a singular event without repetition, the 1920 explosion in the heart of the financial center was far more shocking. The Wall Street bombing, which caused millions of dollars of damage and involved multiple attack sites, was believed to have been planned by Mario Buda, a Galleanist.[13] The Galleanists continued to evade the police manhunt organized to bring to an end the terror they caused, and managed to strike targets for the next decade. The Galleanist cause was echoed in Luigi Galleani's anarchist journal, *Cronaca sovversiva*, which was eventually suppressed by the government because of its open advocacy of revolutionary violence. Their most extraordinary plot was the attempt in 1932 to assassinate Webster Thayer, the judge presiding over the trial of Nicola Sacco and Bartolomeo Vanzetti, anarchist followers of the Galleanists, who were charged with killing a paymaster and his guard in a robbery in Braintree, near Boston, in 1920. Their trial was a media sensation that dragged out over seven years, ending with a sentence of execution in 1927. Doubts about the validity of that judgment, carried out amid the atmosphere of the Red Scare, remain in contention.[14]

The US government reacted strongly and understandably to the threats posed by the insurgent violence. Congress hastily passed a raft of legislation, including the Espionage Act in 1917 and the Sedition Act in 1918. In addition, the Senate and the House passed the Immigration Act (also known as the Anarchist Exclusion Act) that year.[15] As a result, municipal police and government agents were authorized to conduct raids across the country organized by Attorney General A. Mitchell Palmer. Over 5,000 suspected socialists were arrested under the clauses of these laws, of whom 556 were deported.[16] Among those who were sent into exile at this time were the prominent anarchists Emma Goldman and Alexander Berkman, as well as Mario Buda.

[13] The most convincing evidence pointing to Buda as the man who planned and carried out the Wall Street bombing can be found in Avrich, *Sacco and Vanzetti*, 204–7. See also Davis, *Buda's Wagon*, 10–11.

[14] See Avrich, *Sacco and Vanzetti*.

[15] For the terms of these acts, see Murray, *Red Scare*, 13–14.

[16] See Stone, *Perilous Times*, 186–91, 220–6. The eminent judge Learned Hand wrote to Supreme Court Justice Oliver Wendell Holmes of his "dismay" over the spread of fear, demoralization and intolerance across the country as a result of "the Red baiting" attacks, arrests and deportations. Quoted in ibid., 224.

The contagion spread rapidly. In addition to the race riots that broke out in a number of American cities at this time, the labor movement began issuing frequent calls for strikes to win higher wages at factories across the country. A threatened railway strike in 1919 drew the attention of Attorney General Palmer, who joined forces with the railroad company officials in publically denouncing the workers willing to go on strike as sycophants of Bolshevism. A plan brought before Congress to have the nation's rail system operated by a central corporation run by both Washington and company executives produced cries in the Senate that such a proposal "might well have been formulated by a Lenin or a Trotsky," in that it was a naked effort "to sovietize the railroads of this country."[17]

In seeking scapegoats to blame, it was easy to turn against both recent immigrants and African Americans as repositories of Bolshevik conspiracies. Both had joined the labor movement in large numbers during the war years, and were vulnerable to being terrorized. The combined forces of these anxieties collided in Washington in July 1919. The violence was triggered by rumors that a white woman had been assaulted by a number of black men, which led to the formation of hundreds of armed white men, many recently returned from army service, into a lynch mob that marauded its way through the predominantly black areas of the city, destroying property, pulling blacks from cars and buses and beating them brutally, without any attempt by the police to intervene. Eventually, it took 2,000 federal troops who were ordered to end the violence. Newspaper coverage emphasized that the problem was the threat posed by socialist-inspired blacks, who had initiated the riot to undermine the existing system. In fact, once it became clear that the city administration was not ordering the police to restrain the brutalities of the mob, some black citizens did arm themselves and began targeting white rioters on the streets, a turn of events which finally brought out the forces of law and order to end the violence.[18]

In Chicago, neighborhoods where tens of thousands of African American migrants from the South had settled in the city, attracted by the possibilities of employment both during and after the

---

[17] Quoted from the Congressional Record in Read, *The World on Fire*, 255. See also the detailed evidence in McCormick, *Hopeless Cases* and his regional study, *Seeing Reds*.

[18] "Capitol Clashes Increase: Armed and Defiant Negroes Roam about Shooting at Whites," *New York Times*, July 22, 1919; "Race Riot Peril: Radical Propaganda among Negroes Growing," *New York Times*, October 5, 1919.

war, became sites of violent assaults in the summer of 1919. After five days of terror, 38 people were dead, of whom 23 were black. Over 500 required hospitalization for injuries. Similar deadly riots broke out in smaller cities like Omaha and Knoxville. In all of these cases, the press and the government came to similar conclusions to justify the violence: "Negro agitators, supported by the Bolsheviki" were responsible. The Bureau of Investigation (the ancestor of the FBI) went further in asserting that Soviet Russia was actually funding the effort to stimulate racial conflict in the US, thereby provoking white citizens to act in self-defense.[19]

The campaign against communism intensified over the next two decades, creating a variant that might be best termed "soft terror" that was characterized by severe psychological and economic consequences for its targets, rather than actual violence. The fear of communist subversion was sufficiently widespread to engender an overall atmosphere of political insecurity that generated its own forms of repression. For the victims, these years were dominated by fear and terror, as they faced rejection by neighbors, schools and employers in the effort to blacklist anyone suspected of political radicalism. One of the most stunning examples of this effort to denounce and punish the specter of domestic communist influence was *The Red Network*, a hugely influential book by Elizabeth Dilling, published soon after President Franklin Roosevelt took office and recognized the Soviet Union for the first time since the 1917 revolution. This 354-page compendium named and described, with profusely detailed entries, the activities of 460 groups, clubs, organizations and publications that, she argued, propounded the dangerous principles of Marx and Lenin in the US. A separate section of the book listed hundreds of individuals, with their locations and activities prominently identified. She had enthusiastic endorsements from congressmen as well as such influential figures as Robert McCormick, publisher of the *Chicago Tribune*. Funded by the Daughters of the American Revolution, Dilling lectured across the country on the dangers of the communist menace,

---

[19] Read, *The World on Fire*, 257–61. One of the most horrific assaults of violence on a black community in the US occurred in Tulsa in 1919, though it appears not to have been affected by the fear of incipient communism. For a comprehensive account, see Hirsch, *Riot and Remembrance*. The eminent historian John Hope Franklin was a young witness to the destruction of the entire African American neighborhood in Tulsa that year by white mobs. See his memoir, *Mirror to America*.

at churches, schools, colleges, American Legion posts and military bases, where she reached many thousands of ordinary citizens responsive to the call to action in their neighborhoods.[20]

Weimar violence and the Nazi prelude

Germany emerged from the Great War with its own vulnerabilities in the wake of the collapse of the entire structure of imperial authority. As the primary defeated power, questions about legitimacy of the new form of government preoccupied the statesmen gathered at the postwar Versailles Peace Conference in 1919. The decision reached was that the victors would decide what form of governance would be imposed upon Germany. Not surprisingly, resentments surfaced across the country, as well as anxieties and uncertainties that led a number of factions to contemplate violent measures to undermine the new regime. For them, the treatment Germany received as the defeated power in the war was experienced as a moment of national humiliation. The imperial regime was replaced by a republic, without an election or plebiscite. The new German constitution was to be written by a National Assembly meeting in the city of Weimar, instead of the traditional capital, Berlin. The German delegates at Versailles, as representatives of the defeated war power, had to accept the harsh conditions of the treaty, which included a war guilt clause, accepting the stationing of French, Belgian and British troops in the Ruhr Valley while agreeing to its own demilitarization, and paying costly reparations primarily to France and Britain to compensate the damage it caused during the war as the aggressor. The appeal of expressing discontent with the situation by resorting to acts of violence soon gained wide support.

Few witnesses to the emergent terror of this period perceived the danger to the fledgling democratic system in Germany as clearly and as early as did Emil Julius Gumbel. In 1922, Gumbel, a socialist, pacifist and aspiring academic statistician, published a book that not only comprehensively recorded the huge number of assassinations that had already taken place in Germany since the end of the war, but also

---

[20] Dilling, *The Red Network*. The book was in its fourth reprinted edition within a year, and continued its popularity up to the wartime alliance with the Soviet Union.

categorized them. The writing was direct, passionate and even cynical in its outrage at the course of events so vividly described.

Gumbel was convinced that the killings were largely the work of fanatical nationalist factions targeting socialists whom they believed were plotting to take over the weak administration in Weimar in order to institute a communist regime in Germany. In addition, they were motivated by the drive for revenge against the German statesmen who signed the Versailles Treaty which, they believed, was an admission of national betrayal and humiliation. By the time Gumbel was composing his narrative, Karl Liebknecht and Rosa Luxemburg, the primary leaders of the radical Spartacist League and the newly established Communist Party of Germany, had been brutally murdered in Berlin by an armed faction of the rightist Freikorps in January 1919. Barely a month later, the Independent Socialist Party leader and Bavarian premier, Kurt Eisner, was fatally shot in Munich by an aristocrat, Count Anton von Arco auf Valley.[21] In April, Otto Neuring, the socialist minister of war in Saxony was murdered by a group of soldiers, and in September, nationalists fatally shot Hugo Haase, another Independent Socialist. Perhaps more shocking was the 1921 assassination of Matthias Erzberger, head of the Catholic Center Party, who was one of the signers of the Versailles Treaty. However, the event that seems to have most disturbed Gumbel was the assassination on June 24, 1922 of Walter Rathenau, the country's widely respected foreign minister and highest ranking Jewish government official, by members of the nationalist group Organization Consul.

Gumbel recognized the terrible problem facing the inexperienced German government. In France in 1871 when the imperial regime came to an end, there had been precedents from 1789 and 1848 for the re-establishment of a democratic republic, and a strong republican tradition had managed to compete against the forces favoring monarchical restoration. Germany had no such past, leaving the weak Weimar republic extremely vulnerable to the proponents of the nationalist right. Moreover, the political terrain in postwar Germany was marked by the emergence of underground factions

---

[21] Commonly known as Anton Arco-Valley, he claimed he had killed Eisner because, being both Jewish and a socialist, he was a double danger to Germany. Arco-Valley's mother, it should be noted, was Jewish. Though sentenced by a court to death for his crime, the verdict was overturned by the Bavarian cabinet.

making use of the latest weaponry to sabotage the regime. Gumbel called these illegal activist cells "assassination organizations," operating under their own rules of political violence to achieve their aims. He divided them into nationalist categories of monarchist (seeking a return of the Hohenzollern dynasty), imperialist (restoring the territories of the Reich dismembered by the Versailles Treaty) and anti-Semitic (the myth of Jewish control of both the banking system as well as the revolutionary movement). Although divided in terms of ultimate strategy, these groups were frequent allies in the wave of terrorism that shook the foundations of the Weimar republic.

Further, Gumbel was quite aware of the wide network in society sympathetic to these groups and their destructive tactics, which existed in military circles, sports clubs and even in schools, where young students were still using textbooks extolling the glory of the Bismarckian era. The Weimar administration was, as a consequence, seen as "a regrettable aberration to be corrected as soon as possible" by "young terrorists acting in absolute good faith" in killing "the few republicans that Germany possesses."[22] Gumbel was merciless in his treatment of the press, which he saw as conspiring in the wave of killings. He quoted from newspaper headlines and articles that ostensibly condemned the assassinations but in fact were expressing measures of satisfaction that Germany's version of the Red Scare was having positive results by removing from positions of influence communists, Jews and treasonous signers of the despised Versailles Treaty. The correspondents of the press, he concluded, found it acceptable to overlook both "paid *agents provocateurs* who deliberately stir up unrest and also the provocative behavior of the police" who ensure that the responsibility for the violence is deflected to the victims instead of the actual perpetrators.[23]

Gumbel charted the thousands of incidents and victims of the violence that took place as a result of the street wars, shootings, bombings and outright summary executions. He also followed the course of events into the court system, where he found judicial gridlock and partisanship instead of justice. He documented hundreds of political murders between 1919 and 1921, and compared the

---

[22] Gumbel, "Organized Murder," 128. This is an excerpt from Gumbel's *Vier Jahre politischer Mord.*
[23] Gumbel, "Organized Murder," 130.

treatment of those on the political right and the left in the courts. By his count, 326 of the 354 assassinations committed by nationalists went entirely unpunished. By contrast, of the 22 socialists charged with such crimes, ten were sentenced to execution and three received life sentences in prison.[24]

Foreign observers were well aware of the political chaos in Germany described by Gumbel, but chose to see it in terms of the threat from the East. Stephen Pichon, foreign minister of France, wrote to his British counterpart that Germany was "as full of Bolshevism as Russia itself was before the Revolution, and [revolt] may break out at any time." He expressed further concern that because "Bolshevism is very contagious," it was capable of spreading to France as well.[25] There were specific contemporary events that alarmed Pichon and others, rooted in their fears of any kind of a revived powerful German state that would again threaten Europe. Above all, they were deeply concerned about the consequences of the 1918 dockyard strike in Kiel, which spread to other cities with the activist support of radical Spartacists. In the political confusion, red flags were hoisted atop public buildings in Berlin, Munich, Hamburg and elsewhere, signaling the advent of a number of socialist-oriented administrations across the country, while Western governments watched anxiously from afar.

The country's first postwar president, the moderate socialist Friedrich Ebert, attempted to steer a middle course between the radical demands of the Spartacists and their loyalists in workers' councils and circles sympathetic to the Bolshevik regime in Moscow on the one side, and the ultra-nationalists on the other. Rightists led by Wolfgang Kapp took advantage of the unstable situation in 1920, marching on Berlin and seizing control of the Reichstag. He was supported by a number of Freikorps units who were strongly opposed to the clause in the Versailles Treaty demanding a substantial reduction in the regular army and the virtual elimination of their units.[26] The coup attempt failed in large measure because of a strike called by the workers' councils to

---

[24] Brenner, *Emil J. Gumbel: Weimar German Pacifist and Professor,* 72–3. See also the documentation in Gumbel, *Denkschrift des Reichjustizministers.*

[25] Quoted in Read, *The World on Fire,* 25.

[26] The Versailles treaty called for the reduction of the Reichswehr, the regular army, from 350,000 to 100,000, and for the abolition of the 250,000-member Freikorps. Kapp and his co-conspirators were also concerned that the National Assembly in Weimar might assume full authority as the republic's capital in place of Berlin.

protest the seizure of power. There were casualties as violence broke out, before the Ebert administration was finally able to resume control of the government.

This street warfare conducted by outlawed political organizations on a widespread basis was a relatively new development in the continuing evolution of the tactics of political violence. In contesting the fundamental validity of the state, these factions regarded the entire political and legal framework of the Weimar regime as illegitimate, and intended it to be replaced by a new order that combined elements of the grandeur of the fallen imperial era with a militant German nationalism. Indeed, there were aspects of this campaign of terror that perversely incorporated components of the ancient theme of tyrannicide into the planning strategy of an emerging structure of political parties forming outside of the existing political system and dedicated to replacing it with a new anti-republican ideology.

Similar currents of ideological and nationalist terror were at work elsewhere in Europe as well. In France in 1936, the prominent socialist statesman Léon Blum was wounded in a failed assassination attempt perpetrated by activists loyal to the fascist Croix de Feu and the extreme nationalist Action Française parties, the culmination of a decade of violence in the streets. In Ireland, the long and violent struggle of the Fenians, the Irish Invincibles and their offshoots to remove British control from the island won a partial victory with the creation of the Irish Free State in 1921. However, the struggle over the remaining province still under British rule, Ulster, would see sectarian agony and many more deaths as the outlawed Irish Republican Army (seeking an end to British rule in Ulster) and the paramilitary Ulster Resistance (the Protestant counterpart, resisting Catholic and republican opposition to the status quo) played out their violent struggle for decades, until the apparent resolution of the conflict at the end of the twentieth century. The republic established in Spain in 1931 after the collapse of the monarchy was under attack from anarchist opponents on one side, and the far more lethal threat posed by the fascist Falange Party on the other.

The crises that weakened the Weimar regime led to a renewal of German nationalism, but one that would essentially redefine the concept. Unlike the situations that brought Lenin to power in Russia and Mussolini in Italy, where outlaw parties took over the state in violent confrontations that produced other varieties of state terrorism, the German National Socialist Workers (Nazi) Party, over the course of a decade, transformed itself from an underground, conspiratorial set of factions into a powerful legal political party able to compete in elections. Headed by Adolf Hitler, who had already served a brief jail term for his involvement in a failed coup attempt, the Nazi Party constructed an appealing ideological narrative that won increasingly wide support in local and national elections in the late 1920s. That narrative promised the restoration of German honor by nullifying the terms of the Versailles Treaty, halting the spread of the communist threat from within, and the restoration of the economy, which had been so severely damaged by the Great Depression and the burdens placed upon it by the postwar arrangements.[27]

The violence that had been so integral to the nationalist factions earlier was now put into full force by the state. After his appointment as chancellor in January 1933, Hitler began a systematic campaign of spreading fear and, on occasion, creating public disturbances which he then claimed to have suppressed in the name of re-establishing order. The Reichstag was burned by the Nazis but blamed on the communists, who were arrested en masse. Hitler brutally purged his own party's ranks, once again claiming that lurking dangers had been avoided. Above all, he revived the deeply rooted anti-Semitic trope by identifying the Jews of Germany as responsible for the economic disasters of the Depression and the political dangers of Soviet influence. The Enabling Act of 1933 dispensed with the need for parliamentary approval of laws, permitting the government to decree laws which it used repeatedly to repress those it deemed enemies of the state.

The trajectory of violence intensified throughout the decade as the Nazi Party declared all other political groups and parties to be illegal, and, following the passing of the Nuremburg Laws in 1934, moved to marginalize and later to eliminate socialists, homosexuals, patients suffering from mental illnesses (the "defectives"), Gypsies and Jews within the country. Society's complicity and support from the media were critical in making the repression so effective so quickly. Anyone who has seen Leni Riefenstahl's compelling documentary footage of Hitler's arrival in Nuremburg for the 1934 Nazi Party rally, in "Triumph of the Will," can readily comprehend the charismatic appeal

---

[27] For a good, recent analysis of the rise of the Nazi Party and Hitler's leadership within the larger historical context of German politics, see Baranowski, *Nazi Empire.*

Hitler obviously had for so many Germans. His political fantasies seem to be engraved in the mesmerized faces of the throngs who lined the streets to get a fleeting glimpse of his motorcade into the city, as Leni Riefenstahl made so vividly clear in her film. The former political outlaws had come to power by means of the democratic process, which they promptly set out to destroy with forms of violence that included world war, mass extermination and genocide.

In spite of the highly centralized effort by the ruling Nazi Party to dominate all aspects of political life, making forceful use of both propaganda and violence, forms of resistance did exist throughout the period. To be sure, the forces of the opposition were severely circumscribed and their chances of success were minuscule. Nevertheless, there were even a number of attempts to assassinate Hitler, to bring an end to the ruinous war as well as to the political fantasy of an Aryan Reich controlling the world, that would last a thousand years.

The resistance groups represented a wide spectrum of ideological antagonisms to the National Socialist agenda. Although the left had been weakened by the assaults upon communists soon after Hitler came to power, some socialists survived and worked secretly against the regime, such as the group around Julius Leber, former editor and Social Democratic Party Reichstag deputy. Leber was jailed during the 1930s for political writings unacceptable to the Nazi Party, but after his release joined Claus von Stauffenberg's group as part of a plot to assassinate Hitler. Leber was ultimately betrayed by a former communist spying for the Nazis, arrested in 1944 and executed on January 5, 1945.[28]

The extraordinary courage of the pacifist student group, White Rose, ended in tragedy as their anti-Nazi agitation campaign was uncovered and every member was executed in 1943.[29] Some churches, both Catholic and Lutheran, also worked quietly in the shadows, secretly protecting Jews and criticizing the state's policies at great risk. Another effort was made by the group known as the Red Orchestra, which sought to communicate valuable information on Hitler's terrorism to the Allies, including the Soviet Union. Activists in this group were also eventually located, arrested and executed.[30]

---

[28] Kershaw, *Hitler*, 431–2.
[29] On the leader of the White Rose circle, see McDonough, *Sophie Scholl*. See also Michalczyk, "The White Rose Student Movement in Germany," 49–57.
[30] Nelson, *Red Orchestra* and Brysac, *Resisting Hitler*.

Mention should also be made of the astonishing career of Carl Friedrich Goerdeler, who, as mayor of Leipzig, criticized Nazi Party policies and mobilized civilian support in a search for political alternatives, which took him throughout Germany and abroad. His reception was less than sympathetic outside the country, where he was either regarded as an official of the Reich or as a politician without a legitimate portfolio. Churchill, in particular, was dismissive when Goerdeler sought his aid in the 1930s. Eventually Goerdeler went underground to escape the warrant for his arrest, but was caught, tried and executed in February 1945 after suffering months of interrogations and torture.[31] The bitter irony about the timing of his death and Leber's is that they took place just a season away from the complete collapse in defeat of the Third Reich itself. However, this was true of many others as well who perished from illness and disease in concentration camps, death marches and executions.

Finally, another kind of terrorism went on after the war, but this one was carried out by the Allies. The horrors inflicted on the Germans by the Red Army during their advance into Berlin at the end of the war and in the immediate aftermath have been narrated in detail elsewhere.[32] However, the brutality of the Western Allies occupying Germany after the war has only recently begun to receive the same attention. The motive of revenge for Nazi atrocities was used to justify years of mistreatment, outright torture and abuse meted out against Germans during the late 1940s. Many Germans were herded into former concentration camps where they were treated with contempt, neglect and abuse, in addition to those who were simply murdered. Propaganda films made the rounds showing the horrors of the death camps to arouse further reprisals against the German survivors of the Allied bombing campaigns. Red Cross statistics, among the most reliable from this period, list over one million German soldiers who surrendered or were taken prisoner as "missing." Other data suggest that the numbers were much higher, as some changed their identities, hid underground or fled abroad; others who were actually imprisoned

---

[31] On Goerdeler, see Ritter, *The German Resistance*; the futile contact with Churchill is cited on p. 131. Other useful studies of the efforts to oppose the state violence of the Third Reich include Hoffman, *The History of the German Resistance* and Mommsen, *Alternatives to Hitler*, esp. ch. 3 "The Social Vision and Constitutional Plans of the German Resistance," pp. 42–133.

[32] Naimark, *The Russians in Germany*.

in displaced persons detention centers died there after being tortured, left to rot without food or shot. Diaries and letters from survivors express the extreme fear they felt of the occupying authorities. Fantasies abounded among the Allies, including plans to force the POWs into slave labor camps and to reduce Germany to a pre-industrial condition to punish it for its war crimes.[33]

The Nazi experience was one in which the regime terrorized its opponents to an extraordinary degree. Those who were selected for repression and death were guilty only of being the object of a vast imagination of paranoia by officials who were never secure in their authority. The terror was necessary as state policy as a means to fortify that vulnerable sense of legitimacy. That is why the list of targets was infinitely expansive, and virtually limitless in its range of categories. The millions, primarily Jews, who perished in labor and death camps across Germany and occupied Poland are salient testament to the ultimate tragedy of the Nazi regime's dependency on policies of excessive state terror. The immensity of the violence, memorialized within the singular terms of Shoah and Holocaust, still defies efforts to place its horrors within the rational and moral framework of a modern, civilized society.

At the same time, those who were denounced as enemies of the Reich, whether real or imagined for the purposes of maintaining the regime's authority, had a strange and unacknowledged power to terrorize the state that so cruelly punished them. The fantasy of the Aryan future was the unrealizable goal that every threat had to be violently extinguished, and done so completely, no matter how many millions of lives were involved. That form of terror could only end with the demise of the regime itself.

State terror in the Stalin era

Meanwhile, the Soviet Union, so feared by governments across the Western world, spent the decade of the 1930s mainly engaged in massive forms of political terror within its own borders. Analyses of this period, dominated as it was by the supremacy of Stalin and his trusted circle, have understandably emphasized the violence of the state

---

[33] See the recent study by MacDonagh, *After the Reich*, esp. 78–9, 342–4, 392–428.

over all other aspects of daily life. Among scholars, disputes have erupted over the years as to exactly how many victims there were, how to categorize them, and the ways in which the Soviet terror resembled or differed from its Nazi counterpart in Germany.[34] Some specialists of the period have tried to show that many, and perhaps most, Soviet citizens lived relatively normal lives, even during the worst excesses of the arrests and executions.[35]

Nevertheless, there is no denying the reality of the utilization of violence as a matter of state policy. From the moment Lenin and the Bolsheviks assumed power at the end of October 1917, debates raged over how to deal with the perceived threats to the new regime. One version was recorded by I. N. Steinberg, a former commissar who joined the first Bolshevik administration along with other Left Socialist Revolutionaries and even a number of anarchists, all of whom were enthusiastic supporters of the revolution at the time. Among the many disagreements that soon broke out among the factions, one of the most divisive was the matter of establishing a department responsible for exercising "revolutionary justice" against those who opposed the government. Lenin's argument was that victory could not be assured "without the cruelest revolutionary terror." When Steinberg asked, with evident sarcasm and resignation, "Then why do we bother with a Commissariat of Justice? Let's call it frankly the *Commissariat for Social Extermination* and be done with it," Lenin replied, according to Steinberg's memoir, "Well put ... that's exactly what it should be ... but we can't say that."[36]

There is little dispute over the fact that this program of state repression was firmly in place over the next two decades, based on the foundational elements established by Lenin and his commissars. To be sure, there was a pretense of supporting the principle of justice through public trials. However, the nature of those trials was rarely in doubt,

---

[34] One epicenter of these debates over the number of victims is the differential analysis in Conquest, *The Great Terror* and Getty and Manning, *Stalinist Terror*. The comparison between the police states in Germany and Russia in the 1930s has stirred contradictory responses from Hannah Arendt's founding study, *The Origins of Totalitarianism*, to the more recent book by Michael Geyer, *Beyond Totalitarianism: Stalinism and Nazism Compared*.

[35] See Robert Thurston's book, *Life and Terror in Stalin's Russia* in which he quotes from the early correspondence of Alexander Solzhenitsyn, who seemed blissfully unaware of the denunciatory drama orchestrated from the Kremlin.

[36] Steinberg, *In the Workshop of the Revolution*, 145.

and they actually had greater similarities with the ruthless revolutionary tribunals of the French Terror in 1793–4 than they did to any court
system sponsored by the postwar republics in Europe or the US. After
Stalin consolidated power, he developed an even more extreme version
of preordained trial outcomes, as the lists of the state's enemies
expanded exponentially along with the number of suspects sentenced
either to execution or to hard labor in the Siberian gulag system.

That said, there were also examples of participants in the
political violence in Soviet Russia who are harder to categorize as either
simply supporters or opponents of the regime. Moreover, the shifts and
struggles that exemplify their careers tell us something of the more
neglected currents of the time. Indeed, they illuminate a particular
characteristic of so many of the participants in this revolutionary era,
namely a continual shifting of self-identity. More than merely adopting
a new *nom de guerre*, they literally repeatedly reinvented themselves, in
part to find a way to keep pace with the shifting sands of the transformative political situation that they tried so desperately to influence.
The role of violence, however, remained a constant presence.

Boris Savinkov was one prominent case in point. He began as a
prominent SR terrorist during the height of the violence directed
against the tsarist regime in the 1905 revolutionary period. Among
his many "actions," he was responsible for the high-profile assassinations of Prime Minister von Plehve and Grand Duke Alexander. He
was arrested and imprisoned but escaped and fled to France. After the
collapse of the tsarist regime in February 1917, he returned to Russia
and sufficiently transformed himself into a statesman to be appointed
Deputy Minister of War in Kerensky's Provisional Government. After
the October seizure of power by the Bolsheviks, Savinkov became a
strong opponent of the Bolsheviks, actively fomenting resistance to
Soviet power during the Civil War.

He turned up later in Poland during the Red Army's invasion in
1920 organizing defense groups and also spent considerable time trav-
eling throughout Europe, speaking with statesmen and politicians
about the dangers posed by the authoritarian regime in Moscow.
A few years later, he switched dramatically again, claiming loyalty to
the Soviet state after being betrayed by a comrade who inveigled him to
return to Soviet Russia to confront his destiny. He was arrested, but the
party leadership was divided on whether to trust him or prosecute him.
Stalin argued strongly for executing him. After a special trial, he was

sentenced to death, but that was commuted to a ten-year prison term. While in detention in the notorious Lubianka prison, Savinkov mysteriously found a way to leap from a prison window to his death on May 7, 1925. His biographers still express doubts over whether this was a political murder or a suicide.[37]

Another case of the reinvented revolutionary personality involved with political violence in Russia is that of Victor Serge. Born in Brussels as Victor Lvovich Kibalchich, Serge inherited a familial terrorist myth of political martyrdom. His uncle was N. I. Kibalchich, who was sentenced to death in 1881 at the trial of the Executive Committee of People's Will in St Petersburg. Fearing arrest because of his own involvement in the anti-tsarist underground, Serge's father moved his family to Brussels, where his son Victor grew up. In his insightful memoir, Serge describes the influence of his uprooted family life, his search to create coherence out of the reality of his radical family values and the difficulties of realizing these fantastic dreams of structural transformation. Serge's initial foray into the world of the political opposition occurred when he was 15. While working as an apprentice at a photographic plant in Brussels, one of his close friends was arrested, charged with being "an anarchist gangster" and executed.[38]

Serge was deeply influenced by the violent exploits of the Socialist Revolutionary Party in Russia in the years surrounding the 1905 revolution, and decided to move to Paris because of the many legendary Russian revolutionaries who either had been, or were at that time, working there as political exiles to undermine the Russian government from afar. Once in Paris, however, he abandoned the socialist-populist ideology of the Russian movement and instead responded to the charismatic appeals of the transnational anarchist revolutionaries. He joined the notorious Bonnot Gang whose members brazenly confronted the police in gun battles, robbed the wealthy in the name of the suffering masses, and

---

[37] See Spence, *Boris Savinkov: Renegade on the Left*, 355, 357 and Wedziagolski, *Boris Savinkov: Portrait of a Terrorist*, xxvii. Also relevant is his own book: Boris Savinkov, *Memoirs of a Terrorist* and the documents in Savinkov, *Vospominaniia*. He also published the novel, *Pale Rider* (1909), which remains one of the most vivid and tense fictional descriptions of an insurgent terrorist cell in action.

[38] Serge, *Memoirs of a Revolutionary, 1901–1941*, 8–9.

pioneered the use of the first generation of motorized vehicles to launch insurgent attacks and rapid escapes.

Following a jail term for these activities, Serge, now inspired by the transformation of political authority in Russia, went to his father's homeland, where he hoped to participate in the Bolshevik experiment. The anarchist in Paris reinvented himself to accommodate the ideology of Soviet Marxism as interpreted in Petrograd in 1918–19. He quickly found himself involved in irresolvable political conflicts. To be sure, he was on personal terms with prominent writers like Maxim Gorky, and his association with Grigorii Zinoviev led to his appointment as a leading journalist for the newly established Communist International. Nevertheless, he retained his critical stance against state authority and disagreed openly with Trotsky over the latter's justification for the Red Terror. Finally, facing the defeat of Trotsky's Left Opposition and Stalin's ascent to the position of supreme leadership, Serge was expelled from the party in 1928, arrested and imprisoned but allowed to emigrate in 1936.[39] Serge was forced to confront the fact that his utopian vision of fusing anarchism with Bolshevism had been crushed by a far more powerful socialist fantasy supported by Stalin's unrelenting use of violence in the service of enforcing his authority.

There were, of course, significant individuals playing out the policies of state violence that turned Savinkov against the revolutionary regime and that so appalled Serge. From the very start of the Bolshevik era, Feliks Edmundovich Dzerzhinskii was at the top of this administration of terror as a result of his being appointed to head a special branch for state security, the All-Russian Extraordinary Commission for the Struggle against Counter-Revolution and Sabotage, known by its Russian acronym, the Cheka.[40] There certainly were real threats to the Bolshevik acquisition of power, including the attempted assassination of Lenin, the conspiracies of a host of political parties hostile to Bolshevism on any level that spiraled into a full-scale civil war, and the

[39] In addition to Serge's *Memoir*, see his critiques of Stalinism in *From Lenin to Stalin* and *Russia Twenty Years After*, both of which contain valuable information on the "Soviet Anarchists" who sought a similar accommodation with Bolshevism. He also published a number of penetrating political novels based on his political experiences; among the most memorable are *Conquered City* (1932), *The Case of Comrade Tulayev* (1949) and *The Unforgiving Years* (1971). The best biography in English is Weissman, *Victor Serge*.

[40] The name comes from a combination of the first syllables of the Russian words for Extraordinary Commission.

widespread chaos of criminal social disorders in the absence of coherent and stable authority at the local levels. All this was in addition to the rumors that turned into reality when the Anglo-American Expeditionary Force invaded Soviet territory to overthrow the Bolshevik government.[41] To battle against these challenges to Bolshevik legitimacy, the Cheka was called into being in 1918 with Dzerzhinskii as its chief officer.[42]

Dzerzhinskii was never a theorist. He was steeled in the cause of Marxism, according to his own personal account, by the tsarist regime's inhumane treatment of its political opponents as well as of the Russian people. His diary entries and letters to his wife while in tsarist prisons, years before he could even imagine he would later become the head of that very prison system in its Bolshevik incarnation, are dominated by his efforts to convince himself of the need to survive, and "the righteousness of our cause." He was capable, however, of envisioning a utopian future with which he could emotionally identify: "I visualize the vast masses now coming into action and shattering the old system ... I am proud that I, one of them, see, feel, and understand them and that I and they have suffered much."[43]

Once in power, his discipline and commitment dominated every policy he established for his subordinates in the expanding security agency, as evidenced by his early directives. One of these declared that there existed "no other way to combat counter-revolutionaries, spies, speculators, burglars, hooligans, saboteurs and other parasites than their merciless annihilation at the scene of the crime."[44] When opposition stood in his way, as it did when he was challenged by the Commissar of Justice, the Left SR Isaac Steinberg, Dzerzhinskii went directly to Lenin to force Steinberg out of office. "The Cheka is not a court of law," he proclaimed at the dismissal meeting. "The Cheka is the defense of the revolution, as is the Red Army ... The Cheka must

[41] A recent study based on new archival information places renewed emphasis on policing the problems of crime, massive law-breaking activities and population control as critical in understanding the origins of the Stalinist era of terror. See Hagenloh, *Stalin's Police*. In a related archival study, Sheila Fitzpatrick has demonstrated the huge role of public denunciations as a dynamic force in the trajectory of terror in her book, *Tear Off the Masks: Identity and Imposture in Twentieth Century Russia*.
[42] The decree forming the Cheka can be found in Lenin, "To Comrade Dzerzhinskii," 156–8.
[43] Dzherzhinskii, *Dnevnik. Pis'ma k rodnym*, 17–18. This diary notation is dated December 31, 1908.
[44] McDaniel, "Political Assassination and Mass Execution," 243.

protect the revolution and annihilate the enemy – even if its sword should by chance descend on the heads of the innocent."[45]

Another episode in the contestation over the survival of the Bolshevik regime that emerged soon after the revolution centered on the charges leveled against the British Vice-Consul in Moscow, Bruce Lockhart, in 1918. Lockhart was arrested, accused and sentenced to death for his alleged participation in a conspiracy to assassinate Lenin. The official who headed the case for the government was Iakov K. Peters, a member of Dzerzhinskii's All-Russian Cheka Presidium, the branch of the administration responsible for setting police policy for the district Cheka units in other cities. Lockhart, in his memoir, describes his experiences in the Lubianka prison where he joined the first prisoners assigned to be executed according to the recently established policies of the Red Terror. He managed to have conversations with some of them, and learned that they covered the spectrum from ordinary "bandits" to members of the clergy and, above all, opposition political activists. Lockhart was also important enough to be interrogated by Peters himself, who, interestingly, bared a bit of his own soul to his prisoner. Like so many Bolsheviks struggling at the time to remain in power, Peters related how his rage against the *Ancien Régime* was forged in a Riga prison where he had been sentenced for revolutionary activities. More than anything else, he recalled the periods when he had been tortured by the authorities, and displayed his stunted fingernails that had been ripped off his fingers at that time. Yet, here he was now carrying out similar policies against those opposing his government's authority. In response, "he told me that he suffered physical pain every time he signed a death sentence." To make sense of this, Lockhart believed that he was speaking to a man with a divided personality. On the one hand, Peters possessed "a strong streak of sentimentality in his nature, but he was a fanatic as far as the clash between Bolshevism and Capitalism was concerned, and he pursued his Bolshevik aims with a sense of duty which was relentless," Lockhart concluded.[46]

---

[45] Steinberg, *In the Workshop of the Revolution*, 226.
[46] Lockhart, *Memoirs of a British Agent*, 328. For Peters' account, see Peters, "Vospominaniia o rabote v VChK v pervyi god revoliutsii," 5–32. Lockhart was eventually freed in an exchange with Britain, where the Soviet diplomat Maxim Litvinov had been arrested in a reprisal. This was the first such high-level prisoner exchange, in what would become a practice that lasted over six decades of conflict between the West and the USSR. For a recent and objective account of the central events of the Lockhart Affair, see Rabinowitch, *The Bolsheviks in Power*, 322–3, 335–6, 338–9.

The ruthlessness with which Lenin and his commissars dealt with those they believed were state enemies continued without respite during the transitional 1920s. The security agency responsible for protecting the political order changed its name over the course of the decades of Soviet power – the Cheka morphed into the NKVD (People's Commissariat for Internal Affairs), which in turn shifted through other appellations into its final Soviet title, the KGB (Committee for State Security). Its chiefs also changed each time one of them was eliminated, but the victims of the violence found little change whether it was Nikolai Ezhov, Lavrenty Beria or any of the others who headed the agency.

Students of the Stalinist era of state terror have debated how to count these victims. Should the huge numbers of people who starved to death during the famine in the Ukrainian Republic of the USSR in 1932–3 be included? Should the prisoners who died in the Gulag camps be considered in the same category as those who were condemned to death by tribunals across the country and then executed by firing squad? What about the massive deportations to Central Asia and the Soviet Far East, as well as the destruction wrought in the countryside during the violent "collectivization campaign" in 1930 against the kulak peasantry?[47] All of this preceded what has come to be known as "The Great Terror" of 1937–8, when the last of the prominent Old Bolsheviks were condemned to death after confessing their crimes against the party and the nation, some in full view of members of the international press, who were permitted to selectively cover these sensational trials. Nevertheless, in whatever way the numbers are put together, we end up with statistics in the millions.[48]

In most instances of modern political violence involving states and societies, the media play an important role. In the Soviet era, when newspapers were entirely removed from private ownership and controlled by the state, the portrayal of terrorism was unidirectional and extreme. Throughout the first decades of the consolidation of power in

[47] See Werth, "The Crimes of the Stalin Regime: Outline for an Inventory Classification," 400–19 and also Werth's "The Mechanism of a Mass Crime," 215–39.
[48] For recent data on the victims, see Getty, *The Road to Terror*, 241–5 and Goldman, *Terror and Democracy in the Age of Stalin*, 1–2, 5, both of which have rich bibliographic references to explore. As a contrast, the satirical scene in Lev Kuleshov's film, *The Extraordinary Adventures of Mr. West in the Land of the Bolsheviks* (1924), in which he presents a mock trial of the gullible visitor from America conducted by a group of Bolsheviks made to look like cannibalistic barbarians would have been unthinkable in such an atmosphere.

Moscow, the national newspaper of the ruling Communist Party, *Pravda* (with its Orwellian title: Truth), hammered away at the theme of internal threats to the country. While, on the one hand, the danger was portrayed as never ceasing and always lurking below in the shadows of ordinary people, on the other, the nation was constantly reassured that the security organs of the party were in constant and victorious battle with these "wreckers," "saboteurs" and outright "traitors." The atmosphere that this created was one of perpetual vigilance and anxiety. As one scholar has put it, "readers were to see that they could be safe from terror with no one, in no place, at no time. Their fear was to be boundless."[49]

This constant menace thus required not only the participation of ordinary citizens but also the ruthlessly protective actions accorded the police to achieve what was described incessantly as "the liquidation of terrorists." All Soviet citizens were in this way enjoined daily to participate collectively in the struggle against opponents of the proletarian state. The judgment of the Party was not publically questioned or seriously criticized, for to do so was to risk being identified as part of the problem. Yet, the criteria for assessing threats were continually changing and were often extremely vague. The less clear the directives were, the more inclusive they could become. Witness the following document from a local collective farm official who was trying to master the linguistic jargon of Bolshevism as well as to find favor for denouncing the enemies in his midst: "It is not a *kolkhoz* [collective farm] but a nest of gentry and gendarmes ... Degenerate elements have wormed their way onto the *kolkhoz* board ... We are now waging war against the grabbers ... Revolutionary legality was brazenly violated ... He took the path of terror ... An incorrigible opportunist and hidden Trotskyite ... This handful of *kulak* holdouts ... White-guardists, Trotskyites and wreckers."[50]

The result was the establishment of a permanent policy of state violence that was normalized as the first response to any form of resistance to the political order. The fact that the government in the Soviet Union felt the need to resort to violence as matter of official state policy reflects the pervasive insecurity of the ruling party. Stalin and his associates had little trust in their own citizenry. At the same time, everyone's nightmare was that the notorious Black Marias would pull

[49] Young, "Terror in *Pravda*," 180.   [50] Fitzpatrick, *Tear Off the Masks*, 171.

up to their apartments in the dead of night and police storm up the stairs to carry out orders for the arrest and disappearance of a member of the family. For the regime, the permanent fear was rooted in an incessant inability to define what appeared to be a limitless stream of potential opponents whom they had to ruthlessly repress. There was a certain amount of realism to the Stalinists' fears. There were cases of recalcitrant factory workers, embittered peasants after the violence of the collectivization campaign, students who wrote and distributed pamphlets criticizing the party's policies at various times, and continual intrigues within the party leadership.[51] Also, as many memoirs have shown, privately, in kitchens and during outdoor walks in the snow, devastating criticism of the party's authoritarianism was voiced among trusted friends that could never be put into print.

There is perhaps no better example of the insecurities of power than Stalin's fear of the criticism of poets. At least since the time of Pushkin, the written word, particularly when penned by poets, had a reverence in Russian culture whose authority and charisma are difficult to transmit out of its context. Once invited to write odes to the tsars in past centuries, during Stalin's time, some poets found it necessary to take the incredible risks involved either by overtly speaking against the ruler or manifesting their opposition in coded language. Anna Akhmatova and Boris Pasternak spent a good part of their creative years terrorized by the regime that constantly sought various ways to curb their daring creativity.

They, however, managed to live out their lives in spite of the repressive obstacles placed in their way. The case of the extraordinary poet, Osip Mandelstam, is another matter. In an unguarded moment, at a reading in 1933 at his apartment of a poem he had recently composed, one of his guests reported to the Kremlin security personnel the content of the verse, which enraged Stalin to the degree that Mandelstam was arrested, confined, and ultimately sent to the gulag, where he died in 1940 after being tortured and left to languish in the brutal Siberian winter. The poem, hardly subtle, which so threatened Stalin that he essentially condemned the poet to death, reads as follows:

> We live not knowing the country beneath us
> At ten feet away you can't hear the sound
> Of any words but "the wild man in the Kremlin,

[51] Getty, *The Road to Terror*, 233.

slayer of peasants and soul-strangling gremlin."
Each thick finger of his is as fat as a worm,
To his ten-ton words we all have to listen
His cockroach whiskers flicker and squirm
and his shining thigh-boots shimmer and glisten...
At each execution he belches his best.
This Caucasian hero with his broad Ossetian chest.[52]

The manner in which Stalin dealt with the legacy of Vladimir Mayakovsky presents another variant on the theme of literary terrorism. Mayakovsky, like Mandelstam, was a gifted poet with an ambivalent attitude toward literary conformity and the shift toward authoritarian party sovereignty in spite of his initial post-revolutionary enthusiasm. After Mayakovsky's suicide in 1930, Stalin established a hagiographic interpretation of his career that was highly selective in what it emphasized. To heighten and enforce the sense of fear among Soviet writers, he went so far as to proclaim a law in 1935 that made opposition as well as demonstrative indifference to the official Mayakovsky canon a crime against the state.[53]

This war against poets and writers was another aspect of the mood of uncertainty that pervaded the Kremlin. Unable to achieve the framework of a legitimate system of authority acceptable to the rank and file of the social order, Stalin and his political intimates were driven to continually invent new enemies of the state, and to terrorize them into loyal submission. In time, the regime grew dependent on them because it needed threatening opponents to stabilize its own power, in the absence of a genuinely representative legal system. The mistrust and anxiety that the party leadership felt toward its citizenry was, to some extent, a projection of its own sense of instability and questionable legitimacy, and policies of terror were its effort to master and control these fears. In the words of one scholar of this period, "what particularly distinguished the Bolsheviks is the extent to which

---

[52] Quoted in Boym, *Another Freedom*, 69. The Russian critic Benedict Sarnov wrote that "Stalin knew perfectly well that the opinion future generations would have of him depended to a large degree on what poets wrote about him." Quoted in Prieto, "Reading Mandelstam on Stalin," 68–72, where the Mandelstam poem is commented on exhaustively, with special attention to the meaning of the words the poet chose.

[53] See the discussion in Urbaszweski, "Canonizing the 'Best, Most Talented' Soviet Poet," 635–66, esp. 652, and 664, fn. 81 for the evidence.

they turned tools originally intended for total war to the new ends of revolutionary politics."[54] To convince Soviet citizens that the promise of their utopian political fantasy of a classless society had a realistic basis, all weapons at the disposal of the regime were necessary.

Moreover, although the portrait of the future was painted in terms of inevitability, this was a war without either a foreseeable or predictable end in terms of timing. As the head of the state, Stalin was certainly responsible for the level of violence maintained, but it could not have functioned without loyal subordinates. In fact, the terror was facilitated by a wide network of people, all of whom had a specific interest in the repression in terms of their own professional advancement, maintaining job security, removing competition for their posts, or simply revenge for past actions directed against them. Fears of losing control or being targeted themselves led many to support the unifying cult around Stalin and the widening boundary of intolerance for alternative perspectives.

The disorderliness of the period suggests that the regime could not have known in advance what its future policies would be, in spite of its explicit commitment to Marxist eschatology. One after another, policy decisions were reversed due to the disapproval of results. War Communism was officially replaced in 1921 by the New Economic Policy, which in turn was ended after widespread criticism. Stalin's program of massive national industrialization in the Five Year Plans was set in motion in 1928. The following winter, the excessively violent campaign of collectivization was ordered, with Red Guard squads assaulting kulaks in the countryside, but then was suddenly halted by Stalin in the spring of 1930 with his ironically titled "Dizzy with Success" article in *Pravda* that mainly covered up the widespread and counterproductive rural violence. Satisfied that the two goals of seizing grain believed to have been hoarded by peasants seeking profits, and expropriating the remaining areas of private landholding, had been sufficiently realized, Stalin did not end the use of political violence, but shifted it to other targets with the intention of achieving other goals. These included rapid turnover in the party's ranks, to maintain control from the top. Officials at various levels were hired, promoted and then arrested and executed within the space of a few years, in many instances. Also, left and right factions within the ruling Communist

[54] Holquist, "Violent Russia, Deadly Marxism?," 651.

Party, which had been declared the only legal party in the country in 1921, were initially supported, permitting instances of interesting political and economic debate. This, however, was followed by a period of support for one over the other. Finally, Stalin had both eliminated prior to the purge trials of 1937–8, where many "Old Bolsheviks" were falsely charged with having committed crimes against the state, and executed. What mattered, as it turned out, was not what they had actually done or even why, but rather how those actions were being interpreted at the present moment of judgment.

The terror continued to find new victims. During the Second World War, Stalin mobilized a Jewish Anti-Fascist Committee that was permitted to establish a very public international presence as a rallying force for allies globally to join with the Soviet Union in defeating Nazi Germany. After the war, he ruthlessly suppressed them. His purpose had been achieved, and now that the war was over, he feared that such a group, tainted by its involvement with "capitalist contacts" developed during the war years with many Jewish members abroad, could turn into an independent faction with questionable loyalty to his authority.[55]

While these lurches seemed to consolidate increasing authority for Stalin and his frequently changing security chiefs, and certainly brought untold tragedy to the victims and their families, the shifts also made visible a deep sense of "nervousness, indecision and even frequent panic" that lay beneath the public face of optimism and ideological righteousness.[56] This unease was not Stalin's alone but affected the choices made by members of the Central Committee, the Politburo, district party secretaries and the entire bureaucracy. Everyone could easily be persuaded to imagine the enemies threatening their positions, and identify with the need to consolidate ranks around the directives from the Kremlin, no matter how repressive they were. Stalin's fantasy

---

[55] The committee initially included prominent Jewish intellectuals such as Ilya Ehrenburg and Solomon Mikhoels. Mikhoels was sent to the US to mobilize support there for the Soviet war effort. After the war, the committee members sought to publish material on anti-Semitism and made appeals to Stalin for cooperation. In 1948, Mikhoels was killed in a car accident widely believed to have been ordered by Stalin. In 1952, 13 former members of the disbanded Anti-Fascist Committee were executed for anti-Soviet activities. See Redlich, *Propaganda and Nationalism in Wartime Russia*.

[56] The phrase is from Getty, *The Road to Terror*, 236. For a discussion of further recent research on the Stalin terror, see the forum by Hagenloh, "Terror and the Gulag," and Khlevniuk, "The Stalinist Police State," 627–48.

was to forge his own image as a charismatic leader directing the forces of a powerful communist nation loyal to his will, with dreams of international triumph over the capitalist world. This of course proved impossible to realize. After years in the prerevolutionary underground, living outside the law, with no experience of governance, Stalin and his supporters brought their suspicions and insecurities with them when they came to power in 1917. The ideology of Marxism-Leninism, as interpreted by Stalin in the late 1930s, never succeeded in providing the legitimacy necessary to relax the dynamic of terrorism in state policy.

Perhaps only in literature can we find a truly insightful portrayal of the ordinariness and comprehensiveness of such situations of violence and terror. Vasily Grossman in his last novel, *Forever Flowing*, was virtually obsessed with trying to fathom how it was that both state and society were so complicit in normalizing and legitimizing political crimes in Stalin's time. For Grossman, those who denounced were full participants in the violence, helping the prosecutors fill up the prison cells, the labor camps and the execution sites, all in the name of public security. Most did not think they were committing acts of evil, and most also went to work and ate meals after they reported to the authorities.

> *"Yes," Grossman concludes in his analysis of a fictional trial scene, "yes, they are not guilty; they were forced to it by grim, gloomy, leaden forces, and trillions of tons of pressure were put upon them, and among the living there is no one who is innocent. All are guilty, including you Comrade Prosecutor, and you, defendant, and I, who am considering the defendant, the prosecutor and the judge. But how shamed and how pained we must remain, face to face with our human indecency, unworthiness, obscenity!"*[57]

---

[57] Grossman, *Forever Flowing*, 83. The novel was originally published posthumously in 1970 in Russian; the author, who died in 1964, left this MS as his searing, bitterly critical testament to the failed dreams of his terrorized, socialist-inspired generation.

8 GLOBAL IDEOLOGICAL TERROR DURING THE COLD WAR

The Second World War left in its wake a worldwide disorientation, having revealed the destructive power of nation states on an unprecedented scale. Nothing in the violent past of governments had ever even approached the statistics of mass killings and deportations, in addition to the even larger numbers of physically maimed and psychologically traumatized victims of that war. There are many iconic images that recall the shock of the violence, but among the most infamous remain the firebombing of civilian urban centers like Dresden and Hamburg, the complete devastation resulting from the atomic explosions at Hiroshima and Nagasaki, and the emaciated survivors of the Nazi death camps.[1]

This period also saw, by contrast, a reduction in the number of regimes collapsing, compared to the situation at the close of the Great War.[2] At that time, the defeat and collapse of several major empires had signaled the disappearance of governments across the European continent. In the void created by the vanishing of the Romanov, Ottoman, German and Austro-Hungarian imperial regimes, the victorious allied powers created entirely new states at the postwar Versailles conference in 1919, including Poland (an independent country for the first time since being partitioned among Russia, Austria and Prussia at the end of the eighteenth century), Czechoslovakia, Hungary, Yugoslavia,

---

[1] The numbing statistics of victims have been comprehensively calculated in Rummel, *Death by Government*. See also Snyder, *Bloodlands* for some of the most recent revelations about the war's devastation.
[2] Fazal, *State Death*.

Austria, and the Weimar republic, all of which were vulnerable because they had to consolidate their newly established political legitimacies.

One of the singular achievements of the discussions at Versailles in 1919 was the establishment of the League of Nations, an age-old dream of an institutional framework for resolving international disputes peacefully through negotiations, rather than war. Among its many initiatives, a diplomatic conference met under its auspices in November 1937 to adopt a draft treaty proposing a "Convention for the Prevention and Punishment of Terrorism." The treaty required nation states to individually criminalize terrorist acts and take appropriate measures to identify and judicially deal with them on a case-by-case basis. Twenty-four nations signed up, including 12 from Europe, which led to further meetings. The transcriptions detail the efforts made to consider terrorism as "a special moral crime" and as an international threat, and proposals for prosecution and extradition to facilitate the trial proceedings at an international criminal court. Although much of the discussions focused on acts of violence against governments, there was a draft article proposing the need to consider "terrorist outrages committed by agents of a State," which, if proven guilty of responsibility, should then "be liable for punishment." Eventually, the discussions broke down as the representatives of the participating nations refused to relinquish their sovereign authority to a transnational body. There is evidence, nevertheless, that these important conceptions did have an impact at the Geneva Convention in 1949 and also at a number of productive debates at the United Nations.[3]

The delegates to the postwar Versailles conference cannot be faulted for proposing solutions to the problems plaguing international affairs. However, much criticism has emerged as to how appropriate and effective their model was for replacing the fallen empires with new nationality-based states, as well as the Middle East mandates that many viewed as holdovers from the colonial era. Similar intentions were at work once again at the postwar discussions in 1945. Once the Axis powers had surrendered unconditionally to the Allied command and codified the terms in postwar agreements, the triumphant alliance splintered into disagreements between the Soviet Union and the West.[4] Although this is usually considered the period in which the Cold War

---

[3] Saul, "The Legal Response of the League of Nations to Terrorism," 78–102.
[4] See the comprehensive treatment in Judt, *Postwar: A History of Europe since 1945*.

came into existence, in fact it signaled a resumption of the tensions and antagonisms that had dominated much of Great Power diplomacy and strategy since the initial appearance of the "Bolshevik menace" in 1917. Nevertheless, it is virtually impossible to discuss the problems of political violence, whether on the national or international levels, without making reference to the implacable hostility and suspicion that existed after 1945 between what became enshrined as the communist and the free worlds. One country after another, on continent after continent, found itself forced to choose sides. Both sides offered attractive rewards for joining up, and the stakes were high. Once committed, that country was considered a lost nation by the other side, no longer trustworthy, and subject to vilification, censorship and exclusion.

Congo and Algeria

The African continent, with its stirrings of liberation from colonial rule, became one significant area of contestation in the Cold War rivalry, with elements of terrorism always in evidence. The Congo, long Belgium's colonial resource, declared independence in 1960 and elected Patrice Lumumba as its political leader. Internal conflicts raged, eventually consuming Lumumba himself. Although there remains a good deal of unresolved controversy about his demise, it is clear that he was supported by the Soviet Union and considered a political liability by Allen Dulles, head of the CIA. After being forcibly removed from office, Lumumba was executed on January 17, 1961 by Belgian mercenaries and local Congolese opponents, with the tacit permission of the American authorities, who saw this act as a victory in preventing the Soviet Union from gaining control over the rich mineral resources of the Congo.[5]

An even more dramatic story, with far greater implications for future developments in the spread of political violence, had been taking place in Algeria at that time. From 1954 to 1962, a brutal campaign of reciprocal terror dominated the country, with its central cauldron in the capital city, Algiers. The French, who had governed Algeria since the early nineteenth century, were determined to maintain it as an integral part of the nation. The most devastating terror from above was carried out by the Organisation de l'Armée Secrète (OAS), which, under the

[5] For an analysis, see de Witte, *The Assassination of Lumumba*.

command of General Jacques Massu, carried out a massive campaign of repression, torture and executions with the full cooperation of the notorious police chief, Maurice Papon.

Struggling against this hegemony, members of the Algerian National Liberation Front (FLN) made use of every weapon at their disposal to end what they understood as a continuation of the colonial occupation of their country. Tens of thousands of people, mostly Algerians, died in the struggle for independence, which was finally achieved in 1962 when General Charles de Gaulle negotiated the Evian Accords to end the presence of French political authority there.[6] It was a battle that revealed examples of "exceptional cruelty" on both sides of the combat lines.[7] Both the FLN and the OAS were masters of the process of dehumanization, seeing each other more as beasts than as people. At the same time, the French proclaimed themselves as representatives of the "free world" against the threatening socialist forces of the Algerian resistance, who, according to Massu, could not have put up such a battle without inspiration and aid from Moscow.[8]

The Algerian rebellion found perhaps its most eloquent and influential interpreter in the person of Frantz Fanon. Born in the French colony of Martinique, he was educated in France, where he studied medicine and did a residency in psychiatry before deciding to accept a position at the Blida-Joinville Hospital in Algiers in 1953. Although he clearly sympathized with the nascent National Liberation Front, he accepted for treatment in his hospital both French and Algerian patients who had suffered psychological traumas and disorders from the violence.[9] Once the authorities learned of his sympathies for the FLN, in 1957 he was expelled from Algeria and spent the next several years mainly in Tunis where he became an important advocate of the emerging colonial resistance in Africa. Although the French attempted several times to kill him, he ultimately died of leukemia in 1961.

---

[6] The classic account remains Horne, *A Savage War of Peace*.
[7] The phrase is from Thomas, Moore and Butler, *Crisis of Empire*, 205.
[8] On this linkage, see Connelly, *A Diplomatic Revolution*.
[9] His "case studies" are detailed in Fanon, "Colonial War and Mental Disorders," *Wretched of the Earth*, 181–233. Though compelling, persuasive and even prophetic in various ways, his diagnostic categories of psychiatric illnesses have never been included in the profession's textbooks. The reasons given are that they are unscientific in that they have never been duplicated in other studies, and because they are seen to be unacceptably ideological in orientation, rather than objective findings.

Fanon's opening essay in one of his most influential books, *Wretched of the Earth*, has become one of the foundational texts in the history of modern insurgent terrorism. In the essay "On Violence," Fanon's justification for the use of the tactics of terrorism goes beyond Karl Heinzen's position of a century earlier. Whereas Heinzen moved the discourse from the utility of killing a tyrannical ruler to validating a frontal assault against the state's brutality, Fanon turned his attention to the psychological motivation for, and collective benefit of, employing violence against the regime. For Fanon, the evil to be eradicated, which was responsible for the wretchedness of the Algerians' lives, was the colonial occupation under which they lived. "Europe's well being and progress were built with the sweat and corpses of blacks, Arabs, Indians, and Asians," then historically frozen in place by the regime's "sweeping powers of coercion," he wrote. Europe could never have achieved its supremacy without "plundering the underdeveloped peoples." For too many centuries, he continues, "capitalists behaved like war criminals," making use of "deportation, massacres, forced labor and slavery" in order to extract valuable minerals and precious metals with the complicity of their governments.[10]

Fanon delves into the motives of the colonized natives in order to both portray and legitimate their arousal to rebellion. After so many years of repression and restriction, they had come to realize that there were essentially three choices available to them. First, they could continue to passively accept the status quo, hoping that obedient, non-political behavior would at least allow them to have jobs and provide some modicum of food and shelter for their families. Second, they could decide to emigrate and try to live more successfully elsewhere, although the consequences of having the stain of color in a white world would never, Fanon reminds his reader, entirely disappear. Finally, there was the path of resistance, which is what Fanon advocated in order to bring an end to the injustice of the existing system of authority, not only in Algeria, but across the continent of Africa as well.

Here too he paints a portrait of the gradual realization on the part of the native that he possesses righteous indignation against the ruling settlers from France, and that he can act on that sentiment to ameliorate his condition. "When the colonized subject is tortured, when his wife is killed or raped, he complains to no one," because no

[10] Fanon, "On Violence," *Wretched of the Earth*, 53–7.

one will listen. Of all the crimes committed in Algeria, "not a single Frenchman has been brought before a French court of justice for the murder of an Algerian." With all avenues to justice closed, the native turns to justifiable violence. "On the individual level," Fanon writes, "violence is a cleansing force. It rids the colonized of their inferiority complex, of their passive and despairing attitude. It emboldens them, and restores their self-confidence." When enough individuals come to this commitment, "armed struggle for national liberation" becomes necessary, legitimate and in the end, satisfying once victory has been achieved.[11]

Fanon was also deeply aware of the continent-level nature of his critique, and the larger Cold War context of which it was a component part. He wrote of the Sharpeville massacre in apartheid South Africa, as well as of similar atrocities committed by imperialist government troops and their surrogates in Madagascar, Morocco and Kenya, which permitted him to conceptualize a pan-African liberation struggle. Moreover, he was cognizant of the impact of the rivalry between the US and the Soviet Union in Africa. From his vantage point as theorist and activist, Fanon saw the role of the US as spreading fears about how, without the protection of regimes in their orbit, "the communists will very likely take advantage of the unrest in order to infiltrate these regions," with "liberation movements masterminded by Moscow."[12] The only legitimate response, according to Fanon, was for the colonized to liberate themselves through violence, and, in the process, to regain their humanity by cleansing themselves of the residue of imperialism.

In spite of Fanon's passionate commitments, there were many aspects of the Algerian terrorist situation that he either was unaware of or chose not to deal with. The responses to the violence were far more complicated and nuanced than the stark dialectic that he described between the forces of victims and oppressors. In reality, there were many divisions on both sides of the struggle. Although a minority in the general population, there were significant numbers of Algerian Muslims who actually fought with the French army. In the aftermath, they suffered the fate of complete outcasts. Those who remained following independence were regarded as traitors by their fellow citizens; those who took refuge in France suffered racism and neglect

[11] Ibid., 49–51.   [12] Ibid., 34–5.

as discarded refugees.[13] Further divisions over the use of terror were rife among the ranks of the FLN, including the assassination of members who tried to find pathways to negotiate a peaceful settlement with President de Gaulle, and severe humiliations imposed upon Muslim women who had been raped by French soldiers during the war. There were also cases in which the French OAS detained and tortured French Algerians suspected of being sympathetic to Algerian independence.[14]

South Africa

The decolonization struggle in South Africa was also fraught with internecine violence that ultimately had an even greater global impact by comparison with Algeria. Just as the French in Algeria continued to believe in the possibility that they could exercise political hegemony there in perpetuity, the South African political fantasy was embedded in the narrative that the white Afrikaans elite would eternally rule over the black majority of the country. Also, not unlike the Algerian case, beneath the regime's very visible and repressive authority lay a deep insecurity and mistrust of the population over which it ruled. The prejudice that informed the moral code of the French authorities was even more starkly evident in South Africa. In both instances, the native population was considered to be a backward, primitive race that operated according to cultural values that were considered well beneath the ethical conduct of the higher civilization that the governing officials presumed to represent.

White settlers began to colonize the territory of the southern African continent as early as the 1650s, coming mainly from Holland and England, although Huguenots fleeing persecution from Catholics in France also established a community there. The disparities between white settlers and black natives were starkly present from the outset of the immigration, providing the foundation for the emergence of the violent racial conflicts of the twentieth century. The Dutch and British communities functioned as separate entities until the Second Boer War

---

[13] Crapanzano, *The Harkis.*
[14] Evans, *Algeria: France's Undeclared War.* For the broader context of these conflicts, see Connelly, *A Diplomatic Revolution.*

(1899–1902). Afrikaner influence remained powerful enough over the course of decades to gradually reverse the situation of local political domination. By the 1950s, the Afrikaner National Party had gained a political majority in Parliament.

The postwar ideology of the state was in large measure a product of the worldview of the Afrikaner *Broederbond*, founded in 1918. The claims to racial superiority of this organization, which developed into a large network of allied groups, were rooted in the desire to create a pathway toward achieving a national identity for the white Dutch immigrants in an alien setting as they competed with the British for control of territory, resources and native labor. Beneath the heroic narrative of struggle that they created lay a host of collective insecurities and a defensive self-portrait, articulated in the framework of a separate culture of hierarchical racial superiority, justified by Biblical references designed to illustrate the project of an advanced Christian civilization.[15] Violence was a crucial ingredient in the realization of this political goal well before there was an official state policy of apartheid. As early as 1922, the South African military forces conducted an aerial bombardment in Bondelzwaarts that resulted in over 100 deaths of blacks native to the region. The bombing, which foreshadowed similar tactics that would dominate the next world war, was a deliberate part of the strategy of enforcing the domination of the white race in the effort to create the dream of a Greater South Africa.[16]

The party leadership quickly mandated a series of laws that created a legal system in 1948 of "separate development" or "apartness," which became known as the apartheid system of institutionalized racism. In 1950, the party legislated the Population Registration Act which essentially classified the entire citizenry of the Republic of South Africa into racial categories as white, black or colored, with the latter referring to people of Asian or mixed Asian-African ancestry. Blacks were required to carry "pass books" which contained, in addition to the usual personal data, fingerprints, photographs, indications of tribal origin and criminal records where relevant. In 1951, the Bantu Authorities Act became law, creating four separate "homelands" for blacks. This had the effect of completely disenfranchising blacks by establishing their rights as solely related to their tribal homelands, and inventing a new class of internal exiles that had to essentially obtain

[15] Bell, *Unfinished Business*, 28.   [16] Mazower, *No Enchanted Palace*, 51.

visas from the government in Pretoria to travel from their homeland to any city or village in South Africa.[17]

Far worse than confronting this repressive legal structure was the physical violence that spread paralyzing fear among the black villages and townships. Physicians examining former prisoners who had been released found huge numbers of injuries from whips, sticks and rifle butts, in addition to evidence on some of electric shocks and humiliating exposures of their bodies to the whims of sadistic guards. Even children were not spared the violence if there was suspicion of their involvement in aiding the opposition.[18] For the regime, the application of violence was a war against terrorism in which it portrayed itself as the victim acting in self-defense, not as the perpetrator of torture and terror.

The repressive power of these racial laws of the Afrikaner state soon called forth a response which took two forms – a resistance emphasizing non-violence, such as the women in the Black Sash group,[19] and another tendency in which violence played the leading role. In 1953, the Public Safety Act and its Criminal Law Amendment were accepted by the South African parliament, which essentially gave standing permission to the government to proclaim states of emergency of unspecified duration and with severe penalties for disobedience. The bloodshed that followed made headlines around the world. In 1960 at Sharpeville, 69 blacks were shot to death for refusing to carry their passes. In 1976, an uprising against the apartheid regime in the Johannesburg black township of Soweto led to the deaths of 575 blacks. A prominent casualty of this carnage was the resistance activist Steve Biko, who, after being wounded in a shootout with police, was tortured and killed a year later by the authorities while in detention.[20]

Further violent protest against policies of apartheid through strikes and sabotage organized by the African National Congress, the

---

[17] On this period, see the following: Greenberg, *Legitimizing the Illegitimate*; Muthien, *State and Resistance in South Africa*; Noval, *Deconstructing Apartheid Discourse*; Posel, *The Making of Apartheid*.

[18] The evidence discussed here can be found in Purdue, *Terrorism and the State*, 93–4. Purdue calls this "institutional terror," pp. 96–7.

[19] The Black Sash movement, founded in 1955 by Jean Sinclair, was a resistance organization of white women who demonstrated against the Pass Laws and the apartheid legal system, and offered counseling to victimized black families. Despite harassment, it functioned until the end of the Afrikaner regime.

[20] Biko, *No Fears Expressed*.

Pan-African Congress and the South African Communist Party all led to enhanced terror on the part of the state. The violence of the insurgents was an integral component of the larger context of South African terrorism. One of the most notorious examples was the Church Street bombing in Pretoria on May 20, 1983. The military faction of the ANC, Umkhonto we Sizwe (Spear of the Nation), carried out a car bombing targeting the central offices of the South African Air Force command center, which was situated on Nedbank Square, a prominent area of the city crowded with pedestrians. The bomb claimed at least 19 victims, all civilians except for two ANC operatives who also died in the huge blast. Over 200 people were wounded, many quite seriously. The ANC claimed that the action was retaliation for the raid conducted the previous December in Lesotho by the South African police in which 42 ANC supporters and party members were shot to death, and also for the assassination of Ruth First, anti-apartheid activist and wife of South African Communist Party leader Joe Slovo, that month by the security forces in Maputo, Mozambique.

Indeed, these struggles too, like those in Algeria and the Congo, could not escape the bipolar tensions of the Cold War. To be sure, the racial ideology that characterized the legal system under all South African prime ministers, had its roots in the earlier, formative years before the National Party took control. Nevertheless, there is little doubt that the apartheid administrators saw themselves engaged in a virtuous, defensive struggle against the infusion of Soviet influence via the South African Communist Party, and against the growing influence of the American civil rights movements, also viewed as communist-inspired, which provided additional evidence of the grave threat posed by blacks seeking their rights as equal citizens with whites.

The Robben Island prison near Cape Town, one of the world's most notorious at the time, was filled to capacity with arrested blacks forced to endure decades of hard labor, abuse and torture.[21] What took place there over the decades of confinement reveals yet another example of interactive relationships between officials of the state and

---

[21] Nelson Mandela was imprisoned on Robben Island after his arrest in 1963 and kept in virtual isolation for much of the time he was there in an effort to avoid his charismatic influence on the other prisoners. He has written eloquently of his years there in his autobiography, Long Walk to Freedom. Until his release in 1990, the primary available photograph of him was the black and white picture from his law school graduation. On the resistance groups, see Ellis, Comrades Against Apartheid.

oppositional insurgents. The wretched conditions of the island jail and the torturous daily existence that the prisoners experienced relentlessly every day for decades provided a formative collective experience. In spite of the physical and mental abuse suffered daily, the prisoners managed to find innovative ways to construct a complex social structure that included a wide variety of activities from sports to governance. Individuals and small groups of prisoners found ways, after repeated attempts that were rejected, to gain privileges that led to consequences that the regime officialdom could not have imagined.

With regard to sports, there was an obvious desire among the prisoners to play football within the prison walls as a form of exercise. The first step was finally getting permission to have a soccer ball. This in turn led to the establishment of a number of teams that trained and practiced on the prison playing field. Eventually, the teams organized regular games and competed in prison soccer leagues. Disputes were resolved by writing a constitution that included a functioning judicial board whose purpose was to resolve players' disagreements.[22]

No less significant were the examples of Afrikaner guards who agreed to attend weekly lessons to improve their reading skills in which their "teachers" were ANC prisoners. This in turn led to more books being brought to the island's growing prison library. At the same time, correspondence was conducted, often in code, between the prisoners and their comrades abroad, linking the communities of internal and external exile. The results of all these activities were monumental in that they constituted competing strategies of resistance to the power of the apartheid government that were quietly argued out on Robben Island. In the process, a vital political education in self-governance evolved in an unlikely environment, which would be of enormous value when, and if, liberation was achieved. As one specialist on Robben Island has put it, "the relationship between power and resistance [on Robben Island] was closer to a continuum than a relationship between opposites." This phenomenon further suggests the presence of "dialectical play between the state's will and society's response," meaning that the actions of each side determined the options available to the other in the space where they interacted.[23]

---

[22] Korr and Close, *More Than Just a Game.*
[23] Buntman, *Robben Island and Prisoner Resistance to Apartheid*, 195, 269.

This historical episode of the dominance by terror of whites over blacks finally came to an end with the unexpected collapse of the apartheid regime in 1994, amidst a multitude of ironies. The illegal and banned ANC became the ruling party in power. Nelson Mandela, viewed by the apartheid regime as one of the most dangerous persons in the country, moved from his confinement in an isolated cell block on Robben Island, to head the Pretoria parliament, in a stunning change that few could have predicted. The former insurgent terrorists, whose lives had been decimated by exile and killing, now found themselves organizing commissions of "truth and reconciliation" in which victimized family members faced their former masters in courtrooms without the authority to sentence, a place where words and tears replaced guns and bombs.[24]

Latin America

One of the most violent arenas of the continuing conflicts between governments and their opponents during the ideological Cold War years was Latin America. Few countries on the continent managed to avoid being swept up in the combat. Although each national narrative had its own distinctive features, there were many common characteristics to be found as well. Marxism was both the great fear of governments and the militant inspiration of the insurgents in a struggle that literally was about life and death. This ideological context permitted a principled justification for the terrorism that became an addictive tactic on both sides of the barricades. Government leaders remained insecure in terms of justifying their authority, since they had often come to power in illegal or contestable circumstances, leading them to order policies of repression to enforce their claim to legitimacy.

In Argentina, the term "Dirty War" first was utilized by the state to describe the need for the police to soil themselves in the process of cleansing society of the plague of insurgents who sought to bring revolutionary chaos to the fatherland. In the aftermath of a brutal military dictatorship, the term shifted to become a description of the acts of the death squads that "disappeared," at a minimum, between 10,000 and 30,000 citizens between 1976 and

---

[24] See Doxtader and Salazar, *Truth and Reconciliation in South Africa.*

1983.[25] Few were as violent in carrying out these policies of state terror as the Argentine Task Force 3.3.2, which has been characterized as "the most notorious group of torturers and murderers of the most notoriously murderous junta in modern Latin American history."[26] Its successor, the Anti-Communist Alliance (a.k.a. the Triple A), continued these government policies of violent repression. At the same time, the insurgency led by the Montoneros and the allied People's Revolutionary Army (ERP) was responsible for hundreds of kidnappings, tortures and killings of government operatives, business leaders and police officials.[27]

One of the early leaders of the Montoneros, Mario Firmenich, directed two spectacular kidnappings in 1974. In July, the Montoneros kidnapped and murdered former minister Arturo Roig, and in September they held John and Jorge Born, two industrialist millionaires, for ransom, receiving $60 million in exchange for their return. Firmenich began his career as a Catholic nationalist but gradually drifted into the radical camp during the military dictatorship. He was eventually tracked down, arrested in Brazil, and extradited back to Argentina where he was sentenced to 30 years in prison.[28]

The violence of this era had its roots in earlier conflicts that took place during the two terms of President Juan Peron, an enthusiast of Benito Mussolini's fascist policies. In subsequent years, Peronistas divided into factions with armed militants in both the government and in labor unions acting in his name. However, the Cold War context for the Dirty War was firmly established by the shock of the Cuban revolution in January 1959, which was interpreted in Argentina as an existential threat to the nation in a manner not unlike the way in which

---

[25] The authoritative *Nunca Mas* (Argentine National Commission on the Disappeared), which collected 50,000 pages of testimonies of participants and witnesses, concluded that it could verify 10,483 disappearances that were, in most of the cases cited, preceded by indescribable methods of torture. The larger figure of 30,000 is cited in Marchak, *God's Assassins*, 5. Marchak (p. 338) also praises the *Nunca Mas* report as a national self-examination that "is unique in its honesty and comprehensiveness."

[26] Rosenberg, *Children of Cain*, 82.

[27] Sloan, "Political Terrorism in Latin America," 312–13.

[28] Firmenich was eventually amnestied by President Carlos Menem in 1990 and went on to start a new career as an academic economist. There are reports that he was a double agent during the latter part of his Montonero career, but these remain in dispute. See Moyano, *Argentine's Lost Patrol*, 91–2, 191 (fn. 9).

the Bolshevik seizure of power in 1917 had generated hysterical waves of fear from Berlin to Washington.

The US became increasingly involved in the Argentine anti-communist campaign. The leader of the junta that came to power in the aftermath of the collapse of the Peron regime in 1976, General Jorge Rafael Videla, had received training in "counterinsurgency leadership" at the School of the Americas in Fort Benning, Georgia, an agency of the Department of Defense. Admiral Emilio Massera, who oversaw the prison system where insurgents were detained, graduated in 1963 from the Inter-American Defense College in Washington.

The well-planned crusade against communist subversion was gradually put in place by Videla, Massera and their military advisers, who ordered their security forces to adopt all necessary tactics of violence against the domestic enemy. Once the arrests were ordered in massive numbers, the prisoners were detained in the Marine Mechanics School buildings (ESMA) under the authority of Massera. Prisoners were often coerced into tasks of complicity, before they were disposed of. Some of the university graduates were forced to translate material of interest to the regime into Spanish from foreign languages, while others were compelled to become ghost writers for members of the junta, composing the text of speeches and newspaper articles designed to appear in publications abroad that presented benign views of the country for purposes of diplomacy and tourism.

Other tactics involved soldiers raping wives after their husbands were arrested. In a related operation, in cases where both parents were taken away, the infants and children left behind were placed with families selected by the regime, and brought up without ever knowing who their biological parents were. In recent years, some of these children, decades later, have found their way back to either their surviving parents or grandparents in scenes of tearful reunions that would have been unimaginable in the past.[29] Disposing of the bodies of the prisoners became a problem, as the number of mass graves expanded to capacity near the prison where they were shot by firing squads. This difficulty was resolved by an innovative technique: following a period of torture, the condemned prisoners were drugged

[29] See, e.g., Forero, "Argentina's Dirty War Still Haunts Youngest Victims," and Warren, "Son Lost to Torturers Reappears." For a narrative of some of these harrowing prison experiences, see Lewis, "The Inferno," 147–62.

into virtual unconsciousness, their bodies were then wrapped in burlap bags with heavily weighted chains, and dropped from the cargo hatch of military aircraft over the South Atlantic Ocean for the sharks to feed on. According to a former naval commander, ESMA was responsible for killing "between 1,500 and 2,000 in this manner."[30]

The regime was clear about the purpose, necessity and morality of its mission from the start. The day after the military takeover of the government on 25 March 1974, Videla justified his new regime:

> The armed forces have assumed the direction of the state in fulfillment of an obligation from which they cannot back away. They do so only after calm meditation about the irreparable consequences to the destiny of the nation that would be caused by the adoption of a difference stance. This decision is aimed at ending misrule, corruption and the scourge of subversion.
>
> During the period which begins today, the armed forces will develop a program governed by clearly defined standards, by internal order and hard work, by the total observance of ethical and moral principles, by justice, and by the integral organization of Man and by the respect of his rights and dignity ... and the task of eradicating, once and for all, the vices which afflict the nation.[31]

In a chilling statement of support for this alleged republic of virtue, General Iberico St Jean, governor of the huge and strategically vital Buenos Aires province, spoke with unmistakable clarity of the junta's responsibilities: "First we must kill all the subversives, then their sympathizers; then those who are indifferent; and finally, we must kill all those who are timid."[32]

The junta's dictatorship did come to an end, but not because of an Algerian-style triumph from below. The regime collapsed because of its own miscalculation in foreign affairs. Perhaps overconfident

---

[30] Lewis, *Guerrillas and Generals*, 157–8. An unforgettable scene of an Argentine soldier struggling to push a prisoner out of the plane into the ocean who was still alive, desperately holding on and crying out for mercy can be found in Nathan Englander's novel, *The Ministry of Special Cases*.
[31] Quoted in Rosenberg, *Children of Cain*, 123.   [32] Quoted in ibid., 124.

because of the demonstration of its supreme power in dealing with Marxist subversives at home, the foreign ministry recommended contesting Britain's control of the Falkland Islands (Malvinas). A bravado assault to invade the islands ended in humiliating defeat. General Leopoldo Galtieri, who was president at the time, resigned. Elections were held and won by Raul Alfonsin, who had campaigned on a platform that included a focus on human rights for all Argentines. Alfonsin organized the arrests of the junta leaders, who were tried on multiple charges of abuse of power, murder, torture and illegal arrests. Both Videla and Massera were sentenced to life in prison, though many of the functionaries of the Videla regime were pardoned by President Carlos Menem in 1990 after he was elected to office.

In Chile, the narrative played out somewhat differently, though the ideological context justifying political violence sounded strikingly similar to the junta's rhetoric in Argentina. Chile before Pinochet had been one of South America's most durable democracies. In the 1970 elections, a veteran socialist candidate, Salvador Allende, defeated former president Eduardo Frei, becoming the hemisphere's first democratically elected Marxist. Allende had run without success in three previous elections, but had decades of experience in a variety of government posts.

Once in office, he moved quickly to establish a socialist economy for Chile that included a vast nationalization project in which the state took control of the country's valuable copper industry, expropriated farmland to be run by peasant collectives, and ordered the construction of low-income housing projects. There was immediate opposition from across the spectrum of Chilean society. Truckers working for private companies went on strike and refused to deliver goods, factory owners torched their own plants rather than turn them over to the government, and businessmen fled the country in large numbers. What Allende did *not* do was to censor the opposition press, arrest his enemies, establish revolutionary tribunals and establish a state police militia to strengthen his power through violence and repression.

Most disturbing, especially to the Nixon administration in Washington, was the direction of Allende's foreign policy. The Cuban government was officially recognized and Fidel Castro was invited to Santiago for a state visit, in flagrant opposition to the isolation of Cuba insisted on by the Organization of American States. In addition,

Allende was in dialogue with officials in Moscow, including the KGB, to organize the shipment of both money and arms to bolster Chile's faltering economy. Shortly after Allende was awarded the Lenin Peace Prize in Moscow, he was criticized by his own Supreme Court for judicial misrule and by the Chamber of Deputies for ruling by decree, thereby undermining the democratic foundation of the state.

The opposition to Allende went further by planning a *coup d'état*, which was being openly discussed in the press and in diplomatic circles. On September 11, 1973, with the enthusiastic support of the CIA, General Augusto Pinochet ordered the aerial bombardment of La Moneda, the presidential palace, arresting or shooting members of the Allende administration. Allende is believed to have committed suicide rather than surrender, though in the absence of an impartial investigation, many remain convinced he was assassinated. His successor ruthlessly and quickly reversed the political and economic direction of the country. Pinochet proclaimed his intention to establish a commission that would consider a new constitution after the seizure of power was complete, but that its main task was to silence all aspects of the Allende regime. That administration, he stated, remained a threat as "an enemy that did not exist before but today infiltrates, divides and corrodes the government and has brought about violence and terrorism. If democracy was an instrument that fitted its times, today, it is not adequate to survive in such a world. Traditional democracy is no longer able to face an adversary that has destroyed the state."[33]

Pinochet abolished the congress, ended all political party competition for elections and assumed control of both the media and the judiciary, prior to inaugurating a brutal campaign of state terror. The categories of enemies of the new regime expanded as labor leaders, newspaper editors, and university activists among many others were arrested and disappeared, usually after a period of torture for information on suspected subversives still at large. To streamline his program, Pinochet established one of the world's most feared national police forces, the National Intelligence Directorate (DINA), which was replaced in 1977 by the National Information Center (CNI), which continued the repression despite its benign-sounding title.

---

[33] Quoted in ibid., 345. See also Pion-Berlin, *The Ideology of State Terror*, and Sloan, "State Repression and Enforcement Terrorism in Latin America," 83–98.

Activities against the regime went on throughout the period, though largely in highly clandestine situations. There were public demonstrations, defacing of government buildings with black paint slabs during the night, and occasional acts of violence against the police. Periodically the government claimed to have uncovered caches of arms from Cuba destined for insurgent Marxist groups operating underground. None of this, however, remotely compared to the violence of the state against its own people. The toll was enormous, with the most recent studies concluding that there were over 40,000 cases of arrest, torture, disappearance and murder by the security forces during the military dictatorship.[34] The terror finally came to a climax in the 1988 plebiscite, in which over 50 percent of the voters rejected Pinochet's request for another eight years in power. Criminal charges were brought against him once out of power, but he died before any of the numerous prosecutions were able to bring him to justice.[35]

In Peru, yet another violent combat zone developed involving the state and an insurgent opposition. The militant Shining Path (*Sendero Luminoso*) (the name was taken from a Marxist phrase, the shining path leading to revolution) was founded by the Marxist theorist and teacher Abimael Guzman, a professor of philosophy who taught at a regional university in the province of Ayacucho. Radicalized in the 1960s and with a strong admiration for the manner in which Mao had captured power in China from the countryside (as opposed to the Leninist urban model), Guzman built an influential organization dedicated to the creation of a peasant-based "new democracy" socialist society. In the 1970s, he formed a "revolutionary directorate" with training centers for militias to lead the armed struggle against the Peruvian government.

Peru during these years was ruled by a military administration. Under the dictatorial rule of General Francisco Morales Bermudez,

---

[34] The 2004 Chilean National Commission on Political Prisoners and Torture listed 35,000 cases of abuse under Pinochet's rule from 1973 to 1990. In 2011, further analyses of police files documented a new total of 40,018 cases of abuse under detention, disappearance and death. Among these files was the record of the arrest and torture of Alberto Bachelet, father of the Chilean president, Michelle Bachelet (2006–10).

[35] For the discussion on Chile, I have relied on Kornbluh, *The Pinochet File*, Dinges, *The Condor Years*, and the Latin American section of the National Security Archive website organized by Kate Doyle, whose research is of inestimable value. On the conflicts embedded in national memory regarding these and related events in the region, see Lessa and Druliolle, *The Memory of State Terrorism in the Southern Cone*.

elections had not been permitted in the 12 years prior to the 1980 campaign, when the regime allowed acceptable candidates to seek public support.[36] Guzman's response was to urge a nationwide boycott against "all the bourgeois candidates," and went further by ordering the burning of ballot boxes in a number of villages. At the same time, the group began a concerted effort, which achieved some success, to mobilize impoverished peasants with promises of social reform programs. In some areas, local authorities were encouraged to implement these programs almost immediately, since the central government had paid little attention to the villagers' needs and discontents. As this competing influence increased, the administration recognized the threat to its power, and took action. Army and police units were dispatched to universities to silence the Shining Path's influence there, destroying property as well as making mass arrests. In February, 1987, 4,000 troops invaded the university in San Marcos, arresting over 500 students, trashing dorm rooms, stealing computers and burning piles of books in their rooms.[37]

Both sides committed assassinations and massacres in rural areas. If a village was suspected of cooperating with the government, Shining Path squads would invade with brute force, often executing landowners and local officials in these operations. Peasants who resisted were publically punished to set an example. If, on the other hand, a village was considered sympathetic to the insurgents, the army was equally ruthless in its violent response, indiscriminately killing and raping defenseless residents.[38] Guzman in turn became increasingly bold, proclaiming the need for the exploited masses to "arm themselves and rise in revolution to put the noose around the neck of imperialism and the reactionaries, seizing them by the throat and garroting them."[39]

Throughout the 1980s, the battleground expanded. Having consolidated a huge swath of the Peruvian countryside, Guzman adopted a new strategy by assaulting the capital, which had previously been outside the zone of conflict. Shining Path forays into Lima were

---

[36] General Morales Bermudez was involved with the large transnational operation called Operation Condor which involved officials in Argentina, Bolivia, Brazil, Chile, Paraguay and Uruguay as well as Peru who were cooperating in secretly shuttling disappeared prisoners to torture centers, with the complicity of the US government. See Campbell and Brenner, *Death Squads in Global Perspective*, 314, and Kornbluh, *The Pinochet File*, 331–402.

[37] Rosenberg, *Children of Cain*, 186.   [38] Taylor, *Shining Path*, 102–46.

[39] Quoted in Gorriti, *The Shining Path*, 35.

successful in achieving the bombing of wealthy neighborhoods and the blowing up of power stations, plunging the city into periods of frightening darkness.[40] There were inevitably casualties, intended or otherwise. Included among the former were the Shining Path's 1985 assassination of several US and French government officials as well as a number of aid workers in Lima.

Alberto Fujimori, elected president of Peru in 1990, committed himself to the eradication of the Shining Path by any means necessary. Toward that end, he created the *Grupo Colina* death squad, which was responsible for a number of massacres in insurgent-controlled village areas. Guzman was finally caught, arrested, brought to trial in 1992 and imprisoned with a life sentence. The Shining Path soon dissolved without his leadership, and the fears engendered by its militant interpretations of Marxist ideology dissipated amid the void left by the collapse the year before of the center of global communism in Moscow.

The combat between Fujimori and Guzman ultimately was one which neither of them won. Each was responsible for mass killings and an absence of concern for basic human rights. Fujimori gloated as he had Guzman paraded through Lima in a truck on his way to court, so the public could find satisfaction in the humiliation of such a feared militant leader. But in 2000, Fujimori's abuse of the law brought down his administration, forcing him to flee into exile in Japan. He eventually returned to restore his name, but was sentenced to 32 years in prison for illegally ordering the killing, disappearing, kidnapping and torturing of Peruvian citizens. In a further development, the 2003 Peruvian Truth and Reconciliation Commission's final report concluded that there were nearly 70,000 deaths and disappearances between 1980 and 2000, attributed in equal measure to the Fujimori regime and to Guzman's Shining Path.[41]

Similar conflicts of terrorism occurred elsewhere in Central and South America. Guatemala experienced years of violent convulsions as the government militias destroyed much of the indigenous population, always justifying the killings and disappearances with either silence

---

[40] Smith, "Shining Path's Urban Strategy: *Ate Vitarte*," 145–65.
[41] Brett, *Peru Confronts a Violent Past*. Most of the atrocities described above are documented in this astonishingly revealing report. For further references, see Stern, *Sendero Luminoso*.

or the rhetoric of anticommunism.[42] In Nicaragua, the Marxist Sandinistas actually did gain power, alarming the US to such an extent that the Reagan administration was willing to participate in the illegal and secret transport of weapons to the anticommunist Contras, in the Iran-Contra Affair.[43] The government fought the militant Tupamaros in Uruguay.

In Brazil, President Getulio Vargas is generally regarded as one of the country's most important leaders, ruling in two separate periods encompassing the years between 1930 and 1952. The instability and vulnerability of the governing structure of Brazil throughout this period is reflected in the fact that Vargas was in and out of power in a variety of formats, from actual elections to arranged accessions in cooperation with the military authorities. His opponents emerged from both extremes of the political spectrum, but his main adversaries were on the left. The main force of his regime's repression was directed against suspected communist subversion. To deal with what he believed was a mortal threat to the government, he directed a massive police dragnet that utilized nationalist propaganda to defend as necessary the policies of arrest, torture and imprisonment. At the same time, Vargas introduced reforms during his years in power which have left a positive legacy in Brazil, in spite of his periodic sponsorship of terrorist policies. The Vargas era eventually came to an end not as a result of insurgent victories, but because of irresolvable internal factionalism in his party, that led to his suicide in 1952.[44]

From the beginning to the end of his years in office, Vargas insisted on the need for his authoritarian regime. His fantasy included a radiant future for Brazilians once he was able to dispense with the conflicted factionalism and competing political parties that characterized the problems of democracy. "The rights of individuals have to be subordinate to the obligations to the nation," he proclaimed, on assuming power. In addition to suspending payments of foreign debt, he defended the "abolition of political parties, the reorganization of the

---

[42] Wilkinson, *Silence on the Mountain.*
[43] For a contextual analysis of these Cold War conflicts and terror regimes in Central America, see the introduction in Grandin, *The Last Colonial Massacre.*
[44] See the account in Loewenstein, *Brazil under Vargas.* Other useful studies of the repressive tactics employed under Vargas include McCann, "The Military and the Dictatorship: Getulio, Goes and Dutra," 109–42; Dulles, *Sobral Pinto, "The Conscience of Brazil"*; Rose, *One of the Forgotten Things.*

218 / The Foundations of Modern Terrorism

national court, and regulation of pensions in the public, civil service" in order to end "the fractious interests" sabotaging the country's progress. Vargas saw no need for what he called these "political inter- mediaries" standing between the state and its people. His measures, he further stated, had a moral purpose, which was "the abolition of all situations of privilege." The state would also "attend to the imperative of social justice" by being "vigilant in the repression of extremism." Indeed, the government was prepared to establish new "fortified mili- tary prisons and agricultural colonies" for the internment of "all those agitating elements recognized by their seditious activities or condemned by their political crimes." In this way, the administration would be better able to safeguard its citizens from "the ideological madness of false prophets and vulgar demagogues."[45]

At the end, before his suicide, Vargas left behind a letter explaining his own assessment of what he had achieved. "I made myself chief of an unconquerable revolution. I began the work of liberation and I instituted a regime of social liberation." Evil forces, referred to as "birds of prey," operating behind his back and beyond his control, were responsible for his inability to realize the noble policies he had attempted with his reform program. "To those who think that they have defeated me, I reply with my victory ... My sacrifice will remain in your souls."[46]

The situation in Brazil hardly improved after Vargas. He was succeeded as president by João Goulart, who attempted to introduce new policies amid the Cold War rivalries. He reversed Brazil's foreign policy stance by establishing relations with socialist countries gener- ally considered loyal to the Soviet Union, openly opposed sanctions against Cuba, and permitted communists to work in positions of authority in government agencies. All of this antagonized the Johnson administration in Washington, which helped organize a coup to remove Goulart from power, which was accomplished on the night of March 31, 1964. For the next two decades, Brazil was under the control of military dictatorships, with strong anti-communist com- mitments. Civil liberties were suspended, the political party system was neutered to eliminate serious opposition factions, and repressive strikes were carried out in the cities as well as in the countryside.

---

[45] Vargas, "New Year's Address, 1938," in Levine and Crocitti, *The Brazil Reader*, 186–9.
[46] "Vargas's Suicide Letter, 1954," in Levine and Crocitti, *The Brazil Reader*, 222–4.

There were instances of protests on university campuses, and a number of kidnappings of diplomats and ambassadors during the late 1960s, all of which convinced the government to act even more decisively. Villages believed to be harboring opponents and insurgents were burned to the ground, and clerics suspected of being critical of the government were subjected to threats and even torture. Aiding in the repression, the Brazilian government welcomed General Paul Aussaresses, the French veteran of the Algerian campaigns of terrorism, in 1973. For some years, he trained the police and military intelligence services in methods of torture, disappearance and body disposals.[47]

Brazil also provides yet another example of the ongoing interaction between a regime of terror and the violent insurgent militants seeking its overthrow. One of the leading opponents of the regime was Carlos Marighella, who grew up in a remote Brazilian village. His father was an Italian immigrant worker in search of a better future in Brazil, while his mother traced her ancestry back to slaves in Sudan who were brought across the Atlantic involuntarily. Carlos, attracted to the appeals of Brazilian communists, was arrested and charged with political subversion in 1936 during the early years of the Vargas dictatorship. He was released, rearrested, tortured, and finally amnestied in 1945.

He became more deeply immersed in the ideology of Marxism during visits to China in 1953 and 1954. In 1966 he published a long essay, "The Brazilian Crisis," which brought him to wider attention. As Fanon had argued for the necessity of armed struggle against the French occupation of Algeria, Marighella applied the argument to Brazil, interpreting the Vargas regime as the occupiers of his homeland, so ruthless that only armed resistance could repel its brutality. He was also fiercely critical of the Brazilian Communist Party for its condemnation of the tactics of armed struggle against the state and the middle classes. His radicalism went beyond the orthodoxies of the Party, which expelled him in 1968. He also went to Cuba at this time, inspired by Che Guevara's calls for rebellion in Latin America. Returning clandestinely to Brazil, he headed the militant Action for National Liberation (ALN) which organized a series of bank robberies, explosions at army barracks and foreign companies, the kidnapping of the American

---

[47] See Kirsch, *Revolution in Brazil*; Rose, *One of the Forgotten Things*; French, *Drowning in Laws*; and Hentschke, *Vargas and Brazil*.

ambassador, Charles Elbrick, and the assassination of Charles Chandler, an American army captain accused of being a double agent. Hunted day and night by the authorities, Marighella was fatally shot in a police ambush in November 1969, exposed by a double agent while walking alone on a street in São Paulo.[48]

Before his death, he wrote "For the Liberation of Brazil" and an influential text that has become a seminal document in the history of insurgent terror, "The Minimanual of the Urban Guerrilla." The "Manual" has been translated into more than 20 languages around the globe and copies of it were found in the course of police raids during the 1960s in the apartments of members of the Baader-Meinhof Group in West Germany, the Red Brigades in Italy, the IRA in Northern Ireland, the Basque ETA organization in Spain and the Popular Front for the Liberation of Palestine in Beirut, to name only a few of the most prominent.

Terrorism, Marighella wrote, no longer implies evil. "It does not dishonor one. It is rather the focus of mass action." Indeed, this form of resistance "ennobles the spirit. It is an act worthy of all revolutionaries engaged in armed struggle against the shameful military dictatorship and its monstrosities."[49] The urban guerrilla is defined as "the implacable enemy of the government, systematically inflicting damage on established authority and those who exercise power to exploit the nation."[50] The guerrilla's purpose is to demoralize, dismantle and destroy the existing political system. Marighella, following in the tradition of Heinzen, Nechaev and Fanon, describes the profound challenges that must be overcome to achieve success, as well as the personal qualities one must have. He devotes attention to tactics, strategy, weapons, the targets of armed attacks, the execution of enemies and spies, and the liberation of prisoners languishing in police dungeons. Taking up arms for this cause is "the reason for being," and terrorism "is a weapon you cannot do without."[51]

Radical violence in the US

The connections linking the confrontations between regimes and insurgents in Latin America to the transatlantic revolts that took place in the

---

[48] Hanrahan, "Marighella: Father of Modern Terrorism," 13–34.
[49] Marighella, *The Manual*, 40.   [50] Ibid., 46.   [51] Ibid., 55, 84.

1960s "from Berkeley to Berlin" cannot be fully understood without placing them squarely within the defining context of the Cold War. To put it another way, the militant theorists like Fanon, Marighella and Guzman were inspired by new and more radical interpretations of the generation of Mao, Ho Chi-Minh and Che Guevara as much as they were by Marx or Lenin; moreover, they admired the examples in reality of leaders of socialist states in the USSR and the People's Republics in China, Cuba and Vietnam who were engaged, in their view, in realizing the utopian predictions of communism. These experiments in state communism soon found their appeal on the other side of the Cold War, as insurgent organizations emerged in West Germany, Italy, France and the US that were willing to turn to violence to achieve their goals.

At the same time, the governments in these countries were deeply influenced negatively by the propaganda and rhetoric of communist states. The free world stood virtuously as the protector of democratic values against the threat of the dictatorial force of collectivism, while the socialist world on the other side of the Iron Curtain presented its future as one in which class divisions, exploitation and the injustices of capitalism would finally be abolished. Both the Soviet Union and the US provided assistance in many ways to areas of the world where they competed with one another for political control and economic resources, from offers of political asylum to those willing to cross the divide, to outright gifts of weapons and money. In addition, the security agencies on both sides were engaged in violent acts of sabotage, assassination and the overthrow of governments around the world considered threatening to their respective ideological causes.

Not surprisingly, this international context of ideological combat played a strong role in much of the political violence that rocked the Western world during the 1960s and 1970s. Confronted by movements dedicated to national liberation, decolonization, anti-imperialism or Marxist-inspired fantasies of heroic revolutions to ameliorate the condition of the masses, anticommunist-oriented governments acted under the traditional assumption that their central responsibility was to defend their citizens against the threat of all forms of insurgent terrorism. However, they seem to have rarely understood their own contributions to the violence. Simultaneously, communist states enforced rigid policies to guard against capitalist and imperialist threats to their legitimacy.

Framed within the context of these larger international forces that deeply influenced the political violence during the era of the 1960s, every country where insurgent terrorism threatened statesmen and citizens alike had its own national conflicts to confront. The danger posed by Marxist ideology and communism, in one form or another, seemed to appear almost everywhere. In the US, prominent blacks such as Paul Robeson and W. E. B. Du Bois were placed under constant surveillance in the 1950s by the FBI and its stridently anticommunist director, J. Edgar Hoover. Both Robeson and Du Bois had spent time in the Soviet Union, and neither hid their sympathies for that country's proclaimed ideals.[52] Also in the 1950s, African Americans began, at first quietly and then more vociferously, to assert the right to register at regional polling centers, where their voting privileges had been blocked by adherents of the culture of Jim Crow, as well as to seek equal access to traditionally segregated public institutions. All of these efforts were watched closely by the local agencies of the FBI.

Inspired in part by these acts of civil disobedience, a group of students at the University of Michigan established an organization called Students for a Democratic Society (SDS) in 1960. Two years later, the SDS leadership issued a statement of purpose voted on at the SDS Port Huron convention, which emphasized the commitment to ending racism, militarism and the exploitation of the poor in America. By mid-decade, a plethora of groups emerged with similar commitments, including the Congress on Racial Equality (CORE), the Southern Christian Leadership Conference (SCLC) led by Martin Luther King, and the Student Non-Violent Coordinating Committee (SNCC). With the assassinations of Medgar Evers and Malcolm X, two leaders with contrasting reputations within the African American population, a range of institutions, including army recruiting centers, corporate headquarters and universities became targets for rising rage and calls for vengeance, as cities across the country erupted in spasms of violence.

The efforts at enrolling blacks to vote in the South, which had provoked violent reactions since the initial efforts at the beginning of the decade, became literally deadly as well. During the "Freedom Summer" of 1964, three young civil rights workers were murdered in Philadelphia, Mississippi. Branded as "outside agitators" and "communists" by local citizens, their brutalized bodies were not discovered for two months, as few residents were willing to speak about the event. Years later, it was proven that members of the Ku Klux Klan were responsible and that the

---

[52] Baldwin, *Beyond the Color Line and the Iron Curtain.*

killings were planned with the explicit approval of the town's sheriff, Lawrence Rainey. The consensus of his constituency was grounded in the fear of the consequences of black political empowerment.[53]

In 1968, the Mississippi Democratic Party refused to seat black representatives as delegates, fomenting protests that fused with antiwar disturbances and reached a climax in Chicago's Grant Park, near the hotel where the Democratic National Convention was in progress. Mayor Richard Daley ordered the police to clear the park after first forcing the television media out of the area. The result was a violent police crackdown that left scores of protestors bloodied.[54]

In Oakland, California, another violent drama was in progress as the police clashed with members of the recently formed Black Panther Party. Led by Huey Newton, Bobby Seale and Eldridge Cleaver, the Panthers in their signature black leather uniforms, armed with rifles and revolvers, reversed the earlier stereotype of the humiliated, obsequious Negro. Centered in Oakland, the organization began by running soup kitchens and literacy programs for blacks in the Bay Area, but soon aroused suspicion and antagonism when they announced that they were obtaining arms to defend the black community from police brutality and abuse. They further declared the party's commitment to the confrontational ideology of Black Power with its Marxist and Maoist overtones. The police and the Panthers engaged in a number of shootouts, with casualties on both sides. Between 1967 and 1970, ten Panthers and nine policemen were killed in these street battles in Oakland. The FBI closely monitored the Panther organization as it developed chapters across the country. The bureau's tactics included planting informants and provoking incidents of violence. In 1969, the Panthers tortured and murdered Alex Rackley, identified as a police spy in the New York chapter of the organization. By the end of the 1970s, the Black Panther Party

---

[53] See McAdam, *Freedom Summer*; McClymer, *Mississippi Freedom Summer*; Watson, *Freedom Summer: The Savage Season that Made Mississippi Burn*, 205–14.

[54] Although the television and media crews were ordered out of the park so that the police could clear it using methods that might have been seen as unnecessarily brutal, footage of the ensuing carnage was recorded by a film director, Haskell Wexler. Wexler was completing the last scene in "Medium Cool," which was staged in Grant Park. He requested permission to stay, provided he focus only on the fictional story and his actors. The result is a documentary backdrop of the police violence that Wexler clearly intended to include. The completed film, starring Robert Forster, was screened in theaters in 1969.

was decimated by the loss of many of its leaders as a result of killings, self-imposed exile or imprisonment.[55]

Support for the Black Panther Party, however, did emerge within the ranks of one of the most prominent radical groups of the period, the Weathermen, a relatively small organization of former members of SDS impatient with the tactics of nonviolence to achieve political goals. They came to national attention in Chicago during the "Days of Rage" in October 1969, when, in retaliation for the police assassination of a local Black Panther leader, Fred Hampton, they torched much of the downtown area for four days and nights. They then went into covert operations, renaming themselves the Weather Underground, taking responsibility for 19 bombings at symbolically selected targets. They justified their deeds with rhetoric from the essays of Marxist theoreticians, particularly Fanon and Marighella. Their fantasy of power, inspired by the insurrectionary successes of Mao and Castro, was clearly articulated in their clandestinely produced publications. In one instance, they stated that their "intention is to disrupt the empire ... to incapacitate it, to put pressure on the cracks, to make it hard to carry out its bloody functioning against the people of the world ... Our intention is to forge an underground ... protected from the eyes and weapons of the state, a base against repression, to accumulate lessons, experience and constant practice, a base from which to attack."[56]

The relentless surveillance and repression by law enforcement authorities at both the federal and local levels, combined with the ending of the war in Vietnam, left the Weather Underground isolated. Demonstrations on their behalf and funding from sympathizers declined, and the "safe houses" that once provided a support network of clandestine planning centers across the country also diminished. They were on the FBI's most wanted list, with their photos pasted on the walls of post offices across the country, and were the objects of a massive, nationwide manhunt. By the middle of the 1970s, only a small group of the Weather Underground leaders were still at large. They did

---

[55] See, among a large literature, Ogbar, *Black Power* and Williams and Lazerow, *In Search of the Black Panther Party.*

[56] Dohrn *et al., Prairie Fire,* 1. The leadership of the Weather Underground included Bernadine Dohrn, Mark Rudd, William Ayres, Jeff Jones, Cathy Boudin and Kathy Wilkerson. For a succinct history of the group, including its fragmented survival into the 1980s, see Smith, *Terrorism in America,* 95–107, and Varon, *Bringing the War Home,* esp. 20–195.

manage to make a documentary film to explain the reasons for their tactics of violence, and conduct a few final "actions" before dissolving within the next decade.[57]

The American government played a crucial role in all of these developments, primarily through a secret FBI unit that was established as part of the Bureau's Counter Intelligence Program (COINTEL) in 1956. These undercover agents operated under a wide mandate that permitted them to disrupt, discredit, provoke and ultimately eliminate dissident groups considered subversive of the national interest. Initially, their actions were directed toward silencing the influence of the Communist Party (CPUSA), but soon their successes encouraged Hoover to expand their tactics of surveillance and repression to include the Socialist Party and, though with far less force, the Ku Klux Klan.

In the 1960s, COINTEL agents shifted their attention to the civil rights and radical organizations, from Martin Luther King's Southern Christian Leadership Conference, the NAACP and the Congress on Racial Equality, to the Black Panthers and Weathermen. Their methods included aggressive beatings, torture and assassinations. They had the full cooperation of most local police officials, all of whom shared the same insecurities, fears and prejudices about the dissident groups. One of the glaring examples of this joint effort was the night raid on the home of Chicago Black Panther leader, Fred Hampton. With intelligence supplied by the FBI, the Chicago police stormed Hampton's house and shot him to death in his bed, with his wife and infant child in the room, on December 4, 1969 in an alleged act of self-defense. In this case, the press prominently covered the story but the interpretation centered on the killing as a justified necessity to end a threat to American society by preventing a dangerous militant from committing further violence. The media's emblematic photograph of the event showed the policemen leaving Hampton's house, smiling with satisfaction for having courageously and successfully responded to a mortal threat.[58]

---

[57] *Underground*, made by Emile de Antonio, Mary Lampson and Haskell Wexler, was filmed in 1974 at a Los Angeles safe house, and remains an important source both for the interviews conducted with the militants then still at large and the rare documentary footage included. In 2005, Sam Green and Bill Siegel directed a follow-up documentary film, *The Weather Underground: A Look Back at the Antiwar Activists who Met Violence with Violence*.

[58] See Churchill and Wall, *The COINTEL Papers* and Jeffrey-Jones, *The FBI*. Re-examinations of the forensic evidence showed that the official story of self-defense was highly unlikely since all bullet remains were of police issue.

Elsewhere, similar coordination took place between the COINTEL agents and law enforcement officials in cities around the country throughout the decade. In San Diego, undercover units managed to provoke competing militant groups into attacking one another, which, in one instance, led to the killing of Jim Huggins and Sylvester Bell, two local leaders of the Black Panther Party. In addition, the units regularly engaged in home invasions searching for drugs they themselves often had planted, and conducted robberies of stores and banks which were then blamed on the dissidents. Yet another instance of this cooperation involved the key role played by FBI agent Thomas Rowe, Jr. in the murder of civil rights worker Viola Liuzzo. Rowe, a COINTEL informant, spread rumors that Liuzzo was an active member of the Communist Party and involved with seditious activities in Mississippi. Local Klan members, including Rowe, planned and carried out the drive-by shooting when they found Liuzzo in her car accompanied by Leroy Moton, a young African American local resident, who survived the attack.[59]

In many respects, the ideological conflicts driving the terrorism of this period came to an end on November 3, 1979 in a violent event that took place in Greensboro, NC. Overshadowed by the invasion of the US Embassy in Teheran the same day, it received little contemporary coverage in the media. Less understandable is the fact that it has gone unmentioned in all the histories of terrorism. The participants included Virgil Griffin, Imperial Wizard of the North Carolina Ku Klux Klan; Brent Fletcher, head of the regional American Nazi Party: Eddie Dawson, an informant working as a double agent in touch with the Greensboro police department while reporting to the FBI as a mole inside the Klan; and local members of the Communist Workers Party (CWP).

Rarely has there been a more convincing portrait of the violent consequences of a clash of mutually antagonistic and entangled political interests. November 3 had been chosen by the CWP for a "Death to the Klan March" in a predominantly black neighborhood in Greensboro. The activists in the CWP had worked in the city for

---

[59] Hewitt, *Understanding Terrorism in America from the Klan to Al Qaeda*, 90, 98, 104.
In this case, her children sued the federal government and won a conviction against Rowe. For a fuller account of the Liuzzo affair, see May, *The Informant, the FBI, KKK and the Murder of Viola Liuzzo*.

months to further a variety of causes, including union organizing in textile mills, improved health care and civil rights legislation for minorities. They had applied for, and were granted, a permit for their demonstration. What they didn't realize was that Dawson had transmitted their route from the police to Griffin and Fletcher. On the day before the scheduled march, the CWP organized a demonstration on the front lawn of the Klan's meeting house where they shouted taunting threats and burned a confederate flag. Infuriated, Griffin and Fletcher used this as the excuse to take action. On November 3, as the marchers proceeded along the prescribed route, the police had been instructed to "take an extended lunch period." Several cars with Klan members and Dawson drove into the area of the march, got out of their cars with pistols and rifles, and fired on the CWP leaders. Five CWP demonstrators were shot to death at point blank range, and ten other people were wounded. The assassins returned to their cars and drove off without obstruction. In spite of extensive TV newsreel coverage showing exactly who fired the weapons, the killers were exonerated of all criminal charges after two trials with all-white juries.[60]

The intertwined nature of the violence continued into the 1980s, with right-wing groups also participating in significant numbers. Although they received far less attention in the media, religiously oriented and extreme nationalist organizations were very active during this period. The Klan played a key role in the racist reaction to the 1954 School Desegregation Act and the civil rights movement that emerged soon after. During the 1960s, reports from both the FBI and the Southern Poverty Law Center, which has kept a vigilant watch and compiled comprehensive records on the violent activities of the extreme right for decades, show that there were 588 violent incidents of bombings, shootings and maiming of victims, primarily in the South, with at least 65 recorded deaths.[61]

---

[60] The best account of the affair is Bermanzohn, *Through Survivors' Eyes*. There are valuable additional visual sources: *Lawbreakers: The Greensboro Massacre* (The History Channel, 2000) provides the context of the affair; *88 Seconds in Greensboro* (UNC-TV, 2003) focuses on the role of Eddie Dawson; and *Closer to the Truth*, directed by Adam Zucker (Filmmakers Library, 2008) which centers on the more recent Truth and Reconciliation hearings on the 1979 murders. We owe the existing footage of the shootings in these documentary films to several courageous Greensboro news reporters who hid underneath cars across the street to film the carnage.

[61] Hewitt, *Understanding Terrorism in America*, 16–17. Klan membership, always in dispute due to the secrecy involved, has been estimated by the Anti-Defamation League as

Other significant right-wing violent militant organizations flourished as well, with FBI infiltration a constant ingredient. The Sheriff's Posse Comitatus (SPC) was formed in 1969 in Portland, Oregon, inspired by the 1878 congressional act of that name which limited the role of the federal government in local law enforcement. The SPC leaders declared war on federal authorities, who challenged their right to deputize posses. According to Henry Beach, one of the organization's founders, members intended to arrest and prosecute "officials of the government who commit criminal acts or who violate their oath of office ... He shall be removed by the posse to the most populated intersection of streets in the township and, at high noon, be hung by the neck, the body remaining until sundown as an example to those who would subvert the law."[62]

Other groups with similar ideologies of anticommunism, anti-Semitism and racism against African Americans include the Aryan Nation and the militia organizations that were particularly strong in Arizona and Michigan in these years. Most of the members of these groups were influenced by the apocalyptic violence in William Pierce's *The Turner Diaries*, which depicted a decisive race war in which white citizens tortured, killed and hung mutilated bodies of blacks from neighborhood lampposts in genocidal violence. A copy of this book was found in the truck driven by Timothy McVeigh, who had trained with the Michigan Militia, after he blew up the Alfred Murrah Federal Building in Oklahoma City in 1995, killing 185 people.

Political violence in Western Europe

Europe was not spared the experience of coping with the problems created by the ideological perpetrators of terrorism from above and below. The situation in West Germany was particularly chaotic. Although student groups formed organizations in support of the international causes of the time – protesting the war in Vietnam and apartheid in South Africa, in particular – the main issues of concern that led to the outbreak of violence in the 1960s were specific to the country itself.

---

peaking at 57,000 in 1967, and declining to around 5,000 by 1973. Ibid., 25. By contrast, the Weather Underground's numbers are generally cited at around 300 members.
[62] Smith, *Terrorism in America*, 58.

Of these national peculiarities, none rankled more than the political continuities that were left unresolved after the demise of the Third Reich. Major industries and companies that had supported Hitler's economy before and during the war remained in place, with, in some cases, the same executives still at their helm. There are estimates that as many as 75 percent of the West German judges in the Adenauer administration had formerly been active Nazi Party members, some even having served in high positions in the judicial system or secret services. Further, many officers in the federal police force had been hired and promoted because of their "prior experience" in security matters.[63]

Disagreements over crucial political problems were further enflamed by each side's unwillingness to compromise in their demands on one another. Rather, each sought the dissolution of the other. Particular discontent on the part of opposition student political groups in 1966 was directed against the Emergency Laws. The West German government justified these laws on the basis of having the responsibility to protect its citizenry against the communist threat from the German Democratic Republic. To accomplish this task, comprehensive security measures were enacted and the Communist Party was declared illegal in the Federal Republic, despite its constitutional commitments to the principles of a democratic republic. Rudi Dutschke, one of the leaders of the Socialist Student Association (German SDS), actively campaigned for the repeal of these restrictive laws. The reaction was "a rigidly authoritarian response of police, city, and university authorities," which had the effect of provoking rather than subduing the student groups. As one specialist has assessed the conflict, it was very difficult, if not impossible, to justify, especially in a democratic republic built upon the ruins of a genocidal regime of fascism, "chasing and clubbing demonstrators, and, of course, even less the killing of student demonstrator Benno Ohnesorg by the police after he had already been forced into submission."[64] The death of Ohnesorg occurred during a demonstration protesting the visit of the Shah of Iran to Berlin on June 2, 1967, and was the triggering event that set the opposed forces into an escalation of violent acts.

Police violence was swiftly employed with a brutality that had not been seen since the war years. In 1968, Dutschke narrowly survived

---

[63] Kellen, "Ideology and Rebellion," 46.
[64] Merkl, "West German Left-Wing Terrorism," 175, 176.

an assassination attempt on his life. The assailant, Josef Bachmann, was a house painter with strong anticommunist convictions and believed to have been a police informant by SDS members.[65] Fires broke out at several prominent department stores in Frankfurt. In addition, the editorial offices of the Springer Press, which severely criticized the militants in its publications in caricatured terms, were attacked with firebombs. Demonstrations involving thousands of people became monthly events in many cities, frequently broken up by the police amidst a hail of Molotov cocktails and bullets.

Two years later, the Red Army Faction (*Rote Armee Fraktion*, or RAF) was formed by Horst Mahler, an attorney, and Ulrike Meinhof, an editor on the staff of the left-leaning journal, *Konkret*. They were soon joined by a number of other radicals, including Andreas Baader, a charismatic figure with much more underworld experience in criminal theft than he had with political involvements at that point. Their commitments were to a socialist ideology based on interpretations of the liberation movements of the Third World, urban guerrilla theory from Marighella and the Tupamaros, and acknowledged inspiration from the writings and activities of Che Guevara, Ho Chi Minh, Frantz Fanon, Antonio Gramsci and Herbert Marcuse.

Their tactics ranged from daring assaults on American military bases to the kidnapping of powerful business executives and bombings of selected "bourgeois and fascist" targets. Some of their "actions" were spectacular events designed to draw support for their cause and expose the survivals of fascism in West Germany. In addition to planting explosive devices at large banking facilities, American military installations, buildings housing NATO offices, and the Springer Press network, members of the Red Army Faction and its affiliates kidnapped and executed a number of federal prosecutors, prominent industrial officials and diplomats. In some of these cases, drivers, bodyguards and policemen were killed in the ensuing shootouts. Perhaps the most symbolic act of the RAF was the seizure in broad daylight on September 5, 1977 of Hans Martin Schleyer, a wealthy industrial executive who during the war had been a member of the Nazi

---

[65] Bachmann was arrested and sentenced to a seven-year prison term. He committed suicide in 1970. Dutschke partially recovered from the assault but suffered irreparable brain damage and died as a result of his injuries in December 1979.

Party and an SS officer responsible for "crimes against humanity" according to the manifestoes of his captors. After a protracted period of time dominated by fruitless negotiations between the RAF and the West German government over the release of political prisoners, Schleyer was executed on October 18.

The police were given greater latitude to investigate, raid and arrest suspected and actual members of the RAF following the murder of Schleyer. By the 1980s, most of the leaders of the RAF had been killed in police shootouts or arrested, although small factions continued to commit acts of violence in diminishing numbers until the formal dissolution of the organization in 1998. Baader and Meinhof died earlier in their prison cells, either from successful suicide attempts or, as their followers continue to believe, at the hands of their jailors. Meinhof's body was found dangling from the bars on her high cell window, suspended by a series of knotted jail towels on May 9, 1976.[66]

In Italy, the political violence of the Cold War era also had its mix of international causes and specific endogenous conflicts. Statistically, more insurgent terrorist acts took place there than in any other single country in Europe. Between 1969 and 1986, there were 14,569 violent attacks committed by militant groups of the left and the right, causing 415 fatalities and nearly 1,200 injuries to victims.[67]

Some of the major problems facing Italy in the 1960s were unresolved issues dating back to the end of the Second World War. One was the factionalism of the competing parties, which extended from the Communist Party (PCI) on the left to neo-fascist and monarchist parties on the right. Italy's transition from dictatorship to democratic republic in 1945 was the result of a very close national plebiscite, leaving many on the more extreme right and left frustrated, with intentions to undermine the new postwar republic. Indeed, the country has rarely experienced political stability in the postwar era, with the political parties, the church and the mafia all contributing to the fact that Italy went through 48 distinct coalition governments between the creation of the postwar republic and the 1980s. The second problem was economic in nature, pitting the wealthier north, mainly the area above Rome,

---

[66] For a full account of Meinhof's career, see Colvin, *Ulrike Meinhof and West German Terrorism*. On the wider political and cultural impact of the movement, consult the essays in Berendse and Cornils, *Baader-Meinhof Returns*.

[67] Ferracuti, "Ideology and Repentance: Terrorism in Italy." Somewhat different data can be found in della Porta, "Left Wing Terrorism in Italy," 106.

against the more impoverished south. One consequence of this division between rich and poor was the emergence of a powerful labor movement, at times militant in its calls for better working conditions.

As for the outbreak of widespread terrorism in Italy, although the Marxist-inspired acts of labor violence of this period received the headlines, the fact is that the more serious "black terrorism" attacks from below were initiated by fascist activists who were outraged by the government's acceptance of socialists and communists in their ruling coalitions.[68] Throughout the 1960s, rightist groups exploded bombs at anti-fascist demonstrations in Milan and Rome, and regularly assaulted university buildings in those cities in violent events that saw students severely beaten and their classrooms trashed and burned. The bombings by rightist groups with names like "New Order" spread into public space, where indiscriminate violence led to numbers of civilians becoming victims. Their intention was not only to eliminate the left but also to expose the weakness of the coalition government and create the chaos that would lead to an authoritarian leadership. In the mid-1970s, neo-fascists took responsibility for bombs killing at least 20 people in several cities.[69] Street clashes between rival ideological gangs and shootouts with the police became increasing dangers in public manifestations, including election campaigns.

There were frequent votes of no confidence by antagonistic parties in the parliament in Rome, leading to constant breakdowns of government coalitions. In addition, officials in the military and the security services made it known that they were not satisfied with having socialists as state ministers and members of parliament, able to shape national policy with what appeared to be attitudes that were responsive to Moscow's side of the Cold War competition. They therefore were more than permissive toward the neo-fascist groups responsible for the attacks on the left, because of their shared strategic agendas.[70]

Despite these facts of political cooperation, the center of the narrative of what Italians refer to as "the years of lead" has been focused almost exclusively on the "red terror" of the insurgent left. In

[68] See, for a detailed account, Rimanelli, "Italian Terrorism and Society, 1940s–1980s," 260–7.
[69] Marwick, *The Sixties*, 621–2, 748.
[70] Meade, *Red Brigades* 35. According to Meade's data, he concluded that during the 1960s and 1970s, "the majority of those killed by terrorists in Italy were the victims of the extreme right-wing groups."

the winter of 1969–70, labor activists organized crippling strikes at factories in and around industrial Milan, which also attracted a number of radicalized university students committed to Marxist ideologies. In 1970, Renato Curcio from the University of Trento and Alberto Franceschini, a member of the Young Communist League, formed an organization called the Red Brigades which took the old "propaganda by deed" concept to new levels of terror. During the next several years, they set off bombs in the cars of factory owners and union members identified with neo-fascist parties and engineered kidnappings of factory and union officials. By 1974, they turned their attention from industrial targets to attacks against the state, kidnapping magistrates and police officials whom they subjected to "alternative trials" at which they were prosecuted as people who escaped justice despite committing misdeeds daily against the poor. The symbolic intention behind these coercive trials, according to Red Brigade communiqués, was to demonstrate the hypocrisy and social class prejudices of the ruling legal system to the country at large. They also turned their violence against Italian Communist Party members and labor activists affiliated with their policies. From the perspective of the Red Brigades, the PCI was essentially a participant in supporting the state system they so deeply resented.

Although Curcio and Franceschini were arrested in 1974, the Red Brigades continued to operate under new leadership and with related combat squads across the country. The police were unable to stem the tide of shootings, kidnappings, and robberies. One of the more innovative and painful tactics developed by the insurgents was that of "kneecapping" targets. The technique required weeks of detailed surveillance of the daily routines of judges, bankers, industrialists and gendarme officers, in order to locate the periods of time when they were left unguarded or exposed in public. Usually a car or motor-scooter pulled up alongside the target, who was shot with precision in the knees, often damaging them for life. During kidnappings, photographs were taken of the victims, who were forced to hold the morning newspaper with the date visible on their chests; the photos were sent to local papers where the cooperative media distributed them around the country. The return of the kidnapped prisoner was usually dependent upon the release of Red Brigade members serving time in jails, including, above all, Curcio. Red Brigade manifestoes were published, explaining their intention to bring down the bourgeois state and its imperialist alliances, and end exploitation by corporate capitalism.

In 1978, these tactics were taken one step too far with two actions. The first involved the decision by Mario Moretti, who succeeded Curcio as one of the main Red Brigades leaders, to kidnap Aldo Moro, a former prime minister from the Christian Democratic Party and one of the most revered politicians in the country. He was held in humiliating conditions for 54 days while the government continued to refuse demands that he be exchanged for a prisoner release. The tense situation came to an end when Moretti had Moro shot and then dumped his corpse in front of Rome's Trevi Fountain. The second occurred a year later when the Red Brigades assassinated a popular labor leader and Communist Party member, Guido Rossa. This murder provoked a nationwide revulsion against the Red Brigades from all sides of the political spectrum. The PCI joined with the Christian Democrats in a "historic compromise" that eventually led to a mass of arrests and defections under a government amnesty program that severely weakened the ability of the Red Brigades to threaten civilians and state officials with acts of violence.[71]

There were other participants in the violence. A separate communist-inspired group, *Autonomi*, was even more brutal in its tactics of terror than the Red Brigades, despite their smaller numbers. Their signature event was to provoke street mayhem with rocks, Molotov cocktails and bombs hurled at selected targets such as newspaper buildings, state offices and the detested Communist Party headquarters, whose members were considered sell-outs because of their participation in the ruling coalitions of "the bourgeois state." The police in these cases reacted with their own forms of brutality as they sought to stem the overturning of cars and blocking of trams by using tear gas and guns, in the process harming passers-by as well as perpetrators.[72] Isolated incidents of insurgent terror from Red Brigade members still at large and militants in other groups continued throughout the next decade, but the violence of the "years of lead" as a dynamic movement with channels of recruitment and ideological appeal had been seriously diminished by the early 1980s.[73]

---

[71] Farracuti, in Reich, *Origins of Terrorism*, 83–5; della Porta, "Left Wing Terrorism in Italy," 153–4.

[72] Meade, *Red Brigades*, 88.

[73] See the anthology of articles on this period in Catanzaro, *The Red Brigades and Left Wing Terrorism in Italy* which includes valuable statistical data and additional source material

Finally, the postwar unrest in France merits inclusion. Here also the ideological battles of the Cold War were fought out in a familiar trajectory rooted in a combustible mixture of specifically French issues and international causes, which moved inexorably toward violence within a short space of time in the 1960s. Students at the Sorbonne and also at the suburban campus of the University of Paris at Nanterre had grown increasingly active in forming groups opposing the war in Vietnam and the refusal of the French and American administrations to impose sanctions on the apartheid regime in South Africa. However, the galvanizing force that radicalized many students into action was the Fouchet Law, the project of the minister of education, Christian Fouchet. This legislation essentially restricted matriculation in French higher education, at a time when there were increasing calls to relax admissions requirements to include minorities (such as the children of large numbers of Algerians who had fled to France to escape the instability and violence before and after liberation) and graduates of high schools outside the small network of elite academies that had always dominated the university system.

From the moment the press notified the public that the law was to be implemented at the end of the spring term in 1968, the protests generated were immediate, huge, and far wider than the authorities had expected. At Nanterre, Daniel Cohn-Bendit emerged as the charismatic and bold leader of these protests, which quickly involved thousands of students. Strikes and massive demonstrations became weekly events as demands grew for the repeal of the Fouchet Law. The press and the university administration treated the student demands with disparaging and sometimes insulting responses. Rumors began to take on a major role. One that was pervasive was the fear that Cohn-Bendit, who held a West German passport, would be deported from France. The police were given orders to use violence if necessary to end the demonstrations, which they employed with particular brutality on occasions.

Further fuel was added to the fires when the January 1968 Tet Offensive against the American army was announced in Vietnam, and led to the creation of support groups among the French students on

gathered from interviews and interrogations. A valuable and extensive bibliography on this period of Black and Red Terror can be found in the notes compiled in Rimanelli, "Italian Terrorism and Society," 283–96.

behalf of the Vietnamese Communists. "The Movement of 22 March" emerged in Nanterre on that day after the police arrested militants of the National Vietnam Committee, following a demonstration to celebrate the forthcoming "victory of the Vietnamese people against American imperialism."[74] News of the attempted assassination of Rudi Dutschke had the effect of both further attracting militants and emboldening right-wing groups to attack the offices of their despised Marxist-inspired antagonists on the left. The government's response was to close down Nanterre and the Sorbonne. In May, the violence reached unprecedented levels, with demonstrators taking over whole neighborhoods using cobblestone barricades ripped up from the streets, and the police becoming more ruthless in their assaults with gas grenades as well as firearms. The violence cooled only at the end of May with the intervention of General de Gaulle, legislation by the National Assembly to address the problems of the university system, and the signing of the Grenelle Agreements, which were directed at satisfying demands of the labor unions who had joined the struggle.[75]

The "texte du jour," which for a time joined Fanon's writings as the inspiration for socialist-oriented militants in the student movements of the late 1960s and 1970s, was Daniel Cohn-Bendit's *Obsolete Communism: The Left Wing Alternative*. Written in the heat of the moment, the book is a treatise on the crisis affecting governments and societies in the West in general, but is specifically an analysis of the antagonisms that brought about the 22 May Movement in France. Unlike the manifestoes of Fanon or Marighella, to which his book is sometimes linked, Cohn-Bendit does not focus on violence as a necessary tactic in the struggle against the state. For him, it is the terror of bureaucracy that exercises its stranglehold on the strivings of ordinary people to improve the quality of their lives. Cohn-Bendit indicts structures of authority, and the educational administration from Fouchet down to the deans at Nanterre as self-serving guardians of tradition with little interest in the daily problems of their constituents. More devastating, given his political role in the demonstrations, was his critique of both the French Communist Party and the heads of their allied labor unions, whom he

---

[74] Marwick, *The Sixties*, 604.
[75] Ibid., 617–18. For a cautious but comprehensive and sympathetic look back at the French crisis and its legacy, see Singer, *Prelude to Revolution*.

saw essentially as alternative versions of authoritarian capitalism that participated fully in the corrupt practices of the existing regime. Their efforts at conciliation and reformism, he argued strongly, were not only unrevolutionary, but antirevolutionary. His preference was for an anarchist-inspired mass movement that refused to compromise with the state in all its guises, and one that would resort to violence only when repressed and provoked into desperation.[76]

By the time the Berlin Wall fell in 1989, and certainly before the demise of the Soviet Union two years later, most of the ideological violence of the Cold War era had waned if not vanished entirely. The situations differed from country to country in spite of what appeared to be similar commitments and intentions on the part of both governments and insurgents throughout the period. The terrorist situation lessened largely as a result of a combination of repression, exhaustion and failure on both sides to achieve their desired outcomes. Governments remained in place, though quite altered by the violence; insurgents retreated only to re-emerge with new agendas to challenge existing authorities. These new battles of the next period of terrorisms already existed in a minor key but would soon dominate in the period to follow.

Nevertheless, in virtually every instance of struggle during the period now designated as "the sixties," unrealizable political fantasies continued to predominate as they had in the past among those who saw the use of violence as the means to their ends. On one side, the visions of socialist utopian futures continued to inflate the hopes of radical protesters and militants, while, on the other, it haunted the corridors of power in government cabinets across the Western world. At the same time, the very real problems of inequality and injustice that desperately needed to be addressed were left to fester while the responsible authorities and their radicalized competitors for power competed with one another using increasingly violent means. A continuing aspect of this culture of terror was the compulsion to invent, imagine and symbolically empower a collective enemy. No radical movement came close to

---

[76] Cohn-Bendit and Cohn-Bendit, *Obsolete Communism*. The last section of the book is a searching examination of the roots of Communist Party failures in the period between the Bolshevik seizure of power and the crushing of the anarchist rebellion at Kronstadt in 1921. See pp. 199–245. For a companion contemporary account which emphasizes extensive press sources covering the events in Paris, see Seale and McConville, *Red Flag/Black Flag*. On 1968 in its larger global context, see Kurlansky, *1968: The Year that Rocked the World*. Also very useful for a transatlantic perspective is Horn, *The Spirit of '68*.

posing the kind of threat to the state that rulers and their security chiefs envisaged, making the states of emergency declared in response, more often than not, experiments in excessive repression. Similarly, the brutality and evil ascribed to even the most feared dictators of the period proved frequently to be exaggerations of the enforcement powers they possessed and the longevity of their presence, horrific as many of their crimes were. To be sure, there were always some individuals in government who sought to lessen the terror from above, and many in society who found benign alternative explanations and justifications for their harsh rulers. So too, radical opposition movements rarely were able to win the social support they needed to be successful since too many people could not morally accept the tactics of violence used as reprisals.

Nevertheless, militants, fired with visions of revolutionary insurrections, took to the streets, occupied public buildings, overran university administrations, bombed their way to prominence and proclaimed demands that the state could not accept. The police carried out the assignments from their superiors in departments and ministries, infiltrating, provoking and using extreme violence, when permitted, to quell the tide of discontent.

Ultimately, the problems that fuel periods of extensive terrorism cannot easily be disentangled from the legal systems of the countries where the events occur, and the powerful interests that are served by engaging in the violence. To a great extent, this is due to the fact that the very measures enacted that are designed to protect citizens from fear and violence also contain provisions to provide security for the enforcement of the authority of the state. The Cold War era complicated this relationship further because of the dominating influence of the two competing superpowers. Too often, statesmen, security forces, insurgents and ordinary citizens on both sides of the divide found themselves caught up in what appeared to be a moral struggle against an implacably ruthless ideological enemy willing to use any means to achieve tactical advantage or strategic victory. Given such stark choices, governments from Moscow to Pretoria, and from Berlin to Santiago, permitted temporary emergency measures to be extended indefinitely to deal with the crisis at hand. In some extreme cases, the states of emergency lasted for many years, as they did under Stalin and Pinochet, making the regimes dependent upon the use of terrorism to attempt to totally eliminate the threat from below. Often, these tactics generated more problems than they solved. Because the agents of violence on both sides had such an abiding interest in maintaining terrorist tactics to achieve unrealistic ends, the trajectories of political violence at the level of both governments and insurgencies in the era of ideological terror remained inextricably intertwined. The ancient problems of validating state legitimacy for both rulers and the ruled, finding a polity that could minimize the unacceptable conditions of inequality, intolerance and injustice in society, and establishing a polity which permitted governments to retain power without fear of their own citizens, all remained unsolved. The variables for the continuing presence of terrorism therefore remained where they had been for two centuries, at the heart of modern political culture, always within reach for those desiring its embrace.

9 TOWARD THE PRESENT: TERRORISM IN THEORY AND PRACTICE

The transition from the modern to the contemporary is one in which the challenges to the historian are the most difficult, since we lack much of the empirical evidence necessary for a proper historical analysis that remains unavailable due to its sensitive connection to ongoing terrorist campaigns. We may well be concerned about the conclusions we may be approaching because we are still engaged in the enterprise as representatives of one side or another with interests in the competing currents involved. For decades of the twentieth century, the Cold War presented exactly such restrictions, and it is only in its aftermath that we can obtain the evidence to answer questions about which formerly we could provide little more than knowledgeable speculation. To take one example, we no longer have to rely on estimates made by Sovietologists about the structure of the USSR's power elite by watching where they are positioned in relation to one another atop the Lenin Mausoleum during the annual Revolution Day celebrations; we now have access to previously unavailable records of party meetings, diplomatic cables, and secret security archives, which permits us to arrive at both new and more accurate findings. Now that the Cold War era has run its course, it appears that it can be moved out of the historical category of the contemporary and appropriately consigned to an expanded version of the period since the French Revolution that we have been referring to as the modern era.

Despite this urge to historicize with the advantages of greater degrees of objectivity, we must recognize that some of the contested issues of that period, rather than vanishing, instead reappeared with greater force in the aftermath. With regard to the specific problematic of political violence, we see not so much an entirely new landscape as a cinematic fade in and fade out of certain trends, many of which were already in progress before 1991 when the bipolar superpower struggle that defined the previous period ended. Alignments were reconfigured between the antagonistic forces at work, but significant elements remained as part of transmitted cultures of violence. The nation state did not vanish, nor did its generic hegemony even weaken despite certain predictions to the contrary. Insurgencies were not conquered; on the contrary, in some ways they have strengthened in the post-Cold War transition. Above all, terrorism became a central feature of foreign policy in government circles, a leading agenda for active insurgencies, and the paramount concern of citizens globally, perhaps even more so than in the past.

The grand narrative of the victory of the free world over Soviet communism notwithstanding, the forces at work in the preceding years require far more complex consideration. The important role that the tropes of Marxism played in justifying the need for violent tactics that were adopted by both governments (which feared it) and insurgents (who embraced it) gradually exhausted themselves in the corridors of combat that dominated Western political and cultural life in the decades after the Second World War. The perceived danger of communist subversion, which had been the justification for so much of the violent repression by governments of their own citizens across entire continents, gradually ceased to function as an engine of fear capable of mobilizing forms of state terror. Similarly, Marxism, in its various redemptionist and insurrectionist interpretations, which included resorting to tactics of violence, also waned as an ideology with the capacity to attract large numbers of adherents with an appeal of charismatic inspiration. This also influenced the fact that Marxism, in the modes in which it was applied as state authority, achieved only a temporary status of legitimacy as a form of governance (with the continuing notable exceptions of China, North Korea and Cuba). However, the structures of antagonism that had fueled the terrorisms of the Cold War era remained, with new ingredients and components for each side to sort out. The interdependencies between those with interests in the maintenance of terrorism in both governments and insurgencies, so central to the past political conflicts in which violence was utilized, remained.

The reasons for this continuity lie in the persistence of the problems that engendered the terrorisms of the past. Above all, the question of state legitimacy re-emerged, thinly disguised, in changing sites of contestation. The US, widely recognized as the sole remaining superpower, assumed the responsibility of controlling global security by expanding its influence as "the empire of liberty."[1] American intervention abroad had been an important part of the country's foreign policy since its inception as a republic, and thus continued this assertion of authority as the twentieth century waned. In place of a communist threat, the new menace was characterized as a religious subnational network organized by al-Qaeda and its affiliates.

From the start of al-Qaeda's appearance in diplomatic cables and the international press, terrorist acts, unprovoked and barbaric in nature, were foregrounded in the analysis of this network as the justification for what were described as counter-terrorist policies by the US government. The possibility of the US playing an important role in fostering the violent acts it was seeking to crush was not part of the official narrative. In fact, the issue at the core of the emerging post-Cold War conflict with al-Qaeda as a phenomenon was one of political legitimacy. The US assumed it had an obligation to counteract forces that threatened its interests, particularly in the Middle East, and to respond with violence. This new insurgency reacted in ways that insurgencies so frequently have in the past when contesting the intrusion of an outside power asserting its sovereignty. As a consequence, Iraq and Afghanistan became the post-Soviet battlefields of terrorism for the US and its NATO allies. Further, the ideological threat posed by al-Qaeda was defined primarily as a religious danger that menaced the fundamental liberties of the secular democratic world. In fact, there was a crucial political foundation to the al-Qaeda proclamations that received far less attention from the defenders of Western sovereignty. The network was from the start dependent on military armaments from private suppliers, financial support from states like Iran, and safe harbor for their strategic bases in Sudan, Pakistan and Afghanistan, at different time periods. Beyond that, setting up al-Qaeda's future fantasy order once victory over the infidels was achieved, according to the vision described by Ayman Al Zawahari, who worked closely with Osama Bin Laden, involved creating a modern version of the medieval

[1] Westad, *The Global Cold War*, 8–38.

Muslim caliphate, which would have to involve many governmental institutional structures carrying out Islamic policies, including the repressive security apparatus so familiar to the modern secular state it was designed to replace.[2]

One of the most prescient observers of this need to enforce the sovereignty of the state was the political theorist, Harold Lasswell, who as early as 1937 formulated the concept of "the garrison state." As he watched the world slide toward global war, Lasswell noted a particularly insidious and threatening current that was forming within governments, regardless of whether they were democratic or authoritarian, that he believed was both new and influential. Policies, he noted, were increasingly being made by a rising group of specialists whose expertise was violence. Particularly alarming to Lasswell was the fact that these were not only elected or appointed officials at the state level, but also groups that had taken command in military strategy offices, scientific institutes and in the boardrooms of significant corporate enterprises. To combat threats, he argued, governments were establishing zones of "battle potential" involving a wide array of specializations, with priorities given to technical services, personnel management and entrepreneurial profit. Lasswell referred to this tendency as "the socialization of danger" which was enforced by a permanent perpetuation of the threat of violence, from within and without, that required the overall protection of scientific, corporate and governmental specialists in violence – "the political elite of the garrison state."[3]

In such circumstances, intelligence becomes a principal feature of state policy and social consciousness. Increasing numbers of people are recruited from universities and corporations and placed in positions where their expertise can be of service to those in positions of authority in government, the military or security agencies. As this process expands, according to Lasswell, laws are passed to legitimize their powers of surveillance in order to facilitate their ability to locate the vulnerabilities of the antagonists of the state who threaten its security, integrity or territory. He called this "the civilianization of the garrison state" as ordinary citizens were encouraged to be suspicious of the

---

[2] Ayman Al Zawahiri, "Knights Under the Prophet's Banner," in Laqueur, *Voices of Terror*, 426–33.

[3] Lasswell, *Essays on the Garrison*, 56, 59, 64. The essays in this edition were first published in 1940 and 1941; Lasswell used the term "garrison state" initially in his article, "Sino-Japanese Crisis: The Garrison State versus the Civilian State," 643–9.

loyalty of their peers and to rely on the government's specialists in violence for the resolution of doubt.[4]

Some of the security agencies Lasswell anxiously predicted came into full force, under their various notorious acronyms, before fading out with the collapse of their governmental patrons.[5] Those feared names include the KGB of the USSR; the Stasi of the German Democratic Republic; Romania's Securitate; the Shah of Iran's Savak force and Saddam Hussein's Revolutionary Guards in Iraq, among many others. Others continue to function with increased capacities in the bureaucracy of terror, ranging from the Inter Intelligence Agency of Pakistan, the Israeli Mossad, and the powerful military-security agencies in Iran, Egypt, Syria and Saudi Arabia, to the global operations of the CIA in the US and MI6 in the UK.

Meanwhile, the lineups from the insurgencies also changed. The IRA and the PLO shifted from violent militants to inchoate state administrators. The Turkish PKK along with the Tamil Tigers in Sri Lanka, the November 17 group in Greece, and the Shining Path in Peru were either severely repressed or wiped out by systematic efforts of the security agencies and military forces. In their place around the world, governments and citizens faced the wrath of Hezbollah, Hamas, al-Qaeda, Abu Sayyaf and the Taliban.[6] The conditions for terrorism continue unabated, with new personnel to act out the entanglements of violence over the unresolved problems between governments and their oppositions, nationally and transnationally.

Whether we are talking about a garrison state, security state, or perhaps the milder term, vigilant state,[7] we cannot escape the role of the chief source of political authority if we are to understand the very significant role that violence has come to play in our lives. It is the state, after all, which remains the repository of people's hopes, aspirations and well-being, fashioned within legal frameworks that increasingly involve the participation of the social order in their applications. This has been true for the last two centuries, since the secular nation state

---

[4] Lasswell, *Essays on the Garrison State*, 97, 98, 107. The concept has been used more recently and in a different interpretation in Friedberg, *In the Shadow of the Garrison State*.

[5] See the interesting analysis of the phenomenon of state demise in historical perspective in Fazal, *State Death*, esp. 169–228.

[6] For a recent comprehensive survey of the insurgencies, see Burleigh, *Blood and Rage*, chs 7 and 8.

[7] I take this term from Porter, *The Origins of the Vigilant State*.

assumed these responsibilities from the monarchies that dominated the Western world before the era of the French Revolution.

The dilemma at the core of the relationship between the state and the presence of political violence is intimately bound up with the manner in which governments and citizens carry out their responsibilities with regard to one another. Early in the twentieth century, Heinrich von Treitschke brought fresh relevance to Hobbes' classic notion of the state as a Leviathan, protecting its subjects in return for limitations on their liberty, by interpreting the modern state as supreme, benign and omnipotent of necessity. "The idea of a positive right of resistance" was, for him, an indefensible absurdity that could only lead to the disruption of the governing process, bring harm to the civil order, and thereby extinguish the realization of a free citizenry.[8] Harold Laski, writing between the world wars and citing many of the same sources that Treitshchke used, came to a different conclusion. He understood the importance of balancing the power of the government with the expression of the citizenry in a manner that avoided the authoritarian state on the one hand, and violent revolution on the other.[9]

While it may appear understandable for Treitschke in Germany and Laski in England to have written as they did, their interpretations have retained a durable presence. Theorists have always conceptualized within the framework of their own nation's values, and it is not surprising to see that they still do. For much of the Western world, and beyond it as well, the presumption that one's own government is acting in the interests of its citizenry is common, even among critics. Even when policies of violence are called into action, society will be prone to understand that this is necessary to crush a clear and present internal or external danger. To assume otherwise is to wander into the territory reserved for the categories of the subversive and the dangerous rebel who seeks not to reform but to overthrow the existing order. The state, which has always held a monopoly on advanced weaponry over its citizens, also has always had on its side cooperation with, if not outright control over, both the legal system and the economy within its territory. The values of patriotism and national loyalty cannot be discounted as additional bulwarks in generating mass support for governments, regardless of whether they are acting within the

---

[8] von Treitschke, *Politics*, 191–2.   [9] Laski, *The State in Theory and Practice*, 178–9.

constitutional limits of the prescribed legal system to which their leaders are formally committed.

There have been many good recent studies on the problem of terrorism within democratic states. Almost without exception, the content of all these efforts, however conceptually interesting and convincingly evidenced they may be, is remarkably similar. The democratic republic, flaws notwithstanding, remains in symbol and reality the institutional embodiment of societal protection, defense and security against violent threats from below and without.

There are many recent examples of this perspective. For the political theorist John Keane, violence, simply put, is "the greatest enemy of democracy as we know it." Democracy, he argues, is "marked by an inner tendency to non-violence," rooted in deep suspicions about the power of the police and the military. Violence "in mature democracies" is understood as "the unlawful use of force," for which there are legal mechanisms in place with constitutional guarantees to ensure that the boundaries are not crossed.

At the same time, Keane is hardly denying the presence of terrorism in our time, especially since the September 11 attacks. His point, however, is that it is born elsewhere, metastasizes in lawless territories, and is imported into civilized, democratic space packaged as what he calls "surplus violence." Threatening though it is, terrorism is not an insurmountable problem. Keane classifies three main categories of terror, which include nuclear-armed non-democratic governments, stateless areas harboring fanatic militants, and mobile terrorist organizations driven by apocalyptic visions of transformation. Each of the forms in his taxonomy can be minimized or eliminated by what he calls the tactics of "democratizing the violence," a process which involves patient efforts to listen, communicate and present responsible moral positions in order to overcome the threat, rather than declaring wars on terror.[10]

This faith in democratic institutions to transcend the arenas of political violence except when threatened by them is a prevalent theme in the literature on terrorism. A prominent American scholar in the field, Leonard Weinberg, has argued a similar interpretation for many years. In a recent essay that seeks to shed light on the sources of terrorism within democracies and why democracies are targeted by

[10] Keane, *Violence and Democracy*, ch. 1.

terrorists, the problematic is already freighted in a specific orientation by the nature of the very questions asked. Nevertheless, the author is concerned about the fact that violent incidents continue to plague democratic republics.

His answers revolve around a set of conditions that character-ize the multi-ethnic nature and global positions of the most powerful nations in the Western world. First, politically, the citizenry of the US is a diverse mix of colliding interest groups that, though normally able to resolve differences without violence, are vulnerable to periods of ter-rorism. The system survives without losing its democratic essence due to its strong constitutional structure, which is not fundamentally chal-lenged except by a minority of extreme opponents. Thus, the "permis-sive conditions" that define democracies may provide more opportunities for political violence to occur, but less chance that such tactics will succeed. Second, with regard to the international system, the US is "an attractive target" for terrorists from a variety of orienta-tions because of its wealth, power and influence around the world. Though cognizant of the fact that "terrorists attack the United States and Western European countries because they oppose the economic and cultural penetration of their homelands by the West," statistical studies show, Weinberg argues, that the "explanation for the current wave of international terrorism based on reaction against globalization and countries identified as globalization's sponsors and beneficiaries is not supported by the available evidence." In short, there is a huge distinction between being vulnerable to terrorism on the one hand, and being responsible for it on the other. In Weinberg's analysis, the former takes exclusive priority over the latter.[11]

David Rapoport, whose prolific work has greatly influenced terrorism studies, reflects a broader approach with his wave theory. Rapoport sees terrorism evolving historically in terms of four conceptu-ally distinct waves or "cycles of activity" expanding and contracting in

---

[11] Weinberg, "Democracy and Terrorism," in Louise Richardson (ed.), *The Roots of Terrorism*, 45–56. Richardson has assembled a rich array of contemporary terrorist scholars in this volume. In the same vein, Tal Becker has characterized the various ways in which states may be involved in terrorism, which is most often largely as support networks for the private anti-state insurgencies that pose, he argues, the real threat to security. His point is that governments must take responsibility for such policies and be held accountable in order to bring this non-state terror under control. See Becker, *Terrorism and the State*. Boaz Ganor has done similar insurgent oriented terrorism analysis. See his "Defining Terrorism: Is One Man's Terrorist Another Man's Freedom Fighter?," 287–304.

specific time periods dominated primarily by insurgent movements, beginning in the 1880s in Russia, and driven by "a common predominant energy." These waves of terrorism, frequently composed of a multitude of insurgent organizations, last until they cease to inspire new groups with common purposes, and then disappear. The main waves have been organized around appeals to anarchist, nationalist, ideologically internationalist, and, most recently, transnational religious orientations, with each deeply influenced by the specific historical conflicts of their time periods. Rapoport sees the cycles of violence as intimately tied to the successes and failures of democratic reform programs of nation-states. Although the role of governments in the violence is acknowledged, the main thrust of the wave theory points to the dangers historically posed by the insurgencies to both states and societies.[12]

European scholars have also made inquiries into many of these problems. In particular, Blandine Kriegel and Giorgio Agamben, two theoretically oriented writers interested in the historical origins of the phenomenon of terrorism and its relationship to the state well before the French Revolution, deserve attention. Although both cite their intellectual debt to Michel Foucault, their interpretations of the problem of violence and the state could not be more opposed. Kriegel's thesis focuses on the fact that the state was the responsible agent in bringing about the widespread rule of law by gradually replacing the abuses, violence and capricious rule of the feudal monarchies. Rights were granted, over time, by state authorities and their parliaments that, while limited at first, eventually were expanded to cover all social classes. The state, she argues, was itself subject to the law, which provided "constraints on power and limitations on human uses of things and of other human beings." In addition, while she recognizes that the state has always had a legal commitment to the preservation and protection of life, she does not deny that it also retained "the right to mete out life and death to citizens."[13] Nevertheless, it is clear from her analysis that she feels the critique of the state, which has dominated postmodern theory, has been exaggerated and one-sided.

[12] Rapoport, "The Four Waves of Modern Terrorism," 3–30.
[13] Kriegel, *The State and the Rule of Law*, esp. 11, 24–32, 41–2, 63.

Agamben is also very interested in the evolution of the European legal system within the framework of the nation state. However, he is far more concerned than Kriegel about the extent to which the state was able to make use of the law in order to justify acts of violence against its own citizens. For him, the state's "right to violence" has not only been exercised from the earliest period of its existence in the post-feudal world, but legal systems have supported its use against declared domestic dangers as well. He cites the jurisprudence that established what he calls the hegemony of "sovereign violence" and "sovereign terror" as the precedents for modern forms of nation state violence. However, his main contention is that rulers have always found ways to use violence against their subjects and citizens extra-judicially by making controlling use of "judicial power not mediated by law." This is what he calls the "state of exception," a policy which states call into being to confront a crisis, but which in many instances remains in place as a permanent part of the legal system, and thus, "becomes the rule."[14]

A related concern in any discussion of terrorism is that of its relationship to morality. Many scholars have tried to answer the question of whether there is an ethical justification to the use of political violence in any form. The answers have not been conclusive. Indeed, unless we take partisan sides in a struggle, we still cannot easily find our way out of the simple logic of one person's terrorist being another's freedom fighter (and vice versa). The case for moral violence, eloquently and passionately formulated at the dawn of the modern discourse on the subject, by St-Just at the state level and by Heinzen at the insurgent level, still remains with us in its refined and revised forms. Governments continue to explain the need to do battle with the insurgents on moral grounds, while the militants justify their violence with their own moral claims. The issues may concern concrete spaces such as territory (whether regarded as religiously sacred, historically significant for ethnic or other reasons, or endowed with economic resources), or more abstract concerns about dignity, honor and the legitimacy of a political system. They are driving forces nonetheless, regardless of whether they are expressed by an underground movement's leadership or a government in power, Still, the distinction between what is in fact a privilege (I am entitled to...) as

---

[14] Agamben, *State of Exception*, esp. 20, 32–5, 40–2, 64.

opposed to a right (I deserve...) is obscured in the fire and smoke of moral antagonisms.[15]

Although there are no easy solutions to the issues embedded within the framework of defining ethical terrorism, the criteria offered by the British moral philosopher Stuart Hampshire some time ago are still worth considering. He proposed four considerations that he believed were possible justifications for committing acts of political violence, or, as he put it, "justified killing in very extreme situations in peacetime," although they refer exclusively to insurgencies reacting to the abuse of state power. They include the following:

> *First, that it is a response to a great injustice and oppression, as of a resistance movement against a foreign power ruling by force and terror so that the victim is the reverse of innocent; secondly, that it is certain that no lawful and non-violent means of remedying the injustice and oppression will be given; thirdly, that the political killing will cause far less suffering, and less widespread suffering than the present injustice and cruelty are causing; lastly that it really is very probable that the killing will end the oppression, and that it will not provoke more violence and more horror.*[16]

Yet another category of analysis that has attracted increasing attention might be termed "the end of terrorism." Historically, insurgencies have sought to end the violence of the state, and governments with their security forces have devoted much of their annual budget allotments on efforts to eradicate those same insurgencies. Neither side has managed to abolish the existence of the other, since rulers and militants capable of brutalities seem to have been inexhaustibly replaceable over the last two centuries. Governments have fallen, and movements have been brought to an end, but the phenomenon of terrorism, state and insurgent, continues. Studies that have primarily identified insurgencies as the violent threat, have indeed focused on the manner in which states have repressed their activities. These include the arrest of the leaders of

---

[15] For an interesting discussion of these and related issues, with a good bibliography of the relevant literature, see Held, *How Terrorism is Wrong*.

[16] Quoted in Honderich, *Terrorism for Humanity*, 212, fn. 9.

militant groups, which usually severely weakens the movements, as well as repression by brute force. In some cases, militants find their way to negotiations and even into power (the FLN in Algeria, the Palestinian PLO, the Provisional IRA in Northern Ireland and the ANC in South Africa, among others). [17] However, once the leaders of an insurgency manage to obtain political power, there are no guarantees that they will not resort to policies of violence to legitimate and consolidate their authority at some point. Nor can we ever be certain that new oppositions will not arise, in the time-honored manner in which they always have, to raise questions about abusive government policies and unaddressed problems facing multitudes of their fellow citizens, if not the very legitimacy of the regime. Given the possibility of these developments, the insurgent-focused and security-oriented literature does not present us with a reliable formula for ending terrorism.

Nevertheless, most of the discussions of these matters tend to be resolved (at least to the satisfaction of their authors) in favor of seeing the problems from the perspective of the state. This main interpretive orientation in terrorism studies, characterized in one recent analysis as "orthodox terrorism theory," "favors the illegal and illegitimate approach to explaining terrorism that mirrors the realist, state-centric understanding." The other prominent schools of thought revolve around "radical terrorism theory," which focuses on insurgent justifications of political violence by the state's antagonists, and "moderate terrorism theory," which emphasizes the structural problems of a political, social or economic nature that play a leading role in creating mobilizing cadres that activate terrorism.[18] If we add to these the two categories of totalitarian/authoritarian terrorism (Stalin, Hitler, Pol Pot, etc.) and what is referred to frequently by the awkward term "state-sponsored terrorism" (Iran supporting Hezbollah, or the CIA arranging the overthrow of Allende, Mossedegh and others), we have a fairly complete picture of the available choices in the literature.[19]

---

[17] Cronin, *Ending Terrorism*, ch. 2 ("Historical Patterns in Ending Terrorism"), 23–49. The author also applies these lessons from the past into a futurist scenario of how al-Qaeda can be defeated and what a post-al-Qaeda world might look like. See also Jones and Libicki, *How Terrorist Groups End: Lessons for Encountering al-Qa'ida*, 9–44 for the discussion, and 143–88 for the extensive worldwide data set compiled by the authors.

[18] Franks, *Rethinking the Roots of Terrorism*, 46.

[19] For a thorough discussion of this earlier point of view, see Wardlaw, *Political Terrorism*.

If there is an "orthodox" perspective, it rests on the unexamined assumption that defensive state violence is legal terror, while opposition violence is automatically illegitimate. Such an understanding is usually acceptable to the majority of citizens in a given country so long as the enemy is clearly identified as a threat to the nation's overall security and any individual's well-being. This faith in the state also has permitted, in the polite phrase of James Scott, its ability to make "quite discriminating interventions of every kind," from public health measures to political surveillance and beyond. Scott further reminds us that the state is neither wholly benign nor evil, but "is a vexed institution that is the ground of both our freedoms and our unfreedoms." He asks us to "weigh judiciously the benefits of certain state interventions against their costs,"[20] and this is nowhere more vital than when the government uses its awesome authority to sanction violence against its own, or anyone else's, citizens.

There are now efforts being made to critically revise these predominating categories. Most importantly, questions are being raised about the validity of seeing the state exclusively as society's protector and justifying its violence as legitimate "counterterrorism," part of a necessary security policy standing as a bulwark against the threat from below. The alternatives to most of the existing literature would seek, as an earlier volume had once attempted, to bring the state back in to the analysis of terrorism.[21] The evidence has always been overwhelming in spite of the long tendency to turn away from its significance. In any historical statistical investigation, the results clearly show exponentially more victims of state political violence than the number of those wounded, tortured and killed by insurgent movements in all categories. During the twentieth century alone, states were responsible, directly or indirectly, for over 179 million deaths, and this does not include the world wars, the Nazi holocaust and the atomic bombing casualties in

---

[20] Scott, *Seeing Like a State*, 3.
[21] Evans, Rueschemeyer and Skocpol, *Bringing the State Back In*. Another book that attempted to crack through the predominant orientation which defined terrorism mainly as the militant insurgent was Falk, *Revolutionaries and Functionaries*. Charles Tilly also recognized the importance of including state violence in his interpretive framework, See, e.g., *The Politics of Collective Violence*, 19–20. See also my discussion in "Ordinary Terrorism," 128–9 and the *European Review of History*, v. 14, n. 3 (September, 2007), a special issue of articles devoted to transnational and comparative perspectives on terrorism, stressing "the interdependent relationship between state violence and terrorism" (p. 276).

Japan.[22] There are very few countries on any continent that have not contributed at some time and in some important way to these morbidity statistics. Also, as this book has tried to demonstrate, every kind of government (not every government), whether authoritarian or democratic, has been complicit in terrorizing its own citizenry in various ways at some point in its history.

Why, then, the resistance to accepting what appears to be the obvious? In part, the objection to including the state in definitions of terrorism is rooted in the acceptance of the notion that the violence of governments is not conducted offensively but is, except in the most apparent cases of authoritarianism, both legal and defensive. Even when discussions do turn toward governments, frequently the focus is on the situational, such as the abuse of human rights in a specific instance, whereupon committees are formed to examine the actions, reports are issued at some point, and officials are on occasion charged with crimes. However, the legitimacy of the institution of the state is often left outside the investigation. It is precisely on this point that the conflict from below surfaces, since the militants do question that very legitimacy. The citizen is left with a choice, and most will stay with the state as it uses its substantial authority to shift full responsibility for the violence onto the shoulders of the underground movement that is contesting the validity of its power and its policies.[23]

The argument made in this book attempts to locate a revisionist position that integrates, rather than separates, the historic antagonists. To be sure, the Italian philosopher Sergio Cotta pointed us in this direction some time ago. Reminding us that the word "violence" should be understood within the framework of its descriptive roots in the act of "violating" another person, Cotta rejects the presumption that it has always been part of the human condition, as well as the notion that it is new to its own time whenever it appears collectively as a social threat. He also finds little use in the notion of terrorism

---

[22] Rummel, *Death by Government*, 1–27. Scholars of the subject are of course aware of this, but simply bypass the issue by stating that their focus is on the underground antistate militant organizations. See, e.g., Chaliand and Blin, *The History of Terrorism*, 6–7.

[23] See the essays in Jackson, Murphy and Poynting, *Contemporary State Terrorism*, and Franks, *Rethinking the Roots of Terrorism*. For a good recent example of the continued focus of terrorism analysis exclusively on the militants assaulting the state, see Ranstorp, *Understanding Violent Radicalisation*.

appearing in separate waves. He instead finds a better metaphor in Vico's notion of the slow course and rapid recourse of historical currents that more resembles the constancy of ocean tides coming ashore ceaselessly.

Not only is the phenomenon of political violence therefore an historical constant, Cotta argues, but it has the tendency to seep into many other aspects of social and institutional existence, which he calls the "field extension of violence" in both space and time. It also has the ability to wound some (its victims) and heal others (its proponents). In one of his more paradoxical passages, Cotta writes that this view forces us to realize that "to eliminate violence, it is necessary to make use of it." To clarify this, he takes us back to the memorable characters in Dostoevsky's novel *The Devils*, where the redemptive, liberating promises of violence that attract the maniacal focus of Alexei Kirillov and Peter Verkhovensky turn out to be "liberation from a false destiny" in which "the new man, free of any bond, finally emerges master of himself." And it was Dostoevsky, Cotta concludes, who also showed us that the antagonists in the terrorist struggle are actually mirror images of one another in certain ways: "The *realpolitiker* and the revolutionary, [though] irreconcilable enemies on the level of praxis, are united to their depths in their common acceptance of, and familiarity with, violence."[24]

As I hope this book has shown, terrorism is a historical phenomenon characterized by the violent combat between elements in governments and societies over unresolved political issues. The combat produces situations in which the consequences of the violence, which is conducted either from above by a variety of political entities or from below directed by equally varied insurgencies, become a dominating factor in the daily functioning of social and political life. The phenomenon is sustained by the dynamic interaction of the combatants and their allies (from supporters to the media) who may be complicit through passive or active engagement, by force or choice. Further, there is increasing reliance on violence as a means either to achieve a desired political goal seen as unattainable by nonviolent methods, or to neutralize the currently perceived threat that may be conjured or real, or contain aspects, as so often is the case, of both. The forces that bring terrorist moments (not movements) to prominence are permanent features of modern nation states, capable of being activated in various

[24] Cotta, *Why Violence?*, 5–6, 12–17, 19, 59.

ways either by government leaders or underground militants in a declared crisis situation. As a result, widespread fear of experiencing the brutalities and atrocities committed by the agents of violence takes its place in the forefront of our consciousness, often determining how we plan our day, what space to choose in order to avoid the danger of becoming a victim of the violence from either side. It is this overwhelming presence in our lives and the determining role it plays in our quotidian decision-making that makes it, not exceptional or extraordinary, but so completely ordinary.[25]

The varieties of political violence that we tend to collect under the emotionally laden concept of terrorism are the product of a long history that stretches back at least to the paradigm-changing era of the French Revolution. With the abolition of one of Europe's most durable and powerful monarchies, the unintended fusion of Enlightenment-inspired ideologues with uprooted rural masses prowling the Parisian streets, motivated by a sense of economic desperation and the psychological willingness to transgress all traditional boundaries, created a new world of unrealizable expectations and a search for new forms of state legitimacy. The document that became the ideological manifesto of these hopes and dreams for better lives was the Declaration of the Rights of Man and the Citizen, promulgated on 26 August 1789 by the newly established and politically unprecedented National Assembly in Paris.

The Declaration of the Rights of Man plays an important role in the emerging world of political violence, despite the fact that the topic is not mentioned in the document. What it did was to open the door to utopian aspirations for the newly empowered citizenries and to their potential realizations by the efforts of governments in the post-monarchical nation state system then dawning. With the collapse of the authority of and symbolic reverence for the *Ancien Régime*'s ruling orders from the royal court to the country's churches and estates, new identities were mobilized by the application of the principles of rights codified in the Declaration.

The significance of this document resides in the way it articulates the changing relationship between state and society. "Men are born and remain free and equal in rights" is the Rousseauian opening flourish. The second clause states that "the purpose of all political association is the

---

[25] I take much of this discussion from my article "Ordinary Terrorism," 125–6.

preservation of the natural and imprescriptible rights of man. These rights are liberty, property, security and resistance to oppression." In contrast to the structures of authority that had dominated for centuries, the nation, not the ruler, was "the source of all sovereignty," invested and legitimized by the people, rather than by God and the Catholic church. The legal system was now to be "an expression of the will of the community" within the nation to which all citizens, through their elected representatives, had the "right to concur."

Two other clauses are significant. The seventh states that because the law is to be made by the people for their security against, among other perils, arbitrary arrest, punishment and abuse, "every citizen called upon or apprehended by virtue of the law, ought immediately to obey and renders himself culpable by resistance." A related matter is raised in clause 12: "A public force being necessary to give security to the rights of men and citizens, that force is instituted for the benefit of the community, and not for the particular benefit of the persons with whom it is entrusted."[26]

The contradictions expressed in these clauses would plague the modern world in ways unimaginable to their idealistic formulators. The transition from the world of absolute monarchies was made clear, but the precise manner in which political power would be shared and exercised between state and society in the new democratic republic was not. While assigning the newly invented conceptions of liberty and rights to the citizenry, the document also makes clear that citizens have an unqualified obligation to obey the law, thereby making resistance essentially a criminal act. More precisely, "resistance to oppression" was expressed as a citizen's inherent legal right, but resistance to obedience to the law rendered him "culpable" before that same legal framework.

At the same time, the elected representatives of the continent's innovative new republic had gained seemingly limitless opportunities to create a polity that would realize these rights in a society that could perhaps achieve the fantastic hopes of the final utopian stage of Condorcet's theory of the historical progress of humanity.[27] They rushed

[26] The document is reproduced in Doyle, *The French Revolution*, 12–15, and Collins, *The Ancien Regime and the French Revolution*, 99. On the controversies over the historical impact of this document, see Moyne, *The Last Utopia: Human Rights in History*.

[27] The Marquis de Condorcet, an important *philosophe* during the French Enlightenment, was elected to the National Assembly but was considered too moderate and untrustworthy

headlong into that future at a furious pace, one that alarmed much of the Western world at the time. It was in the chambers of the House of Commons that Edmund Burke made public his anxieties about the impact of the French experiment. He saw, before many others could, the terrifying potential raised by the effort to create a state based on the contradictory clauses in the Declaration of the Rights of Man. What were the boundary lines on the expectations of ordinary people once armed with such extensive rights? What were the restraints on the state as it used its elected authority to institute the secular paradise of liberty for all citizens?

The terror that Burke feared came into being just three years after he published his *Reflections on the Revolution in France* in 1790. And, in many ways, it has relentlessly expanded its grip throughout the world ever since. Government officials and leaders have never hesitated to use violence to enforce their legitimacy against those believed to be "culpable" in their resistance to authority. Groups of citizens who contest the legitimacy of that authority have committed themselves to tactics of violence as a means of realizing the fantasies of utopian social improvement.[28] Both sides claim they are acting in the name of political progress, human rights and the amelioration of conditions for the less fortunate. Both are possessed by their fantasies of power, by the redemptive power of their goals, and by the unquestioned arrogance that the violent path they have chosen is justifiable. In acting out these interdependent and often mirrored scripts, government specialists in counter-terrorism and insurgents in the underground seek each other out to confront their opponents in public displays of violent duels, often with similar goals in mind and, at times, even imitating each other's tactics. Meanwhile, the terrain of battle expands to include every ordinary aspect of our lives, from work to education and travel. The front no longer has clear spatial limits, since any one of us might be caught in a violent episode of bombing, shooting or kidnapping, in

by the Jacobin regime during the Terror. He was arrested and died in prison in 1794. Much of his multifaceted work was published by his widow during the Napoleonic era, and he is perhaps best known for his optimistic formulation of the idea of progress in his "Sketch for a Historical Picture of the Progress of the Human Mind." See Williams, *Condorcet and Modernity* and Baker, *Condorcet: From Natural Philosophy to Social Mathematics*.

[28] For a useful discussion of the utopian impulse that is both historical and literary, see Kateb, *Utopia and its Enemies* and the essays collected in Kateb, *Utopia: The Potential and Prospect of the Human Condition*.

spite of the fact that security seems to be everywhere.[29] Perhaps no better example exists to illustrate the vast space that political violence now occupies than the fact that, on the one hand, any one of us could choose or be forced to work for the state security agencies, or, on the other, become a member of the militant underground, or both, as has often happened.[30]

Looking back over the last two centuries of political violence, it seems evident that political violence is not yet on the verge of demise. Because it is more like the pain from an incurable medical condition, it may at best be managed. It is an integral part of the body politic, just as illnesses are part of our organic makeup. From a professional standpoint, the historian is not required to find a solution to a problem as complex and difficult as this one is. For that responsibility, we must turn to others, but my hope and intention is that by knowing where we have been, we may learn where we are going more clearly, and, above all, how to get there peacefully.

[29] Savitch, *Cities in a Time of Terror.*
[30] Miller, "The Intellectual Origins of Modern Terrorism in Europe," 61–2.

BIBLIOGRAPHY

2 The origins of political violence in the pre-modern era

Aristotle. *On Man in the Universe*, edited by L. R. Loomis. New York: W. J. Black, 1943.

"Politics." In *Introduction to Aristotle*, edited by R. McKeon. New York: Random House, 1947.

Burgiss, G. "The English Regicides and the Legitimation of Political Violence." In *Terror: From Tyrannicide to Terrorism*, edited by B. Bowden and M. T. Davis, 56–76. St Lucia, Australia: University of Queensland Press, 2008.

Collins, J. B. *From Tribes to Nation: The Making of France 500–1799*. Toronto: Wadsworth, 2002.

Coville, A. *Jean Petit: La Question du Tyrannicide au Commencement du XVe Siècle*. Paris: Auguste Picard, 1932.

Davis, N. Z. "The Rites of Violence." In *Society and Culture in Early Modern France: Eight Essays by Natalie Zemon Davis*, 152–87. Stanford University Press, 1975.

Diefendorf, B. B. *Beneath the Cross: Catholics and Huguenots in Sixteenth-Century Paris*. New York: Oxford University Press, 1991.

Engster, D. *Divine Sovereignty: The Origins of Modern State Power*. DeKalb, IL: Northern Illinois University Press, 2001.

Ford, F. L. *Political Murder: From Tyrannicide to Terrorism*. Cambridge, MA: Harvard University Press, 1985.

Herodotus. *The Landmark Herodotus: the Histories*, edited by R. B. Strassler, translated by A. L. Purvis. New York: Pantheon Books, 2007.

Hogge, A. *God's Secret Agents: Queen Elizabeth's Forbidden Priests and the Hatching of the Gunpowder Plot*. New York: HarperCollins, 2005.

Jászi, O. and Lewis, J. D. *Against the Tyrant: The Tradition and Theory of Tyrannicide*. Free Press, 1957.

Josephus, F. *The Jewish Wars*. New York: Penguin Books, 1989.

Kaplan, B. J. *Divided by Faith: Religious Conflict and the Practice of Toleration in Early Modern Europe*. Cambridge, MA: Belknap Press, 2007.

Kingdon, R. *Myths About the St Bartholomew's Day Massacres, 1572–1576*. Cambridge, MA: Harvard University Press, 1988.

Kirsch, J. *The Grand Inquisitor's Manual: A History of Terror in the Name of God*. New York: HarperCollins, 2008.

Kyle, C. R. "Early Modern Terrorism: the Gunpowder Plot of 1605 and its Aftermath." In *Terror: From Tyrannicide to Terrorism*, edited by B. Bowden and M. T. Davis, 42–55. St Lucia, Australia: University of Queensland Press, 2008.

Laqueur, W., ed. *Voices of Terror: Manifestos, Writings, and Manuals of Al Qaeda, Hamas, and Other Terrorists from Around the World and Throughout the Ages*. New York: Reed Press, 2004.

Laski, H. J., ed. *A Defense of Liberty Against Tyrants*. New York: G. Bell and Sons, 1924.

Luther, M. "Against the Thieving, Murderous Hordes of Peasants. 1525." In *Martin Luther*, edited by E. G. Rupp and B. Drewery, 121–6. London: Edward Arnold, 1970.

Marx, A. W. *Faith in Nation: Exclusionary Origins of Nationalism*. New York: Oxford University Press, 2003.

Plato. *The Republic*, edited by L. R. Loomis, translated by B. Jowett. New York: W. J. Black, 1942.

Rapoport, D. "Fear and Trembling: Terror in Three Religious Traditions." *American Political Science Review* 3-4 (1984): 658–78.

Ruff, J. R. *Violence in Early Modern Europe, 1500–1800*. Cambridge University Press, 2001.

Salisbury, John of. *Policraticus: Of the Frivolities of Courtiers and the Footprints of Philosophers, edited and translated by* C. J. Nederman. Cambridge University Press, 1990.

  The Statesman's Book of John of Salisbury, translated by J. Dickinson. Englewood Cliffs, NY: Prentice-Hall, 1963.

Strauss, L. *Xenophon's Socrates*. Ithaca: Cornell University Press, 1972.

Tacitus. *The Annals of Imperial Rome*, edited and translated by M. Grant. New York: Penguin, 1959.

Thucydides. *History of the Peloponnesian War*, edited by M. I. Finley, translated by R. Warner, revised edn. Harmondsworth: Penguin Books, 1972.

3   Trajectories of terrorism in the transition to modernity

Anderson, F. M., ed. *The Constitutions and Other Select Documents Illustrative of the History of France, 1789–1907*, 2nd edn. New York: Russell & Russell, 1967.

Andress, D. *The Terror: Civil War in the French Revolution*. London: Little Brown, 2005.

Armenteros, C. *The French Idea of History: Joseph de Maistre and His Heirs, 1794–1854*. Ithaca: Cornell University Press, 2011.

Artz, F. B. *Reaction and Revolution, 1814–1832*. New York: Harper & Row, 1963.

Baczko, B. *Ending the Terror: The French Revolution After Robespierre*, translated by M. Petheram. Cambridge University Press, 1994.

Bayly, C. A. *The Birth of the Modern World, 1780–1914: Global Connections and Comparisons*. Oxford: Blackwell, 2004.

Bertoldi, J. S. *Memoirs of the Secret Societies of the South of Italy: Particularly the Carbonari*. London, 1821.

Bessner, D., and M. Stauch. "Karl Heinzen and the Intellectual Origins of Modern Terror." *Terrorism and Political Violence* 22, no. 2 (Spring 2010): 143–76.

Brown, H. G. *Ending the French Revolution: Violence, Justice, and Repression from the Terror to Napoleon*. Charlottesville, VA: University of Virginia Press, 2006.

Chaliand, G., and A. Blin, eds. *The History of Terrorism: From Antiquity to Al Qaeda*. University of California Press, 2007.

Davis, M. T. "The British Jacobins and the Unofficial Terror of Loyalism in the 1790s." In *Terror: From Tyrannicide to Terrorism*, edited by B. Bowden and M. T. Davis, 92–113. St Lucia, Australia: University of Queensland Press, 2008.

Dommanget, M. *Auguste Blanqui et la révolution de 1848*. Paris: Mouton, 1972.

Edelstein, D. "War and Terror: The Law of Nations from Grotius to the French Revolution." *French Historical Studies* 31, no. 2 (March 20, 2008): 229–62.

Emsley, C. *Gendarmes and the State in Nineteenth-century Europe*. Oxford University Press, 1999.

Emsley, C., and B. Weinberger, eds. *Policing Western Europe: Politics, Professionalism, and Public Order, 1850–1940*. Westport, CT: Greenwood Press, 1991.

Engster, D. *Divine Sovereignty: The Origins of Modern State Power*. DeKalb, IL: Northern Illinois University Press, 2001.

Garrard, G. "Isaiah Berlin's Joseph de Maistre." In *Isaiah Berlin's Counter-Enlightenment*, edited by J. Mali and R. Wokler, 117–31. Philadelphia: American Philosophical Society, 2003.

George, D. "Distinguishing Classical Tyrannicide from Modern Terrorism." *Review of Politics* 50, no. 3 (Summer, 1988): 390–419.

Gernet, M. N. *Istoriia tsarskoi tiurmy.* Moscow: Gosizdat, 1951–6.

Goldstein, R. J. *Political Repression in Nineteenth Century Europe.* London: Croom Helm, 1983.

Gough, H. *The Terror in the French Revolution.* New York: Palgrave, 1998.

Greer, D. *The Incidence of the Terror During the French Revolution: A Statistical Interpretation.* Cambridge, MA: Harvard University Press, 1935.

Grob-Fitzgibbon, B. "From the Dagger to the Bomb: Karl Heinzen and the Evolution of Political Terror." *Terrorism and Political Violence* 16, no. 1 (Spring 2004): 97–115.

Gueniffey, P. *La politique de la terreur.* Paris: Fayard, 2000.

Harsin, J. *Barricades: The War of the Streets in Revolutionary Paris, 1830–1848.* New York: Palgrave Macmillan, 2002.

Heinzen, K. "Murder." In *The Terrorism Reader,* edited by W. Laqueur and Y. Alexander. New York: Meridian Books, 1987.

Herzen, A., and D. Macdonald. *My Past and Thoughts: The Memoirs of Alexander Herzen.* New York: Knopf, 1973.

Isabella, M. "Mazzini's Internationalism in Context: From the Cosmopolitan Patriotism of the Italian Carbonari to Mazzini's Europe of the Nations." In *Giuseppe Mazzini and the Globalisation of Democratic Nationalism, 1830–1920,* edited by C. A. Bayly and E. F. Biagini, 37–58. Oxford University Press, 2008.

Laqueur, W. "Karl Heinzen and the Origins of Modern Terrorism." In *The Political Psychology of Appeasement: Finlandization and Other Unpopular Essays,* 89–99. New Brunswick, NJ: Transaction Publishers, 1980.

de Madariaga, I. *Russia in the Age of Catherine the Great.* New Haven, CT: Yale University Press, 1981.

  Politics and Culture in Eighteenth-century Russia: Collected Essays. New York: Longman, 1998.

Mason, L., and T. Rizzo. *The French Revolution: A Document Collection.* Boston, MA: Houghton-Mifflin, 1999.

Mayer, A. J. *The Furies: Violence and Terror in the French and Russian Revolutions.* Princeton University Press, 2000.

von Metternich, R., ed. *Mémoires laissés par le Prince de Metternich.* Vol. III. Paris: E. Plon, 1881.

Miller, M. A. *The Russian Revolutionary Emigres, 1825–1870.* Baltimore, MD: The Johns Hopkins University Press, 1986.

Nechkina, M. V. *Dvizhenie Dekabristov.* 2 vols. Moscow: Nauka, 1987.

Orsini, A. *Anatomy of the Red Brigades: The Religious Mind-Set of Modern Terrorists,* translated by S. J. Nodes. Ithaca, NY: Cornell University Press, 2009.

Raeff, M. *The Well-Ordered Police State: Social and Institutional Change Through Law in the Germanies and Russia, 1600–1800.* New Haven: Yale University Press, 1983.

Rapport, M. *1848 – Year of Revolution.* London: Little, Brown, 2008.

Rath, J. "The Carbonari: Their Origins, Initiation Rites, and Aims." *The American Historical Review* 69, no. 2 (January, 1964): 353–70.

Robespierre, M. *Virtue and Terror,* edited by S. Žižek. London: Verso, 2007.

Robin, C. *Fear: The History of a Political Idea.* New York: Oxford University Press, 2004.

Ruud, C. A., and S. A. Stepanov. *Fontanka 16: the Tsars' Secret Police.* Montreal: McGill-Queen's University Press, 1999.

Scurr, R. *Fatal Purity: Robespierre and the French Revolution.* New York: Henry Holt, 2006.

Slavin, M. *The Hébertistes to the Guillotine: Anatomy of a "Conspiracy" in Revolutionary France.* Baton Rouge, LA: Louisiana State University Press, 1994.

Snyder, L. L., ed. *Documents of German History.* New Brunswick, NJ: Rutgers University Press, 1958.

Soll, J. *The Information Master: Jean-Baptiste Colbert's Secret State Intelligence System.* Ann Arbor, MI: University of Michigan Press, 2009.

Taylor, C. *Modern Social Imaginaries.* Durham, NC: Duke University Press, 2004.

Thorup, M. *An Intellectual History of Terror: War, Violence and the State.* London: Routledge, 2010.

Tilly, C. "War Making and State Making as Organized Crime." In *Bringing the State Back In,* edited by P. B. Evans, D. Rueschemeyer, and T. Skocpol, 169–91. Cambridge University Press, 1985.

Torpey, J. *The Invention of the Passport: Surveillance, Citizenship, and the State.* Cambridge University Press, 2000.

Wahnich, S. *La liberté ou la mort. Essai sur la Terreur et le terrorisme.* Paris: La Fabrique Editions, 2003.

4 Nineteenth-century Russian revolutionary and tsarist terrorisms

Andrieux, L. *Souvenirs d'un Préfet de Police.* Paris: J. Rouff, 1885.

Anisimov, E. V. *Five Empresses: Court Life in Eighteenth-Century Russia,* translated by K. Carroll. Westport, CT: Praeger, 2004.

Ascher, A. P. A. *Stolypin: the Search for Stability in Late Imperial Russia.* Stanford University Press, 2001.

Avrich, P. *Russian Rebels, 1600–1800.* New York: W. W. Norton & Company, 1972.

Belinskii, V. G. *Izbrannye pis'ma*. Moscow: Izdat. Khudozhlit., 1955.

Bergman, J. *Vera Zasulich: A Biography*. Stanford University Press, 1983.

Bordiugova, G. A., ed. *Politicheskaia politsiia i politicheskii terrorizm v Rossii*. Moscow: AIRO-XX, 2001.

Budnitskii, O. V. *Terrorizm v Rossiiskom osvoboditel'nom dvizhenii*. Moscow: ROSSPEN, 2000.

Butterworth, A. *The World That Never Was: A True Story of Dreamers, Schemers, Anarchists and Secret Agents*. New York: Pantheon Books, 2010.

Camus, A. *Les justes*. Paris: Gallimard, 1950.

  The Rebel: an Essay on Man in Revolt. Harmondsworth: Penguin Books, 1962.

Chernov, V. M. "Terroristicheskii element v nashei programme." *Revoliutsionnaia Rossiia* 2 (June, 1902).

Confino, M. *Violence dans la Violence: Le Débat Bakounine-Nechaev*. Paris: François Maspero, 1973.

Conrad, J. *The Secret Agent: A Simple Tale*. London: Penguin, 2011.

  Under Western Eyes. Garden City, NY: Doubleday, 1923.

Daly, J. W. *Autocracy Under Siege: Security Police and Opposition in Russia, 1866–1905*. DeKalb, IL: Northern Illinois University Press, 1998.

  The Watchful State: Security Police and Opposition in Russia, 1906–1917. DeKalb, IL: Northern Illinois University Press, 2004.

Dedkov, N. I., ed. *Politicheskaia politsiia i politicheskii terrorizm v Rossii: Sbornik documentov*. Moscow: AIRO-XX, 2001.

Efremov, P. A. "S. I. Sheshkovskii." *Russkaia Starina* 2, no. 12 (1870).

Figner, V. *Memoirs of a Revolutionist*. New York: International Publishers, 1920.

  Zapechatlennyi Trud. Vol. II. Moscow: Mysl', 1964.

Fischer, B. B. *Okhrana: the Paris Operations of the Russian Imperial Police*. Washington, DC: Center for the Study of Intelligence, Central Intelligence Agency, 1997.

Footman, D. *Red Prelude, the Life of the Russian Terrorist Zhelyabov*. New Haven, CT: Yale University Press, 1945.

Geifman, A. *Entangled in Terror: the Azef Affair and the Russian Revolution*. Wilmington, DE: Scholarly Resources, 2000.

  Thou Shalt Kill: Revolutionary Terrorism in Russia, 1894–1917. Princeton University Press, 1993.

Gelardi, J. P. *From Splendor to Revolution: the Romanov Women, 1847–1928*. New York: St Martin's Press, 2011.

Gross, F. *Violence in Politics. Terror and Political Assassination in Eastern Europe and Russia*. The Hague and Paris: Mouton, 1972.

Guyot, Y. *La Police: Etude de physiologie sociale*. Paris: G. Charpentier, 1884.

Haberer, E. *Jews and Revolution in Nineteenth Century Russia*. Cambridge University Press, 1995.

Hamm, M. F. "Jews and Revolution in Kharkiv: How One Ukrainian City Escaped a Pogrom in 1905." In *The Russian Revolution: Centenary Perspectives*, edited by J. D. Smele and A. Heywood, 156–76. London: Routledge, 2005.

Hardy, D. *Land and Freedom: the Origins of Russian Terrorism, 1876–1879*. New York: Greenwood Press, 1987.

la Hodde, Lucien de. *Histoire des Sociétés Secrètes*. Paris: J. Lanier, 1850.

Hoffman, S., and E. Mendelsohn, eds. *The Revolution of 1905 and Russia's Jews*. Philadelphia, PA: University of Pennsylvania Press, 2008.

Ivianski, Z. "A Chapter in the History of Individual Terror: Andrei Zheliabov." In *Perspectives on Terrorism*, edited by L. Z. Freedman and Y. Alexander. Wilmington, DE: Scholarly Resources, 1983.

"Provocation at the Center: A Study in the History of Counter-Terror." In *Terrorism: Critical Concepts in Political Science*, edited by D. C. Rapoport, 339–368. Vol I. London: Routledge, 2004.

Judge, E. H. *Easter in Kishinev: Anatomy of a Pogrom*. New York University Press, 1992.

Kennan, G. *Siberia and the Exile System*. New York: Century Co., 1891.

Kharkhordin, O. "What Is the State? The Russian Concept of *Gosudarstvo* in the European Context." *History and Theory* 40 (May 2001): 206–40.

Klier, J. D. "Russian Jewry on the Eve of the Pogroms." In *Pogroms: Anti-Jewish Violence in Modern Russian History*, edited by J. D. Klier and S. Lambroza. Cambridge University Press, 1992.

Kravchinskii, S. M. *Smert' za smert': Ubiistvo Mezentseva*. Petrograd: Gosizdat, 1920.

Kronenbitter, R. T. "The Okhrana's Female Agents." In *Okhrana: the Paris Operations of the Russian Imperial Police*, by B. B. Fischer, 81–90. Washington, DC: Center for the Study of Intelligence, Central Intelligence Agency, 1997.

Kropotkin, P. A. *Memoirs of a Revolutionist*. Boston and New York: Houghton, Mifflin and Company, 1899.

In Russian and French Prisons. London: Ward and Downey, 1887.

Lambroza, S. "The Pogroms of 1903–6." In *Pogroms: Anti-Jewish Violence in Modern Russian History*, edited by J. D. Klier and S. Lambroza. Cambridge University Press, 1992.

Laqueur, W., ed. *Voices of Terror: Manifestos, Writings, and Manuals of Al Qaeda, Hamas, and Other Terrorists from Around the World and Throughout the Ages.* New York: Reed Press, 2004.

Lukashevich, S. "The Holy Brotherhood, 1881–1883." *American Slavic and East European Review* 184 (1959): 491–505.

Matlaw, R. E., V. G. Belinsky, N. G. Chernyshevsky, and N. A. Dobrolyubov. *Belinsky, Chernyshevsky, and Dobrolyubov: Selected Criticism.* Bloomington, IN: Indiana University Press, 1976.

McDaniel, J. *"Political Assassination and Mass Execution: Terrorism in Revolutionary Russia, 1878–1938."* PhD dissertation, Ann Arbor: University Microfilms, 1977.

Medzhibovskaya, I. "Tolstoi's Response to Terror and Revolutionary Violence." *Kritika* 9, no. 3 (Summer 2008): 505–31.

Mironov, B. N., and B. Eklof. *The Social History of Imperial Russia, 1700–1917.* Vol. II. Boulder, CO: Westview Press, 2000.

Monas, S. "The Political Police: The Dream of a Beautiful Autocracy." In *The Transformation of Russian Society: Aspects of Social Change since 1861,* edited by C. E. Black, 164–190. Cambridge, MA: Harvard University Press, 1967.

Morozov, N. A. *Povesti moei zhizni.* Moscow: Akademii nauk, 1961.

Terroristicheskaia bor'ba. Geneva and London: Russkaia Tipografiia, 1880.

Mousnier, R. *Peasant Uprisings in Seventeenth-century France, Russia, and China.* Harper & Row, 1972.

Nikitenko, A. V. *The Diary of a Russian Censor,* edited and translated by H. S. Jacobson. Amherst, MA: University of Massachusetts Press, 1975.

Dnevnik. Moscow: Gosizdat, 1955.

Peregudova, Z. I., *Politicheskii sysk Rossii: 1880–1917.* Moscow: Rosspen, 2000.

Pipes, R. *The Degaev Affair: Terror and Treason in Tsarist Russia.* New Haven, CT: Yale University Press, 2003.

Russia Under the Old Regime. New York: Collier Macmillan, 1992.

Pomper, P. *Lenin's Brother: the Origins of the October Revolution.* New York: W.W. Norton & Co., 2010.

"Nechaev and Tsaricide: The Conspiracy Within the Conspiracy." *Russian Review* 33, no. 2 (April 1974): 123–38.

Sergei Nechaev. New Brunswick: Rutgers University Press, 1979.

Raeff, M. "An Early Theorist of Absolutism: Joseph of Volokolamsk." In *Readings in Russian History,* edited by S. Harcave, 177–187. Vol. I. New York: Crowell, 1964.

Russian Intellectual History: an Anthology. New York: Harcourt, Brace & World, 1966.

Romanenko, G. G. *Terrorizm i rutina*. Carouge [Geneva]: Elpidine, 1901.

Ruud, C. A., and S. A. Stepanov. *Fontanka 16: the Tsars' Secret Police*. Montreal: McGill-Queen's University Press, 1999.

Sablinsky, W. *The Road to Bloody Sunday: Father Gapon and the St Petersburg Massacre of 1905*. Princeton University Press, 1976.

Savinkov, B. V, and J. Shaplen. *Memoirs of a Terrorist*. New York: A. & C. Boni, 1931.

Schneiderman, J. *Sergei Zubatov and Revolutionary Marxism: the Struggle for the Working Class in Tsarist Russia*. Ithaca: Cornell University Press, 1976.

Shlapentokh, D. *The French Revolution in Russian Intellectual Life: 1865–1905*. Westport, CT: Praeger, 1996.

Spence, R. B. *Boris Savinkov: Renegade on the Left*. New York: Columbia University Press, 1991.

Squire, P. S. *The Third Department: The Establishment and Practices of the Political Police in the Russia of Nicholas I*. London: Cambridge University Press, 1968.

Stepniak, S. *The Career of a Nihilist; a Novel*. New York; London: Harper & Co., 1889.

Underground Russia; Revolutionary Profiles and Sketches from Life. Westport, CT: Hyperion Press, 1973.

Surh, G. D. "Ekaterinoslav City in 1905: Workers, Jews and Violence." *International Labor and Working Class History* 64 (Fall 2003): 139–166.

"Jewish Self-Defense and Pogrom Violence in 1905." Unpublished paper presented to the annual meeting of the American Association for the Advancement of Slavic Studies (AAASS), Boston, November, 2009.

"Russia's 1905 Era Pogroms Reexamined." *Canadian American Slavic Studies* 44, no. 1–2 (Spring–Summer 2010): 253–95.

Tarnovski, G. [G. G. Romanenko]. "Terrorism and Routine." In *The Terrorism Reader*, edited by W. Laqueur, 79–84. New York: Meridian Books, 1987.

Tikhomirov, L. A. *Vospominaniia*. Moscow: GPIB, 2003.

Zagovorshchiki i politsiia. Moscow: Gosizdat, 1927.

Valk, S. "G. G. Romanenko: Iz istorii Narodnoi Voli." *Katorga i Ssylka*, no. 11 (1928).

Verhoeven, C. *The Odd Man Karakozov: Imperial Russia, Modernity, and the Birth of Terrorism*. Ithaca, NY: Cornell University Press, 2009.

Wedziagolski, K., and T. Swietochowski. *Boris Savinkov: Portrait of a Terrorist*. Clifton, NJ: Kingston Press, 1988.

Weinberg, R. "The Russian Right Responds to 1905: Visual Depictions of Jews in Postrevolutionary Russia." In *Pogroms: Anti-Jewish Violence in Modern Russian History*, edited by J. D. Klier and S. Lambroza. Cambridge University Press, 1992.

Zuckerman, F. S. *The Tsarist Secret Police Abroad: Policing Europe in a Modernizing World.* New York: Palgrave Macmillan, 2003.

5 European nation state terrorism and its antagonists, at home and abroad, 1848–1914

Arcos, Duke of. "International Control of Anarchists." *The North American Review.* In *Early Writings on Terrorism*, edited by R. Kinna. Vol. III. London, New York: Routledge, 2006.

Avrich, P. *The Haymarket Tragedy.* Princeton University Press, 1984.

Begly, L. *Why The Dreyfus Affair Matters.* New Haven, CT: Yale University Press, 2009.

Berkman, A. *Prison Memoirs of an Anarchist.* New York: Schocken Books, 1970 [1912].

Blanqui, A. *Critique sociale. 2 vols.* Paris: Ancienne librairie Germer Baillière et Cie, 1885.

Bramstedt, E. K. *Dictatorship and Political Police; the Technique of Control by Fear.* London: K. Paul, Trench, Trubner & Co., Ltd., 1945.

Burleigh, M. *Blood and Rage: a Cultural History of Terrorism.* New York: HarperCollins, 2009.

Calhoun, A. F. "The Politics of Internal Order: French Government and Revolutionary Labor, 1898–1914." PhD dissertation, Princeton University, 1973.

Carr, M. *The Infernal Machine: a History of Terrorism.* New York: New Press, 2006.

Chaliand, G., and A. Blin, eds. *The History of Terrorism: From Antiquity to Al Qaeda.* Berkeley, CA: University of California Press, 2007.

Christiansen, R. *Paris Babylon: the Story of the Paris Commune.* New York: Viking, 1994.

Clymer, J. A. *America's Culture of Terrorism: Violence, Capitalism and the Written Word.* Chapel Hill, NC: University of North Carolina Press, 2003.

Coats, J. "Half Devil and Half Child: America's War with Terror in the Philippines, 1899–1902." In *Enemies of Humanity*, edited by I. Land. New York: Palgrave/Macmillan, 2008.

Conrad, S. *German Colonialism: A Short History.* Cambridge University Press, 2012

Corbin, J. R. *The Anarchist Passion: Class Conflict in Southern Spain, 1810–1965.* Aldershot: Avebury, 1993.

Deflem, M. "'Wild Beasts Without Nationality': The Uncertain Origins of Interpol, 1898–1910." In *Handbook of Transnational Crime and Justice*, edited by Philip Reichel, 274–85. New York: Sage, 2005.

Edwards, S. *The Communards of Paris, 1871*. Ithaca, NY: Cornell University Press, 1973.

The Paris Commune, 1871. London: Eyre & Spottiswoode, 1971.

Eisenwein, G. R. *Anarchist Ideology and the Working-class Movement in Spain: 1868–1898*. Berkeley, CA: University of California Press, 1989.

Fabijancic, T. *Bosnia: in the Footsteps of Gavrilo Princip*. Edmonton: University of Alberta Press, 2010.

Fellman, M. *In the Name of God and Country: Reconsidering Terrorism in American History*. New Haven, CT: Yale University Press, 2010.

Ford, F. L. *Political Murder: From Tyrannicide to Terrorism*. Cambridge, MA: Harvard University Press, 1987.

Ghosh, T. K., ed. *Science and Technology of Terrorism and Counterterrorism*. Basel and New York: Marcel Dekker, 2002.

Goldman, E. "The Psychology of Political Violence." In *Anarchism and Other Essays*. New York: Dover, 1969.

Goldstein, R. J. *Political Repression in Nineteenth Century Europe*. London: Croom Helm, 1983.

Goodman, J. *The Devil and Mr. Casement: One Man's Battle for Human Rights in South America's Heart of Darkness*. London: Verso, 2009.

Guyot, Y. *La Police: Étude de physiologie sociale*. Paris: G. Charpentier, 1884.

Harris, F. *The Bomb*. New York: Mitchell Kennerley, 1909.

Hochschild, A. *King Leopold's Ghost: a Story of Greed, Terror, and Heroism in Colonial Africa*. Boston, MA: Houghton Mifflin, 1998.

la Hodde, L. de. *The Cradle of Rebellions: A History of the Secret Societies of France*. New York: J. Bradburn, 1864.

Hofstadter, R., and M. Wallace, eds. "Brutalities in the Philippines, 1897–1902." In *American Violence; a Documentary History*. New York: Vintage Books/Random House, 1971.

Itenberg, B. S. *Rossiia i parizhskaia kommuna*. Moscow: Nauka, 1971.

Jellinek, F. *The Paris Commune of 1871*. New York: Grosset and Dunlap, 1965.

Jenkins, B. "1867 All Over Again? Insurgency and Terrorism in a Liberal State." In *Enemies of Humanity: The Nineteenth Century War on Terrorism* edited by I. Land, 81–97. New York: Palgrave/Macmillan, 2008.

Jensen, R. B. "Daggers, Rifles and Dynamite: Anarchist Terrorism in 19th Century Europe." *Terrorism and Political Violence* 10, no. 1 (Spring 2004): 116–53.

"The International Anti-Anarchist Conference of 1898 and the Origins of Interpol." *Journal of Contemporary History* 16, no. 2 (April 1981): 323–47.

"The International Campaign Against Anarchist Terrorism, 1880–1930s." *Terrorism and Political Violence* 21, no. 1 (January 2009): 89–109.

"The United States, International Policing and the War Against Anarchist Terrorism, 1900–1914." *Terrorism and Political Violence* 13, no. 1 (Spring, 2001): 15–46.

Katz, P. M. *From Appomattox to Montmartre: Americans and the Paris Commune*. Cambridge, MA: Harvard University Press, 1998.

Kinna, R. ed. *Early Writings on Terrorism*. Vol. III. London; New York: Routledge, 2006.

Krause, P. *The Battle for Homestead, 1880–1892: Politics, Culture, and Steel*. University of Pittsburgh Press, 1992.

Larson, K. C. *The Assassin's Accomplice: Mary Surratt and the Plot to Kill Abraham Lincoln*. New York: Basic Books, 2008.

Leier, J. M. *Bakunin: the Creative Passion*. New York: St Martin's Press, 2006.

Liang, H. *The Rise of Modern Police and the European State System from Metternich to the Second World War*. New York: Cambridge University Press, 1992.

Lindqvist, S. *Exterminate All the Brutes*, translated by J. Tate. New York: New Press, 1996.

Lippman, J. "Ravachol, King of the Anarchists." *The New York Times*, June 29, 1919.

Maitron, J. *Histoire du mouvement anarchiste*. Vol. II. 2 vols. Paris: François Maspero, 1975.

Ravachol et les anarchistes. Paris: Julliard, 1964.

Mazower, M., ed. *The Policing of Politics in the 20th Century*. Oxford: Berghahn Books, 1997.

Merriman, J. M. *The Dynamite Club: How a Bombing in Fin-de-siècle Paris Ignited the Age of Modern Terror*. New York: Houghton Mifflin Harcourt, 2009.

Michel, L., B. Lowry, and E. E. Gunter. *The Red Virgin: Memoirs of Louise Michel*. University, AL: University of Alabama Press, 1981.

Miller, M. A. "The Intellectual Origins of Modern Terrorism in Europe." In *Terrorism in Context*, edited by M. Crenshaw, 27–62. University Park, PA: Pennsylvania State University Press, 1995.

Morel, E. D. *The Black Man's Burden*. New York: B. W. Huebsch, 1920.

Red Rubber. London: T. F. Unwin, 1907.

Naimark, N. M. *Fires of Hatred: Ethnic Cleansing in Twentieth-century Europe*. Cambridge, MA: Harvard University Press, 2001.

Ouida [pseudonym for Maria Louise de la Ramée]. "The Legislation of Fear." In *Early Writings on Terrorism*, edited by R. Kinna. Vol. III, 265–74. London; New York: Routledge 2006.

Packe, M. St John. *Orsini: the Story of a Conspirator*. Boston, MA: Little, Brown, 1958.

Payne, H. C. *The Police State of Louis Napoléon Bonaparte, 1851–1860.* Seattle, WA: University of Washington Press, 1966.

Pernicone, N. *Italian Anarchism, 1864–1892.* Princeton University Press, 1993.

Perraudin, M., and J. Zimmerer (eds.). *German Colonialism and National Identity.* London and New York: Routledge, 2011.

Pinkerton, A. *Strikers, Tramps, and Detectives* (1878), quoted in R. Jeffreys-Jones, *Cloak and Dollar: a History of American Secret Intelligence.* New Haven, CT: Yale University Press, 2002.

Pinkerton, R. A. "Detective Surveillance of Anarchists." *The North American Review.* In *Early Writings on Terrorism*, edited by R. Kinna, Vol. III, 338–46. London; New York: Routledge, 2006.

Plessis, A. *The Rise and Fall of the Second Empire, 1852–1871*, translated by J. Mandelbaum. Cambridge University Press, 1985.

Porter, B. *The Origins of the Vigilant State: The London Metropolitan Police Special Branch before the First World War.* London: Weidenfeld & Nicolson, 1987.

"Propositions arrêtées par la conférence internationale réunie a Rome." In *Early Writings on Terrorism*, edited by R. Kinna, Vol. III, 326–9. London; New York: Routledge, 2006.

Read, P. P. *The Dreyfus Affair: The Scandal That Tore France In Two* New York: Bloomsbury, 2012.

Rummel, R. J. *Death by Government.* New Brunswick, NJ: Transaction Publishers, 1994.

Schaack, M. J. *Anarchy and Anarchists: a History of the Red Terror and the Social Revolution in America and Europe*, Chicago, IL: F. J. Schulte and Co., 1889.

Schulkind, E., ed. *The Paris Commune of 1871: The View from the Left.* New York: Grove Press, 1974.

Sebald, W. G. *The Rings of Saturn.* New York: New Directions, 1998.

Shafer, D. A. *The Paris Commune: French Politics, Culture, and Society at the Crossroads of the Revolutionary Tradition and Revolutionary Socialism.* New York: Palgrave Macmillan, 2005.

Simpson, F. A. *Louis Napoleon and the Recovery of France.* Westport, CT: Greenwood Press, 1975.

Sonn, R. D. *Anarchism and Cultural Politics in Fin de Siècle France.* Lincoln, NE: University of Nebraska Press, 1989.

Stafford, D. *From Anarchism to Reformism: a Study of the Political Activities of Paul Brousse Within the First International and the French Socialist Movement 1870–90.* Toronto: University of Toronto Press, 1971.

Starr, P. *Commemorating Trauma: the Paris Commune and Its Cultural Aftermath.* New York: Fordham University Press, 2006.

State of New York. *Laws of the State of New York*. Vol. II. Albany, NY: J. B. Lyon, 1902.

Taithe, B. *The Killer Trail: a Colonial Scandal in the Heart of Africa*. Oxford University Press, 2009.

Thomas, E. *Louise Michel*. Montreal: Black Rose Books, 1980.

Thorup, M. "The Anarchist and the Partisan: Two Types of Terror in the History of Irregular Warfare." *Terrorism and Political Violence* 20, no. 3 (September 2008): 333–55.

Tombs, R. *The Paris Commune, 1871*. London, New York: Longman, 1999.

Vincent, K. S. *Between Marxism and Anarchism: Benoît Malon and French Reformist Socialism*. Berkeley, CA: Univ. of California Press, 1992.

6   Terrorism in a democracy: the United States

Anderson, W. L., ed. *Cherokee Removal: Before and After*. Athens, GA: University of Georgia Press, 1991.

Blackhawk, N. *Violence Over the Land: Indians and Empires in the Early American West*. Cambridge, MA: Harvard University Press, 2006.

Boulware, T. *Deconstructing the Cherokee Nation: Town, Region and Nation Among the Eighteenth Century Cherokees*. Gainesville, FL: University Press of Florida, 2011.

Brown, R. M. *Strain of Violence: Historical Studies of American Violence and Vigilantism*. New York: Oxford University Press, 1975.

Brundage, W. F. *Lynching in the New South: Georgia and Virginia, 1880–1930*. Urbana, IL: University of Illinois Press, 1993.

Caroll, J. C. *Slave Insurrections in the United States, 1800–1865*. Mineola, NY: Dover Publications, 2004.

Chardbourn, J. H. *Lynching and the Law*. Chapel Hill, NC: University of North Carolina Press, 1933.

"Crime of Lynching." Hearings Before a Subcommittee of the Judiciary Committee of the US Senate. Washington, DC: Government Printing Office, 1948.

Cutler, J. E. *Lynch-Law: An Investigation into the History of Lynching in the United States*. New York: Longmans, Green, and Co., 1905.

Dray, P. *At the Hands of Persons Unknown: The Lynching of Black America*. New York: Random House, 2002.

Egerton, D. *Gabriel's Rebellion*. Chapel Hill, NC: University of North Carolina Press, 1993.

Fehrenbach, T. R. *Commanches: The Destruction of a People*. New York: Knopf, 1974.

Fellman, M. *In the Name of God and Country: Reconsidering Terrorism in American History.* New Haven, CT: Yale University Press, 2010.

Foner, E. *Give Me Liberty, 1789–1815.* New York: Norton, 2006.

Giddings, P. J. *Ida: A Sword Among Lions.* New York: Amistad/Harper Collins, 2008.

Gwynne, S. C. *Empire of the Summer Moon: Quanah Parker and the Rise and Fall of the Comanche Tribe.* London: Constable, 2011.

Hamalainen, P. *The Comanche Empire.* New Haven, CT: Yale University Press, 2008.

Hochschild, Adam. *King Leopold's Ghost: a Story of Greed, Terror, and Heroism in Colonial Africa.* Boston, MA: Houghton Mifflin, 1998.

Ifill, S. A. *On the Courthouse Lawn: Confronting the Legacy of Lynching in the 21st Century.* Boston, MA: Beacon Press, 2007.

Jacoby, K. *Shadows at Dawn: A Borderlands Massacre and the Violence of History.* New York: Penguin Press, 2008.

Jeffreys-Jones, R. *The FBI: A History.* New Haven, CT: Yale University Press, 2007.

Kappler, C. J., ed. *Indian Affairs: Laws and Treaties.* Washington, DC: Government Printing Office, 1904–1941.

Kolchin, P. *American Slavery, 1619–1877.* New York: Hill and Wang, 1994.

Lear, J. *Radical Hope: Ethics in the Face of Cultural Devastation.* Cambridge, MA: Harvard University Press, 2006.

Linderman, F. B. *Plenty-Coups, Chief of the Crows.* Lincoln, NE: University of Nebraska Press, 1962.

Litwack, L. F. *How Free Is Free?: The Long Death of Jim Crow.* Cambridge, MA: Harvard University Press, 2009.

McGlone, R. E. *John Brown's War Against Slavery.* Cambridge University Press, 2009.

Myrdal, G. *American Dilemma: The Negro Problem and Modern Democracy.* New York: Harper and Brothers, 1944.

Perdue, T., and M. D. Green. *The Cherokee Removal.* Boston, MA: Bedford/St Martin's, 2005.

Raper, A. *The Tragedy of Lynching.* Chapel Hill, NC: University of North Carolina Press, 1933.

Rasenberger, J. *America, 1908.* New York: Scribners, 2007.

Rossiter, C. *Constitutional Dictatorship: Crisis Government in the Modern Democracies.* Princeton University Press, 1948. [Reissued 2002 by Transaction Press.]

Sayles, J. *Moment in the Sun.* San Francisco, CA: McSweeney's Books, 2011.

Smith, D. B. *An American Betrayal: Cherokee Patriots and the Trail of Tears.* New York: Henry Holt, 2011.

Tolnay, S. E., and E. M. Beck. *A Festival of Violence: An Analysis of Southern Lynchings, 1882–1930.* Urbana and Chicago, IL: The University of Illinois Press, 1993.

Trelease, A. W. *White Terror: The Ku Klux Klan Conspiracy and Southern Reconstruction.* New York: Harper & Row, 1971.

Tyson, T. *Democracy Betrayed: The Wilmington Race Riot of 1898 and Its Legacy.* Chapel Hill, NC: University of North Carolina Press, 1998.

Waldrep, C., ed. *Lynching in America: A History in Documents.* New York University Press, 2006.

Whitaker, R. *On the Laps of Gods: The Red Summer of 1919 and the Struggle for Justice That Remade a Nation.* New York: Crown Publishers, 2008.

Wilbarger, J. W. *Indian Depredations in Texas.* Austin, TX: The Steck Company, 1935.

Young, M. "The Exercise of Sovereignty in Cherokee Georgia." *Journal of the Early Republic* 10, no. 1 (Spring 1990): 43–63.

7 Communist and fascist authoritarian terror

Arendt, H. *The Origins of Totalitarianism.* New York: Harcourt Brace Jovanovich, 1976.

Avrich, P. *Sacco and Vanzetti: The Anarchist Background.* Princeton University Press, 1991.

Baranowski, S. *Nazi Empire: German Colonialism and Imperialism from Bismarck to Hitler.* Cambridge University Press, 2011.

Boym, S. *Another Freedom: The Alternative History of an Idea.* University of Chicago Press, 2010.

Brenner, A. D. *Emil J. Gumbel: Weimar German Pacifist and Professor.* Boston and Leiden: Brill Academic Publishers, 2001.

Brysac, S. B. *Resisting Hitler: Mildred Harnack and the Red Orchestra.* New York: Oxford University Press, 2000.

"Capitol Clashes Increase: Armed and Defiant Negroes Roam About Shooting at Whites." *New York Times*, July 22, 1919.

Chamberlain, L. *The Philosophy Steamer: Lenin and the Exile of the Intelligentsia.* London: Atlantic, 2004.

Clymer, J. A. "'Propaganda by the Deed': Plotting Terrorism in American Literature and Culture, 1870–1920." PhD dissertation, Duke University, 1998.

Conquest, R. *The Great Terror: A Reassessment.* London: Pimlico, 2008.

Davis, M. *Buda's Wagon: A Brief History of the Car Bomb.* London: Verso, 2007.

Dilling, E. *The Red Network: A 'Who's Who' and Handbook of Radicalism for Patriots.* New York: privately printed, 1934.

Dzerzhinskii, F. E. "Decree of September 5, 1918, 'On the Red Terror'." In *Ideas and Forces in Soviet Legal History*, edited by Z. L. Zile. New York: Oxford University Press, 1992.

Dnevnik. Pis'ma k rodnym. Moscow: Gosizdat, 1958.

Fitzpatrick, S. *Tear Off the Masks: Identity and Imposture in Twentieth Century Russia.* Princeton University Press, 2005.

Franklin, J. H. *Mirror to America: The Autobiography of John Hope Franklin.* New York: Farrar, Straus, and Giroux, 2005.

Gage, B. *The Day Wall Street Exploded: A Story of America in Its First Age of Terror.* New York: Oxford University Press, 2009.

Getty, J. A. *The Road to Terror: Stalin and the Self-Destruction of the Bolsheviks, 1932–1939.* Revised edn. New Haven: Yale University Press, 2010.

Getty, J. A., and R. T. Manning, eds. *Stalinist Terror: New Perspectives.* New York: Cambridge University Press, 1993.

Geyer, M. *Beyond Totalitarianism: Stalinism and Nazism Compared.* New York: Cambridge University Press, 2009.

Goldman, W. *Terror and Democracy in the Age of Stalin.* New York: Cambridge University Press, 2007.

Goldstein, R. J. *Political Repression in Modern America: From 1870 to 1976.* Urbana, IL: University of Illinois Press, 2001.

Grossman, V. *Forever Flowing.* New York: Harper and Row, 1972.

Gumbel, E. J. "Organized Murder." In *The Terrorism Reader*, edited by W. Laqueur. New York: Meridian, 1987.

Vier Jahre politischer Mord. Berlin, 1922.

trans. *Denkschrift des Reichjustizministers zu "Vier Jahre Politischer Mord".* Berlin: Malik Verlag, 1924.

Hagenloh, P. *Stalin's Police: Public Order and Mass Repression in the USSR, 1926–1941.* Baltimore, MD: Johns Hopkins University Press, 2009.

"Terror and the Gulag." *Kritika* 11, no. 3 (Summer 2010): 627–40.

Hill, R. N. *Men, Mobs, and Law: Anti-lynching and Labor Defense in US Radical History.* Durham, NC: Duke University Press, 2009.

Hirsch, J. S. *Riot and Remembrance: The Tulsa Race War and Its Legacy.* Boston, MA: Houghton Mifflin, 2002.

Hoffman, P. *The History of the German Resistance, 1933–1945.* Montreal: McGill-Queen's University Press, 1996.

Holquist, M. "Violent Russia, Deadly Marxism? Russia in the Epoch of Violence, 1905–21." *Kritika* 4, no. 3 (Summer 2003): 627–52.

Kershaw, I. *Hitler, 1889–1936: Hubris.* New York: Norton, 1998.

Khlevniuk, O. "The Stalinist Police State." *Kritika* 11, no. 3 (Summer 2010): 641–48.

Lenin, V. I. "To Comrade Dzerzhinskii." In *Polnoe sobranie sochinenii.* 5th edn. Moscow: Gosizdat, 1952.

Lockhart, R. H. B. *Memoirs of a British Agent.* London: Putnam, 1932.

MacDonogh, G. *After the Reich: The Brutal History of the Allied Occupation.* Reprint. New York: Basic Books, 2009.

McCormick, C. H. *Hopeless Cases: The Hunt for the Red Scare Terrorist Bombers.* New York: University Press of America, 2005.

   Seeing Reds: Federal Surveillance of Radicals in the Pittsburgh Mill District, 1917–1921. University of Pittsburgh Press, 1997.

McDaniel, J. F. "Political Assassination and Mass Execution: Terrorism in Revolutionary Russia, 1878–1938." PhD dissertation, University of Michigan, 1976.

McDonough, F. *Sophie Scholl: the Real Story of the Woman Who Defied Hitler.* Stroud: History Press, 2009.

Michalczyk, J. J. "The White Rose Student Movement in Germany." In *Resisters, Rescuers, and Refugees: Historical and Ethical Issues*, edited by J. J. Michalczyk. Kansas City, KS: Sheed and Ward, 1997.

Miller, M. A. "Exile's Vengeance: Trotsky and the Morality of Terrorism." In *Just Assassins: The Culture of Terrorism in Russia*, edited by A. Anemone, 209–28. Evanston: Northwestern University Press, 2010.

Mommsen, H. *Alternatives to Hitler: German Resistance Under the Third Reich.* London: Tauris, 2003.

Murray, R. K. *Red Scare: A Study of National Hysteria, 1919–1920.* New York: McGraw-Hill, 1964.

Naimark, N. *The Russians in Germany: A History of the Soviet Zone of Occupation, 1945–1949.* Cambridge, MA: Harvard University Press, 1995.

Nelson, A. *Red Orchestra: The Story of the Berlin Underground and the Circle of Friends Who Resisted Hitler.* New York: Random House, 2009.

Peters, Ia. Kh. "Vospominaniia o rabote v VChK v pervyi god revoliutsii." *Proletarskaia revoliutsiia* 33, no. 10 (1924): 5–32.

Prieto, J. M. "Reading Mandelstam on Stalin." *New York Review of Books*, June 10, 2010.

Rabinowitch, A. *The Bolsheviks in Power: The First Year of Soviet Rule in Petrograd.* Bloomington: Indiana University Press, 2007.

"Race Riot Peril: Radical Propaganda Among Negroes Growing." *New York Times*, October 5, 1919.

Ratshesky, A. C. "Americanization is Cure for Bolshevism." *New York Times*, November 24, 1918.

Read, A. *The World on Fire: 1919 and the Battle with Bolshevism.* New York: Norton, 2008.

Redlich, S. *Propaganda and Nationalism in Wartime Russia: The Jewish Anti-Fascist Committee in the USSR, 1941–1948*. Boulder, CO: East European Quarterly, 1982.

Ritter, G. *The German Resistance: Carl Goerdeler's Struggle Against Tyranny*. New York: Praeger, 1958.

Savinkov, B. *Memoirs of a Terrorist*. New York: Albert and Charles Boni, 1931.

Pale Horse. New York: A.A. Knopf, 1919.

Vospominaniia. Moscow: Moskovskii rabochii, 1990.

Serge, V. *The Case of Comrade Tulayev*, translated by W. R. Trask. NYRB Classics, 2004.

Conquered City, translated by R. Greeman. NYRB Classics, 2011.

From Lenin to Stalin. New York: Pioneer Publishers, 1937.

Memoirs of a Revolutionary, 1901–1941. London: Oxford University Press, 1961.

Russia Twenty Years After. London: Hillman-Curl, 1937.

Unforgiving Years, translated by R. Greeman. NYRB Classics, 2008.

Spence, R. B. *Boris Savinkov: Renegade on the Left*. New York: Columbia University Press, 1991.

Steinberg, I. N. *In the Workshop of the Revolution*. New York: Rinehart & Co., 1953.

Stone, G. R. *Perilous Times: Free Speech in Wartime from the Sedition Act of 1798 to the War on Terrorism*. New York: Norton, 2004.

Thurston, R. W. *Life and Terror in Stalin's Russia, 1934–1941*. New Haven, CT: Yale University Press, 1996.

Trotsky, L. *Military Writings*. New York: Merit Publishers, 1969.

Urbaszewski, L. S. "Canonizing the 'Best, most Talented' Soviet Poet: Vladimir Mayakovsky and the Soviet Literary Celebration." In *Modernism/Modernity*, v. 9, n. 4, 635–65.

Wedziagolski, K. *Boris Savinkov: Portrait of a Terrorist*. Clifton, NJ: The Kingston Press, 1988.

Weissman, S. *Victor Serge: The Course Is Set on Hope*. London: Verso, 2001.

Werth, N. "The Crimes of the Stalin Regime: Outline for an Inventory Classification." In *The Historiography of Genocide*, edited by D. Stone, 400–19. New York: Palgrave Macmillan, 2008.

"The Mechanism of a Mass Crime: The Great Terror in the Soviet Union, 1937–1938." In *The Specter of Genocide: Mass Murder in Historical Perspective*, edited by R. Gellately and B. Kiernan, 215–39. Cambridge University Press, 2003.

Wintz, C. D. *Introduction to The Clansman: An Historical Romance of the Ku Klux Klan, by T. Dixon*. Armonk, NY: M. E. Sharpe, 2001.

Young, G. "Terror in *Pravda, 1917–1939*: All the News That Was Fit to Print." In *The Cultural Gradient, 1789–1991*, edited by C. Evtuhov and S. Kotkin. New York: Rowman and Littlefield, 2003.

8 Global ideological terror during the Cold War

"88 Seconds in Greensboro". UNC-TV, 2003.

Argentine National Commission on the Disappeared. *Nunca Mas: Report of the Argentine National Commission on the Disappeared.* New York: Farrar, Straus, and Giroux, 1986.

Baldwin, K. *Beyond the Color Line and the Iron Curtain: Reading Encounters Between Black and Red, 1922–1963.* Durham, NC: Duke University Press, 2002.

Bell, T. *Unfinished Business: South Africa, Apartheid and Truth.* London: Verso, 2003.

Berendse, G., and I. Cornils, eds. *Baader-Meinhof Returns: History and Cultural Memory of German Left-Wing Terrorism.* Amsterdam: Rodopi, 2008.

Bermanzohn, S. A. *Through Survivors' Eyes: From the Sixties to the Greensboro Massacre.* Nashville, TN: Vanderbilt University Press, 2003.

Biko, S. *No Fears Expressed.* Edited by M. W. Arnold. Houghton, SA: Mutloatse Arts Heritage, 1987.

Brett, S. *Peru Confronts a Violent Past: The Truth Commission Hearings in Ayacucho.* Washington, DC: Human Rights Watch, 2003.

Buntman, F. L. *Robben Island and Prisoner Resistance to Apartheid.* Cambridge University Press, 2003.

Campbell, B. B., and A. D. Brenner, eds. *Death Squads in Global Perspective: Murder with Deniability.* New York: St Martin's Press, 2000.

Catanzaro, R., ed. *The Red Brigades and Left Wing Terrorism in Italy.* New York: St Martin's Press, 1991.

Churchill, W., and J. V. Wall. *The COINTELPRO Papers: Documents from the FBI's Secret Wars Against Dissent in the United States.* Boston, MA: South End Press, 1990.

Cohn-Bendit, D., and G. Cohn-Bendit. *Obsolete Communism: The Left Wing Alternative.* New York: McGraw-Hill, 1968.

Colvin, S. *Ulrike Meinhof and West German Terrorism: Language, Violence and Identity.* Rochester, NY: Camden House, 2009.

Connelly, M. *A Diplomatic Revolution: Algeria's Fight for Independence and the Origins of the Post-Cold War Era.* Oxford University Press, 2002.

Crapanzano, V. *The Harkis: The Wound That Never Heals.* University of Chicago Press, 2011.

de Antonio, E., M. Lampson, and H. Wexler. *Underground*. Sphinx Productions, 1976.

della Porta, D. "Left Wing Terrorism in Italy." In *Terrorism in Context*, edited by M. Crenshaw, 105–159. University Park, PA: Pennsylvania State University Press, 1995.

de Witte, L. *The Assassination of Lumumba*. London: Verso, 2002.

Dinges, J. *The Condor Years: How Pinochet Brought Terrorism to Three Continents*. New York: The New Press, 2003.

Dohrn, B., J. Jones, C. Sojourn, and Weather Underground. *Prairie Fire: the Politics of Revolutionary Anti-imperialism*. Communications Co., 1974.

Doxtader, E., and P. Salazar. *Truth and Reconciliation in South Africa: The Fundamental Documents*. Cape Town: New Africa Books, 2008.

Dulles, J. W. F. *Sobral Pinto, "The Conscience of Brazil": Leading the Attack Against Vargas*. Austin, TX: University of Texas Press, 2002.

Ellis, S. *Comrades Against Apartheid: The African National Congress and the South African Communist Party in Exile*. Bloomington, IN: Indiana University Press, 1992.

Englander, N. *The Ministry of Special Cases*. New York: Knopf, 2007.

Evans, M. *Algeria: France's Undeclared War*. New York: Oxford University Press, 2011.

Fanon, F. *Wretched of the Earth*. New York: Grove Press, 2004.

Fazal, T. M. *State Death: The Politics and Geography of Conquest, Occupation and Annexation*. Princeton University Press, 2007.

Ferracuti, F. "Ideology and Repentance: Terrorism in Italy." In *Origins of Terrorism: Psychologies, Ideologies, Theologies, States of Mind*, edited by W. Reich, 59–64. Baltimore, MD: The Johns Hopkins University Press, 1998.

Forero, J. "Argentina's Dirty War Still Haunts Youngest Victims." *NPR Archive*. 27 February 2010.

French, J. D. *Drowning in Laws: Labor Law and Brazilian Political Culture*. Chapel Hill, NC: University of North Carolina Press, 2004.

Gorriti, G. *The Shining Path: A History of the Millenarian War in Peru*. Chapel Hill, NC: University of North Carolina Press, 1999.

Grandin, G. *The Last Colonial Massacre*. University of Chicago Press, 2004.

Green, S., and B. Siegel. *The Weather Underground: A Look Back at the Antiwar Activists who Met Violence with Violence*. New Video, 2005.

Greenberg, S. B. *Legitimizing the Illegitimate: State, Markets and Resistance in South Africa, 1939–1945*. Berkeley, CA: University of California Press, 1987.

Hanrahan, G. "Marighella: Father of Modern Terrorism." In *The Manual of the Urban Guerrilla*, edited by C. Marighella, 13–34. Chapel Hill, NC: Documentary Publications, 1985.

Hentschke, J. R., ed. *Vargas and Brazil: New Perspectives*. New York: Palgrave Macmillan, 2006.

Hewitt, C. *Understanding Terrorism in America from the Klan to Al Qaeda*. London: Routledge, 2003.

Horn, G. *The Spirit of '68: Rebellion in Western Europe and North America, 1956–1976*. New York: Oxford University Press, 2007.

Horne, A. *A Savage War of Peace*. London: Macmillan, 1977.

Jeffreys-Jones, R. *The FBI*. New Haven, CT: Yale University Press, 2008.

Judt, T. *Postwar: A History of Europe Since 1945*. New York: Penguin, 2005.

Kellen, K. "Ideology and Rebellion: Terrorism in West Germany." In *Origins of Terrorism: Psychologies, Ideologies, Theologies, States of Mind*, edited by W. Reich, 43–58. Baltimore, MD: The Johns Hopkins University Press, 1998.

Kirsch, B. *Revolution in Brazil*. New York: Basic Books, 1990.

Kornbluh, P. *The Pinochet File*. New York: The New Press, 2003.

Korr, C., and M. Close. *More Than Just a Game: Soccer Vs. Apartheid: The Most Important Soccer Story Ever Told*. New York: St Martin's, 2008.

Kurlansky, M. *1968: The Year That Rocked the World*. New York: Ballantine, 2004.

"Lawbreakers: The Greensboro Massacre". The History Channel, 2000.

Lessa, F., and V. Druliolle, eds. *The Memory of State Terrorism in the Southern Cone: Argentina, Chile and Uruguay*. New York: Palgrave Macmillan, 2011.

Levine, R. M., and J. J. Crocitti, eds. *The Brazil Reader: History, Culture, Politics*. Durham, NC: Duke University Press, 1999.

Lewis, P. H. "The Inferno." In *Guerrillas and Generals: The Dirty War in Argentina*, 147–62. Westport, CT: Praeger, 2002.

Loewenstein, K. *Brazil Under Vargas*. New York: Russell & Russell, 1973.

Mandela, N. *Long Walk to Freedom*. Boston, MA: Back Bay Books, 1995.

Marchak, P. *God's Assassins: State Terrorism in Argentina in the 1970s*. Montreal: McGill-Queen's University Press, 1999.

Marwick, A. *The Sixties: Cultural Revolution in Britain, France, Italy and the United States, c. 1958–1974*. New York: Oxford University Press, 1998.

May, G. *The Informant, the FBI, KKK and the Murder of Viola Liuzzo*. New Haven, CT: Yale University Press, 2005.

Mazower, M. *No Enchanted Palace: The End of Empire and the Ideological Origins of the United Nations*. Princeton University Press, 2009.

McAdam, D. *Freedom Summer*. New York: Oxford University Press, 1988.

McCann, F. D. "The Military and the Dictatorship: Getúlio, Góes and Dutra." In *Vargas and Brazil: New Perspectives*, edited by J. R. Hentschke, 109–42. New York: Palgrave Macmillan, 2006.

McClymer, J. F. *Mississippi Freedom Summer*. Belmont, CA: Thompson/ Wadsworth, 2004.

Meade Jr., R. C. *Red Brigades: The Story of Italian Terrorism*. London: Macmillan, 1990.

Merkl, P. H. "West German Left-Wing Terrorism." In *Terrorism in Context*, edited by M. Crenshaw, 160–210. University Park, PA: Pennsylvania State University Press, 1995.

Moyano, M. J. *Argentina's Lost Patrol: Armed Struggle, 1969–1979*. New Haven, CT: Yale University Press, 1995.

Muthien, Y. *State and Resistance in South Africa, 1939–1965*. Aldershot: Avebury, 1994.

Noval, A. *Deconstructing Apartheid Discourse*. London: Verso, 1996.

Ogbar, J. *Black Power: Radical Politics and African American Identity*. Baltimore, MD: Johns Hopkins University Press, 1994.

Pion-Berlin, D. *The Ideology of State Terror: Economic Doctrine and Political Repression in Argentina and Peru*. Boulder, CO: Lynne Rienner, 1989.

Posel, D. *The Making of Apartheid, 1948–1961*. Oxford: Clarendon Press, 1991.

Purdue, W. D. *Terrorism and the State: A Critique of Domination Through Fear*. Westport, CT: Praeger, 1989.

Rimanelli, M. "Italian Terrorism and Society, 1940s–1980s: Roots, Ideologies, Evolution and International Connections." *Terrorism* 12, no. 43 (1989): 249–96.

Rose, R. S. *One of the Forgotten Things: Getulio Vargas and Brazilian Social Control, 1930–1954*. Westport, CT: Greenwood Press, 2000.

Rosenberg, T. *Children of Cain: Violence and the Violent in Latin America*. New York: William Morrow, 1991.

Rummel, R. J. *Death by Government*. New Brunswick, NJ: Transaction Publishers, 1994.

Saul, B. "The Legal Response of the League of Nations to Terrorism." *Journal of International Criminal Justice* 4, no. 1 (2006): 78–102.

Seale, P., and M. McConville. *Red Flag/Black Flag: French Revolution 1968*. New York: Putnam, 1968.

Singer, D. *Prelude to Revolution: France in May 1968*. Cambridge, MA: South End Press, 2002.

Sloan, J. W. "Political Terrorism in Latin America: A Critical Analysis." In *The Politics of Terrorism*, edited by M. Stohl. New York and Basle: Marcel Dekker, 1979.

Smith, B. L. *Terrorism in America*. Albany, NY: State University Press of New York, 1994.

Smith, M. L. "Shining Path's Urban Strategy: Ate Vitarte." In *The Shining Path of Peru*, edited by D. S. Palmer, 145–65. New York: St Martin's Press, 1994.

"State Repression and Enforcement Terrorism in Latin America." In *The State as Terrorist: The Dynamics of Governmental Violence and Repression*, edited by M. Stohl and G. A. Lopez, 83–98. Westport, CT: Greenwood Press, 1984.

Snyder, T. *Bloodlands: Europe Between Hitler and Stalin*. New York: Basic Books, 2010.

Stern, P. A. *Sendero Luminoso: An Annotated Bibliography of the Shining Path Guerrilla Movement, 1980–1993*. Albuquerque, NM: SALALM Secretariat, University of New Mexico, 1995.

Taylor, L. *Shining Path: Guerrilla War in Peru's Northern Highlands, 1980–1997*. Liverpool University Press, 2006.

Thomas, M., B. Moore, and L. J. Butler. *The Crises of Empire: Decolonization and Europe's Imperial Nation States, 1918–1975*. London: Hodder, 2008.

Varon, J. *Bringing the War Home: The Weather Underground, the Red Army Faction and Revolutionary Violence in the Sixties and Seventies*. Berkeley, CA: University of California Press, 2004.

Warren, M. "Son Lost to Torturers Reappears." *Associated Press*, February 2, 2010.

Watson, B. *Freedom Summer: The Savage Season That Made Mississippi Burn*. New York: Viking, 2010.

Wilkinson, D. *Silence on the Mountain: Stories of Terror, Betrayal and Forgetting in Guatemala*. Boston and New York: Houghton Mifflin, 2002.

Williams, Y., and J. Lazerow, eds. *In Search of the Black Panther Party: New Perspectives on a Revolutionary Movement*. Durham, NC: Duke University Press, 2006.

Zucker, A. *Closer to the Truth*. Filmakers Library, 2008.

9   Toward the present: terrorism in theory and practice

Agamben, G. *State of Exception*. University of Chicago Press, 2005.

Baker, K. M. *Condorcet: From Natural Philosophy to Social Mathematics*. University of Chicago Press, 1975.

Becker, T. *Terrorism and the State: Rethinking the Rules for State Responsibility*. Oxford: Hart Publishing, 2006.

Burleigh, M. *Blood and Rage: A Cultural History of Terrorism*. New York: HarperCollins, 2009.

Chaliand, G., and A. Blin. *The History of Terrorism: from Antiquity to Al Qaeda*. Berkeley, CA: University of California Press, 2007.

Collins, J. B. *The Ancien Régime and the French Revolution*. New York: Wadsworth, 2002.

Cotta, S. *Why Violence? A Philosophical Interpretation.* Gainesville, FL: University of Florida Press, 1985.

Doyle, W. *The French Revolution.* New York: Oxford University Press, 2001.

European Review of History 14, no. 3 (September 2007).

Evans, P. B., D. Rueschemeyer, and T. Skocpol, eds. *Bringing the State Back In.* Cambridge University Press, 1985.

Falk, R. *Revolutionaries and Functionaries: The Dual Face of Terrorism.* New York: E. P. Dutton, 1988.

Fazal, T. M. *State Death: The Politics and Geography of Conquest, Occupation and Annexation.* Princeton University Press, 2007.

Franks, J. *Rethinking the Roots of Terrorism.* New York: Palgrave Macmillan, 2006.

Friedberg, A. L. *In the Shadow of the Garrison State: America's Anti-Statism and Its Cold War Grand Strategy.* Princeton University Press, 2000.

Ganor, B. "Defining Terrorism: Is One Man's Terrorist Another Man's Freedom Fighter?" *Police Practice and Research* 3, no. 4 (2002): 287–304.

Held, V. *How Terrorism Is Wrong: Morality and Political Violence.* New York: Oxford University Press, 2008.

Honderich, T. *Terrorism for Humanity.* London: Pluto Press, 2003.

Jackson, R., E. Murphy, and S. Poynting, eds. *Contemporary State Terrorism: Theory and Practice.* London and New York: Routledge, 2010.

Jones, S. G., and M. C. Libicki. *How Terrorist Groups End: Lessons for Encountering al-Qa'ida.* Santa Monica, CA: RAND, 2008.

Kateb, G. *Utopia and Its Enemies.* New York: The Free Press, 1963.

 ed. *Utopia: The Potential and Prospect of the Human Condition.* New Brunswick, NJ: Transaction Publishers, 2008.

Keane, J. *Violence and Democracy.* Cambridge University Press, 2004.

Kriegel, B. *The State and the Rule of Law.* Princeton University Press, 1995.

Kurth, A. *Ending Terrorism: Lessons for Defeating al-Qaeda.* London: Routledge/Adelphi House, 2008.

Laqueur, W., ed. *Voices of Terror: Manifestos, Writings, and Manuals of Al Qaeda, Hamas, and Other Terrorists from Around the World and Throughout the Ages.* New York: Reed Press, 2004.

Laski, H. J. *The State in Theory and Practice.* New York: The Viking Press, 1935.

Lasswell, H. *Essays on the Garrison State.* New Brunswick, NJ: Transaction Publishers, 1997.

 "Sino-Japanese Crisis: The Garrison State Versus the Civilian State." *China Quarterly* 11 (1937): 643–9.

Miller, M. A. "Ordinary Terrorism in Historical Perspective." *Journal for the Study of Radicalism* 2, no. 1 (2008): 125–54.

"The Intellectual Origins of Terrorism in Modern Europe." In *Terrorism in Context*, edited by M. Crenshaw, 27–62. University Park, PA: Pennsylvania State University Press, 1995.

Moyne, S. *The Last Utopia: Human Rights in History*. Cambridge, MA: Belknap Press of Harvard University Press, 2010.

Porter, B. *The Origins of the Vigilant State: The London Metropolitan Police Special Branch Before the First World War*. London: Weidenfeld and Nicolson, 1987.

Ranstorp, M., ed. *Understanding Violent Radicalisation: Terrorist and Jihadist Movements in Europe*. London and New York: Routledge, 2010.

Rapoport, D. C. "The Four Waves of Modern Terrorism." In *Terrorism: Critical Essays in Political Science*. New York: Routledge, 2006.

Rummel, R. J. *Death by Government*. New Brunswick, NJ: Transaction Publishers, 1994.

Savitch, H. V. *Cities in a Time of Terror: Space, Territory and Local Resilience*. Armonk, NY: M. E. Sharpe, 2008.

Scott, J. C. *Seeing Like a State: How Certain Schemes to Improve the Human Condition Have Failed*. New Haven, CT: Yale University Press, 1998.

Tilly, C. *The Politics of Collective Violence*. Cambridge University Press, 2003.

Treitschke, H. von. *Politics*. New York: Macmillan, 1916.

Wardlaw, G. *Political Terrorism: Theory, Tactics and Counter-Measures*. Cambridge University Press, 1989.

Weinberg, L. "Democracy and Terrorism." In *The Roots of Terrorism*, edited by L. Richardson, 45–56. London: Routledge, 2006.

Westad, O. A. *The Global Cold War: Third World Interventions and the Making of Our Times*. Cambridge University Press, 2005.

Williams, D. *Condorcet and Modernity*. Cambridge University Press, 2004.

INDEX

Abu Sayyaf, 244
Action for National Liberation, 219
Action Française, 179
Africa, colonization, 128–34
African National Congress, 205, 207, 208, 251
Afrikaner Broederbond, 204
Afrikaner National Party, 204
Agamben, Giorgio, 248, 249
agents provocateurs, 109
Akhmatova, Anna, 192
al-Qaeda, 242, 244
Al Zawahari, Ayman, 242
Alarm, 119, 120
Albigensian Crusade, 21
Alexander I, 47, 61
Alexander II, 64, 67, 72, 74, 82, 91, 96, 115, 118
Alexander III, 77, 80, 81
Alexandra Feodorovna, Empress of Russia, 167
Alfonsin, Raul, 212
Algerian National Liberation Front, 200–3, 250
Allende, Salvador, 212, 213
Alonso XII, 113
American Federation of Labor, 170
Anabaptism, 22
anarchism, 103
  insurgent violence in America, 118–21
  insurgent violence in Western Europe, 110–18
  states' response to anarchist terror, 123–8
Anarchist Exclusion Act, 172
Anarchist International, 111

Andrieux, Louis, 79
Anti-Communist Alliance, 209
Apache, 144
apartheid, 204–8
Aquinas, Thomas, 18, 20
Arana, Julio Cesar, 131
Arbeiter Zeitung, 119
Argentine Task Force, 209
Aristotle, 13–16, 20
  Politics, 14
Aryan Nation, 228
Aussaresses, Paul, 219
Autonomi, 234
Azev, Evno, 83, 87, 88, 97

Baader, Andreas, 230, 231
Baader-Meinhof Group. *See* Red Army Faction
Babeuf, François-Noel, 40–1, 43
Bachmann, Josef, 230
Bakunin, Michael, 51, 54, 96, 105, 111, 113, 122
Balashov, A. D., 61
Balmashev, Stepan, 83
Bantu Authorities Act, 204
Beach, Henry, 228
Bell, Sylvester, 226
Benkendorff, Alexander K., 47, 61, 62
Benoit, Zéphirin, 115
Berdo, Ia. F., 84
Beria, Lavrenty, 190
Berkman, Alexander, 121, 172
Bermudez, Francisco Morales, 214
Beveridge, Albert, 134
Bin Laden, Osama, 242

Birth of a Nation, 170
Bismarck, Otto von, 102, 103
Black Hand, 111
Black Hundreds, 92, 93
Black Panther Party, 223–5
Black Sash, 205
Blackstone, William, 45
Blanc, Louis, 54
Blanqui, Louis-Auguste, 49, 53, 104
Bloody Sunday, 88
Blum, Léon, 179
Bodin, Jean, 27, 32
Boer War, 203
Bogrov, Dmitry, 89
Bolsheviks, 165, 166, 167, 168, 184, 185,
    190, 193, 195
Bolshevism, 169, 170, 173, 178, 187, 189,
    191, 276
Bonaparte, Louis-Napoleon, 100, 101,
    103
Bonaparte, Napoleon, 42, 44, 46, 48, 100
Born, John, 209
Born, Jorge, 209
Boudinot, Elias, 141, 142
Bracton, Henry de, 19
Brazilian Communist Party, 219
Brilliant, Dora, 88
British Jacobins, 41
Brown, John, 149
Brutus, Junius, 23
    "Vindiciae contra Tyrannos", 23
Buda, Mario, 172
Buonarroti, Filippo, 40, 43
Burke, Edmund, 34, 257
    Reflections on the Revolution in France,
    257
Burke, Thomas Henry, 112
Burton, Scott, 156
Burtsev, Vladimir, 82, 83

cabinet noir, 102
Caesar, Julius, 16
Cafieri, Carlo, 113
Campos, Arsenio Martinez, 114
Canovas, Antonio, 111
Carbonari, 42–5, 49, 57, 163
Carlsbad Decrees, 48, 50, 78
Carnot, Sadi, 111, 118, 128
Casement, Roger, 130, 131
Caserio, Sante Geronimo, 118, 127
Castro, Fidel, 212
Catechism of a Revolutionary, 68–9, 118
Cathars, 21
Catherine the Great, 34, 45–6, 60, 90

Catholic Center Party, 176
Catholic Church, 21, 256
Cavendish, Frederick, 112
Central Intelligence Agency, 199, 213, 244
Chaadaev, Peter, 62
Chadbourn, James, 148
Chandler, Charles, 220
Chanoine, Charles, 132, 133
Charles I, 30
Chase, George K., 151
Cheka, 167, 187, 189, 190
Chernov, Victor, 87
Chernyshevskii, Nikolai, 64–5
Cherokee, 139, 140, 141, 145
Cherokee Nation v. Georgia, 140
Cherokee Removal, 142–3
Chicago Defender, 157
Christian Democracy (Italy), 234
Church Street bombing, 206
Churchill, Winston, 182
Cicero, Marcus Tullius, 17
Civil Constitution of the Clergy, 35
Civil War, 147, 148, 149, 150, 152, 166
civilization programs, 139
Clansman, 170
Clemenceau, Georges, 110
Cohn-Bendit, Daniel, 235, 236
    Obsolete Communism:
    The Left Wing Alternative, 236
Colbert, Jean-Baptiste, 33
Cold War, 8, 198, 199, 202, 206, 208, 209,
    218, 221, 231, 232, 235, 237, 238,
    240, 241, 242, 244
Colfax Massacre, 153
Comanche, 143, 144
Combat Organization, 87, 88–9, 92, 96,
    97, 112
Comintern, 187
Committee of General Security, 61
Committee of Public Safety, 36, 37, 38, 39,
    41, 57, 104
Committees of Surveillance, 38
Communist Manifesto, 53
Communist Party of Germany, 176
Communist Party of Italy, 231, 233, 234
Communist Party USA, 225, 226
Condorcet, Nicolas de, 34, 256
Congo Free State, 129–31
Congress of Vienna, 46, 48, 51
Congress on Racial Equality, 222, 225
Conrad, Joseph, 87
    Heart of Darkness, 133
Constitutional Democratic Party, 94, 166
constitutional dictatorship, 161

Constitutional Union Guard, 152
Contemporary, The 64, 65
conversos, 21
Cook, Marsh, 158
Costa, Andrea, 113
Costigian, Edward P., 159
Cotta, Sergio, 253, 254
Counter Intelligence Program (COINTEL), 225, 226
counterterrorism, 252
Crimean War, 163
Crisis, 157
Croix de Feu, 179
Cronaca sovversiva, 172
Crow, 145, 146
Crow, Joseph Medicine, 145
Cuban revolution, 209
Curcio, Renato, 233
Cutler, James Elbert, 147
Czolgosz, Leon, 121, 126

Danton, Georges, 38, 39
  Dantonists, 37
Daughters of the American Revolution, 174
Decembrist revolt, 46–8, 61, 64, 163
Declaration of the Rights of Man and the Citizen, 255–6
Degaev, Sergei, 82
Deibler, Louis, 81
Delescluze, Charles, 104
Democratic Republic of the Congo, 199
Desmoulins, Camille, 38, 39
Devils, 69, 254
Diderot, Denis, 45
Dilling, Elizabeth, 174
Dixon, Thomas, 170
Dolgorukov, Vasilii A., 64–5
Dostoevsky, Fedor, 63, 69, 90, 254
Douglass, Frederick, 153
Drentel'n, Alexander R., 71
Dreyfus Affair, 132
Du Bois, W. E. B., 222
Dulles, Allen, 199
Duplessis-Mornay, Philippe.
  See Brutus, Junius
Dutschke, Rudi, 229, 236
Dyer, Leonidas C., 159
Dzerzhinskii, Feliks Edmundovich, 167, 187, 188–9

Eastland, James, 161
Ebert, Friedrich, 178
Eisner, Kurt, 176

Elbrick, Charles, 220
Elizabeth, Empress of Austria, 111
Engels, Friedrich, 51, 53, 56
English Civil War, 30
Erzberger, Matthias, 176
Espionage Act of 1917, 172
Essenes, 12
European Restoration, 48–51, 52
Euskadi Ta Askatasuna, 220
Evers, Medgar, 222
Evian Accords, 200
Expedition, 61
Ezhov, Nikolai, 190

Fanelli, Giuseppe, 113
Fanon, Frantz, 57, 200–3, 220, 230
Fawkes, Guy, 28
February Revolution, 164
Federal Bureau of Investigation, 225
Felton, Rebecca, 155
Fenian Brotherhood, 111, 179
Ferdinand, Franz, 111
Ferré, Théophile, 102
Ferry, Jules, 115
Field, Marshall, 120
Fieschi, Giuseppe, 52
Figner, Vera, 86
Firmenich, Mario, 209
Five Year Plans, 194
FLN. *See* Algerian National Liberation Front
Forever Flowing, 196
Foucault, Michel, 248
Fouché, Joseph, 78, 101
Fouchet Law, 235
Fouchet, Christian, 235, 236
Franceschini, Alberto, 233
Francis I, 24
Francis-Joseph, Emperor, 101
Franco-Prussian War, 102, 105, 163
Frederick William IV, 101
Freedmen's Bureau, 150, 152
Freedom Summer of 1964, 222
Frei, Eduardo, 212
Freiheit, 57, 118
French Revolution, 34–41, 167, 185, 255
Frick, Henry Clay, 121, 126
Fujimori, Alberto, 216

Gabriel's Rebellion, 149
Galleani, Luigi, 171
  Galleanists, 172
Gallo, Charles, 115
Galtieri, Leopoldo, 212
Gambetta, Léon, 115

garrison state, 243–4
Gaspard de Coligny, 24
Gaulle, Charles de, 200, 203, 236
Gel'fman, Gesia, 91
General Confederation of Labor, 109, 110
Geneva Convention, 198
German Democratic Republic, 229, 244
German National Socialist Workers Party.
    See Nazi Germany
Girondins, 35
Goerdeler, Carl Friedrich, 182
Goldman, Emma, 106, 121, 127, 136, 172
Gomel Pogrom, 92
Gorky, Maxim, 187
Goulart, João, 218
Gracchus, Tiberius, 16
Gramsci, Antonio, 230
Grant, Ulysses S., 152
Great Terror, 190, 195
Green Book, 46
Greensboro massacre, 226–7
Griffith, D. W., 170
Grossman, Vasily, 196
Grotius, Hugo, 34
Guevara, Ernesto "Che," 219, 221, 230
Guillotin, Joseph-Ignace, 36
gulag, 47, 185, 190
Gumbel, Emil Julius, 175, 176–8
Gunpowder Plot, 28
Guzman, Abimael, 214, 215, 216

Haase, Hugo, 176
Hamas, 244
Hampshire, Stuart, 250
Hampton, Fred, 225
Harting, Arkady M., 83, 84
Hawkes, Albert, 160
Hay, John, 133
Haymarket Affair, 119–20, 137
Hébert, Jacques
    Hébertists, 37, 38
Heine, Heinrich, 51
Heinzen, Karl, 54–7, 66, 78, 110, 118, 165,
    201, 220, 249
    "Murder," 54, 57, 118
Hell, 66
Henry, Emile, 116, 117
Herod, 11
Herodotus, 12
Herzen, Alexander, 51, 64–5, 96
Hezbollah, 244
Hitler, Adolf, 180, 181
Ho Chi Minh, 221, 230
Hobbes, Thomas, 245

Hobson, John A.
    Imperialism, 129
Hoedel, Max, 113
Holmes, Oliver Wendell, 171
Holocaust, 183
Holy Guard, 81
Homestead strike, 137
Hoop Spur massacre, 157
Hoover, John Edgar, 222
Huggins, Jim, 226
Hugo, Victor, 114
Huguenots, 24

Indian Removal Act, 140
insurgent violence, 14
    al-Qaeda, 242–3
    anarchism in America, 118–21
    anarchism in Western Europe, 110–18
    bombing of innocents, 113
    Brazil, 219–20
    Carbonari, 45
    Chile, 213–14
    Cossack and serf revolts, 59–60
    decolonization of Algeria, 199–203
    during the French Revolution, 34
    during the Revolutions of 1848, 57
    in Ireland, 111–12
    Italy, 231–5
    Old Testament, 11
    Paris Commune, 102–8
    Peru, 214–16
    Russia, 59–80, 86–9
    South Africa, 205–7
    United States, 225
Inter Intelligence Agency, 244
International Workers Association,
    105, 106
International Workers of the World, 170
Iran-Contra Affair, 217
Irish Republican Army, 179, 220, 244,
    251
Ivan the Terrible, 60
Izvestiia, 166

Jackson, Andrew, 140
Jacobin Terror. *See* Reign of Terror
Jacobins, 35
Jefferson, Thomas, 148
Jewish Anti-Fascist Committee, 195
Jewish Wars, 12
John of Leyden, 22
John of Salisbury, 19, 20
Jones, Thomas M., 150
Josephus, Flavius, 12

Kadet. *See* Constitutional Democratic Party
Kaliaev, Ivan, 88
Kamorskii, V. M., 84
Kaplan, Fanny, 167
Kapp, Wolfgang, 178
Karakozov, Dmitrii V., 66–7, 71, 85
Keane, John, 246
KGB, 190, 213, 244
Khalturin, Stepan, 72
Kibalchich, Nikolai, 76
Kibalchich, Victor Lvovich. *See* Serge, Victor
King, Jr., Martin Luther, 222, 225
Kirillov, Alexei, 254
Kishenev Pogrom, 92
Kletochnikov, Nikolai, 71
Klobb, Arsene, 132
Knights of White Camelia, 151
Knox, Henry, 139, 140
Koenigstein, François-Claudius.
    See Ravachol
Kolokol, 52
Konkret, 230
Kossuth, Lajos, 51
Kovalskii, Ivan, 86
Kravchinskii, Sergei, 82, 86
Kriegel, Blandine, 248, 249
Kropotkin, Peter, 80, 82, 86, 96, 111, 122
    The Conquest of Bread, 129
Ku Klux Klan, 150–3, 158, 170, 222,
    226, 227
kulak collectivization campaign, 190, 194
Kurdistan Workers' Party (PKK), 244

Lamarque, Jean Maximilien, 50
Land and Liberty, 71, 72, 75, 85
Laski, Harold, 245
Lasswell, Harold, 243, 244
Le Tribun du Peuple, 40
League of Nations, 198
Lear, Jonathan, 145
Leber, Julius, 181
Lecomte, Claude Martin, 104
Lena Goldfield, 94
Lenin, Vladimir, 80, 165, 167, 184, 187,
    189, 190, 221
    *Imperialism, the Highest State of
    Capitalism*, 129
Leopold II, 129
Lépine, Louis, 109
Liceu opera house bombing, 114
Liebknecht, Karl, 176
Linderman, Frank, 145
Liuzzo, Viola, 226
Lockhart, Bruce, 189–90

Loris-Melikov, Mikhail T., 72, 96
Louis XIV, 33
Louis XVI, 35, 37, 45, 73, 167
Louis-Philippe, 50, 52
Lumumba, Patrice, 199
Luther, Martin, 21, 22
Luxemburg, Rosa, 176
Lynch, Charles, 148
Lynch's Law, 148
lynching, 147–9, 156, 158, 159, 160

Macé, Gustave, 81
Mad Summer of 1874, 70, 72, 75
Mahler, Horst, 230
Maistre, Joseph de, 49
Malatesta, Errico, 113
Malcolm X, 222
Mandela, Nelson, 208
Mandelstam, Osip, 192, 193
Manley, Alex, 155
Mao Tse-Tung, 221
Marat, Jean-Paul, 35
Marcuse, Herbert, 230
Maréchal, Sylvain, 41
Marie-Antoinette, 36
Marighella, Carlos, 219, 220, 230
    For the Liberation of Brazil, 220
    The Brazilian Crisis, 219
    The Minimanual of the Urban Guerrilla,
    220
Marx, Karl, 51, 53, 56, 105, 221
Marxism, 113, 164, 168, 187, 188, 196,
    208, 219, 241
Massera, Emilio, 210, 212
Massu, Jacques, 200
Mayakovsky, Vladimir, 193
Mazzini, Giuseppe, 44, 51, 54, 101
McKinley assassination, 57, 111, 121,
    125, 137
McVeigh, Timothy, 228
Meinhoff, Ulrike, 231
Metternich, Klemens von, 48, 49, 51, 56
Meunier, Théodule, 116
Mezentsev, N. V., 86
MI6, 244
Michel, Louise, 106
Mickiewicz, Adam, 51
Mikhailov, Alexander, 71
Mincey, S. S., 158
Moncasi, Juan Oliva, 113
Montesquieu, Charles-Louis, 34, 45
Montoneros, 209
moral violence, 249–50
Morel, Edmond, 130

Moretti, Mario, 234
Morgan, J. P., 171
Moro, Aldo, 234
Moro National Liberation Front, 135
Morozov, Nikolai, 72, 73, 121, 165
    The Terrorist Struggle, 72–3
Morse, Wayne, 160
Mossad, 244
Most, Johann, 57, 118, 127
Moton, Leroy, 226
mouchards, 109

NAACP, 225
Napoleon III. See Bonaparte,
    Louis-Napoleon
Narodnaia Rasprava. See People's
    Vengeance
Narodnaia Volia. See People's Will
National Information Center, 213
National Intelligence Directorate, 213
National Socialism, 180–3
National Vietnam Committee, 236
Native American Removal, 140–3
Nazi Germany, 180–3
Nechaev, Sergei, 67–9, 71, 118, 220
Neuring, Otto, 176
New Economic Policy, 194
New Order, 232
Nicholas I, 47, 61, 64
Nicholas II, 88, 93, 97, 165, 167
nihilists, 116
NKVD, 190
Nobel, Alfred, 121
Nobiling, Karl, 113
Northern Society, 46, 47
Nuremburg Laws, 180

ochlocracy, 13
October Revolution, 168, 184
Ohnesorg, Benno, 229
Okhrana, 79–85, 86, 87, 97, 114, 167
Oklahoma City bombing, 228
Old Testament, 11
oprichnina, 60
Orange Free State, 204
Organisation de l'Armée Secrète, 199–201,
    203
Organization Consul, 176
Organization of American States, 212
Orsha Pogrom, 93
Orsini, Felice, 101

Pahlen, K. I., 69
Pale of Settlement, 92

Palestine Liberation Organization, 244, 251
Pallas, Paulino, 114
Palmer, A. Mitchell, 171, 172, 173
Pan-African Congress, 206
Papon, Maurice, 200
Paris Commune, 40, 102–8, 114, 163
Parsons, Albert, 119, 120
Pasternak, Boris, 192
Peasants' War, 22
People's Revolutionary Army, 209
People's Vengeance, 67, 69
People's Will, 71–7, 80, 82, 83, 86, 96, 112,
    118, 122, 186
Peron, Juan, 209
Perovskii, L. A., 63
Peruvian Amazon Company, 131
Pestel, Pavel, 46, 47, 66
Peter the Great, 33, 45, 59, 60
Peters, Iakov K., 189
Petit, Jean, 20
    "Justification", 20
Petrashevskii, M. V., 63
Pharisees, 12
Philippines, colonization, 133–5
Phoenix Park assassinations, 112, 118
Pichon, Stephen, 178
Pierce, William, 228
Pierrepont, Edward, 151
Pinkerton Agency, 121, 125, 137
Pinkerton, Allan, 125, 126
Pinkerton, Robert, 126, 127
Pinochet, Augusto, 212, 213, 238
Pitt, William, 41
Plato, 14
    The Republic, 16
Plehve, V. K., 83, 88, 96, 185
Plenty-Coups, Chief, 145
pogroms, 91–4
police terrorism, 120
Policraticus, 19
political violence, 3, 5, 8, 10, 11, 12, 16, 17,
    20, 21, 23, 32, 34, 35, 40, 44, 53, 56,
    57, 58, 59, 66, 71, 72, 74, 86, 92, 95,
    107, 120, 128, 129, 137, 138, 153,
    154, 159, 163, 165, 179, 183, 185,
    190, 199, 212, 231, 239, 241, 244,
    245, 246, 249, 254, 255, 258
Pope Gregory XIII, 28
Popular Front for the Liberation of Palestine,
    220
Population Registration Act, 204
Pravda, 166, 191, 194
Preobrazhenskii Prikaz, 60
propaganda by the deed, 111, 113, 233

Protestant Reformation, 21, 22
Proudhon, Pierre-Joseph, 54, 110, 111
Provisional Government, 164, 168
Public Safety Act, 205
Pugachev rebellion, 61
Pullman, George, 120
Purishkevich, Vladimir M., 92
Pushkin, Alexander, 47, 62, 192

race riots, 155–6
Rachkovskii, Peter, 80, 81, 97
Radishchev, Alexander, 46
Ramée, Marie Louise de la, 127, 128
Rathenau, Walter, 176
Ravachol, 115, 116, 117
Reconstruction, 149, 150, 154
Reconstruction Act, 150
Red Army, 165, 166, 182
Red Army Faction, 220, 230, 231
Red Brigades, 220, 233, 234
Red Orchestra, 181
Red Scare, 172
Red Terror, 165–9, 187, 189
Reese v. US, 153
Reflections on Violence, 109
Reign of Terror, 36, 40, 41, 105, 163, 165
Reinforcement Act of 1871, 152
Restoration, 48–51
Révoltés, 116
Revolution of 1905, 88, 90, 92, 93, 96
Revolutionary Guards, 244
Revolutionary Organization 17 November, 244
Revolutions of 1848, 57, 99
  aftermath, 103
Richelieu, Cardinal, 32
Ridge, John, 142
Riefenstahl, Leni, 180
Rigault, Raoul, 102
Riurik dynasty, 59
Robben Island prison, 206
Robeson, Paul, 222
Robespierre, Maximilien, 35–9, 57, 166, 167
Rockefeller, John D., 171
Roig, Arturo, 209
Romanenko, Gerasim, G., 73–4, 121
Romanov dynasty, 59, 167
Roosevelt, Franklin Delano, 160, 174
Roosevelt, Theodore, 130, 134
Ross, John, 140
Rossa, Guido, 234
Rossiter, Clinton, 161
Rousseau, Jean-Jacques, 34

Rowe, Jr., Thomas, 226
Ruge, Arnold, 56
Russell, Daniel L., 154, 155
Russian intelligentsia, 167
Russian Orthodox Church, 59
Russian Revolution, 164–5
Russian Social Democratic Labor Party, 164
Russian Social Democrats, 94

Sacco and Vanzetti trial, 172
Sacred Brotherhood. See Holy Guard
Sadducees, 12
Saint Bartholomew's Day massacre, 23, 24, 26, 27
Saint-Jean, Iberico, 211
Saint-Just, Louis Antoine Léon de, 35, 38, 39, 73, 166, 249
Salvador, Santiago, 114
Savak, 244
Savinkov, Boris, 84, 87, 88, 96, 185, 186
Schleyer, Hans Martin, 230
School of the Americas, 210
Science of Revolutionary Warfare, 118
Scott, James, 252
Second Empire, 100, 102
Secret Expedition, 60
Securitate, 244
Sedition Act of 1918, 172
September 11 attacks, 246
Serge, Victor, 186–7
Sergei Alexandrovich of Russia, Grand Duke, 185
Sharpeville massacre, 205
Sheppard, William, 130
Sheriff's Posse Comitatus, 228
Sheshkovskii, Stepan, 60
Shining Path, 214, 215, 216, 244
Shoah, 183
Sicarii, 12
Simonides of Ceos, 13
Sinitskii, Tikhon, 93
Sipiagin, Dmitrii, 88
Six Books of the Commonwealth, 26
Socialist Revolutionary Party, 83, 84, 87, 92, 94, 121, 166, 167, 168, 184, 186
  terrorist wing, 83–5
Socialist Student Association (German SDS), 229, 230
Society of Seasons, 53
Socrates, 16
soft terror, 174
Soloviev, Alexander, 71
Sorel, Georges, 109
South Africa, 203–8, 228

South African Communist Party, 206
Southern Christian Leadership Conference, 222, 225
Southern Society, 46, 47
Soviet Union, 2, 7, 8, 163, 165–9, 174, 181, 183, 191, 195, 198, 199, 202, 218, 222, 237
Sovremennik. See Contemporary
Soweto uprising, 205
Spanish Inquisition, 21
Spartacist League, 176, 178
Spear of the Nation, 206
Speransky, Michael, 61
Spies, August, 119, 120
Springfield Race Riot of 1908, 156
Stalin, Joseph, 183, 185, 187, 192, 193, 194, 195, 196, 238
Stanley, Henry Morton, 129
Stasi, 244
state of emergency, 4, 7, 37, 79, 161, 205, 229, 238
state of terror, 3
state violence, 14
    against African Americans, 146–61, 173–4
    against anarchism, 123–8
    against Native Americans, 138–46
    Argentina, 208–12
    Brazil, 217–18
    Chile, 212–14
    during Napoleon III's regime, 101–2
    Guatemala, 216
    imperial, 129–35
    Peru, 214–17
    Philippines, 133–5
    psychology of, 15
    Red Terror, 165–9
    South Africa, 207–8
    Stalinist era, 190
    tsarist era, 60–4
    under National Socialism, 180–3
    United States, 228
Stauffenberg, Claus von, 181
Steinberg, I. N., 184
Stennis, John, 161
Stolypin, Peter, 89, 93, 96
Student Non-Violent Coordinating Committee, 222
Students for a Democratic Society, 222
Sudeikin, G. P., 82
Supreme Court, 153, 161

Tacitus, Gaius Cornelius, 17
Taliban, 244
Tamil Tigers, 244

Tarnovskii, G. See Romanenko, Gerasim G.
Taylor, Charles, 32
terrorism
    Catholic, 24
    colonialism as terrorism, 130
    definitions of, 5–7
    during the Protestant Reformation, 23–4
    end of, 250–3
    ethical justifications for violence, 249–50
    Huguenot, 24
    imperial state terror, 129–35
    insurgent terrorism. See insurgent violence
    Ku Klux Klan, 150–3
    literary, 190–4
    moderate terrorism theory, 251
    nationalist violence against Russian Jews, 89–94
    Native American violence, 146
    of the word, 33
    orthodox terrorism theory, 251, 252
    radical terrorism theory, 251
    state terrorism. See state violence
    US justifications, 138
    used as a positive tactic, 73
Tet Offensive, 235
Thiers, Adolphe, 103, 104
Third Reich, 180–3
Third Republic, 108
Third Section, 47, 51, 61–3, 64, 65, 67, 70, 71, 76, 79, 80, 82
Thirty Years War, 21, 23
Three Emperors League, 106
Thucydides, 13
Tiberius, 18
Tikhomirov, Lev, 82
"To The Young Generation," 66
Trail of Tears, 142–3
Transvaal Republic, 204
Treaty of Hopewell, 139
Treaty of New Echota, 140
Treaty of Versailles, 198
Treaty of Westphalia, 21, 23
Treitschke, Heinrich von, 245
Trepov, F. F., 70
Triumph of the Will, 180
Trotsky, Leon, 165, 166, 167, 187
Tupamaros, 217, 230
Turgenev, Ivan, 115
Turner Diaries, 228
Turner, Nat, 149
tyrannicide, 13, 16, 19, 20, 21, 26, 35, 43, 56, 66, 99, 110, 118, 179

US v. Cruikshank, 153
Ulster Resistance, 179
Ulyanov, Alexander, 80
Union of Salvation, 46
Union of the Russian People, 93
Union of Welfare, 46
United Nations, 198
Uritskii, Mikhail, 167

Vaillant, Auguste, 116, 117, 127
Valley, Anton Arco, 176
Vargas, Getulio, 217–18
Vattel, Emmerich de, 34
Verkhovensky, Peter, 254
Versailles Treaty, 175, 176, 178, 180
Vertov, Dziga, 166
Vesey, Denmark, 149
Videla, Jorge Rafael, 210, 211, 212
Vietnam War, 228, 236
Vindiciae, 24, 25, 26, 27
Vock, Mikhail von, 61
Volodarskii, V., 167
Voltaire, 45
Voulet, Paul, 132

Waddell, Alfred, 154, 155
Wagner, Robert, 159
Wall Street bombing, 137, 171
War Communism, 165, 194
Weathermen, 225

Weber, Max, 32
Weimar Republic, 163
Weinberg, Leonard, 246
Wells, Ida B., 153
West Germany, 220, 221, 228, 229, 230
White Army, 165, 167
White Rose, 181
White Terror, 50
Whitley, Hiram C., 151
William of Occam, 19
Williams, George Washington, 130
Wilmington Daily Record, 155
Wilmington Massacre of 1898, 155
Wilson, Woodrow, 171
Witte, Sergei, 93
Wolff, Christian, 34
Wretched of the Earth, 201

Xenophon, 13

Young Italy, 44
Young Russia, 66

Zaichnevskii, Peter G., 66
Zasulich, Vera, 70, 71, 86, 113
Zealots. *See* Sicarii
Zheliabov, Andrei I., 75, 76, 77
Zhuchenko, Zinaida, 84, 85
Zinoviev, Grigorii, 187
Zubatov, Sergei, 83, 84, 94